I0031803

ASIAN ECONOMIC INTEGRATION REPORT 2018

TOWARD OPTIMAL PROVISION OF REGIONAL PUBLIC GOODS IN ASIA AND THE PACIFIC

OCTOBER 2018

ASIAN DEVELOPMENT BANK

ADB

6 ADB Avenue, Mandaluyong City, 1550 Metro Manila, Philippines
Tel +63 2 632 4444; Fax +63 2 636 2444
www.adb.org

ISBN 978-92-9261-354-9 (print), 978-92-9261-355-6 (electronic)
Publication Stock No. TCS189598-2
DOI: http://dx.doi.org/10.22617/TCS189598-2

Notes:
In this publication, "$" refers to United States dollars.
ADB recognizes "China" as the People's Republic of China; "Hong Kong" as Hong Kong, China; "Korea" as the Republic of Korea; and "Siam" as Thailand.
Corrigenda to ADB publications may be found at http://www.adb.org/publications/corrigenda.

Inside photos:
All photos are from ADB: (i) aerial view of Ha Noi; (ii) aerial view of Danang Port; (iii) worker inside one of the factories in the Savan Park Special Economic Zone; (iv) skyscrapers along Singapore's central business district; (v) passengers claiming their baggage at the Mount Hagen Airport (Kagamuga Airport); and (vi) aerial view of the border check point on the Lao People's Democratic Republic side of the Mekong River.

CONTENTS

FOREWORD

Asia's regional integration progresses steadily in flows of goods, services, labor, and other factors of production. However, its pace is divergent across areas, with trade and foreign direct investment (FDI) leading while financial integration lagging. In 2017, Asia's trade (by volume) grew faster than global trade and surpassed its own economic growth for the first time since 2012, which can be attributed to the expansion of the global value chain (GVC)—after a continued slowdown since 2012—with Asia's GVC participation rebounding as well.

In 2017, the Asian Economic Integration Report (AEIR) of the Asian Development Bank unveiled a new composite index—the Asia-Pacific Regional Cooperation and Integration Index (ARCII)—to gauge the degree of regional cooperation and integration in Asia and the Pacific. This year's report presents the time series of the ARCII that shows a broadly steady, yet modestly strengthening, trend of regional integration in Asia and the Pacific over 2006–2016. Infrastructure and connectivity appear to be the most forceful and stable foundation for regional integration in Asia and the Pacific. But, over time, trade and investment have strengthened as a major contributor to regional integration. The extension of the ARCII using a panel data set also allows an empirical exercise to investigate the role of regional integration as an important development strategy. Empirical findings suggest that regional integration has had significant positive impact on economic growth and poverty reduction.

Asia and the Pacific continues to lead the recovery in world trade, while strengthening its intraregional share offers a buffer against the fallout from increasingly inward-looking policies worldwide. Asia's intraregional trade share—measured by value—rose to 57.8% in 2017 from 57.2% in 2016—above the 55.9% average during 2010–2015. Despite a downturn in global investment, FDI in Asia—inward and outward—weakened only slightly. Intraregional FDI increased slightly by both absolute value ($260.0 billion in 2017 from $254.7 billion in 2016) and by share (50.2% from 49.0%). Asia's portfolio investors continue to invest outside the region, with stable intraregional shares of outward equity (debt) investment below 20%—at 18.1% (16.4%) in 2017 from 19.3% (15.3%) in 2016. On the other hand, the region's demand for cross-border bank financing is increasingly met regionally, as the intraregional share of Asia's cross-border bank claims rose from 18.2% in 2012 to 22.6% in 2017. About one in three international migrants are from Asia and the Pacific. The number of international migrants residing in Asia and the Pacific grew from 41.8 million to 42.4 million between 2015 and 2017. The vast majority (78.0%) of international tourism in Asia and the Pacific is also intraregional.

AEIR 2018 includes a special chapter on regional public goods (RPGs). "Toward Optimal Provision of Regional Public Goods in Asia and the Pacific" examines how collective actions among countries can help find solutions to growing transnational development challenges. Increasing regional economic cooperation and integration in Asia and the Pacific has amplified these cross-border challenges and highlights the importance of providing RPGs. RPGs such as cross-border infrastructure, sustainable management of shared natural resources, and cross-border disease surveillance and control offer benefits beyond a single nation's territory. However, independent actions from each nation with different interests may not generate the adequate supply of RPGs to capture their transnational benefits and/or tackle these challenges at the regional level. While quantifying the total benefits of RPGs is challenging given the externalities and spillovers, it is even more difficult to identify and measure specific benefits enjoyed by all individual beneficiaries.

The special chapter discusses appropriate modes of provision as for the type of RPGs to effectively cope with weak individual interests for cooperation that give rise to the so-called "collective action problem." The chapter reviews various case studies from Asia and the Pacific, Europe, and Latin America and the Caribbean that have facilitated RPGs, greater regional cooperation, and collective action. Especially in Asia and the Pacific, the establishment of an integrated tsunami early warning systems illustrates how regional arrangements can effectively complement national and global efforts to reduce the region's vulnerabilities and improve preparedness and response to natural hazards. Finally, the chapter suggests the key roles of multilateral development banks like the Asian Development Bank as an honest broker in enhancing mutual trust and facilitating regional cooperation for the RPG provision through knowledge, finance, and coordination in country efforts.

Yasuyuki Sawada
Chief Economist and Director General
Economic Research and Regional Cooperation Department
Asian Development Bank

ACKNOWLEDGMENTS

The *Asian Economic Integration Report 2018* was prepared by the Regional Cooperation and Integration Division (ERCI) of the Economic Research and Regional Cooperation Department of the Asian Development Bank (ADB), under the overall supervision of ERCI Director Cyn-Young Park. Jong Woo Kang coordinated overall production assisted by Mara Claire Tayag. ERCI consultants under Technical Assistance 9121: Asian Economic Integration—Building Knowledge for Policy Dialogue compiled data and conducted research and analysis.

Contributing authors include Cyn-Young Park, James Villafuerte, Racquel Claveria, and Xylee Javier, with data support from Pilar Dayag (Regional Economic Outlook and Development Challenges); Jong Woo Kang, Suzette Dagli, Dorothea Ramizo, and Paul Mariano (Trade and the Global Value Chain); Fahad Khan, Suzette Dagli, Cindy Jane Justo, with contribution from Elisabetta Gentile, Donald Bertulfo, and data support from David Joseph Anabo (Foreign Direct Investment); Junkyu Lee, Peter Rosenkranz, Bo Zhao, Michael Angelo Cokee, and Clemence Fatima Cruz, with contributions to the boxes from Satoru Yamadera, Kosintr Puongsophol, and Ross Buckley (Financial Integration); and Aiko Kikkawa Takenaka and Ma. Concepcion Latoja, with contribution from Raymond Gaspar (Movement of People). The chapter "Subregional Cooperation Initiatives" was consolidated by Paulo Rodelio Halili based on inputs from Shaista Hussain, Guoliang Wu, and Ronaldo Oblepias (Central and West Asia); the Greater Mekong Subregion Secretariat (Southeast Asia); Ying Qian, Dorothea Lazaro, Stephanie Kamal, Edith Joan Nacpil, Aihua Wu, and Chaoyi Hu (East Asia); Rosalind McKenzie, Jesusito Tranquilino, and Leticia de Leon (South Asia); and Paul Curry, Hanna Uusimaa, and Rommel Rabanal (the Pacific). The global value chain analysis in "Trade and the Global Value Chain" chapter benefited from construction of input-output tables by a team headed by Mahinthan J. Mariasingham from ERCD's Development Economics and Indicators Division.

Junkyu Lee and Kijin Kim coordinated and contributed to the production of the theme chapter, "Toward the Optimal Provision of Regional Public Goods in Asia and the Pacific." Background papers were provided by Todd Sandler, Scott Barrett, John Weiss, Chang-Soo Lee, Guntram Wolff, Gustav Fredriksson, Scott Marcus, Silvia Merle, Simone Tagliapietra, Yikihiro Shiroishi, Junkyu Lee, Kijin Kim, Ricardo Ang, Manuel Albis, and Aiko Kikkawa Takenaka. Benjamin Endriga, Ricardo Ang, Monica Melchor, Alyssa Villanueva, and Mikko Diaz provided research support. Joint collaboration with the Inter-American Development Bank was supported by Antoni Estevadeordal, Joaquim Tres, Matthew Shearer, and Paulo Barbieri.

Guy Sacerdoti and James Unwin edited the report. Ariel Paelmo typeset and produced the layout, with Tuesday Soriano as the proofreader. Erickson Mercado designed the cover and assisted in typesetting. Paulo Rodelio Halili, Aleli Rosario, and Carol Ongchangco helped in proofreading. The Printing Services Unit of ADB's Office of Administrative Services printed the report and the Publishing and Dissemination Unit of ADB's Department of Communications published it. Carol Ongchangco, Pia Asuncion Tenchavez, Maria Criselda Aherrera, and Marilyn Parra provided administrative and secretarial support, and helped organize the AEIR workshops, launch events, and other AEIR-related seminars. Karen Lane of the Department of Communications coordinated the dissemination of AEIR 2018.

DEFINITIONS

The economies covered in the *Asian Economic Integration Report 2018* are grouped by major analytic or geographic group.

- Asia refers to the 48 Asia and the Pacific members of the Asian Development Bank, which includes Japan and Oceania (Australia and New Zealand) in addition to the 45 developing Asian economies.

- Subregional economic groupings are as follows:
  - Central Asia comprises Armenia, Azerbaijan, Georgia, Kazakhstan, the Kyrgyz Republic, Tajikistan, Turkmenistan, and Uzbekistan.
  - East Asia comprises Hong Kong, China; Japan; the People's Republic of China; the Republic of Korea; Mongolia; and Taipei,China.
  - South Asia comprises Afghanistan, Bangladesh, Bhutan, India, Maldives, Nepal, Pakistan, and Sri Lanka.
  - Southeast Asia comprises Brunei Darussalam, Cambodia, Indonesia, the Lao People's Democratic Republic, Malaysia, Myanmar, the Philippines, Singapore, Thailand, and Viet Nam.
  - The Pacific comprises the Cook Islands, the Federated States of Micronesia, Fiji, Kiribati, the Marshall Islands, the Federated States of Micronesia, Nauru, Palau, Papua New Guinea, Samoa, Solomon Islands, Timor-Leste, Tonga, Tuvalu, and Vanuatu.
  - Oceania includes Australia and New Zealand.

Unless otherwise specified, the symbol "$" and the word "dollar" refer to United States dollars, and percent changes are year-on-year.

ABBREVIATIONS

ADB	Asian Development Bank
AfDB	African Development Bank
AEIR	Asian Economic Integration Report
AFC	Asian financial crisis
APEC	Asia-Pacific Economic Cooperation
ARCII	Asia-Pacific Regional Cooperation and Integration Index
ASEAN	Association of Southeast Asian Nations (Brunei Darussalam, Cambodia, Indonesia, the Lao People's Democratic Republic, Malaysia, Myanmar, the Philippines, Singapore, Thailand, and Viet Nam)
ASEAN+3	ASEAN plus Japan, the People's Republic of China, and the Republic of Korea
BOP	balance of payments
BEZ	border economic zone
CAREC	Central Asia Regional Economic Cooperation
CAST	Common Agenda for the Modernization of Sanitary and Phytosanitary Measures for Trade
CBTA	Cross-Border Transport Facilitation Agreement
CEF	Connecting Europe Facility
COP21	21st Conference of the Parties to the United Nations Framework Convention on Climate Change
CPTPP	Comprehensive and Progressive Agreement for Trans-Pacific Partnership
DALY	disability-adjusted life years
DCC	dynamic conditional correlations
DRM	disaster risk management
EEZ	exclusive economic zone
ENPV	economic net present value
ESCAP	Economic and Social Commission for Asia and the Pacific
EU	European Union (Austria, Belgium, Bulgaria, Croatia, Cyprus, Czech Republic, Denmark, Estonia, Finland, France, Germany, Greece, Hungary, Ireland, Italy, Latvia, Lithuania, Luxembourg, Malta, the Netherlands, Poland, Portugal, Romania, Slovak Republic, Slovenia, Spain, Sweden, and the United Kingdom)
EWEC	East–West economic corridor
FDI	foreign direct investment
FFA	Forum Fisheries Agency
FSI	Financial Stress Index
FTA	free trade agreement
GDP	gross domestic product
GFC	global financial crisis
GMS	Greater Mekong Subregion
GPG	global public good
GVC	global value chain
GZAR	Guangxi Zhuang Autonomous Region
ICT	information and communication technology
IDB	Inter-American Development Bank
IMAR	Inner Mongolia Autonomous Region
Lao PDR	Lao People's Democratic Republic
M&A	merger and acquisition
MDB	multilateral development bank
MOU	memorandum of understanding
MW	megawatt
MWh	megawatt-hour
NPG	national public good
ODA	official development assistance
PACER	Pacific Agreement on Closer Economic Relations
PNA	Parties to the Nauru Agreement

PRC	People's Republic of China
RCEP	Regional Cooperation Economic Partnership
RCI	regional cooperation and integration
RPG	regional public good
RKSI	Regional Knowledge Sharing Initiative
ROW	rest of the world
SASEC	South Asia Subregional Economic Cooperation
SASEC OP	SASEC Operational Plan
SDG	Sustainable Development Goal
SMEs	small and medium-sized enterprises
SPS	sanitary and phytosanitary
TPP	Trans-Pacific Partnership
UK	United Kingdom
UN	United Nations
UNEP	United Nations Environmental Programme
US	United States
TVET	technical and vocational education and training
UNESCO	United Nations Educational, Scientific and Cultural Organization
WGPG	Working Group on Performance Standards and Grid Code
WGRI	Working Group on Regulatory Issues
WMO	World Meteorological Organization
WTO	World Trade Organization
WTO TFA	World Trade Organization Trade Facilitation Agreement

HIGHLIGHTS

Regional Economic Outlook and Development Challenges

The Asia and Pacific region maintains healthy economic growth outlook. Excluding high-income economies, the region will grow at 6.0% this year and 5.8% in 2019. However, risks remain tilted to the downside with international trade conflicts escalating and elevated debt levels exposing the region's financial vulnerability as United States (US) monetary policy normalization continues. While volatility of net capital flows across equity, foreign direct investment (FDI), and financial derivatives have declined since 2016, volatility in net debt investment flows increased, reflecting the potential spillovers from US interest rate hikes. With greater economic interdependence and integration contributing to faster transmission of global economic shocks, the region's policy makers should closely monitor the risks rising from global trade and financial market conditions, while remaining vigilant to safeguard financial and economic stability.

The Asia-Pacific Regional Cooperation and Integration Index shows a modestly growing trend in regional integration with positive growth impact. In 2017, the Asian Economic Integration Report of the Asian Development Bank (ADB) unveiled a new composite index—the Asia-Pacific Regional Cooperation and Integration Index (ARCII)—to gauge the degree of regional cooperation and integration in Asia.[1] This year's report presents the extension of the ARCII using a panel data set—the time series ARCII shows a broadly steady, yet modestly strengthening, trend of regional integration in Asia over 2006–2016. Infrastructure and connectivity appear to be the most forceful and stable foundation for regional integration in Asia. Over time, trade and investment have strengthened as a major contributor to regional integration. An empirical exercise reveals that regional value chain, movement of people, and institutional and social integration have been significant drivers of economic growth, while overall regional integration helped reduce poverty.

Trade and the Global Value Chain

Asia continues to lead a recovery in world trade with further strengthening in its intraregional trade in 2017. In 2017, Asia's trade (by volume) grew faster than global trade and surpassed its own economic growth for the first time since 2012. Asia's trade growth accelerated to 7.1% in 2017 from 1.7% in 2016 while world trade growth grew 4.7% from 1.8%. Asia's intraregional trade share—measured by value—also rose to 57.8% in 2017 from 57.2% in 2016—above the average 55.9% during 2010–2015. The simultaneous recovery in global and regional trade can be attributed to the expansion of the global value chain (GVC)—after a continued slowdown since 2012—with Asia's GVC participation rebounding as well.

Escalation of international trade conflict can undermine continued recovery of global and regional trade. The most imminent downside risk to the Asian economy comes from the rise in trade measures from the US and countermeasures from the People's Republic of China (PRC). In fact, international trade conflicts have escalated substantially since the beginning of this year, particularly with the tariffs and countermeasures between the US and the PRC amounting to 25.0% tariff on $50.0 billion worth of each other's imports as of August. Asia's trade growth (by volume) also eased slightly to 6.1% during the first 7 months of 2018. While the direct impact of the new tariffs implemented thus far is estimated to be small, uncertainty about future tariff rates and trade policy could dampen the recovery momentum in global trade. While the region's trade growth can also be affected through potential second-round effect on global supply chains, the real damage could be the impact of trade policy uncertainty on business and consumer confidence, adversely affecting capital spending and other investment decisions.

---

1 Asia refers to the 48 Asia and the Pacific members of ADB, which includes Japan and Oceania (Australia and New Zealand) in addition to the 45 developing member economies.

Foreign Direct Investment

Despite a slowdown in inward FDI to Asia, intraregional FDI continues to rise. Global FDI into the region (measured by gross inward FDI) remains stable at $517.5 billion in 2017 from $519.9 billion in 2016—yet the region's share of global inward FDI rose to 36.2% in 2017 from 27.8% in 2016. Intraregional FDI increased slightly by both absolute value (to $260.0 billion in 2017 from $254.7 billion in 2016) and by share (to 50.2% from 49.0%). Greenfield investments generated some 667,000 jobs in 2017—mainly in India, the PRC, Viet Nam, the Philippines, and Singapore—in real estate, software and information technology (IT) services, and electronic components, among others. Almost half of jobs created through greenfield investments in Asia originated within the region—led by investments from Japan (28.0%), the PRC (15.0%), and the Republic of Korea (14.2%).

Asia's outward FDI moderated by 1.4% in 2017—to $487.9 billion from $494.9 billion in 2016. Asia's global share of outward FDI reached 34.1% in 2017, up from 33.6% in 2016. Japan; the PRC; and Hong Kong, China were among the world's top 10 global investors. Japan was second globally, investing $160.4 billion—30.6% invested in Asia. The PRC's outward FDI slowed by 36.5% from 2016, to $124.6 billion. Emerging Asian investors boosted outward FDI in 2017—with, for example, India doubling its outward investments in sectors such as electronic components and rubber, and Thailand increasing by more than 50% in building and construction material and chemicals, among others.

Financial Integration

Inward portfolio (equity and debt) investment to Asia increased sharply in 2017, driven by a surge in inward equity investment; but the pace will likely moderate in 2018 due to the regional equity markets' relatively tepid performance. International holdings of Asian portfolio equity assets increased by $1.3 trillion in 2017, exceeding the total increase of $954.0 billion over the past 4 years combined. The majority of the surge in 2017 can be attributed to increased inward equity investment by the US ($606.2 billion) and the European Union (EU) ($368.3 billion),[2] with the intraregional share edged down to 15.1%. Ample global liquidity, favorable economic conditions in the region, and investors' appetite for positive equity returns from Asia based on buoyant market performance in 2017 were behind the boost. International holdings of Asian portfolio debt assets also increased by $390.4 billion in 2017, of which $138.7 billion can be attributed to the investment by the rest of the world (excluding the EU and the US), primarily in Japanese debt securities ($78.1 billion), while the intraregional share remains generally stable at 25.5%. However, Asia's cross-border bank liabilities decreased by $107.9 billion in 2017, mainly due to a contraction of bank claims by the EU and the US on Asia—by $78.5 billion from the EU and $42.0 billion from the US—in tandem with the progress in US monetary policy normalization. The intraregional share of Asia's cross-border bank liabilities stands at 27.2%.

Asia's outward portfolio investment and bank claims continue to grow; while the intraregional shares of Asia's international portfolio debt holdings and bank claims have increased, that of its international portfolio equity holdings has decreased. Asia's portfolio investors continue to invest outside the region, with intraregional shares of outward equity (debt) investment below 20%—at 18.1% (16.4%) in 2017 from 19.3% (15.3%) in 2016. Asia's outward equity investment outstanding rose to $4.5 trillion from $3.5 trillion. Outward debt investment outstanding by Asia was $4.2 trillion in 2017, up from $3.9 trillion in 2016—driven largely by a rise in Asian holdings of debt securities issued by regional economies ($92.6 billion) and the rest of the world ($96.2 billion), excluding the EU and the US. Asia's outstanding cross-border bank claims reached $4.6 trillion in 2017, up from $4.4 trillion in 2016, given

2 Japan ($285.3 billion), the Republic of Korea ($134.5 billion), and the PRC ($112.3 billion) were among the major beneficiaries of the inward equity investment by the US and the EU in 2017.

the sizable upturn in global international banking activities in 2017. The increase was predominantly driven by growing overseas bank lending by Japanese banks—the largest foreign lenders globally. The region's demand for cross-border bank financing is increasingly met regionally, as the intraregional share of Asia's cross-border bank claims rose from 18.2% in 2012 to 22.6% in 2017.

Uncertainty surrounding the changes in global financial conditions has led to rising sensitivity to global shocks in Asian equity and bond markets. Both local bond and equity returns have become more sensitive to global shocks since the US monetary policy normalization began. This increasing vulnerability to external shocks is further underpinned by an elevated exposure to international investors, especially from outside the region, whose holdings of Asian portfolio assets grew between 2016 and 2017 from $3.4 trillion to $4.5 trillion in equity and from $1.7 trillion to $2.0 trillion in debt.

Movement of People

Asia continues as the largest source of international migrants globally although the number of Asian migrants headed to regional destinations declined slightly. The global stock of international migrants from Asia rose 3.9% from 83.6 million in 2015 to 86.9 million in 2017. About one in three international migrants are from Asia led by India and the PRC. The number of international migrants residing in Asia[3] also by 1.4%—from 41.8 million to 42.4 million, with more than 70% of them from the region. While Australia tops the list of Asian countries hosting international migrants, India, and Thailand attract the most migrants from their respective subregions, South Asia and Southeast Asia. Outbound migration to the non-regional destinations surpasses intraregional migration, as the region's skilled and unskilled migrant workers continue to favor developed countries and the Middle East over regional host economies. Nevertheless, the region is expected to employ a growing number of migrants as many Asian economies face rapid aging and a declining workforce. As the global economy strengthened its recovery, remittances to Asia surged—to a record $272.5 billion in 2017.

Tourism continues to grow, both within and outside the region. Tourist arrivals in Asia reached 378.5 million in 2016, up 9.3% over 2015 and well above the 3.7% global growth. The vast majority (78.0%) of international tourism in Asia is intraregional—the number of intraregional Asian tourists grew from 235.0 million to 295.3 million between 2012 and 2016. The PRC is by far the most popular destination of Asian tourists, followed by Macau, China; Malaysia; and Thailand. With growing per capita income, Asian tourists heading to non-Asian destinations have grown as well over the past 5 years. Those traveling outside Asia increased 18.6% (16.1 million) to 102.3 million—below the 25.7% growth (60.4 million) in intraregional tourism. International tourism receipts in the region reached a record $346.0 billion in 2016, 5.3% higher than 2015. East Asia and Southeast Asia earned the most from tourism in absolute terms. However, Maldives tops the list of countries most dependent on tourism, with receipts accounting for 68.0% of its gross domestic product (GDP) in 2016.

3 The PRC (5.2 million), the Russian Federation (3.8 million), Bangladesh (3.7 million), and India (3.3 million) are among the top source countries of international migrants to Asia.

Toward Optimal Provision of Regional Public Goods in Asia and the Pacific

With growing economic interdependence and integration, the region increasingly faces development challenges that are transnational in nature, such as infrastructure connectivity within the region, environmental degradation and resource scarcity, and transnational health threats or infectious diseases. Regional public goods (RPGs) such as cross-border infrastructure, sustainable management of shared natural resources, and cross-border disease surveillance and control offer benefits beyond a single nation's territory. While the provision of such RPGs can be shared by multiple countries in the region, collective action by all countries in the region can create spillover effects across the region that are greater than the sum of voluntary contributions by individual countries. On the other hand, independent actions from each nation with different interests may not generate the adequate supply of RPGs to capture their transnational benefits and/or tackle these challenges at the regional level.

Regional arrangements can encourage collective action. Even in the provision of global public goods such as control or elimination of malaria, regional arrangements can complement the global frameworks and help more effective implementation. With fewer nations involved, they reduce uncertainty and take advantage of spatial and cultural proximity in supplying global and regional public goods collectively. In this context, past and ongoing interactions among a smaller group of regional economies facilitate compliance with international arrangements.

However, the challenges in providing RPGs arise from the difficulty of attributing their benefits to specific individual contributions. Quantifying the total benefits of RPGs is extremely difficult given the externalities and spillovers, but it is even more difficult to identify (and estimate the amount of) specific benefits enjoyed by all individual countries. Ideally, if one can identify who benefits and how much from the provision of RPGs, then one can charge each benefit recipient the marginal cost of provision. However, by the nature of public goods, it is very difficult, if not impossible, to exclude individual countries from enjoying the benefits of RPGs once provided. The boundary for the benefits of RPGs is also difficult to define, as the spillover range to which the RPG benefits reach would not be easily identified. The scope of benefits is often and increasingly unclear with growing cross-border linkages, while even national public goods are becoming increasingly interlinked and challenge the domain of regional and global public goods.

Conclusions and Policy Considerations

Understanding how an individual nation's contribution adds to the overall provision of RPGs can help RPG suppliers, including nations and multilateral development banks (MDBs) alike, take the most appropriate modes of provision to avoid the collective action problem. While all regional economies would be better off cooperating to provide RPGs, conflicting interests among them and the cost associated with provision would often discourage mutual cooperation—so called "collective action problem." In this context, the application of appropriate "aggregation technologies" (that is, how individual contributions add up to make the socially available level of the public good) provides the right incentives for collective action to ensure sufficient provision of RPGs.

- For example, when the sum of each nation's contribution would make the overall supply of the RPG, policy intervention should focus on preventing free riding. An example for this type is reducing greenhouse gas emissions. The sum of each contributor's emission reductions would make the overall reduction of the greenhouse gas emissions. The more countries participate and contribute to the emission reduction, the greater is the benefit of climate change mitigation. However, a nonparticipating country can easily enjoy the benefit of emission reductions by participating others; therefore, it is important to prevent free riding.

- When the smallest contribution by the most vulnerable determines the available level of RPG, it would be efficient that policy intervention is directed to assist the most vulnerable countries in need of funding and capacity building. This is known as the "weakest link." An example for this type would be prevention and control of communicable diseases such as malaria.

- When the largest contribution by the leading country determines the available level of RPG, policy support is better dedicated to a leading country with a commitment and ability. This is the "best shot" type. For example, development of vaccines would have the best chance of success if the most technologically advanced country takes a lead.

Regional experiences highlight the important roles of regional institutions in facilitating regional cooperation and coordination; collective action; and complementarity among national, regional, and global efforts in providing adequate level of RPGs.

- **European experiences show that the provision of RPGs can be led and coordinated by regional institutions, including common legislation and regulations.** For example, the EU tries to achieve a fully integrated energy system for the region to ensure energy security such as stable energy supply and affordable prices. The experience illustrates that the EU-wide legislation together with the cooperation of national energy regulators made significant contributions to the progress toward the integrated energy system.

- **The experience of Latin America and the Caribbean illustrates the importance of sequencing and innovations for collective action to promote regional cooperation and facilitate RPG provision.** For many Latin American and Caribbean countries, trade integration has been a common policy priority. Therefore, pursuing trade integration provides an effective first step to foster provision in other related RPG sectors such as cross-border infrastructure. Also helpful in promoting collective action was the adoption of an innovative approach to form a new group for economic cooperation such as the Pacific Alliance based on mutual interests rather than geographic proximity.

- **Experiences in Asia stress the need for regional approaches to tackling common issues that can complement national and global efforts.** For example, the development of the early warning system for tsunamis across the Indian Ocean has improved detection and reporting of disasters significantly, which was complemented by national efforts such as communication and trained responses. Like malaria control in the Greater Mekong Subregion, a stronger regional response could also improve the effectiveness in the prevention of communicable disease outbreaks both regionally and globally.

Developing economies are generally aware of the benefits of RPGs, but view it difficult to contribute to RPG provision. The provision of RPGs by developing economies is often hampered by (i) the difficulty in striking a balance between national and regional interests in development priorities, (ii) the perception of benefits being potentially unequal among contributing economies, and (iii) a shortage of financial resources and capacity to meet the demands for RPGs.

- **Collective action can be promoted if national development priorities align with the need for RPGs.** For example, when a group of countries share better infrastructure connectivity as their respective national development policies, coordinating more cross-border infrastructure investment can be easily facilitated. As such, the region can benefit from having a mechanism in place to share information on national development priorities and the benefits of RPGs among regional stakeholders.

- **It is important to develop better measures to estimate the spillover benefits of RPGs while making more effort to identify potential beneficiary countries who are yet to be included in the group of RPG suppliers.** The perception of free riding and lack of understanding of specific benefits enjoyed by each individual country deter developing countries from making their contributions toward RPGs. More effort to identify and place a value on shared regional benefits, in addition to more information about clear benefits for each individual country, should be made. A guideline or criteria for the design of regional projects with appropriate methodologies to measure their full benefits would further help providers and beneficiaries of RPGs alike.

- **Multilateral development banks (MDBs) can help increase RPG provision via reducing knowledge and financing gaps as well as playing the role of an honest broker to enhance mutual trust and facilitate regional cooperation for the provision of RPGs.** MDBs have been active in RPG provision often reinforced by technical support and capacity building where needed. In addition, they can help facilitate RPG provision of their member economies by strengthening knowledge and information sharing on the benefits and the costs of provision. The strengths of MDBs also build on effective coordination and their role as an honest broker with their accumulated social capital from member countries and local communities. Their in-depth knowledge and experiences in multiple countries and sectors allow a more holistic and integrated approach to address regional and subregional development challenges and hence promote regional cooperation for RPG provision that can complement national efforts.

1

Regional Economic Outlook and Development Challenges

Economic Outlook and Risks

ADB forecasts for developing Asia's economic outlook have improved since the *Asian Economic Integration Report 2017*—economic output is set to grow 6.0% in 2018 from 6.1% in 2017.

Developing Asia's economic growth in 2018 is 0.2 percentage points above the estimate used as a backdrop for last year's Asian Economic Integration Report.[1] Some 26 of the region's 45 developing economies (57.8%) recorded a better-than-expected economic expansion according to the latest forecasts of the Asian Development Bank (ADB) available in the Asian Development Outlook 2018 Update. The People's Republic of China (PRC) is expected to grow 6.6% in 2018, bolstered by strong economic performance in the first half of the year (Table 1.1).

Over the past year, external conditions improved—growth in the euro area has been revised upwards (by 0.2 percentage points) along with the United States (US) (0.4 percentage points). Even as the first quarter 2018 growth in the euro area slowed to 1.6%, it stabilized at 1.5% in the second quarter as labor markets improved, the accommodative monetary policy continued, and fiscal support remained intact. In Japan, growth recovered strongly in the second quarter of 2018, reversing the contraction in the previous quarter. In the US, growth accelerated to 4.2% in the second quarter of 2018 from 2.2% growth in the previous quarter (first half growth reached 3.2%). If this trend continues, the US Federal Reserve may be forced to raise interest rates faster than expected.

Table 1.1: Regional Gross Domestic Product Growth[a] (%, year-on-year)

	2014	2015	2016	2017	Q1 2018	Q2 2018	Forecast[b] 2018	Forecast[b] 2019
Developing Asia[c]	**6.3**	**6.0**	**5.9**	**6.1**	-	-	**6.0**	**5.8**
Central Asia	**5.1**	**3.1**	**2.7**	**4.3**	-	-	**4.1**	**4.2**
East Asia (ex-Japan)	**6.6**	**6.1**	**6.0**	**6.3**	-	-	**6.0**	**5.7**
China, People's Republic of	7.3	6.9	6.7	6.9	6.8	6.7	6.6	6.3
South Asia[d]	**6.9**	**7.4**	**6.7**	**6.5**	-	-	**7.0**	**7.2**
India	7.4	8.2	7.1	6.7	8.2	-	7.3	7.6
Southeast Asia	**4.7**	**4.7**	**4.7**	**5.2**	-	-	**5.1**	**5.2**
The Pacific[e]	**9.6**	**8.1**	**2.4**	**2.4**	-	-	**1.1**	**3.1**
Major Industrialized Economies[f]								
Euro area	1.3	2.1	1.8	2.5	1.6	1.5	2.0	1.9
Japan	0.4	1.4	1.0	1.7	-0.9	3.0	1.1	1.0
United States	2.5	2.9	1.6	2.2	2.2	4.2	2.8	2.4

- = data not available.
[a] Aggregates weighted by gross national income levels (Atlas method, current $) from World Bank, World Development Indicators.
[b] Forecasts based on Asian Development Outlook Update 2018.
[c] Refers to the 45 developing members of the ADB.
[d] Data for Bangladesh, India, and Pakistan are according to their fiscal year. For India, the fiscal year is from April of the specified year through March of the following year. For Bangladesh and Pakistan, the fiscal year is from July of the previous year through June of the specified year.
[e] Excludes Nauru as weights are unavailable.
[f] Quarterly growth rates are based on quarter-on-quarter seasonally adjusted annualized rate.
Sources: ADB (2018); CEIC (accessed September 2018); and World Bank. World Development Indicators. https://data.worldbank.org/products/wdi (accessed September 2018).

[1] Developing Asia includes the 45 developing member countries of the Asian Development Bank (ADB).

Risks to the Outlook

Risks remain tilted to the downside, primarily due to the escalating trade frictions between the US and the PRC; in addition, elevated debt levels could cause greater financial market volatility as US monetary policy normalizes and interest payments rise.

The threat against open, free trade has begun—posing a clear downside risk to developing Asia's growth forecasts. In August, the US launched tariffs on $50 billion of PRC imports, and the PRC countered in kind. The US also canceled country exemptions from steel and aluminum tariffs, prompting countermeasures from Canada, the European Union, Mexico, and the Russian Federation.

Based on recent ADB estimates, the direct impact from the first set of tariffs had very little net effect on growth, investment, and the external current account balance (ADB 2018). But there is no assurance that a further escalation in protectionist measures will not disrupt global supply chains or curb future business expansion plans. Asia is one of the most open regions worldwide—and closely integrated into the global value chain—so a slowdown in global trade or any global shock to trade and investment could easily harm its economic prospects (Box 1.1).

Box 1.1: Trade Volume Outlook for Developing Asia

World trade growth is expected to slow moderately from 4.7% in 2017 to 4.5% in 2018 as growth eases in some advanced economies—likely to affect exports of emerging and developing economies as well.

Developing Asia's trade is also expected to grow but at a slower pace. Trade volume growth is projected to decline from the 7.6% estimate in 2017 to 5.5% in 2018. In the first 5 months of the year, the region's major economies saw trade volume growth moderating. A key risk to the trade volume projection is the escalating trade friction between the United States and the People's Republic of China (PRC) (ADB 2018).

As in previous years, the PRC will remain the key driver of developing Asia's trade growth, while the four middle-income economies of the Association of Southeast Asian Nations (Indonesia, Malaysia, the Philippines, and Thailand) and the newly industrialized economies (Hong Kong, China; the Republic of Korea; Singapore; and Taipei,China) will also provide a boost. Imports to these economies will be buoyed by robust domestic demand, while exports will benefit from growing intraregional demand.

Trade Volume Growth (%, year-on-year)

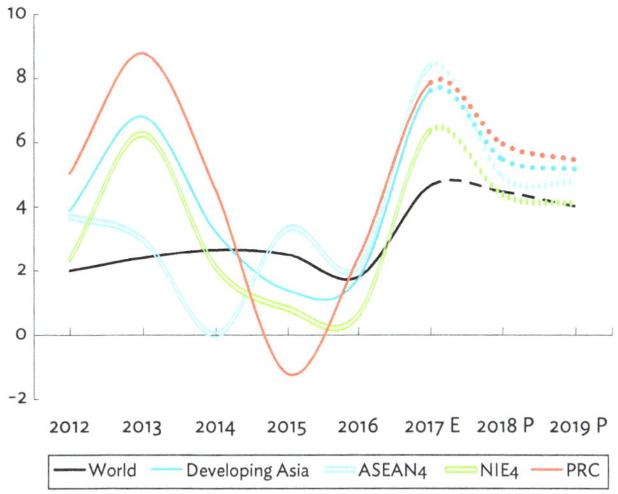

ASEAN = Association of Southeast Asian Nations, E = estimate, GDP = gross domestic product, NIE = newly industrialized economies, P = projected, PRC = People's Republic of China.

Note: ASEAN4 includes Indonesia, Malaysia, the Philippines, and Thailand. NIE4 includes Hong Kong, China; the Republic of Korea; Singapore; and Taipei,China. Trade volume growth projections are calculated using trade volume growth rates of all economies, which were generated using each economy's elasticities-to-real GDP (for imports) and elasticities-to-real GDP of top trading partners (for exports).

Sources: ADB calculations using data from International Monetary Fund. World Economic Outlook April 2018 database. https://www.imf.org/external/pubs/ft/weo/2018/01/weodata/index.aspx (accessed May 2018); International Monetary Fund. Direction of Trade Database. https://www.imf.org/en/Data (accessed August 2018); and World Trade Organization Statistics database. http://stat.wto.org/Home/WSDBHome.aspx (accessed May 2018).

High debt levels can be a destabilizing factor for the financial sector.

Since the 2008/09 global financial crisis, many large developing economies in the region have rapidly accumulated private external debt as a share of gross domestic product (GDP). For example, the PRC's corporate debt rose from 120% of GDP in 2009 to 160% in 2017. The ratio has increased significantly in Thailand; the Republic of Korea; Hong Kong, China; and Singapore. The concern is that these ratios could prove unsustainable should global interest rates rise sharply.

Given this concern and market expectations of further rate rises in the US, many developing Asian currencies weakened relative to the US dollar from early-April 2018 to the end of September. Leading the group is the Indian rupee, which depreciated 11.2% over the period. The PRC yuan fell 9.4%, the Indonesian rupiah 8.4%, Japanese yen 7.4%, and the Malaysian ringgit 7.2%. The Korean won, Taipei,China NT dollar, Singapore dollar, Philippine peso, and Thai baht weakened between 3.8% and 5.0%.

Capital outflows from the region—mostly portfolio investment—have occurred recently.

The regional currency weakness—combined with higher 10-year US Treasury yields—triggered some bouts of capital outflows from emerging markets and the region (Figure 1.1). However, these mostly nonresident portfolio outflows could also be explained by the strong inflows of portfolio investment in 2017—which reached nearly $760 billion (see "Financial Integration", pp. 60–80).

Nonetheless, the decline in portfolio investment flows was far more muted compared with nonresident outflows during the 2013 "taper tantrum" episode. More importantly, nonresident capital outflows were more than offset by stronger inward flows of foreign direct investment and other investments—including bank lending. These inflows contributed to stronger accumulation of international reserves across much of the region, although some economies had foreign exchange reserves decline due to exchange rate volatility.

Still, there has been some market turbulence. For instance, elevated external debt in Argentina and Turkey recently contributed to some financial market turmoil and spillover effects—with the Turkish lira losing more than 40% of its value this year as markets reacted to Turkey's high external debt-to-GDP ratio (over 50%), high and rising inflation (15% in July), and the delayed response from the central bank after it failed to raise interest rates to defend the lira. This turbulence could generate spillover shocks to other emerging markets if confidence suffers, and risk perceptions lead investors to extract their investments.

Figure 1.1: Nonresident Portfolio Capital Inflows—Developing Asia ($ billion)

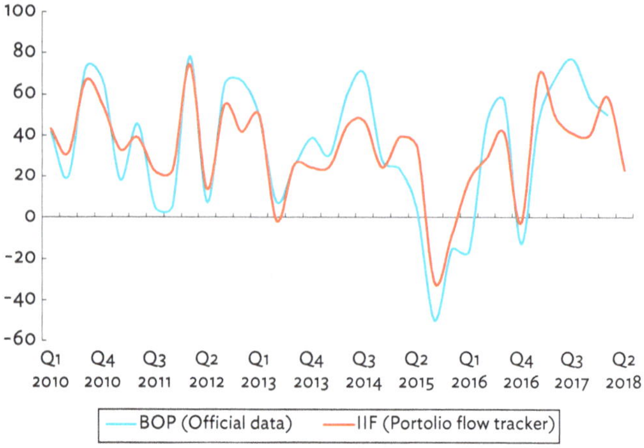

BOP = balance of payments, IIF = Institute of International Finance.
Notes: Portfolio flows are the sum of equity and debt flows. BOP data cover developing Asian economies: Brunei Darussalam; Cambodia; Hong Kong, China; India; Indonesia; the Lao People Democratic Republic; Malaysia; Myanmar; the People's Republic of China; the Philippines; the Republic of Korea; Singapore; Taipei,China; Thailand; and Viet Nam. The IIF data are based on the IIF monthly portfolio flow tracker, which covers India; Indonesia; Malaysia; the People's Republic of China; the Philippines; the Republic of Korea; Taipei,China; Thailand; and Viet Nam.
Sources: ADB calculations using data from CEIC; IIF. Monthly Portfolio Tracker. https://www.iif.com; and International Monetary Fund. International Financial Statistics. https://www.imf.org/en/Data (all accessed August 2018).

Capital flow volatility has subsided in developing Asia during the US monetary policy normalization—except for portfolio debt flows most affected by rising interest rates in the US.

For most subregions, the volatility of net debt investment flows into developing Asia has increased as US monetary policy normalization tightens global financial conditions since 2016. In contrast, during the same period, the volatility of net capital flows—in equity, foreign direct investment, and financial derivatives—has declined (Table 1.2).

Table 1.2: Capital Flow Volatility—Developing Asia (standard deviation of capital net flow levels as % of GDP)

Region	Portfolio (Debt) Pre-GFC Q1 1999–Q3 2007	Portfolio (Debt) Post-GFC Q3 2009–Q4 2015	Portfolio (Debt) MP Normalization Q1 2016–Q4 2017	**	Portfolio (Equity) Pre-GFC Q1 1999–Q3 2007	Portfolio (Equity) Post-GFC Q3 2009–Q4 2015	Portfolio (Equity) MP Normalization Q1 2016–Q4 2017	**
Central Asia	3.9	4.5	6.1	▲	1.8	1.0	0.4	▼
East Asia ex-Japan	1.5	0.7	0.7	▼	1.7	0.8	0.3	▼
South Asia	0.0	0.8	0.9	▲	0.9	1.0	0.6	▼
Southeast Asia	0.9	0.7	0.6	▼	0.8	0.6	0.5	▼
Developing Asia	**1.0**	**0.5**	**0.7**	▲	**1.0**	**0.7**	**0.3**	▼

Region	FDI Pre-GFC Q1 1999–Q3 2007	FDI Post-GFC Q3 2009–Q4 2015	FDI MP Normalization Q1 2016–Q4 2016	**	Financial Derivatives and Other Investments[a] Pre-GFC Q1 1999–Q3 2007	Financial Derivatives and Other Investments[a] Post-GFC Q3 2009–Q4 2015	Financial Derivatives and Other Investments[a] MP Normalization Q1 2016–Q4 2017	**
Central Asia	4.3	2.7	3.9	▲	4.2	6.6	4.9	▼
East Asia ex-Japan	1.6	0.9	0.8	▼	2.2	2.7	1.6	▼
South Asia	0.3	0.5	0.7	▲	1.7	1.3	1.2	▼
Southeast Asia	1.8	1.2	0.8	▼	3.0	2.5	1.9	▼
Developing Asia	**1.1**	**0.7**	**0.6**	▼	**1.7**	**2.0**	**1.4**	▼

** = refers to the direction of capital flow volatility between post-global financial crisis and post-normalization, ▼ = decrease, ▲ = increase, FDI = foreign direct investment, GDP = gross domestic product, GFC = global financial crisis, MP = monetary policy, SDR = special drawing rights.

[a] The category "Other Investments" includes (i) other equity; (ii) currency and deposits; (iii) loans (including use of International Monetary Fund credit and loans); (iv) nonlife insurance technical reserves, life insurance and annuities entitlements, pension entitlements, and provisions for calls under standardized guarantees; (v) trade credit and advances; (vi) other accounts receivable/payable; and (vii) SDR allocations (SDR holdings are included in reserve assets).

Notes: Central Asia includes Armenia, Azerbaijan, Georgia, Kazakhstan, the Kyrgyz Republic, and Tajikistan. East Asia (excluding Japan) includes Hong Kong, China; Mongolia; the People's Republic of China; and the Republic of Korea. South Asia includes India and Sri Lanka. Southeast Asia includes Brunei Darussalam, Indonesia, Malaysia, the Philippines, Singapore, Thailand, and Viet Nam. Data for Brunei Darussalam are only until Q4 2016.

Sources: ADB calculation using data from CEIC; and International Monetary Fund. Balance of Payments and International Investment Position Statistics. http://www.imf.org/external/np/sta/bop/bop.htm (both accessed July 2018).

The Financial Stress Index of developing Asia remains unusually low despite recurring economic and financial events, suggesting that investors have become more complacent toward risk.

Since December 2015, when the US Federal Reserve began normalizing its monetary policy—raising policy rates for the first time since June 2006—developing Asia's Financial Stress Index (FSI)—a composite index that measures the degree of financial stress in four major financial sectors and markets including the banking sector, debt, equity, and foreign exchange markets—has remained very low (Figure 1.2) despite a series of economic, financial, and policy events that have significant implications for financial stability. Though the US Federal Reserve rate hikes in 2017 and 2018 may have contributed to some uptick in the FSI, levels were nowhere near those during the global financial crisis or the 1998/99 Asian financial crisis.

A possible explanation is the wide array of reforms adopted in response to past crises—covering sound macroeconomic fundamentals (budget and foreign reserve management), more flexible exchange rates, stronger financial regulation and supervision, and a stronger regional cooperation framework—which likely contributed to bolstering the region's financial stability and resilience.

Yet, the current low FSI levels may also indicate that investors have become more complacent toward risk—despite looming financial vulnerabilities. Subdued

Figure 1.2: Financial Stress Index—Developing Asia

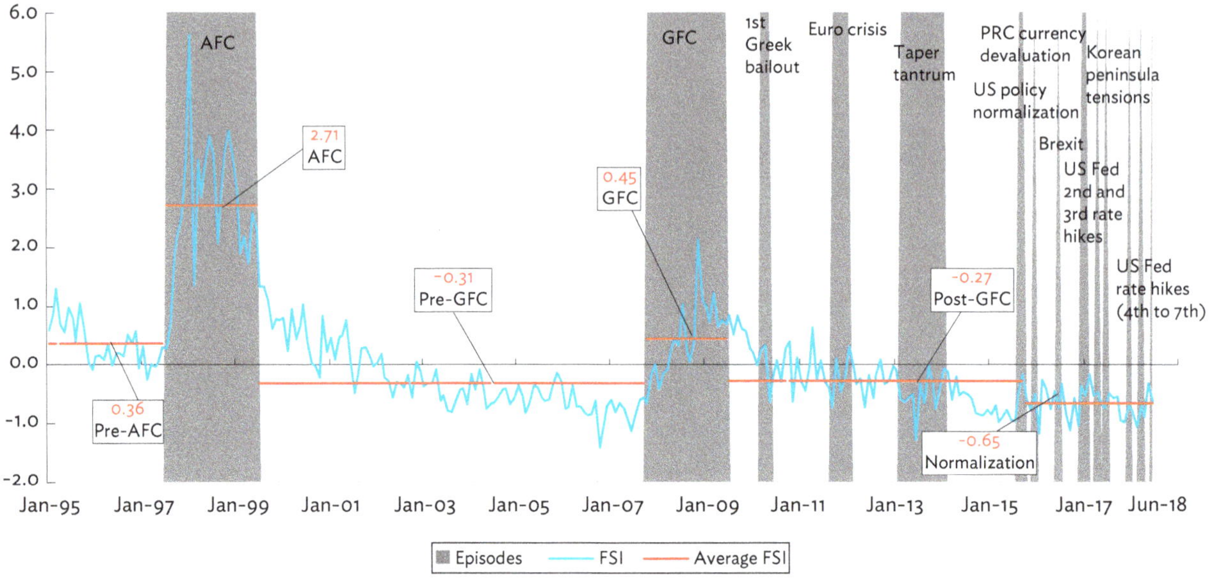

AFC = Asian financial crisis, FSI = Financial Stress Index, GFC = global financial crisis, PRC = People's Republic of China, US = United States, US Fed = United States Federal Reserve System.

Notes:

(i) Pre-AFC = Jan 1995–Jun 1997, AFC = Jul 1997–Jun 1999, Pre-GFC = Jul 1999–Sep 2007, GFC = Oct 2007–Jun 2009, Post-GFC = Jul 2009–Sep 2015, Normalization = Oct 2015–Jun 2018.

(ii) Based on principal components analysis on data from four major financial sectors: the banking sector, debt, equity, and foreign exchange markets. Principal components are based from banking sector price index, sovereign yield spreads, stock market volatility, stock price index, and exchange market pressure index.

(iii) Developing Asia includes Hong Kong, China; India; Indonesia; Malaysia; the Philippines; the PRC; the Republic of Korea; Singapore; Thailand; and Viet Nam.

Sources: ADB calculations using data from Bloomberg; CEIC; Haver Analytics (all accessed August 2018); and methodology by Park and Mercado (2014).

market volatility, coupled with a low risk premium, has often led to a buildup of systemic risks. Investor complacency may contribute to a major price correction in financial markets when investors' risk sentiments suddenly shift due to a worsening growth outlook, or an unexpected change in monetary and credit conditions and policies.

Development Challenges: Vulnerabilities to Economic, Environmental, and Social Shocks

Global economic shocks

Greater economic interdependence and integration is contributing to faster transmission of global economic shocks.

Since the global financial crisis, episodes like the 2010 European debt crisis, the 2013 taper tantrum, this year's sell-off of the Turkish lira, and the threat of escalating US–PRC trade tensions, remind everyone—from policy makers to investors—of the downside risks of a highly interconnected global economy. Until now, global financial and business cycles—and policy adjustments in the US—have largely driven capital flows, asset prices,

Figure 1.3: Percentage of Economies in Recession (%)

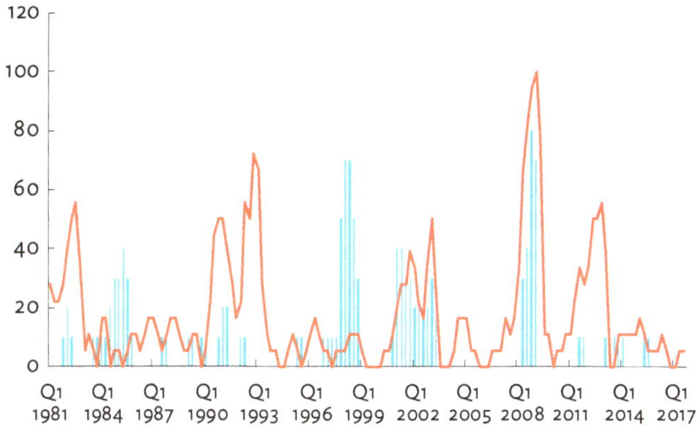

Notes:
(i) A recession is defined as the time (i.e., number of quarters) between the local peak and local trough as defined in ADB Institute (2009).
(ii) The sample for developing Asia includes Hong Kong, China; India; Indonesia; Malaysia; the People's Republic of China; the Philippines; Singapore; Taipei,China; and Thailand. The sample for advanced economies includes Austria, Belgium, Canada, Denmark, Finland, France, Germany, Greece, Ireland, Italy, the Netherlands, Norway, Portugal, Spain, Sweden, Switzerland, the United Kingdom, and the United States.

Sources: ADB calculations using data from data from Oxford Economics (accessed July 2018); and methodology by ADB Institute (2009).

Figure 1.4: Cumulative Output Loss from Recessions, 1981–2017 (% of peak real GDP, median)

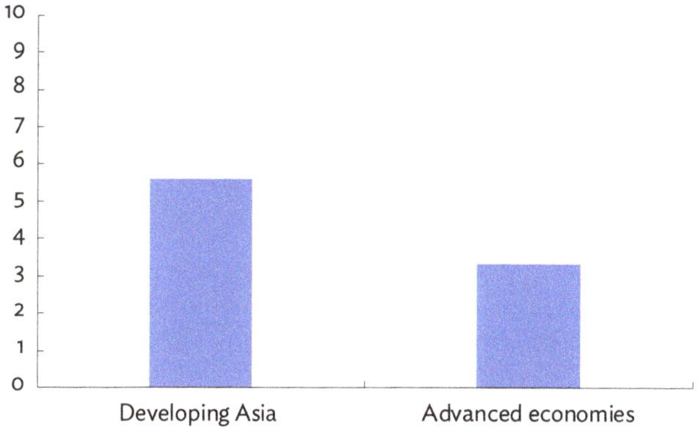

GDP = gross domestic product.

Notes:
(i) A recession is defined as the time (i.e., number of quarters) between the local peak and local trough as defined in ADB Institute (2009).
(ii) The cumulative loss was computed by estimating the median real GDP loss (expressed as % of peak GDP) during the recession periods using quarterly seasonally adjusted real GDP data in $, 2010 prices.
(iii) The sample for developing Asia includes Hong Kong, China; India; Indonesia; Malaysia; the People's Republic of China; the Philippines; Singapore; Taipei,China; and Thailand. The sample for advanced economies includes Austria, Belgium, Canada, Denmark, Finland, France, Germany, Greece, Ireland, Italy, the Netherlands, Norway, Portugal, Spain, Sweden, Switzerland, the United States, and the United Kingdom.

Sources: ADB calculations using data from Oxford Economics (accessed July 2018); and methodology by ADB Institute (2009).

and risk premia on a global scale, sometimes harming national economies.

This is evident from the strong correlation—since the Asian financial crisis—between the incidence of developing Asia's recessions with those globally; possibly a consequence of the region's deepening integration with the global economy (Figure 1.3). Generally, developing Asia's recessions do not last very long—their median duration is about 3 quarters. However, the cost of recessions to developing Asia is proportionately larger than those in advanced economies. For instance, the cumulative output losses from recessions in developing Asia have a median of around 5.6% of peak GDP compared with 3.3% for advanced economies (Figure 1.4). This validates the findings of Aghiar and Gopinath (2007), which attributed the large and persistent volatility in emerging markets to their less diversified economic structures and limited ability to tap the international financial system.

Moreover, the median cost of a recession also masks an important fact—that some of developing Asia's recessions have also been both deep and long. For instance, out of the 36 recorded recessions in the region since 1981, 6 episodes lasted more than a year and entailed cumulative output losses above 24% of peak GDP—about 4 times the median recorded loss.

Often, these long and deep recessions are associated with financial stress and banking crises—a direct offshoot of unfettered capital flows across borders, which fuels excessive global capital market volatility. The increasing pace of globalization, interconnectedness, technological advancements, and geopolitical dynamics could contribute to more frequent and debilitating global economic shocks, which will inevitably trigger economic fallout in the region. In short, today contagion is a given; and building resilience is therefore imperative.

Shocks from natural hazards

Economic costs from the loss of life and damage to property and natural resources caused by natural hazards are rising.

Developing Asia is one of the most disaster-prone regions worldwide—with devastating earthquakes, volcanic eruptions, tsunamis, typhoons, floods, drought, and landslides. Historically, the frequency of disasters

Table 1.3: Number of Disasters and Resultant Deaths, by Type—Developing Asia

Period	All Types		Climatological		Geophysical		Meteorological		Hydrological	
	Number of Disasters	Number of Deaths	Number of Disasters	Number of Deaths	Number of Disasters	Number of Deaths	Number of Disasters	Number of Deaths	Number of Disasters	Number of Deaths
1901–1910	5	20,806	–	–	4	20,566	1	240	–	–
1911–1920	12	844,235	1	500,000	5	193,235	3	51,000	3	100,000
1921–1930	10	3,318,211	1	3,000,000	5	212,211	4	106,000	–	–
1931–1940	24	4,517,576	–	–	9	155,718	10	1,358	5	4,360,500
1941–1950	14	67,931	–	–	5	4,141	5	3,060	4	60,730
1951–1960	58	2,054,809	–	–	11	4,581	32	9,742	15	2,040,486
1961–1970	71	40,683	3	–	13	14,195	41	24,997	14	1,491
1971–1980	143	318,073	10	–	19	283,141	70	4,327	44	30,605
1981–1990	349	37,212	14	1,591	54	5,651	163	16,102	118	13,868
1991–2000	537	64,726	29	2,353	71	6,435	222	22,542	215	33,396
2001–2010	773	245,118	31	156	95	208,556	262	13,920	385	22,486
2011–August 2018	612	39,728	22	35	84	11,736	239	15,878	267	12,079
Total	**2,608**	**11,569,108**	**111**	**3,504,135**	**375**	**1,120,166**	**1,052**	**269,166**	**1,070**	**6,675,641**

– = not available.

Notes: Climatological disasters include drought, forest fires, and land fires. Geophysical disasters consist of ash fall, associated avalanches, earthquakes or other ground movements, landslides, lava flows, rockfalls, and tsunamis. Hydrological disasters include associated avalanches, coastal floods, flash floods, landslides, mudslides, riverine floods, rockfalls, and subsidence. Meteorological disasters include cold waves, convective storms, heat waves, severe winter conditions, and tropical cyclones.

Source: EM-DAT: The Emergency Events Database–Université catholique de Louvain–Centre for Research on the Epidemiology of Disasters, D. Guha-Sapir, Brussels, Belgium. https://www.emdat.be (accessed September 2018).

from natural hazards has been increasing; and the swathe of their impact has been growing (Table 1.3). This trend primarily reflects the exponential increase in the velocity, volume, and intensity of economic development, human interactions, as well as the concentration of human and physical assets in limited geographical spaces—the result of urbanization and agglomeration. In addition, climate change has also caused extreme weather events which sometimes lead to widespread disasters.

Compared with other regions, developing Asia has been more exposed to the impact of disasters.

Over the past 20 years, for example, developing Asia has borne almost one-fifth (17%) of the estimated cost of global natural hazards—equivalent to $29 billion annually. Moreover, while 19.9% of disasters due to natural hazards occur in developing Asia, 31.4% of the people affected live in the region. In general, the distribution of disasters by category is largely dominated by floods and storms (hydrometeorological), which account for over three-quarters of all disasters. Storms and floods have the highest human impact, although mortality from flooding has been decreasing recently.

Natural hazards often cause massive loss of life, destruction of livelihoods, and destruction of tangible community and national assets—which can permanently affect long-term growth prospects.

Natural hazards such as earthquakes, tsunamis, tropical storms, floods, and landslides cause death; harm human lives and livelihoods; and destroy tangible assets such as buildings, property, and other capital assets. The loss of life and associated occupational skills, along with the destruction of school buildings, also disrupts education and diminishes overall human capital. Natural resources such as forests, farms, land, and soil quality are also affected. Together they can reduce the productive capacity of an economy—both short and long term. Furthermore, recurring exposure to natural hazards can also lead to adaptive but unproductive "behavior" by individuals or communities. For example, they may invest less in capital goods for fear of losing them again to another disaster.

Low-income countries or communities are often most affected by natural hazards for several reasons.

First, poorer countries have limited means to restore and rebuild destroyed assets. Second, poorer communities are also often located in hazard-prone areas or communities, have fragile housing or community infrastructure, and have few functioning early warning systems. Third, the poor also suffer disproportionately from loss of economic assets—whether farms, livestock, tools, or equipment. Due to their limited means and access to financial resources, the poor are often unable to replace these income-generating assets—falling into a long-term "poverty trap."

Evidence from the Philippines—Balisacan and Fuwa (2001), and Balisacan and Pernia (2002)—showed that the occurrence of typhoons or disasters are significantly related with increased poverty rates among disaster-affected provinces. The economic consequences of these disasters from natural hazards often span generations: the poor in frequently hit areas may lead to poverty traps, as people and communities in these areas cannot easily bounce back from economic shocks from these natural hazards. Therefore, transformative and social protection policies are needed to make poorer communities more resilient to natural hazards—particularly in keeping their risk assessment strategies current.

Rising inequality

Rising inequality within many Asian economies skews development.

Since the 1990s, inequality—as measured by the Gini coefficient—has been rising in many developing Asian countries. For instance, an ADB (2012) report noted that of 28 countries with comparable data between the 1990s and 2000s, 11—accounting for 82% of developing Asia's population—experienced rising inequality in per capita expenditure or income as measured by the Gini coefficient. Similarly, using household per capita consumption expenditure data, the developing Asia-wide Gini coefficient rose from 38 in the 1990s to 44 in the 2010s—despite improvement of Gini coefficients in the Philippines, Thailand, Viet Nam, Nepal, and Pakistan. The study further noted that had inequality not widened in the economies where it increased, similar growth in 1990–2010 would have lifted an estimated additional 240 million people out of poverty (or 6.5% of developing Asia's 2010 population).

Governments can play an important role in ensuring greater equality of opportunity.

Governments can contain rising inequality by improving redistributive policies and making growth more inclusive. First, it can ensure that growth is more employment-friendly to increase labor's income share. This can be achieved by strengthening labor market institutions, reducing distortions that discourage the use of labor, and supporting the growth of small and medium-sized enterprises. Second, it can work to reduce spatial inequality by improving subnational connectivity, developing growth centers in lagging regions, and extending transfers to those regions to develop human capital. Third, it can apply efficient fiscal measures to reduce inequality in human capital. This entails the use of targeted transfers rather than general price subsidies, prioritizing human capital and social protection expenditures, and greater and more equitable revenue mobilization.

Given these long-term economic, environmental, and social challenges, it is important that Asia strengthen its regional development strategy to deliver better outcomes across the three dimensions and ensure that growth is more inclusive, with benefits for everyone.

Regional Integration as Development Strategy[2]

Regional integration is a dynamic process where a group of neighboring countries cooperate to achieve common goals for mutual benefit. Depending on the purpose and goal, a multitude of regional integration initiatives have emerged globally; and Asia is no exception. Regional

2 This section draws on two working papers: Park and Claveria (2018a, 2018b).

integration can encompass many different facets—such as promoting trade and investment, developing infrastructure, improving people's mobility, strengthening provision of regional public goods, and providing the legal and institutional basis for international policy cooperation. Often, the dynamic effects of regional integration support economic growth and development, particularly when accompanied by increased market size, exploitation of economies of scale, enhanced competition, increased investment, and technical or technology transfer.

As a result, regional integration has become a useful development strategy for many global and regional institutions. For example, the United Nations recognized regional integration as an important tool to support national efforts in implementing the 2030 Agenda for Sustainable Development.

Asia-Pacific Regional Cooperation and Integration Index

The Asia-Pacific Regional Cooperation and Integration Index shows a steady trend of regional integration in Asia and the Pacific, led by East Asia and Southeast Asia.

In 2017, ADB unveiled its Asia-Pacific Regional Cooperation and Integration Index (ARCII)—to gauge the degree of regional cooperation and integration in Asia and the Pacific (ADB 2017).[3] A panel approach is used to extend the ARCII over 2006–2016—to monitor how the index evolved and identify the different drivers of regional integration over time (Park and Claveria 2018a).

The ARCII time series shows modest growth of regional integration in Asia over 2006–2016 (Figure 1.5). Southeast Asia had the highest degree of integration among subregions for the sample period, except in 2016, with an average score of 0.590. East Asia closely followed, scoring higher than Southeast Asia in 2016.

Figure 1.5: Asia-Pacific Regional Cooperation and Integration Index—Asia Subregions

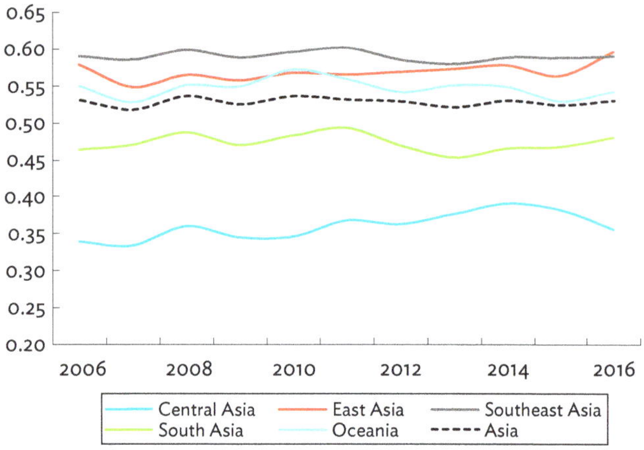

Note: The Index combines 26 indicators categorized into six regional cooperation and integration dimensions: (i) trade and investment, (ii) money and finance, (iii) regional value chains, (iv) infrastructure and connectivity, (v) movement of people, and (vi) institutional and social integration. The overall index cannot be computed for the Pacific due to lack of data in the money and finance dimension.
Source: Park and Claveria (2018a).

Oceania closely trailed East Asia and even surpassed the latter in 2010. Meanwhile, South Asia and Central Asia scored well below—placing fourth and fifth—throughout the sample period.

Progress in regional integration over time is most volatile in trade and investment and money and finance, while largely stable in regional value chain and the movement of people, among others.

By dimension, the trade and investment index was most volatile, along with money and finance (Figure 1.6). In contrast, the remaining four subindexes—namely, regional value chain, infrastructure and connectivity, movement of people, and institutional and social integration—were relatively stable across all subregions. Southeast Asia scored highest in regional integration for the dimension of trade and investment; movement of people; and regional value chain, which was overtaken by Central Asia in 2012 and East Asia in 2013. East Asia also maintained relatively high degrees of regional

[3] The ARCII aims to assess the extent to which each economy is integrated into the region, to identify strengths and weaknesses of multiple regional integration drivers, and to comprehensively and systematically track progress. Given the complex nature of regional integration, the ARCII combines 26 indicators categorized into six regional cooperation and integration dimensions: (i) trade and investment, (ii) money and finance, (iii) regional value chains, (iv) infrastructure and connectivity, (v) movement of people, and (vi) institutional and social integration. It covers the Asia and the Pacific members of the ADB (45 developing member economies plus Australia, Japan, and New Zealand), where data are available.

Figure 1.6: Dimensional Subindexes—Asia Subregions

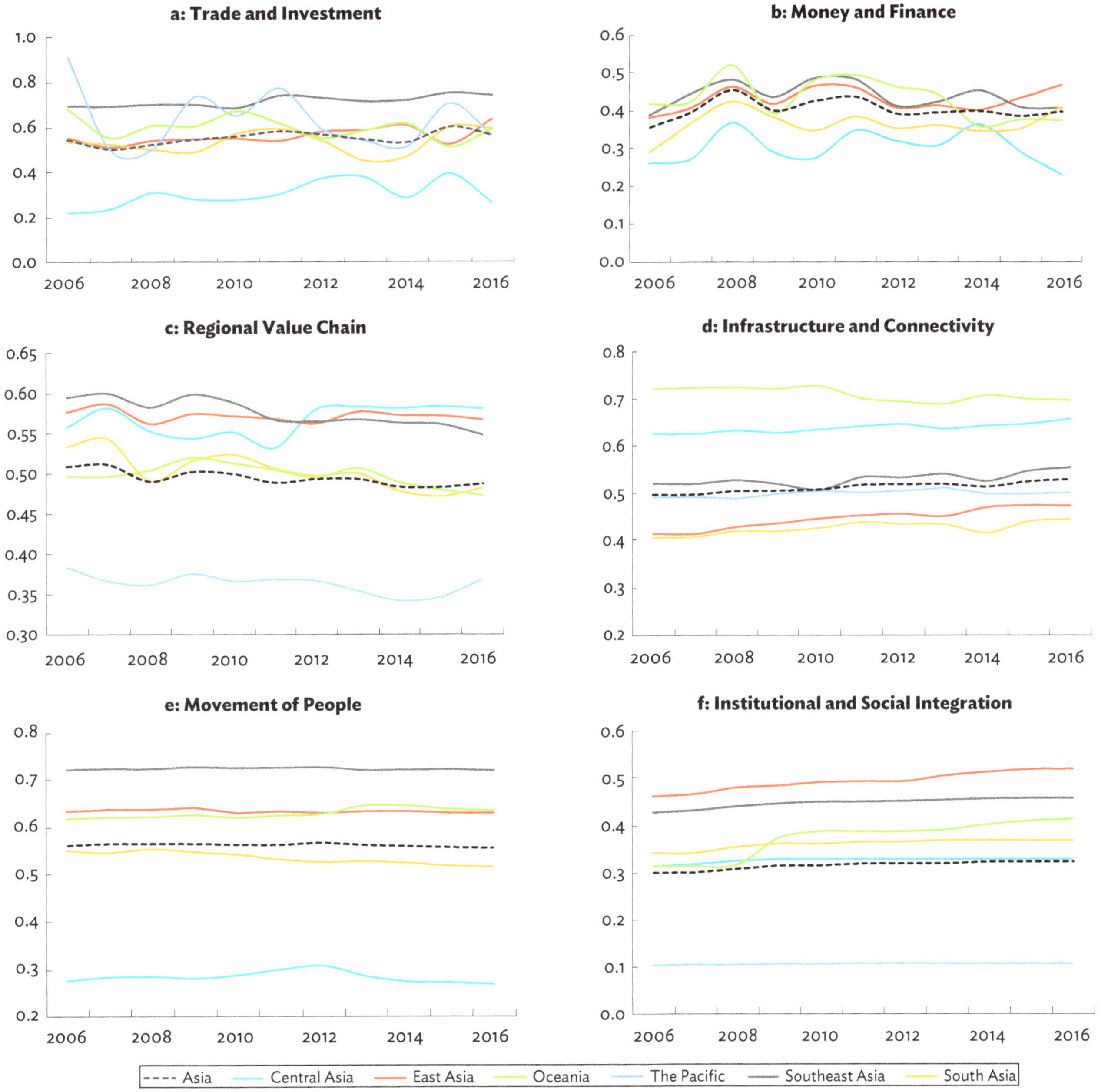

Source: Park and Claveria (2018a).

integration among all subregions, showing modest upward movements in all six dimensions. Oceania led in regional integration for infrastructure and connectivity, although the subregional index comprises Australia and New Zealand only due to lack of data for the Pacific developing member countries. Subregional variations in the movement of people and institutional and social integration were particularly large across the sample period. Regional integration for the movement of people was dominated by Southeast Asia, while particularly weak in Central Asia. East Asia exhibited consistently higher institutional and social integration among other subregions, with the Pacific scoring lowest.

Estimating the Impact of Regional Integration on Economic Growth and Poverty Reduction

Many empirical studies have analyzed the link between regional integration and economic growth.

As a development strategy, regional integration brings economic benefits by promoting greater economies of scale in common markets and production networks, as well as through technology diffusion and knowledge spillovers, often generated by free trade and investment flows. Greater regional integration—by removing barriers to trade, competition, capital, and labor mobility—can improve the overall efficiency with which labor combines with capital to produce output (Baldwin 1989). As a result, regional integration has been adopted as an important, actively pursued development strategy in many developing regions globally—including Asia, Africa, and Latin America and the Caribbean.

Using the ARCII and its six dimensional subindexes—capturing its multidimensional nature—an ADB study investigated how these regional integration dimensions, individually and together, impact economic growth and poverty reduction (Box 1.2).

Regional integration—as measured by the modified ARCII indexes—has a significant and positive effect on economic growth, and a negative impact on poverty.

The study found that the dimensions of regional value chain, movement of people, and institutional and social integration played an important and positive role in shaping the economic growth of the region. Among the dimensions of regional integration—and passing a series of robustness tests—regional value chain continues to show a significant and positive impact on economic growth. Regional integration also appears to provide the greatest opportunity to reduce poverty. Overall, integration and the dimensions of trade and investment, money and finance, and institutional and social integration are significant and robust drivers of poverty reduction. Their impact in curbing poverty is even more pronounced for lower-income countries. Furthermore, the overall degree of regional integration appears to exert more influence on poverty alleviation compared with efforts at individual dimensions promoting regional integration.

However, while regional integration is an important factor for economic growth and development, country-specific institutional and governance factors should not be overlooked. The regression results show that—together with certain dimensions and overall integration—investment in human capital (as measured by secondary education), macroeconomic stability (inflation), and institutional quality (control of corruption index) significantly impact economic growth and poverty reduction.

Box 1.2: Assessing the Impact of the Asia-Pacific Regional Cooperation and Integration Index on Economic Growth and Poverty

Another set of Asia-Pacific Regional Cooperation and Integration Index (ARCII) and its six dimensional subindexes have been estimated using the globally consistent weights and standardization methodology for the regression. Using the modified ARCII, infrastructure and connectivity appear to be the most forceful and stable foundation for regional integration in Asia compared with other regions including the European Union (EU), Latin America and the Caribbean, and Africa. But, over time, trade and investment have strengthened as a major contributor to regional integration, compensating for a modest weakening in movement of people (box figure). In the EU, the contributions of all dimensions are broadly balanced, although money and finance, infrastructure and connectivity, movement of people, and institutional and social integration contribute a bit more than the other two remaining dimensions. Institutional and social integration support regional integration the most in Latin America and the Caribbean, while regional value chain contributes the most to regional integration in Africa.

To assess the impact of ARCII that is extended globally (ARCII') on economic growth and poverty, an unbalanced panel data set for 156 countries for the period 2006–2016 was used to run a growth regression that includes ARCII'

Dimensional Contribution to Regional Integration Index—Asia versus Other Regions

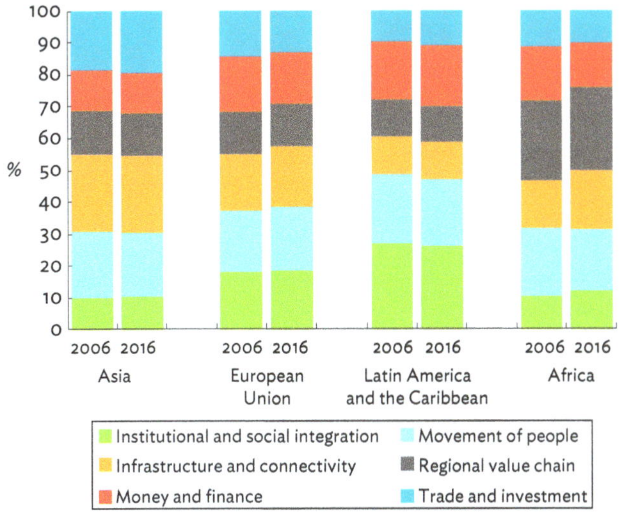

Source: Park and Claveria (2018b).

as another explanatory variable, in addition to other macroeconomic control variables. The choice of control variables was guided by economic theory and relevant empirical literature that are often cited as major drivers of economic growth.

The estimation was based on the following growth equation:

$$y_{i,t} = \beta_0 + \beta_1 y_{i,t-1} + \beta_2 X_{i,t} + \beta_3 ARCII'_{i,t} + \mu_i + \varepsilon_{i,t} \quad (1)$$

where $y_{i,t}$ is the logarithm of the dependent variable of interest (growth and poverty) for country i at time t, $y_{i,t-1}$ is the initial level of per capita income, $X_{i,t}$ is a vector of control variables, $ARCII'_{i,t}$ is the modified ARCII, μ_i is the unobserved country-specific effect and $\varepsilon_{i,t}$ is the error term.

For the estimation, a system generalized method of moments (GMM) procedure was adopted. The system GMM employs fixed effects (a dummy for each country) to capture time invariant country heterogeneities. To control for persistence, lagged values of the dependent variable are included as additional independent variables in system GMM estimation.[a] In addition, system GMM addresses the endogeneity of the regressors by instrumenting them with their own lagged values.

Regional value chain, infrastructure and connectivity, and institutional and social integration exert a positive impact on per capita GDP growth.

The baseline model, used control variables such as secondary school enrollment, investment (represented by gross fixed capital formation) as percentage of gross domestic product (GDP), government consumption as percentage of GDP, inflation rate, and control of corruption index. Education and good governance (in accord to theoretical expectations) impact positively on growth as indicated by the significant positive coefficients of secondary school enrollment and control of corruption index. Nevertheless, government spending seems to dent economic growth as shown by the significant negative coefficient of government consumption.

The impact of government consumption is not obvious a priori. As noted by Dreher (2006), a large government sector may induce inefficiencies and crowd out the private

Continued on next page

[a] Some dependent variables may also display persistence; for example, income inequality tends to change slowly over time with very minimal within-country variation, reflecting some unobserved state-dependent factors (Coady and Dizioli 2017).

Box 1.2 *continued*

sector, while the provision of efficient infrastructure and proper legal framework by government may enhance growth. The result indicates that the crowding-out effect of government consumption dominates its growth-enhancing impact. This is in line with the negative coefficient of a government consumption measure that eliminated spending on productivity-enhancing sectors such as defense and education (Barro 2003).

However, when the dimensional subindexes enter the growth regressions separately, three dimensions of regional integration showed significant positive impact on economic growth: regional value chain, movement of people, and institutional and social integration (box table 1). Moreover, secondary school enrollment and control of corruption retain their significance in these specifications. On the other hand, the significance of government consumption vanishes when infrastructure and connectivity is included as a separate regressor.

Overall ARCII' index shows a significant and negative impact on poverty.

Based on the baseline specification of the poverty regression, higher income reduces poverty, while greater inequality and increased government consumption are associated with higher poverty. As indicated in box table 2, the overall ARCII' index yielded a significant and negative coefficient, which indicates that broad-based regional integration could help reduce poverty. The significant positive coefficient of its interaction with the logarithm of GDP per capita implies that the poverty-increasing impact of regional integration tends to be greater at high income levels. Moreover, the dimensions of trade and investment, money and finance, and institutional and social integration and their interactions with real GDP per capita were significant and similarly signed as the overall ARCII' index and its interaction with real GDP per capita. In addition, the greater magnitude (in absolute value) of the coefficient of the overall ARCII' indicates that regional integration efforts would be more effective in reducing poverty when undertaken in an integrated rather than piecemeal fashion.

1: Summary of ARCII-Augmented Growth Regression Results
Dependent variable: Log(Real GDP per Capita)

	Baseline	Baseline with Financial Openness	Baseline with Financial and Trade Openness
Log(Regional value chain)	0.462*	0.871**	0.871**
	(0.254)	(0.371)	(0.419)
Log(Movement of people)	0.167	0.545**	0.525*
	(0.145)	(0.271)	(0.284)
Log(Institutional and social integration)	0.501***	0.467***	0.494***
	(0.139)	(0.136)	(0.170)
With control variables	Yes	Yes	Yes

*** = significant at 1%, ** = significant at 5%, * = significant at 10%. Windmeijer robust standard errors in parentheses.
ARCII = Asia-Pacific Regional Cooperation and Integration Index, GDP = gross domestic product.
Notes: Table indicates summary of results when the dimensional subindexes enter the growth regressions separately.
Source: Park and Claveria (2018b).

2: Summary of ARCII-Augmented Poverty Regression Results
Dependent variable: Log(Poverty Headcount Ratio)

	Baseline	Baseline with Trade Openness
Log(Overall ARCII')	-19.340**	-16.420*
	(7.819)	(8.442)
Log(Overall ARCII') x log(Real GDP per capita)	2.047**	1.734*
	(0.827)	(0.897)
Log(Trade and investment)	-2.106*	-2.237**
	(1.082)	(1.031)
Log(Trade and investment) x log(Real GDP per capita)	0.223*	0.236**
	(0.119)	(0.114)
Log(Money and finance)	-13.940***	-13.370***
	(4.876)	(4.810)
Log(Money and finance) x log(real GDP per capita)	1.440***	1.370***
	(0.502)	(0.497)
Log(Institutional and social integration)	-9.311***	-9.460***
	(2.849)	(2.928)
Log(Institutional and social integration) x log(Real GDP per capita)	1.032***	1.051***
	(0.312)	(0.322)
With control variables	Yes	Yes

*** = significant at 1%, ** = significant at 5%, * = significant at 10%. Windmeijer robust standard errors in parentheses.
ARCII' = Modified Asia-Pacific Regional Cooperation and Integration Index, GDP = gross domestic product.
Notes: Table indicates summary of results when the dimensional subindexes enter the poverty regressions separately.
Source: Park and Claveria (2018b).

Source: Park and Claveria (2018b).

References

Aghiar, M. and G. Gopinath. 2007. Emerging Market Business Cycles: The Cycle is the Trend. *Journal of Political Economy*. 115(1). pp. 69–102.

Asian Development Bank (ADB). 2012. *Asian Development Outlook 2012: Confronting Rising Inequality in Asia*. Manila.

———. 2017. *Asian Economic Integration Report 2017: The Era of Financial Interconnectedness– How Can Asia Strengthen Financial Resilience?* Manila.

———. 2018. *Asian Development Outlook 2018 Update*. Manila.

Asian Development Bank Institute (ADBI). 2009. Recessions and Recoveries in Asia: What Can the Past Teach us About the Present Recession? *ADBI Working Paper Series*. No. 150. Tokyo.

Baldwin, R. 1989. On the Growth Effects of 1992. *NBER Working Paper Series*. No. 3119.

Balisacan, A. and N. Fuwa. 2001. Growth, Inequality, and Poverty Reduction in the Philippines. *UPSE Discussion Paper*. No. 0109. Manila: UP School of Economics.

Balisacan, A. and E. Pernia. 2002. What Else Besides Growth Matters for Poverty Reduction? *ERD Policy Brief*. No. 5. Manila: ADB.

Barro, R. J. 2003. Determinants of Economic Growth in a Panel of Countries. *Annals of Economics and Finance*. No. 4. pp. 231–274. Peking University Press.

Coady, D. and A. Dizioli. 2017. Income Inequality and Education Revisited: Persistence, Endogeneity, and Heterogeneity. *IMF Working Paper*. No. 17/126. International Monetary Fund.

Dreher, A. 2006. Does Globalization Affect Growth? Evidence from a New Index of Globalization. *Applied Economics*. No. 38. pp. 1091–1110.

EM-DAT: The Emergency Events Database–Université catholique de Louvain–Centre for Research on the Epidemiology of Disasters, D. Guha-Sapir, Brussels, Belgium. https://www.emdat.be (accessed September 2018).

Institute of International Finance. Monthly Portfolio Tracker. https://www.iif.com (accessed August 2018).

International Monetary Fund (IMF). Balance of Payments and International Investment Position Statistics. http://www.imf.org/external/np/sta/bop/bop.htm (accessed July 2018).

———. Direction of Trade Database. https://www.imf.org/en/Data (accessed August 2018).

———. International Financial Statistics. https://www.imf.org/en/Data (accessed August 2018).

———. World Economic Outlook April 2018 Database. https://www.imf.org/external/pubs/ft/weo/2018/01/weodata/index.aspx (accessed May 2018).

Park, C. Y. and R. Claveria. 2018a. Constructing the Asia-Pacific Regional Cooperation and Integration Index: A Panel Approach. *ADB Economics Working Paper Series*. No. 544. Manila.

———. 2018b. Does Regional Integration Matter for Inclusive Growth? Evidence from the Multidimensional Regional Integration Index. *ADB Economics Working Paper Series*. No. 559. Manila: Asian Development Bank.

Park, C. Y. and R. Mercado. 2014. Determinants of Financial Stress in Emerging Market Economies. *Journal of Banking and Finance*. 45(C). pp. 199–224.

World Bank. World Development Indicators. https://data.worldbank.org/products/wdi (accessed September 2018).

World Trade Organization Statistics Database. http://stat.wto.org/Home/WSDBHome.aspx (accessed May 2018).

Trade and the Global Value Chain

Recent Trends in Asia's Trade

The recovery in global trade strengthened during 2017 with Asia leading the pace.[4]

By volume, global trade growth accelerated to 4.7% in 2017 from 1.8% in 2016, surpassing global economic growth for the first time since 2012 (Figure 2.1a). The broad-based upturn of the global trade was buoyed by economic recovery in advanced economies and strengthening global manufacturing output—also giving a significant boost to trade globally. Asia remained the key driver of the global trade recovery, contributing about 61.7% of volume growth. The region's trade volume expanded by 7.1% in 2017, the highest since 2011 (Figure 2.1b). Trade volume also grew strongly in North America (4.1%) and the European Union (EU) (2.9%) but at a slower pace in the Middle East (0.7%). The recovery also reached Latin America and the Caribbean (up 3.4%) and Africa (0.5%). Asia's trade growth was highest mostly due to the region's robust gross domestic product (GDP) growth.

Exports and imports contributed equally to Asia's accelerated trade volume growth.

Strengthening private consumption, along with strong domestic and cross-border investment, powered the region's import volume to grow by 7.7% in 2017, up from 1.6% in 2016. Strong external demand from within the region and developed economies boosted Asia's exports—with volume growth rising to 6.7% in 2017, well above the 1.8% growth in 2016. The People's Republic of China (PRC) accounted for 35.2% of the region's total trade volume growth (Figure 2.2). Japan; the Republic of Korea; Taipei,China; and Hong Kong, China are also largely credited for the increase in Asia's exports. India; Hong Kong, China; the Republic of Korea; and Australia likewise posted significant contributions in import growth.

Figure 2.1: Merchandise Trade Volume and Real GDP Growth—Asia and World (%, year-on-year)

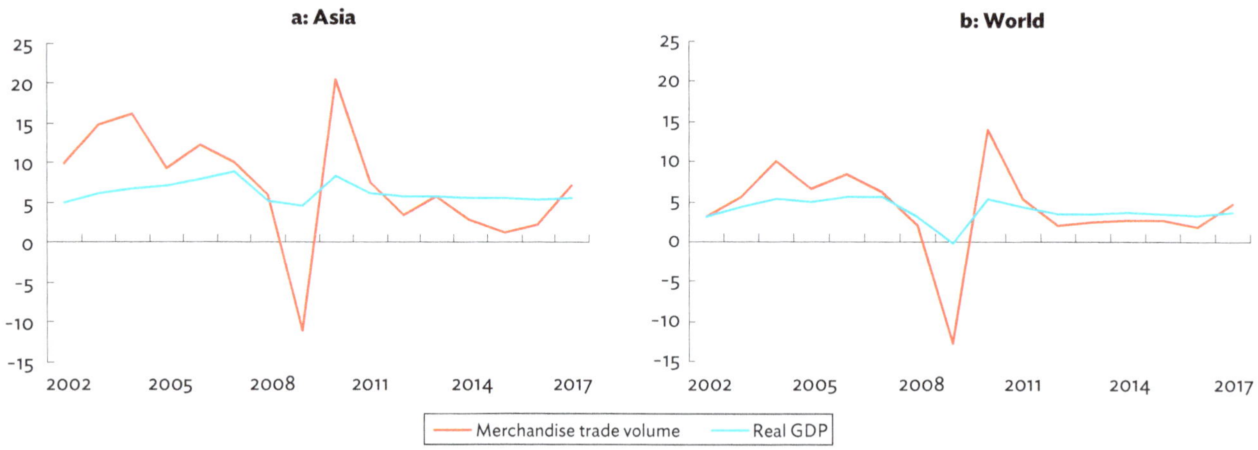

GDP = gross domestic product.
Note: Real GDP growth is weighted using nominal GDP in purchasing power parity.
Sources: ADB calculations using data from International Monetary Fund. World Economic Outlook April 2018 Database. https://www.imf.org/external/pubs/ft/weo/2018/01/weodata/index.aspx; and World Trade Organization. Statistics Database. http://stat.wto.org/Home/WSDBHome.aspx (both accessed May 2018).

4 Asia refers to the 48 Asia and the Pacific members of the Asian Development Bank (ADB), which includes Japan and Oceania (Australia and New Zealand) in addition to the 45 developing Asian economies.

Figure 2.2: Sources of Trade Volume Growth—Asia

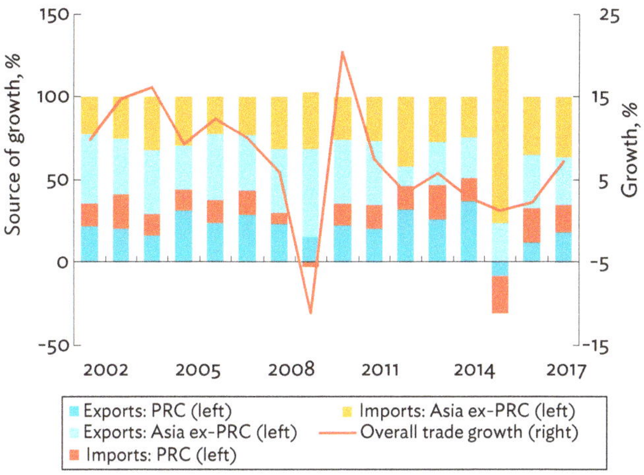

PRC = People's Republic of China.
Source: ADB calculations using data from World Trade Organization. Statistics Database. http://stat.wto.org/Home/WSDBHome.aspx (accessed May 2018).

The value of Asia's merchandise trade growth also rebounded strongly.

After contracting in 2015 and 2016, the region's merchandise trade value grew by 12.6% in 2017 (Figure 2.3). Aside from the volume increase, the growth in value also benefited from increased global commodity prices, such as energy and crude oil. This helped commodity-exporting countries like Malaysia, Indonesia, Mongolia, the Lao People's Democratic Republic (Lao PDR), Kazakhstan, Azerbaijan, and Papua New Guinea—all of which saw strong export growth. By contrast, commodity-importing economies like Bangladesh, India,

Figure 2.3: Trade Value—Asia and World

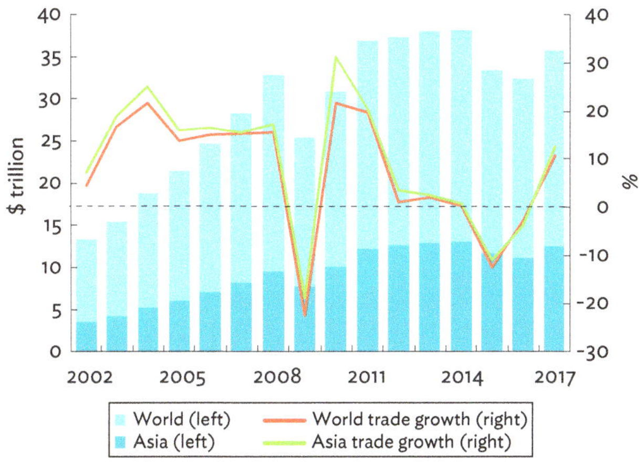

Source: ADB calculations using data from World Trade Organization. Statistics Database. http://stat.wto.org/Home/WSDBHome.aspx (accessed May 2018).

Sri Lanka, the Philippines, and Thailand saw imports grow due to strong domestic expenditures.

Intermediate goods drove merchandise export growth across much of the region.

The growth in intermediate goods contributed most to the 2017 export rebound (Figure 2.4). As mentioned, commodity exporters gained from global price increases. For manufacturing export-oriented economies (such as the PRC, Japan, the Republic of Korea, Singapore, Malaysia, and Cambodia) strong external demand for electronic raw materials and products, machinery and equipment parts, and other industrial supplies—from both within the region and advanced economies—led to the export recovery.

Asia's import growth was also propelled by intermediate goods, and capital goods to a lesser extent.

In most economies, the decline in import growth in 2016 reversed in 2017 (Figure 2.5). Imports of oil and industrial metals increased in countries where manufacturing expanded, while intermediate inputs to manufacturing for assembly into electronic products, machinery, and equipment also led to rapid import growth. This also reflected the rebuilding of raw material inventories for near-term production. The strong growth in both exports and imports of intermediate goods implies a strengthening of Asian economic integration into global and regional value chains. Also, capital goods imports grew in most Asian economies, suggesting continued near-term expansion in domestic investment.

Asia's trade growth remained robust in recent months, and will likely continue if current risks can be contained.

After record highs in the first half of 2017, Asia's trade sustained its growth momentum in the second half of 2017 and the first half of 2018 (Figure 2.6). In January 2018, trade value growth reached 20.7%, the highest since August 2012. Trade volume growth, on the other hand, kept its pace at more than 5% and peaked at 9.0% in February 2018. However, the region's trade expansion gradually moderated in the first half of 2018. Meanwhile, the global environment, in general, remains favorable on Asia's trade, but heightened risks could undermine trade prospects. Downside risks include the possible softening

Figure 2.4: Contribution to Exports Growth, by Commodity Type—Asia (%)

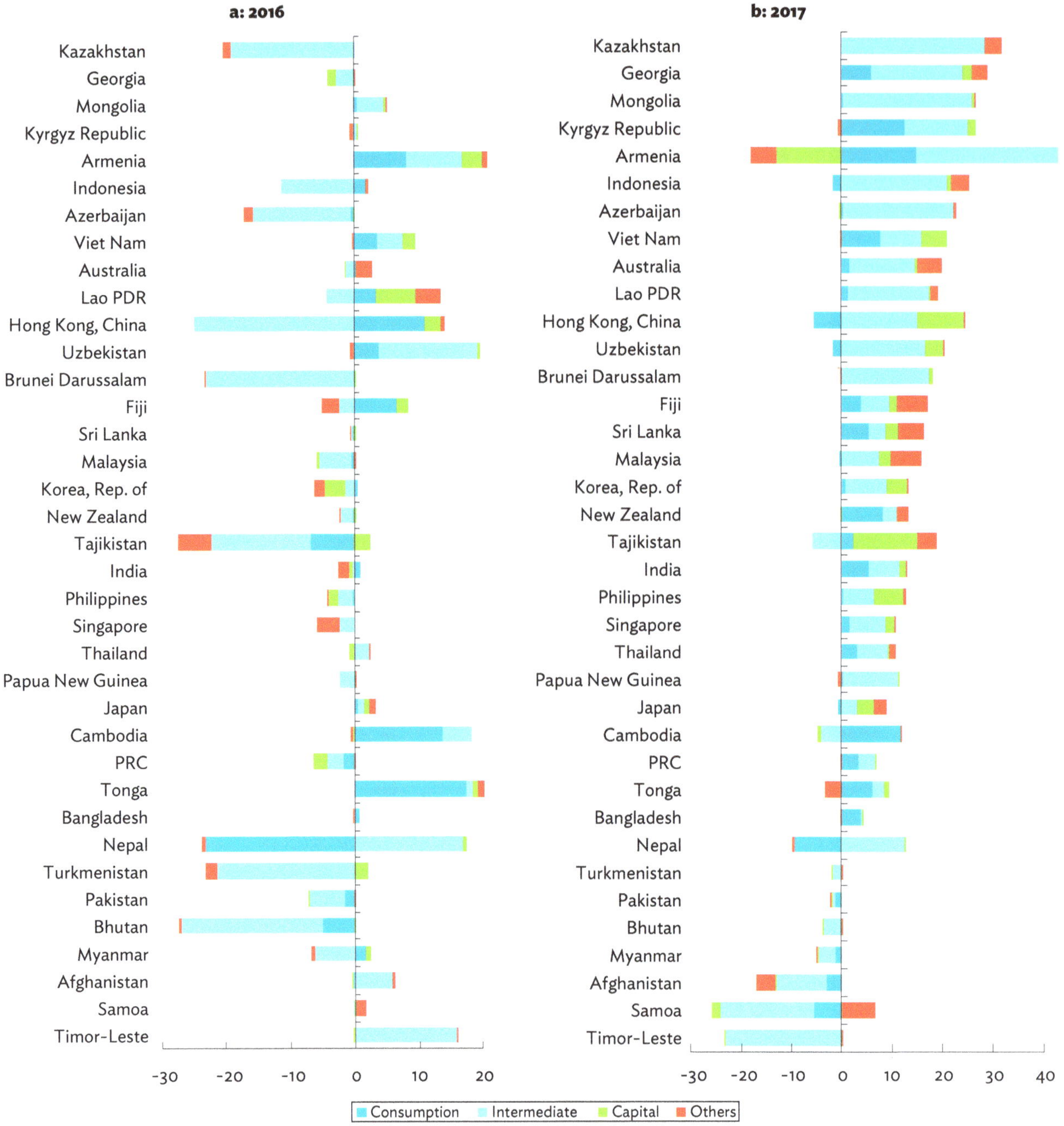

Lao PDR = Lao People's Democratic Republic, PRC = People's Republic of China.
Notes: Based on Broad Economic Categories. Sorted by 2017 values.
Sources: ADB calculations using data from International Monetary Fund. Direction of Trade Statistics. https://www.imf.org/en/Data (accessed August 2018); and United Nations. Commodity Trade Database. https://comtrade.un.org (accessed May 2018).

Figure 2.5: Contribution to Imports Growth, by Commodity Type—Asia (%)

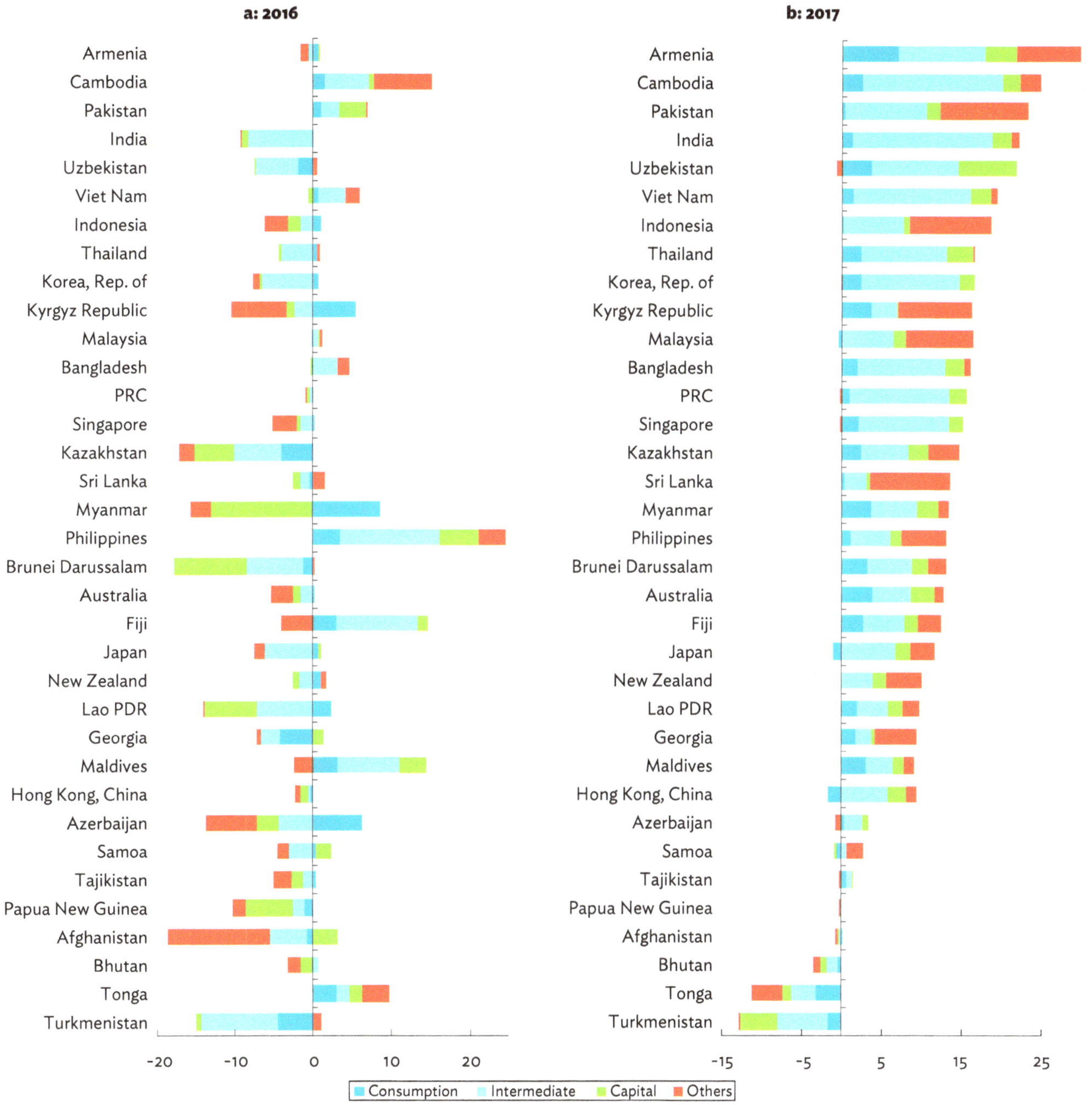

Lao PDR = Lao People's Democratic Republic, PRC = People's Republic of China.
Notes: Based on Broad Economic Categories. Sorted by 2017 values.
Sources: ADB calculations using data from International Monetary Fund. Direction of Trade Statistics. https://www.imf.org/en/Data (accessed August 2018); and United Nations. Commodity Trade Database. https://comtrade.un.org (accessed May 2018).

Figure 2.6: Monthly Trade, by Value and Volume—Asia

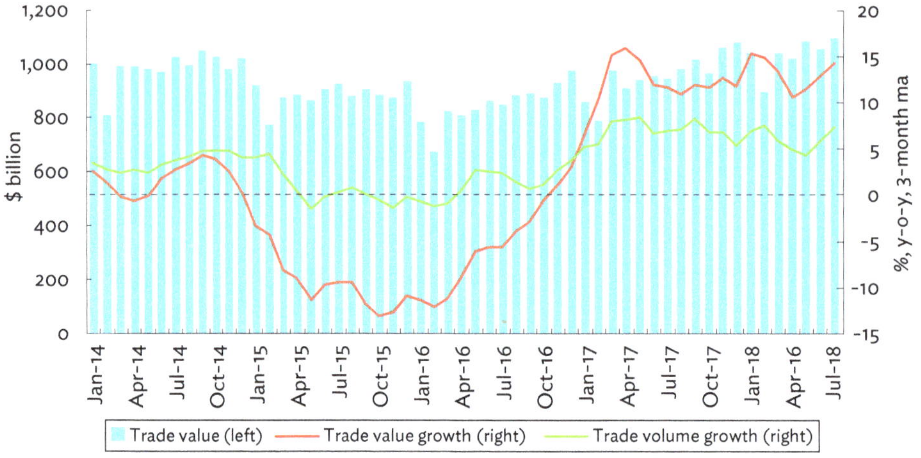

ma = moving average, y-o-y = year-on-year.

Notes: Trade volume growth rates were computed using volume indexes. For every period and trade flow type (i.e., imports and exports), the available data include an index for Japan and an aggregate index for selected Asian economies, which include Hong Kong, China; India; Indonesia; Malaysia; Pakistan; the People's Republic of China; the Philippines; the Republic of Korea; Singapore; Taipei,China; Thailand; and Viet Nam. To come up with an index for Asia, trade values were used as weights for the computations. On the other hand, trade value levels and growth rates were computed by aggregating import and export values of the same Asian economies.

Sources: ADB calculations using data from CEIC; and CPB Netherlands Bureau for Economic Policy Analysis. World Trade Monitor. https://www.cpb.nl/en/data (both accessed September 2018).

of global economic growth, intensifying bilateral trade frictions between the world's major trading countries, escalating trade policy uncertainty, and stagnation in the global value chain expansion. The trade conflict between the United States (US) and the PRC has escalated since early 2018, with the US imposing tariffs mostly on industrial inputs, such as machinery and transport equipment and parts, while the PRC mostly on agricultural products. The impact of tariffs on Asia's trade is estimated to be small, but persistent and deeper trade frictions could exert growing strains on Asia's trade growth. Further strengthening trade ties intraregionally could help shield Asia from these potential headwinds.

Figure 2.7: Intraregional Trade Share—Asia, European Union, North America (%)

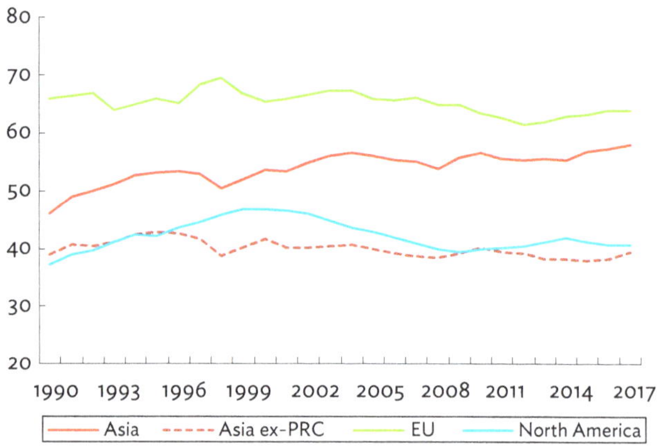

EU = European Union, PRC= People's Republic of China.

Notes: EU refers to aggregate of 28 EU members. North America covers Canada, Mexico, and the United States.

Source: ADB calculations using data from International Monetary Fund. Direction of Trade Statistics. https://www.imf.org/en/Data (accessed August 2018).

Asia's Intraregional Trade

Along with its strong trade performance in 2017, Asia's trade integration continues to strengthen.

Bilateral trade within the region increased further. By value, the intraregional trade share reached a record 57.8% in 2017, above the 57.2% recorded in 2016—and 55.9% average during 2010–2015 (Figure 2.7). In contrast, intraregional trade share in the EU (63.8%) declined slightly by 0.1 percentage point in 2017 from 2016, while it remained the same at North America (40.7%). Trade linkages in Asia remained solid, as the region's intraregional trade grew by 13.9% in 2017 after 2 years of contraction—excluding the PRC, growth was 16.8% (Figure 2.8). The region's trade to non-Asian economies increased at 11.1% in 2017.

Figure 2.8: Trade Value Growth, Intraregional and Extraregional—Asia (%)

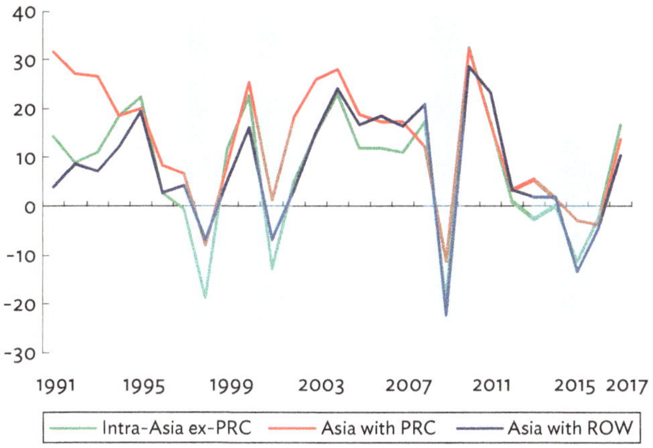

PRC = People's Republic of China, ROW = rest of the world.
Note: Shaded areas indicate 1997/98 Asian financial crisis, 2000/01 "dot.com" recession, 2008/09 global financial crisis, and the recent global trade growth slowdown.
Source: ADB calculations using data from International Monetary Fund. Direction of Trade Statistics. https://www.imf.org/en/Data (accessed August 2018).

Figure 2.9: Intraregional Trade Shares—Asia Subregions (%)

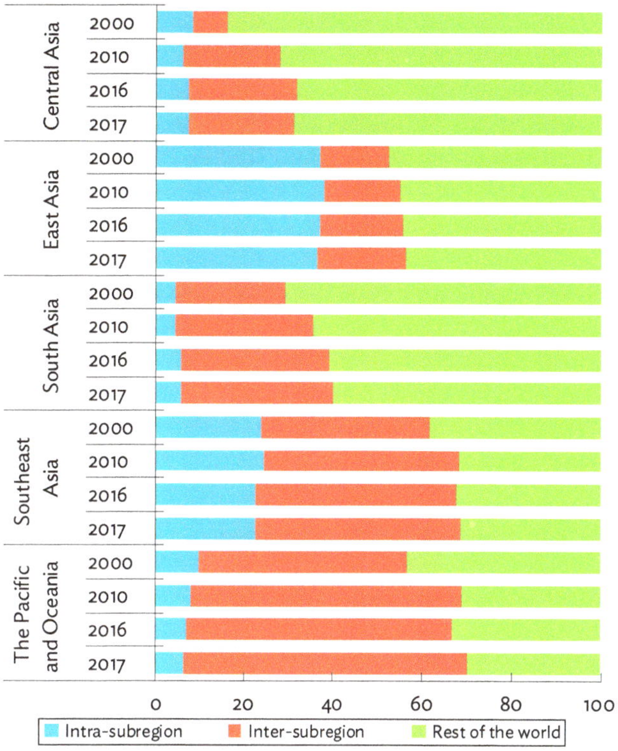

Source: ADB calculations using data from International Monetary Fund. Direction of Trade Statistics. https://www.imf.org/en/Data (accessed August 2018).

Nonetheless, trade relationships within Asia vary considerably, indicated by large differences between intra- and inter-subregional trade shares.

Intraregional trade grew across all subregions in 2017, except for Central Asia. In South Asia, Southeast Asia, and the Pacific and Oceania,[5] inter-subregional trade shares increased in 2017, supported by robust trade with regional trading partners. By subregion, East Asia consistently holds the highest intra-subregional trade share—although it declined slightly to 36.3% in 2017 from 36.9% in 2016 (Figure 2.9). Southeast Asia's intra-subregional trade share was second at 22.4% in 2017.

Inter-subregional trade shares remain much higher than intra-subregional trade shares in the Pacific and Oceania (64.0% inter-subregional share), South Asia (34.5%), and Central Asia (24.1%). Further analysis using gravity model estimation indicates similar results (Box 2.1).

[5] The Pacific and Oceania subregion includes ADB's Pacific developing member countries plus Australia and New Zealand.

Box 2.1: Gravity Model Estimation of Bilateral Exports

A gravity model on Asia's bilateral exports is estimated to give a snapshot of recent progress in regional trade integration. The model includes a dummy variable for "both in Asia" if both economies come from the region. The coefficient can be viewed as a trade integration index. The estimation implements a 5-year rolling panel regression using annual data (box table 1).

Asia's intraregional trade bias is strong and gained strength in 2017—although the coefficient of the intraregional trade dummy remains insignificant. Across all subregions, the intra-subregional trade bias strengthened in 2017 except for South Asia (box table 2). Inter-subregional trade bias is particularly significant in South Asia and Southeast Asia, strengthening further in 2017.

1: Gravity Model Estimation Results, 2013-2017
Dependent variable: Log(Bilateral Exports)

Variables	All Goods	Capital Goods	Consumption Goods	Intermediate Goods
Log(Distance)	-1.66***	-1.64***	-1.73***	-1.70***
	(0.02)	(0.02)	(0.02)	(0.02)
Colonial relationship dummy	0.84***	0.88***	0.94***	0.86***
	(0.09)	(0.09)	(0.10)	(0.10)
Common language dummy	0.99***	0.93***	1.07***	0.90***
	(0.04)	(0.04)	(0.04)	(0.04)
Contiguity dummy	0.98***	1.14***	1.19***	1.07***
	(0.10)	(0.10)	(0.10)	(0.11)
Regional dummies (base: Asia to ROW)				
Both in Asia dummy	0.45 [0.43]	0.11 [0.33]	0.40 [0.41]	-0.09 [-0.31]
	(0.35)	(0.36)	(0.41)	(0.34)
Importer in Asia dummy	2.44***	-2.24**	0.74	2.28***
	(0.66)	(0.97)	(0.82)	(0.72)
Both in ROW dummy	1.65***	-2.71***	-0.18	2.01***
	(0.51)	(0.84)	(0.64)	(0.64)
Rho (sample selection term)	0.14***	0.30***	0.21***	0.18***
Sample size	277,280	277,280	277,280	277,280
Censored observations	138,937	179,383	158,525	155,202
Uncensored observations	138,343	97,897	118,755	122,078

*** = significant at 1%, ** = significant at 5%, * = significant at 10%, ROW = rest of the world. Estimates for 2012–2016 are in brackets. Robust standard errors in parentheses.

Notes: Time-varying economy dummies are included but not shown for brevity. Heckman sample selection estimation was used to account for missing economy pair data. Data cover 173 economies, of which 43 are from Asia. Trade data are based on Broad Economic Categories.

Sources: ADB calculations using data from Institute for Research on the International Economy. http://www.cepii.fr/CEPII/en/cepii/cepii.asp (accessed May 2018); and United Nations. Commodity Trade Database. https://comtrade.un.org (accessed May 2018).

2: Gravity Model Estimation Results, 2013-2017: Intra- and Inter-Subregional Trade (All Goods)

Variables	Central Asia	East Asia	South Asia	Southeast Asia	The Pacific and Oceania
Intra-subregional trade dummy	4.54***	6.46***	0.49	4.93***	1.79**
	[3.80***]	[6.40***]	[0.49]	[4.83***]	[1.23*]
Inter-subregional trade dummy	-0.15	0.30	4.28***	0.22***	-0.31
	[-0.11]	[0.27]	[4.21***]	(0.34)	[-0.38]

*** = significant at 1%, ** = significant at 5%, * = significant at 10%. Estimates for 2012–2016 are in brackets.

Notes: Base category (benchmark) is the subregion's trade with economies outside Asia. The usual gravity model variables and time-varying economy dummies are included but not shown for brevity. Heckman sample selection estimation was used to account for missing bilateral economy-pair data. Data cover 173 economies, of which 43 are from Asia. Trade data are based on Broad Economic Categories.

Sources: ADB calculations using data from Institute for Research on the International Economy. http://www.cepii.fr/CEPII/en/cepii/cepii.asp (accessed May 2018); and United Nations. Commodity Trade Database. https://comtrade.un.org (accessed May 2018).

Sources: ADB staff using data from Institute for Research on the International Economy. http://www.cepii.fr/CEPII/en/cepii/cepii.asp (accessed May 2018); and United Nations. Commodity Trade Database. https://comtrade.un.org (accessed May 2018).

Progress of Global and Regional Value Chains

Global and regional value chain expansion returns.

The *Asian Economic Integration Report 2017* reported a continued slowdown in global and regional value chains in 2016. Asia's global value chain (GVC) participation—measured by the share of value-added content in gross exports used for further processing through cross-border production networks—indicated a deepening of GVC participation since 2000. It reached a peak of 74.5% in 2011, but slowed afterward through 2016. The latest ADB Multi-Regional Input–Output Tables—covering 62 economies including 26 economies in Asia—shows a new trend developing. Value-added components of gross exports globally showed signs of GVC expansion in 2017 (Figure 2.10a)—share of domestic value added declined between 2016 and 2017 (returned domestic value added declined slightly), while foreign value added and purely double counted terms increased. The GVC participation rate rose from 73.3% to 73.6%.

In Asia, the GVC participation rate peaked at 69.7% in 2011, but gradually declined to 67.4% in 2016. The trend reversed in 2017, with Asia's GVC participation climbing back to 68.0% (Figure 2.10b). Foreign value-added exports share also increased in 2017 compared with 2016, while domestic value added declined. This indicates that Asian firms imported more intermediate inputs for exported goods and services. The other two components of gross exports—returned domestic value added and purely double-counted terms—also hint at better GVC prospects. Box 2.2 analyzes GVC linkages at bilateral levels at greater length.

Evolution of GVC and its changing patterns are deeply inbred into the economic activities of individual economies and characterize the breadth and depth of international trade. While this might be a stern reality, less attention has been paid to the economic impact of expanding GVCs. Box 2.3 attempts to shed some light on this issue.

Figure 2.10: Components of Gross Exports (%)

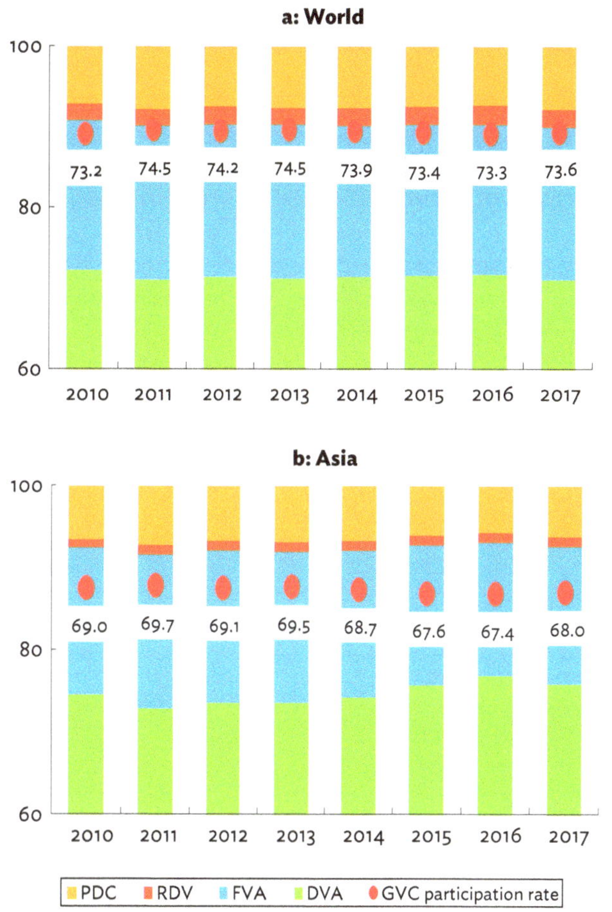

DVA = domestic value added, FVA = foreign value added, GVC = global value chain, PDC = purely double-counted terms, RDV = returned domestic value added.

Notes: The GVC participation rate is measured by the share of value-added contents of gross exports used for further processing through cross-border production networks. It is computed as the ratio of GVC components of exports (gross exports less domestic value added in final goods exports data from 2010 to 2017 to gross exports).

Sources: ADB calculations using data from 2010–2017 ADB Multi-Regional Input-Output Tables; and methodology by Wang, Wei, and Zhu (2014).

Box 2.2: Analysis of Bilateral Value Chains of Selected Asian Economies, European Union, Latin America, and North America

Based on the global value chain (GVC) decomposition methodology of Wang, Wei, Zhu (2014) and the 2010–2017 ADB Multi-Regional Input–Output Tables—covering 62 economies, including 26 economies in Asia—bilateral value chain participation ratios were calculated to analyze the changing patterns of production networks since 2010. The bilateral value chain participation ratio is computed as the ratio of GVC components of exports (gross exports less the sum of domestic value added in final goods exports) to gross exports. In addition to bilateral value chain linkages, this ratio also tracks how much each partner helps each other to be linked to the third countries through their value chain network. The lines on box figure 1 show the bilateral value chains ratio for 2010 and 2017 grouped into low, medium, and high scores. The thickest and densest lines pertain to a high bilateral value chain participation ratio above 80%, the medium lines correspond to ratios from 50% to 79%, and the thin and least dense lines to ratios of 49% and below.

1: Production Networks of Selected Asian Economies, European Union, Latin America, and North America

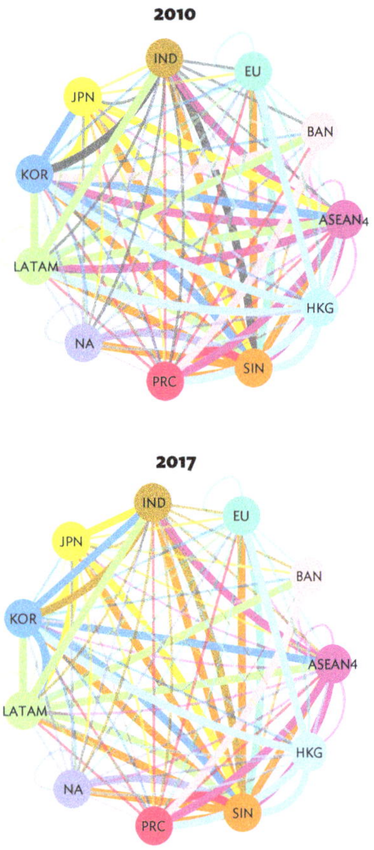

ASEAN4 = Indonesia, Malaysia, the Philippines, and Thailand; BAN = Bangladesh; EU = European Union; HKG = Hong Kong, China; IND = India; JPN = Japan; KOR = Republic of Korea; LATAM = Latin America (Brazil and Mexico); NA = North America (Canada and the United States); PRC = People's Republic of China; SIN = Singapore.
Note: Value chain participation ratio = Gross exports – Final goods exports for consumption in importing economy / Gross exports.
Sources: ADB calculations using data from the 2010–2017 ADB Multi-Regional Input–Output Tables; and methodology by Wang, Wei, and Zhu (2014).

Between 2010 and 2017, bilateral value chain links—as measured by the value chain participation ratio—among economies in Asia and other regions evolved differently for each pair. While some pairs showed stronger value chain links in 2017 than in 2010, others had weaker connections.

The Republic of Korea forged stronger value chain links with its partners, especially with India—increasing from 72.0% in 2010 to 85.4% in 2017 (box table). Japan strengthened value chain links with Latin America in 2017—rising from 77.4% to 80.7%—while its link with the Republic of Korea weakened slightly. Singapore and India maintained their value chain links with partners over the period. However, links between the ASEAN4 (Indonesia, Malaysia, the Philippines, and Thailand) and Hong Kong, China with trade partners had weakened by 2017 compared with 2010. ASEAN4 value chain links with Japan and the Republic of Korea weakened, while strong links remained with the PRC, India, and Singapore. The value chain link between Bangladesh and the Republic of Korea declined in 2017 from 2010, where the former's GVC linkage to the latter fell from 82.5% to 78.4%, and the latter's to the former fell from 69.0% to 64.4%. Hong Kong, China—a financial and production hub—had weaker links with the ASEAN4 and Latin America. North America and the European Union (EU) had strong links only with Singapore among Asian economies.

Apart from these notable shifts in value chain participation ratios between pairs, most of the links—especially medium links—remained the same. It is therefore more useful to look at the year-on-year changes (box figure 2). The thickness and density of the lines are configured the same way as box figure 1, except that box figure 2 only shows lines that have positive developments over the prior year. For example, the 2011 chart only shows the lines of bilateral value chain participation ratios that increased compared with 2010, while the 2012 chart only shows links that have increased or strengthened compared with 2011.

Thus, from 2011 to 2015, bilateral value chain links have weakened—as there are fewer and fewer lines (box figures 2a–2e). There were 66 visible lines in 2011, meaning there

Continued on next page

Box 2.2 *continued*

1: Value Chain Participation Ratio

a: 2010

Exporter/ Importer	ASEAN4		BAN		PRC		EU		HKG		IND		JPN		KOR		LATAM		NA	
ASEAN4	0.76																			
BAN	0.73	0.66																		
PRC	0.68	0.84	0.52	0.90																
EU	0.77	0.76	0.51	0.28	0.65	0.60	0.74													
HKG	0.88	0.55	0.59	0.67	0.92	0.49	0.84	0.62												
IND	0.76	0.88	0.58	0.63	0.55	0.61	0.65	0.72	0.36	0.79										
JPN	0.80	0.75	0.47	0.45	0.71	0.50	0.67	0.71	0.45	0.80	0.73	0.77								
KOR	0.83	0.81	0.69	0.83	0.77	0.75	0.67	0.70	0.61	0.91	0.72	0.92	0.81	0.85						
LATAM	0.87	0.80	0.86	0.46	0.77	0.64	0.71	0.73	0.44	0.84	0.88	0.80	0.65	0.77	0.88	0.73	0.66			
NA	0.77	0.63	0.51	0.24	0.66	0.43	0.74	0.70	0.54	0.66	0.76	0.65	0.68	0.54	0.69	0.65	0.78	0.68	0.68	
SIN	0.89	0.90	0.70	0.40	0.93	0.87	0.90	0.90	0.71	0.98	0.83	0.87	0.83	0.92	0.92	0.88	0.88	0.91	0.82	0.87

b: 2017

Exporter/ Importer	ASEAN4		BAN		PRC		EU		HKG		IND		JPN		KOR		LATAM		NA	
ASEAN4	0.72																			
BAN	0.64	0.63																		
PRC	0.65	0.85	0.48	0.91																
EU	0.73	0.75	0.53	0.22	0.66	0.57	0.77													
HKG	0.80	0.51	0.60	0.47	0.90	0.46	0.81	0.60												
IND	0.73	0.90	0.51	0.52	0.53	0.60	0.64	0.72	0.37	0.76										
JPN	0.79	0.70	0.53	0.35	0.73	0.46	0.68	0.68	0.44	0.73	0.81	0.75								
KOR	0.80	0.80	0.64	0.78	0.79	0.75	0.72	0.69	0.58	0.83	0.85	0.90	0.79	0.87						
LATAM	0.85	0.76	0.92	0.42	0.70	0.62	0.73	0.74	0.45	0.78	0.88	0.77	0.57	0.81	0.80	0.80	0.72			
NA	0.71	0.65	0.45	0.22	0.64	0.46	0.75	0.70	0.57	0.62	0.75	0.64	0.66	0.59	0.69	0.70	0.80	0.68	0.70	
SIN	0.88	0.89	0.73	0.27	0.93	0.84	0.90	0.88	0.73	0.98	0.81	0.83	0.83	0.91	0.90	0.86	0.86	0.94	0.82	0.86

ASEAN4 = Indonesia, Malaysia, the Philippines, and Thailand; BAN = Bangladesh; EU = European Union; HKG = Hong Kong, China; IND = India; JPN = Japan; KOR = Republic of Korea; LATAM = Latin America (Brazil and Mexico); NA = North America (Canada and the United States); PRC = People's Republic of China; SIN = Singapore.

Notes: Value chain participation ratio = (Gross exports – Final goods exports for consumption in importing economy)/Gross exports. Value chain exports and gross exports used for computation exclude the exports of agriculture, mining, and fishery; mining and quarrying; and other nonmetallic mineral sectors.

Sources: ADB calculations using data from the 2010–2017 ADB Multi-Regional Input–Output Tables; and methodology by Wang, Wei, and Zhu (2014).

were 66 links that strengthened between 2011 and 2010, that fell to 46 in 2012 and 34 in 2015.

The weakening trend of bilateral value chain links reversed in 2016 (box figure 2f). Hong Kong, China and the Republic of Korea's value chain links strengthened, while all of ASEAN4's weakened. Stronger links were also formed between Latin America and India, Latin America and Bangladesh, as well as North America and India. Singapore's value chain links surged in 2016. This suggests bilateral GVC linkages already started to recover in 2016 before the aggregate GVC participation ratio showed a broader recovery in 2017.

In 2017, 62 bilateral value chain links strengthened (box figure 2g). Notably, ASEAN4 and the EU regained strong value chain links with trade partners. For the ASEAN4, value chain exports of food, beverages, and tobacco; basic metals and fabricated metals; as well as wholesale trade boosted the group's links—especially with the PRC and Singapore. The EU increased GVC exports of transport, electrical and optical equipment, and renting of machinery equipment including other business activities to Singapore; the PRC; Hong Kong, China; and the Republic of Korea. In 2017, among Asian economies, the PRC, Singapore, and ASEAN4 showed the most progress in building value chain linkages with trading partners.

Continued on next page

Box 2.2 *continued*

2: Trends in Production Network of Selected Asian Economies, European Union, Latin America, and North America

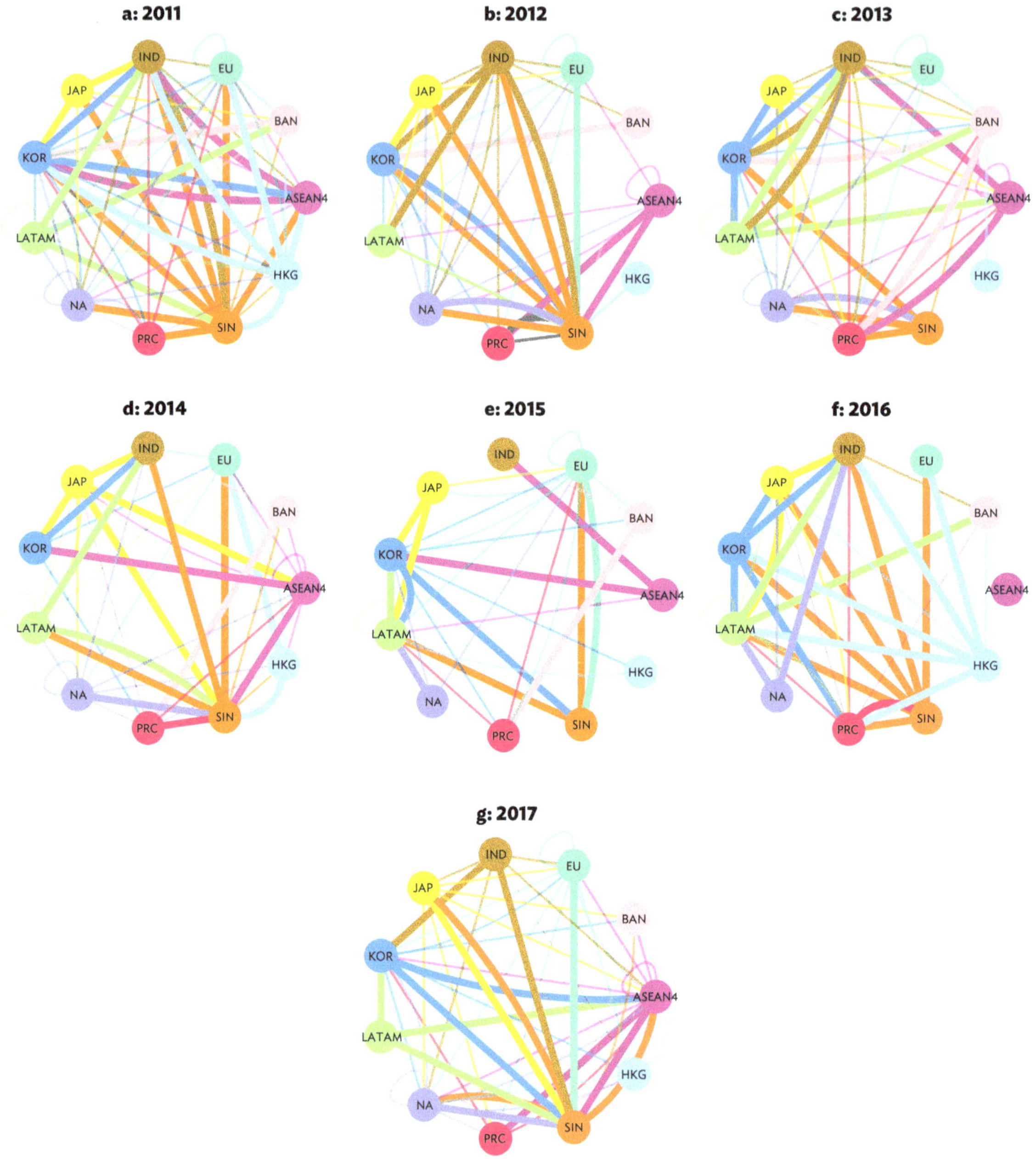

ASEAN4 = Indonesia, Malaysia, the Philippines, and Thailand; BAN = Bangladesh; EU = European Union; HKG = Hong Kong, China; IND = India; JPN = Japan; KOR = Republic of Korea; LATAM = Latin America (Brazil and Mexico); NA = North America (Canada and the United States); PRC = People's Republic of China; SIN = Singapore.

Notes: Value chain participation ratio = Gross exports – Final goods exports for consumption in importing economy / Gross exports.

Sources: ADB calculations using data from the 2010–2017 ADB Multi-Regional Input–Output Tables; and methodology by Wang, Wei, and Zhu (2014).

Sources: ADB staff using data from the 2010–2017 ADB Multi-Regional Input–Output Tables; and methodology by Wang, Wei, and Zhu (2014).

Box 2.3: Impact of the Global Value Chain on Productivity Growth

Expanding global value chain (GVC) is known to contribute to productivity growth—by prompting innovation and technological intensity and leveraging economies of scale and specialization. Most empricial studies focus on the country or industry level impact of GVC participation. Here, the impact of GVC expansion on productivity growth using cross-country panel data is explored. Based on a standard Cobb–Douglas production function,[a] the regression equation is:

$$\ln y_{it} = \beta_0 + \beta_1 \ln IGDPC_i + \beta_2 INF_{it} + \beta_2 AGRI_{it} + \beta_3 GOV_{it} + \beta_4 \Delta \ln AWGI_{it} + \beta_5 FDI_{it} + \beta_6 FGCF_{it} + \beta_7 FL_i + \beta_8 EDUC_i + \beta_9 \ln FTAit + \beta_{10} \ln GVC_{it} + \delta_{it}$$

where $\ln y_{it}$ is the natural log of labor productivity, $\ln IGDPC_i$ is natural log of initial gross domestic product (GDP) per capita, INF_{it} is the inflation rate, $AGRI_{it}$ is the share of agriculture to total value added of economy *i*, GOV_{it} is government expenditure expressed as share of total GDP, $\Delta \ln AWGI_{it}$ is the change in natural log of the average World Governance Index score, FDI_{it} is net foreign direct investment inflow expressed as a share of GDP, $FGCF_{it}$ is gross fixed capital formation (% of GDP), FL_i is the initial level of female labor participation rate as share of total labor force, $EDUC_i$ is the initial level of labor force with advanced education as share of total working age population, $\ln FTA_{it}$ is the natural log of cumulative number of counterpart countries in free trade agreements, and $\ln GVC_{it}$ is the natural log of GVC exports. The GVC participation ratio is computed using the gross export decomposition methodology of Wang, Wei, and Zhu (2014) and data from the 2010–2017 ADB Multi-Regional Input–Output Tables.

The results of the ordinary least squares (OLS) panel regression are in Annex Table 2a.1. Model 1 shows the results of the random effects regression, while Model 2 shows the fixed effects results. Initial GDP per capita has the expected sign and significance. A 1% increase in $IGDPC_i$ leads to a 0.9% increase in productivity growth. This suggests that a higher initial level of income results in higher labor productivity growth.

Meanwhile, $\ln AWGI_{it}$, which measures the quality of institutions, has a positive coefficient indicating that the quality of governance and institutions matters for labor productivity. Inflation has a negative and significant coefficient of 0.02. A 1 percentage point increase in capital formation, $FGCF_{it}$, results in 0.5% increase in labor productivity.

$\ln GVC_{it}$ has a positive and significant effect on labor productivity growth. Exporters with higher GVC exports are expected to have higher labor productivity growth, holding other factors constant. A 1% increase in GVC_{it} results in 0.04% increase in productivity based on the random effects regression results and 0.4% based on the fixed effects regression.

To test for the robustness of these results—and to control for possible endogeneity due to omitted variable bias—a Two Stage Fixed Effects Least Squares estimation is used. The $\ln GVC_{it}$ was instrumented by ln *total trade*$_{it}$ in Model 3 which is the natural log of total exports and imports of country *i*. Using ln *total trade*$_{it}$ as instrument variable in the first stage estimation for the $\ln GVC_{it}$ yields a coefficient of 0.9 and is significant at the 1% level. This means that a 1% increase in GVC_{it} will likely result in 0.9% increase in labor productivity. An additional instrument for $\ln GVC_{it}$ is introduced in Model 4, *CA/Exports*$_{it}$, which is the current account balance as share of exports to further check the robustness of the results. In this model, a 1% increase in GVC_{it} results in 1.0% increase in labor productivity and significant at the 1% level.

---

[a] Y_i is the output of country *i* at time *t*, and the production function is specified as follows:

$$Y_i = K_i^{\alpha} (A_i H_i)^{1-\alpha} \quad (1)$$

where K_i is physical capital, H_i is human capital augmented labor utilized in production. A_i is the labor-augmenting measure of productivity, defined as $A_i = f(GVC_i, X_i)$. GVC_i is GVC exports and X_i is a vector of other specific control variables affecting A_i. It is assumed that labor, L_i, is homogenous and each unit of labor has been endowed with education, E_i. The human capital-augmented labor is defined as

$$H_i = e^{\phi (E_i)} L_i \quad (2)$$

where $\phi (E_i)$ is the efficiency of labor with education compared to the case where education is zero, $\phi(0)=0$. Equation (1) is rewritten and expressed as output per worker, $y_i \equiv Y_i/L_i$, as follows:

$$Y_i = \left(\frac{K_i}{Y_i}\right)^{\frac{\alpha}{1-\alpha}} h_i f_i(GVC_i, X_i) \quad (3)$$

and $h_i \equiv H_i/L_i$ is human capital per unit of labor. For the empirical analysis, equation (3) is expressed in natural logarithmic form. For a given time *t*,

$$\ln y_i = \left(\frac{K_i}{Y_i}\right)^{\frac{\alpha}{1-\alpha}} \ln h_i + \ln GVC_i + \ln X_i) \quad (4)$$

The level of labor productivity, $\ln y_i$ is modeled as a function of formation of physical and human capital, GVC exports and other control variables such as macroeconomic stability, quality of institutions, and trade liberalization. Note that here $y_i = \left(\frac{Y_i}{L_i}\right)$ where Y_i is nominal gross domestic product and L_i is the total labor force of economy *i*.

Sources: ADB staff using data from 2010–2017 ADB Multi-Regional Input-Output Tables; and methodology by Wang, Wei, and Zhu (2014).

Updates on Regional Trade Policy

Despite a slowdown of the region's growth in free trade agreements, Asia's push for greater market access through extraregional trade ties and deepening existing free trade agreements gives fresh impetus to trade openness.

The slowdown in the growth of Asia's free trade agreements (FTAs) in effect continued in 2017 (Figure 2.11). Using the World Trade Organization Regional Trade Agreements database, however, the share of Asian FTAs to the world total increased slightly in 2017, from 25.0% to 28.6%. Two Asian FTAs took effect in 2017 (down from three in 2016)—between Hong Kong, China and Macau, China; and between the European Free Trade Association (EFTA) and Georgia. The FTA between the People's Republic of China (PRC) and Georgia came into force 1 January 2018. Two more bilateral FTAs took effect in 2018, namely those between (i) Tapei,China and Paraguay; and (ii) Singapore and Sri Lanka. The plurilateral FTA between the Philippines and the EFTA also entered into force in 2018.

There was a slight rebound in the number of FTAs signed in 2017 (Figures 2.12, 2.13), including the plurilateral Pacific Agreement on Closer Economic Relations (PACER) Plus 10[6] and the FTA between ASEAN and Hong Kong, China—the first ASEAN FTA signed in a decade. As of August 2018, three bilateral FTAs between the following economies were signed: (i) Singapore and Sri Lanka which also took effect on 1 May 2018; (ii) Hong Kong, China and Georgia; and (iii) Australia and Peru. During the same period, five plurilateral FTAs were also signed between the following economies and trade blocs: (i) the Republic of Korea and Central America,[7] (ii) Eurasian Economic Union[8] and the PRC, (iii) Eurasian Economic Union and Iran, (iv) Japan and the European Union (EU), and (v) the Comprehensive and Progressive Agreement for Trans-Pacific Partnership (CPTPP). The FTA signed between Japan and the EU, which have a combined GDP accounting for about a quarter of the world GDP, reaffirms these big economies commitment to open and rules-based trade.

Two key trends continue to shape Asia's FTA landscape. First, Asia's push for market access in economies outside the region continues unabated (Figure 2.14). In the last quarter of 2017, the PRC launched negotiations for bilateral FTAs with Mauritius and Moldova. It has also initiated a joint feasibility study with Panama in

Figure 2.11 Newly Effective Free Trade Agreements—Asia

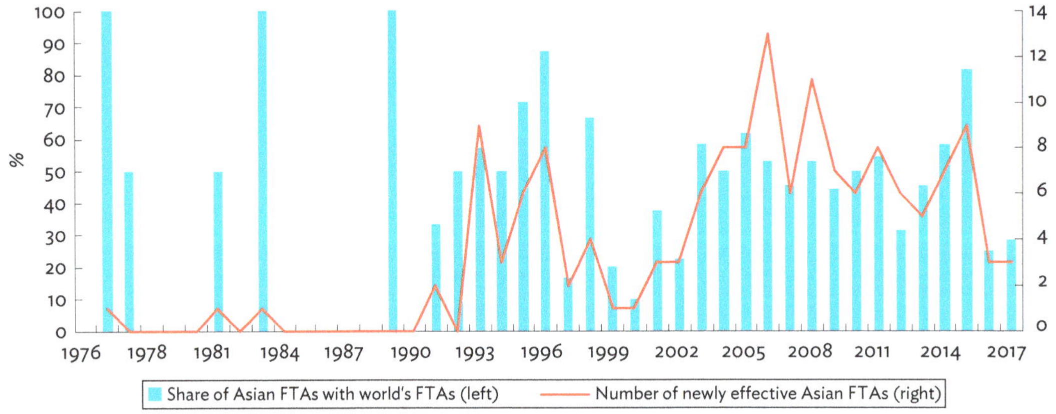

FTA = free trade agreement.
Sources: ADB calculations using data from ADB. Asia Regional Integration Center FTA Database. https://aric.adb.org/fta; and World Trade Organization. Regional Trade Agreement Information System. http://rtais.wto.org (both accessed August 2018).

6 PACER Plus 10 includes Australia, the Cook Islands, the Federated States of Micronesia, Kiribati, the Marshall Islands, Nauru, New Zealand, Niue, Palau, Samoa, Solomon Islands, Tonga, Tuvalu, and Vanuatu.

7 Central America is a trading bloc consisting of Costa Rica, El Salvador, Guatemala, Honduras, Nicaragua, and Panama.

8 The Eurasian Economic Union is composed of Armenia, Belarus, Kazakhstan, the Kyrgyz Republic, and the Russian Federation.

Figure 2.12: Number of Proposed and Signed Free Trade Agreements—Asia

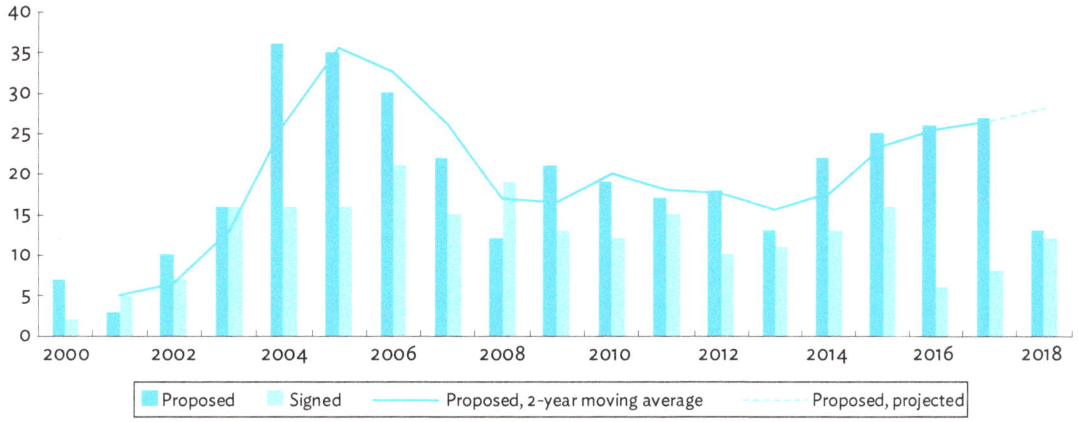

FTA = free trade agreement.
Notes: Includes bilateral and plurilateral FTAs with at least one of ADB's 48 regional members as signatory. "Signed" includes FTAs that are signed but not yet in effect, and those signed and in effect. "Proposed" includes FTAs that are (i) proposed (the parties consider an FTA, governments or ministries issue a joint statement on the FTA's desirability, or establish a joint-study group and joint-task force to conduct feasibility studies); (ii) framework agreements signed and under negotiation (the parties, through ministries, negotiate the contents of a framework agreement that serves as a framework for future negotiations); and (iii) under negotiation (the parties, through ministries, declare the official launch of negotiations, or start a first round of negotiations). 2018 covers FTAs that are signed and proposed from January to July.
Source: ADB. Asia Regional Integration Center FTA Database. https://aric.adb.org/fta (accessed August 2018).

Figure 2.13: Number of Signed Free Trade Agreements—Asia (cumulative since 1975)

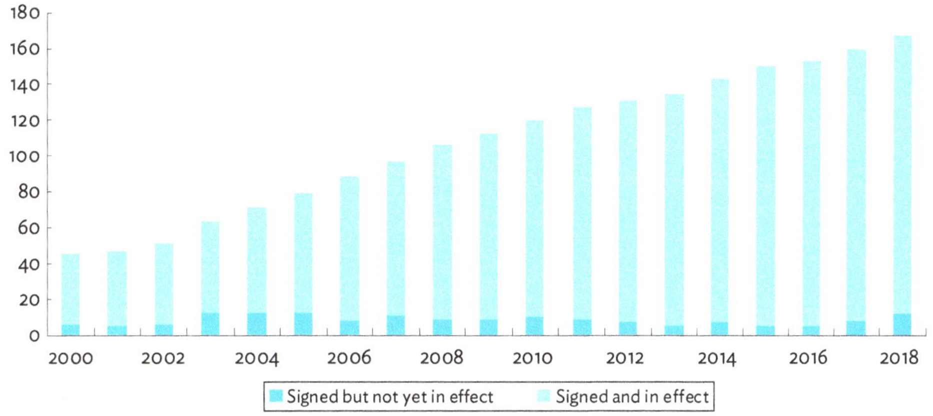

FTA = free trade agreement.
Notes: Includes bilateral and plurilateral FTAs with at least one of ADB's 48 regional members as signatory. 2018 covers FTAs that are signed from January to July.
Source: ADB. Asia Regional Integration Center FTA Database. https://aric.adb.org/fta (accessed August 2018).

early 2018. Six of the eight FTAs signed in 2018 involve non-Asian partners. Meanwhile, Indonesia has launched FTA negotiations with African economies such as Mozambique and Tunisia. Australia has started FTA talks with the EU, while Singapore and the Republic of Korea are currently negotiating bilateral FTAs with Mercosur.[9] In addition, the Republic of Korea had initiated the process of seeking associate membership of the Pacific Alliance[10] trade bloc, which will result in an FTA with Mexico. Bilateral FTAs exist between the Republic of Korea and Chile, Colombia, and Peru, but none with Mexico, the largest economy in the alliance. Asia's drive

9 Mercosur or *Mercado Comun del Sur* (Southern Common Market) is a subregional bloc composed of Argentina, Brazil, Paraguay, and Uruguay.

10 The Pacific Alliance is a Latin American trading bloc consisting of South American neighbors Chile, Colombia, and Peru, and non-neighbor Mexico.

Figure 2.14: Number of Signed Free Trade Agreements, Intraregional and Extraregional (cumulative since 1975)

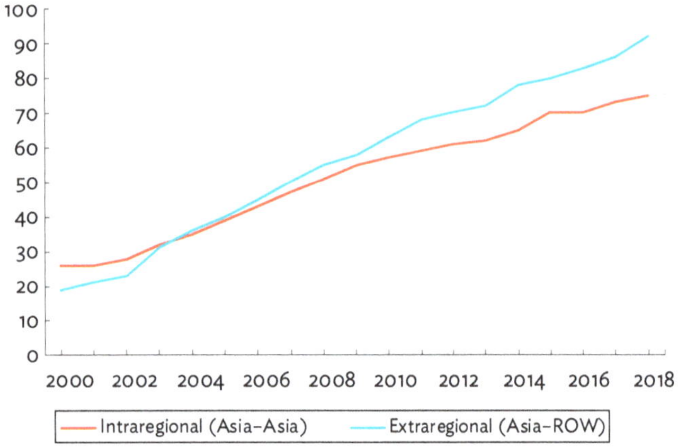

FTA = free trade agreement, ROW = rest of the world.
Notes: Includes bilateral and plurilateral FTAs with at least one of ADB's 48 regional members as signatory. "Signed" includes FTAs that are signed but not yet in effect, and those signed and in effect. 2018 covers FTAs that are signed from January to July.
Source: ADB. Asia Regional Integration Center FTA Database. https://aric.adb.org/fta (accessed August 2018).

to strengthen trade links with non-Asian partners and nontraditional markets reflects its close GVC links and its commitment to trade openness.

Second, there is a sharp upsurge in the number of Asian FTAs in various stages of being upgraded or the deepening of existing liberalization commitments to include "behind-the-border" issues such as investment, trade facilitation, competition, and government procurement. While a staggered improvement toward greater trade openness is not a new strategy, the growing trend of Asian FTA upgrading is fairly new—and intensified in the last 2 years. The upgraded FTA between Singapore and Australia—which originally took effect in 2003—came into force 31 December 2017. The upgraded FTA between the PRC and Chile was signed in 2017, while the FTA between the Republic of Korea and the United States (US) clinched renegotiations this year. Overall, 15 Asian FTAs are currently going through an upgrading process. Although the growth of Asia's FTAs seems to be reaching a plateau, the deepening of existing FTA commitments is a new way of advancing trade openness and creating new trade opportunities despite global trade uncertainties.

Comprehensive and Progressive Agreement for Trans-Pacific Partnership

Following the US departure from the Trans-Pacific Partnership (TPP) agreement, the remaining 11 TPP members signed the CPTPP on 8 March 2018 in Chile.[11] The ministers who signed the CPTPP "expressed their determination to complete their domestic processes to bring the Agreement into force expeditiously" (New Zealand Government Official Website 2018). The ministerial statement also welcomed the expression of interest of several other economies to join in the future. The CPTPP will enter into force 60 days after at least six (over 50%) signatories ratify the agreement. At present, three CPTPP members—Japan, Mexico, and Singapore—have completed the respective domestic processes necessary to ratify the trade deal.

Regional Cooperation Economic Partnership

Another "mega" trade deal, the Regional Cooperation Economic Partnership (RCEP),[12] remains under negotiation. RCEP would cover the 10 ASEAN members and six economies with existing FTAs with ASEAN. In the Joint Media Statement of the Sixth RCEP Ministerial Meeting held on 30–31 August 2018 in Singapore, RCEP ministers "welcomed the conclusion of two additional chapters at the 23rd round of negotiations, namely the Chapters on Customs Procedures and Trade Facilitation and Government Procurement, bringing the total concluded chapters to date to four" (ASEAN Secretariat 2018). They adopted "a package of year-end deliverables" and "expressed the hope that completion of the package would signify the substantial conclusion of the RCEP negotiations this year."

11 The 11 TPP members include Australia, Brunei Darussalam, Canada, Chile, Japan, Malaysia, Mexico, New Zealand, Peru, Singapore, and Viet Nam.

12 RCEP is composed of 10 ASEAN members, and its six FTA partners namely, Australia, India, Japan, New Zealand, the People's Republic of China, and the Republic of Korea.

Trade Remedies

Significant administrative tariff and nontariff barriers remain.

The increase in administrative tariff and nontariff measures continued into 2018 (Figure 2.15). New tariffs imposed may reduce trade and damage GVC exports (see Box 2.4 for analysis of the impact of antidumping duties on GVC exports).

Not all nontariff measures, however, are intended to impede trade. Some have legitimate purposes, such as sanitary and phytosanitary measures that protect food safety for consumers and prevent or limit the spread of pests and diseases among plants and animals. Antidumping duties remain the most widely used trade remedy globally against Asia's exporters (Table 2.1).

Figure 2.15: Trade-Related Measures—Asia

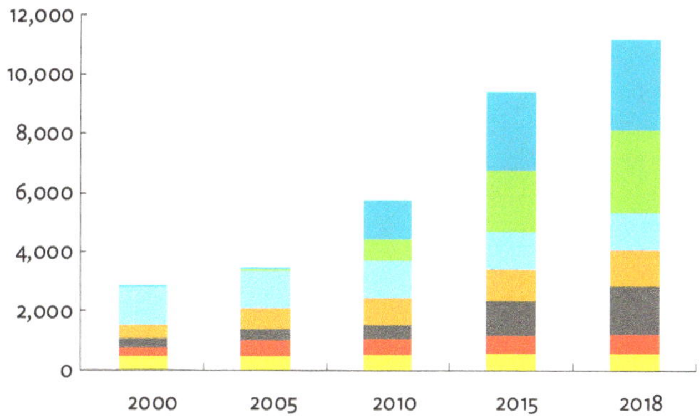

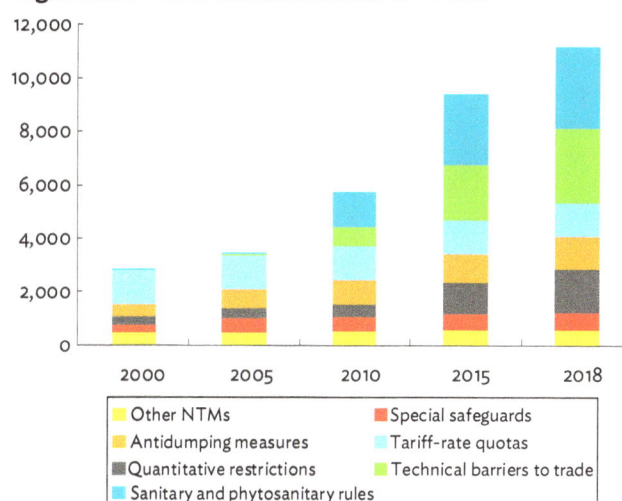

NTM = nontariff measures.
Notes: Based on cumulative number of measures in force as of end of each year. 2018 covers measures that are in force and will be enforced in 2018. Other NTMs include countervailing measures, safeguards, and export subsidies.
Source: ADB calculations using data from World Trade Organization. Integrated Trade Intelligence Portal. https://www.wto.org/english/res_e/statis_e/itip_e.htm (accessed August 2018).

Table 2.1: Trade Remedy Measures[a] and World Trade Organization Cases,[b] 2010–2018

Measures	World Total	Asia[c] Total	**Asia** (Complainant / Affected)– **ROW** (Respondent / Imposing)	**ROW** (Complainant/ Affected)– **Asia** (Respondent / Imposing)	**Asia** (Complainant/ Affected)– **Asia** (Respondent/ Imposing)
Anti-dumping (Article VI of GATT 1994)					
Number of measures implemented	1,303	1,033	478	145	410
Number of cases	46	33	18	9	6
	(3.5%)	(3.2%)			
Subsidies and Countervailing Measures					
Number of measures implemented	122	104	82	8	14
Number of cases[d]	36	23	11	11	1
	(29.5%)	(22.1%)			
Safeguards[e]					
Number of measures implemented	81	48[f]	33[f]	48[f]	48[f]
Number of cases	23	10	7	0	3
	(28.4%)	(20.8%)			
Total					
Number of measures implemented	1,506	1,257	593	201	463
Number of cases	105	66	36	20	10
	(7.0%)	(5.3%)			

GATT = General Agreement on Tariffs and Trade, ROW = rest of the world.
Notes: Numbers in parentheses are percentage share of cases to total measures implemented. 2018 covers trade remedies in force as of February 2018 and WTO dispute settlement cases that have requested consultation as of July 2018.
[a] Trade remedy measures are trade rules or policies implemented by an economy. In the table, trade remedies include measures which are in force.
[b] WTO cases are disputes on trade measures among WTO members that are brought before the WTO Dispute Settlement Body.
[c] Asia as implementing/affected region equals the number of global trade remedy measures minus ROW–ROW measures (not shown in table).
[d] Includes cases involving complaints on the grant of subsidies and countervailing measures.
[e] Safeguard measures are imposed on all WTO members; no bilateral data available.
[f] Includes multilateral safeguard measures affecting all WTO members.
Sources: ADB calculations using data from WTO. Disputes by agreement. https://www.wto.org/english/tratop_e/dispu_e/dispu_agreements_index_e.htm; and WTO. Integrated Trade Intelligence Portal. https://www.wto.org/english/res_e/statis_e/itip_e.htm (both accessed August 2018).

Box 2.4: Impact of Antidumping Duties on Global Value Chain Exports

Since the beginning of 2018, global trade tensions have escalated. An initial series of tariffs on washing machines and solar cells in January was initiated by the United States, followed by tariffs on aluminum and steel announced early March. A further $34 billion of products imported from the People's Republic of China (PRC) was targeted in July, with an additional $16 billion in August. The tariffs triggered immediate tit-for-tat countermeasures by those affected—particularly Canada, the PRC, and the European Union.

Most economists and policy makers are deeply concerned about how rising tariffs will affect global trade—and in particular their impact on global production networks. Assessing their potential impact is difficult due to a lack of historical data—given that global tariff rates have declined significantly over time and remain low. Thus, there is no plausible benchmark for assessing the impact of higher tariff rates.

One alternative is to use antidumping (AD) cases, as they are levied as duties against specific sectors. Nevertheless, the purpose and level of AD duties could be quite different from those of the tariffs under implementation and contemplation recently. In this sense, the empirical exercise below, while providing some analogy in understanding the potential impact of tariff barriers, needs to be viewed mainly from the angle of impact of trade remedies. The impact of AD on targeted imports has long been a popular topic for researchers. However, less frequent are studies on their impact on global value chains (GVCs). Here, empirical work is conducted to assess whether importing countries' AD case initiations in a sector harms their own GVC exports in other sectors due to industrial linkages and spillover effects.

The fixed effects panel ordinary least squares (OLS) model estimated takes the following form:

$$\ln X_{odt}^{j} = \beta_1 + \beta_2 \ln IO_{ot}^{j} + \beta_3 \ln IO_{dt}^{j} + \beta_4 \ln dist_{od} + \beta_5 contig_{od} + \beta_6 comlangoff_{od} + \beta_7 col_{od} + \beta_8 \ln tar_{odt}^{j} + \beta_9 AD_{odt}^{i} + \mu_o fe_o^{j} + \gamma_d fe_d^{j} + \alpha_t year_t + \varepsilon_{odt}^{j} \quad (1)$$

where fe^j= importer or exporter fixed effects alone or interacted with International Standard Industrial Classification (ISIC) 3 sections and subsections, depending on the model specification. To measure the lagged impact of initiating AD on GVC exports, the antidumping variable AD^i_{odt} is equal to 1 if the importer (d) initiates AD on exporter (o) in sector i at least once during the past 3 years, and 0 otherwise. X^j_{odt} is the GVC exports of AD initiating country d to country o in sectors other than i at period t. Other country bilateral variables follow the general gravity model specification (i.e., $dist_{od}$, $contig_{od}$, $comlangoff_{od}$ and col_{od}) except for IO^j_{ot} and IO^j_{dt}, which control for industrial output of the exporter and importer, respectively, at time t. The $year_t$ dummy controls for time-specific cross-country common factors. The bilateral GVC exports data are derived from the ADB Multi-Regional Input–Output Table, which covers 48 economies and spans the years 2000, 2005, 2008, 2011, and 2015.

The fixed effects panel OLS regression results indicate a significantly negative impact of AD cases on GVC exports of the AD initiating countries in other sectors (Annex Table 2c.1). When a country initiates an AD case on coke, for example, its GVC exports in other sectors decline between 9% and 30%, depending on the fixed effects model (Annex Table 2c.1, columns 4 to 6). Other sectors could have a variety of industrial linkages with the AD initiating sector through backward and forward linkages. Thus, protecting a specific sector through AD can make GVC exports of other sectors suffer.

A generalized method of moments (GMM) regression is used to check for robustness. Equation (1) is revised to include a one-period lag GVC exports as an explanatory variable and reestimated using the system GMM regression technique developed by Blundell and Bond (1998), which combines the regression in first differences with an estimation run in levels, using both lagged levels and lagged differences as instruments. Equation (1) is rewritten as:

$$\ln X_{odt}^{k} = \beta_1 + \beta_2 \ln X_{od(t-1)}^{k} + \beta_3 \ln IO_{ot}^{k} + \beta_4 \ln IO_{dt}^{k} + \beta_5 \ln tar_{odt}^{k} + \beta_6 AD_{odt}^{i} + \alpha_t year_t + \varepsilon_{odt}^{k} \quad (2)$$

where k is a specific sector other than sector i.

The complete set of time-invariant gravity variables is not included in the specification because, with the system GMM estimator, we can obtain efficient estimates while controlling for time-invariant unobserved heterogeneity, simultaneity, and the dynamic relationship between current values of the explanatory variables and lagged values of the dependent variable. In effect, this addresses omitted variables bias. The autocorrelation test and the robust estimates of the coefficient standard errors rest on the assumption of no correlation across individuals in the idiosyncratic disturbances. To make this assumption likely to hold, we include time dummies $year_t$.

System GMM results show that the AD initiating country's GVC exports in other sector can suffer when AD is initiated (Annex Table 2c.2). Given the short production network involved, however, agricultural products and wood do not seem to cause significant negative spillovers to GVC exports in other sectors.

Sources: ADB staff using data from 2015 ADB Multi-Regional Input–Output Table; Bown (2016); Institute for Research on the International Economy. http://www.cepii.fr/CEPII/en/cepii/cepii.asp (accessed May 2018); United Nations Statistics Division. National Accounts Main Aggregates Database. https://unstats.un.org/unsd/snaama/dnlList.asp (accessed January 2018); and World Integrated Trade Solutions. https://wits.worldbank.org/ (accessed February 2018).

Based on the latest data on trade remedies notified to the World Trade Organization, antidumping measures against Asia increased to 132 in 2017 from 121 in 2016 (Annex Table 2b.1). Base metals and chemicals were the most targeted (Annex Table 2b.2). The PRC; the Republic of Korea; and Taipei,China were most affected (Annex Table 2b.3).

References

ADB. Asia Regional Integration Center FTA Database. https://aric.adb.org/fta (accessed August 2018).

———. 2010–2017 Multi-Regional Input–Output Tables.

———. 2015 Multi-Regional Input–Output Tables.

———. 2017. *Asian Economic Integration Report 2017: The Era of Financial Interconnectedness: How Can Asia Strengthen Financial Resilience?* Manila.

Association of Southeast Asian Nations (ASEAN) Secretariat. 2018. The Sixth Regional Comprehensive Economic Partnership Ministerial Meeting. https://asean.org/storage/2018/10/RCEP-ISSL-MM-6-JMS-FINAL.pdf

Blundell, B. and S. Bond. 1998. Initial Conditions and Moment Restrictions in Dynamic Panel Data Models. *Journal of Econometrics*. 87 (1998). pp. 115–143.

Bown, C. P. 2016. Global Antidumping Database. http://econ.worldbank.org/ttbd/gad/ (accessed February 2017).

CPB Netherlands Bureau for Economic Policy Analysis. World Trade Monitor. https://www.cpb.nl/en/data (accessed August 2018).

Institute for Research on the International Economy. http://www.cepii.fr/CEPII/en/cepii/cepii.asp (accessed May 2018).

International Monetary Fund. Direction of Trade Database. https://www.imf.org/en/Data (accessed August 2018).

———. World Economic Outlook April 2018 Database. https://www.imf.org/external/pubs/ft/weo/2018/01/weodata/index.aspx (accessed May 2018).

New Zealand Government Official Website. 2018. Comprehensive and Progressive Agreement for Trans-Pacific Partnership Ministerial Statement. https://www.beehive.govt.nz/sites/default/files/2018-03/CPTPP%20Ministerial%20Statement.pdf

United Nations. Commodity Trade Database. https://comtrade.un.org (accessed May 2018).

United Nations Statistics Division. National Accounts Main Aggregates Database. https://unstats.un.org/unsd/snaama/dnlList.asp (accessed January 2018).

Wang, Z., S. J. Wei, and K. Zhu. 2014. Quantifying International Production Sharing at the Bilateral and Sector Levels. *NBER Working Paper*. No. 19677. Cambridge, MA: National Bureau of Economic Research.

World Bank. World Governance Index. http://info.worldbank.org/governance/wgi/#home (accessed March 2018).

———. World Development Indicators. http://databank.worldbank.org/data/source/world-development-indicators# (accessed March 2018).

———. World Integrated Trade Solutions. https://wits.worldbank.org/ (accessed February 2018).

World Trade Organization. Disputes by agreement. https://www.wto.org/english/tratop_e/dispu_e/dispu_agreements_index_e.htm (accessed August 2018).

———. Integrated Trade Intelligence Portal. https://www.wto.org/english/res_e/statis_e/itip_e.htm (accessed August 2018).

———. Regional Trade Agreement Information System. http://rtais.wto.org (accessed August 2018).

———. Statistics Database. http://stat.wto.org/Home/WSDBHome.aspx (accessed May 2018).

Annexes

Annex Table 2a: Impact of Global Value Chain Exports on Labor Productivity Growth

Table 2a.1: Regression Results
Dependent variable: Log(Labor Productivity$_{it}$)

Variables	Random Effects (1)	Fixed Effects (2)	Fixed Effects 2SLS (1 IV) (3)	Fixed Effects 2SLS (2 IV) (4)
Log(Initial GDP per capita)$_i$	0.873***			
	(0.050)			
Inflation$_{it}$	-0.019***	-0.011	0.001	0.003
	(0.007)	(0.008)	(0.006)	(0.006)
Government expenditure/GDP$_{it}$	-0.015	-0.008	0.015	0.018**
	(0.010)	(0.012)	(0.009)	(0.009)
D.Log(Ave. WGI)$_{it}$	0.061***	0.060**	0.070*	0.071
	(0.022)	(0.029)	(0.042)	(0.044)
Agriculture VA/Total VA$_{it}$	-0.009	-0.012	-0.0007	0.001
	(0.012)	(0.016)	(0.016)	(0.017)
FDI net inflows/GDP$_{it}$	0.068	0.004	-0.071	-0.082
	(0.087)	(0.072)	(0.061)	(0.064)
Initial female LF participation/LF$_i$	-0.003			
	(0.008)			
Initial LF with advanced education/LF$_i$	0.001			
	(0.001)			
Log(Cumulative number of FTAs)$_{it}$	-0.008	-0.269	-0.116	-0.093
	(0.024)	(0.242)	(0.174)	(0.181)
Gross fixed capital formation/GDP$_{it}$	0.006**	0.006***	0.010***	0.010***
	(0.002)	(0.001)	(0.002)	(0.003)
Log(GVC exports)$_{it}$	0.035*	0.396***	0.945***	1.025***
	(0.019)	(0.124)	(0.179)	(0.173)
Constant	1.841***	7.627***		
	(0.591)	(2.185)		
Time fixed effects included	Yes	Yes	Yes	Yes
Observations	237	237	237	237
R-squared within	0.567	0.665	0.503	0.452
F-statistic			31.64	18.95
Anderson canonical correlation LM statistic			28.89	33.78
Sargan Statistic				1.237

*** = significant at 1%, ** = significant at 5%, * = significant at 10%. Robust standard errors are in parentheses.
2SLS = two-stage least squares, FDI = foreign direct investments, FTA = free trade agreement, GDP = gross domestic product, GVC = global value chain, IV = instrumental variable, LF = labor force, OLS = ordinary least squares, VA = value added, WGI = World Governance Index.
Notes: In column (3), the instrument used is the total trade expressed in natural logarithm. The same variable is also used for column (4), as well as the current account.
Sources: ADB calculations using data from 2010–2017 ADB Multi-Regional Input-Output Tables; World Bank. World Development Indicators. http://databank.worldbank.org/data/source/world-development-indicators# (accessed March 2018); World Bank. World Governance Index. http://info.worldbank.org/governance/wgi/#home (accessed March 2018); World Trade Organization. Disputes by agreement. https://www.wto.org/english/tratop_e/dispu_e/dispu_agreements_index_e.htm (accessed August 2018); and methodology by Wang, Wei, and Zhu (2014).

Annex Table 2b: Trade Remedy Measures—Asia

Table 2b.1: Number of New Trade Remedy Measures Involving Asia

	a: Asia as Imposing Party				b: Asia as Affected Party			
Year	**AD**	**CV**	**SG**	**Total**	**AD**	**CV**	**SG**	**Total**
2010	59	3	1	63	99	13	5	117
2011	57	3	10	70	77	6	11	94
2012	62	2	3	67	81	10	6	97
2013	70	3	2	75	135	13	4	152
2014	62	2	11	75	108	7	19	134
2015	70	2	11	83	135	11	18	164
2016	78	2	5	85	121	20	7	148
2017	97	5	5	107	132	16	9	157

AD = antidumping, CV = countervailing measures, SG = safeguards, WTO = World Trade Organization.
Notes: Trade remedy measures include measures which are in force. Safeguard measures are applied to all WTO members, hence the number of measures implemented include measures that are applied to all WTO members.
Source: ADB calculations using data from WTO. Integrated Trade Intelligence Portal. https://www.wto.org/english/res_e/statis_e/itip_e.htm (accessed August 2018).

Table 2b.2: Number of Trade Remedy Measures Affecting Asia, 2010-2018—Top Affected Sectors

HS Product Description	Total	Antidumping Duties	Countervailing Duties	Safeguards
Base metals and articles	443	362	54	27
Products of the chemical and allied industries	184	164	12	8
Resins, plastics and articles; rubber and articles	124	113	9	2
Machinery and electrical equipment	101	84	11	6

HS = harmonized system, WTO = World Trade Organization.
Notes: Trade remedy measures include measures which are in force. Safeguard measures are applied to all WTO members, hence the number of measures implemented include measures that are applied to all WTO members. 2018 covers trade remedies in force as of February 2018.
Source: ADB calculations using data from WTO. Integrated Trade Intelligence Portal. https://www.wto.org/english/res_e/statis_e/itip_e.htm (accessed August 2018).

Table 2b.3: Number of Implemented Trade Remedy Measures, 2010-2018—Top Affected Asian Economies

	Number of Measures Implemented		
Economy Affected	**ROW**	**Asia**	**Total**
People's Republic of China	338	205	543
Republic of Korea	87	99	186
Taipei,China	76	87	163

ROW = rest of the world, WTO = World Trade Organization.
Notes: Trade remedies include measures which are in force. 2018 covers trade remedies in force as of February 2018.
Source: ADB calculations using data from WTO. Integrated Trade Intelligence Portal. https://www.wto.org/english/res_e/statis_e/itip_e.htm (accessed August 2018).

Annex 2c: Impact of Antidumping Case Initiations on Global Value Chain Exports

Table 2c.1: Panel Ordinary Least Squares (All countries)
Dependent variable: Log(Bilateral GVC Exports ISIC 3 level)

Sector Initiated with AD case	Basic Metals and Fabricated Metal			Coke, Refined Petroleum and Nuclear Fuel			Chemicals and Chemical Products			Electrical and Optical Equipment		
Variables	(1)	(2)	(3)	(4)	(5)	(6)	(7)	(8)	(9)	(10)	(11)	(12)
Contiguity (=1 or 0)	1.010***	1.505***	0.677***	0.992***	1.499***	0.729***	0.797***	1.254***	0.681***	0.950***	1.442***	0.692***
	(0.191)	(0.239)	(0.218)	(0.168)	(0.204)	(0.183)	(0.188)	(0.233)	(0.212)	(0.184)	(0.228)	(0.197)
Common official language (=1 or 0)	-0.146	0.201	-0.112	-0.228	0.129	-0.090	-0.163	0.228	-0.184	-0.108	0.303**	-0.118
	(0.177)	(0.17)	(0.219)	(0.149)	(0.144)	(0.186)	(0.164)	(0.160)	(0.213)	(0.152)	(0.149)	(0.200)
Colonial relations (=1 or 0)	0.388**	0.753***	0.356*	0.422***	0.727***	0.311	0.402**	0.772***	0.384*	0.320**	0.686***	0.323*
	(0.164)	(0.203)	(0.204)	(0.150)	(0.164)	(0.190)	(0.168)	(0.200)	(0.210)	(0.158)	(0.180)	(0.192)
Log(distance)	-0.816***	-0.519***	-0.906***	-0.874***	-0.518***	-0.900***	-0.915***	-0.564***	-0.979***	-0.984***	-0.593***	-1.011***
	(0.067)	(0.061)	(0.093)	(0.064)	(0.055)	(0.076)	(0.068)	(0.063)	(0.088)	(0.066)	(0.058)	(0.084)
Bilateral applied tariff (simple average)	-0.021***	-0.016***	-0.020***	-0.025***	-0.018***	-0.025***	-0.022***	-0.017***	-0.020***	-0.020***	-0.015***	-0.018***
	(0.005)	(0.004)	(0.005)	(0.005)	(0.004)	(0.005)	(0.005)	(0.004)	(0.005)	(0.005)	(0.004)	(0.004)
Industrial output (exporter)	0.570***	0.566***	1.095***	0.550***	0.538***	1.055***	0.520***	0.514***	1.078***	0.513***	0.524***	1.090***
	(0.103)	(0.102)	(0.04)	(0.094)	(0.093)	(0.030)	(0.092)	(0.090)	(0.038)	(0.094)	(0.093)	(0.037)
Industrial output (importer)	0.417***	0.911***	0.410***	0.408***	0.924***	0.388***	0.473***	0.935***	0.401***	0.405***	0.913***	0.374***
	(0.101)	(0.022)	(0.096)	(0.097)	(0.021)	(0.093)	(0.095)	(0.022)	(0.091)	(0.093)	(0.022)	(0.089)
AD case initiation on sector (=1 or 0)	-0.047	-0.229***	-0.127*	-0.151***	-0.301***	-0.092**	-0.137**	-0.096*	-0.275***	-0.160***	-0.209***	-0.240***
	(0.070)	(0.068)	(0.070)	(0.049)	(0.052)	(0.047)	(0.057)	(0.053)	(0.054)	(0.061)	(0.059)	(0.060)
Constant	-16.80***		-25.91***	-9.859***	-27.23***	-24.56***	-10.55***	-26.56***	-24.41***	-7.951**	-26.04***	-23.94***
	(3.617)		(2.526)	(3.434)	(2.381)	(2.394)	(3.381)	(2.394)	(2.372)	(3.351)	(2.421)	(2.309)
No. of observations	3,892	3,892	3,892	4,254	4,254	4,254	4,202	4,202	4,202	4,401	4,401	4,401
Exporter - ISIC 3 FE	Yes	Yes	No	Yes	Yes	No	Yes	Yes	No	Yes	Yes	No
Importer - ISIC 3 FE	Yes	No	Yes	Yes	No	Yes	Yes	No	Yes	Yes	No	Yes
Year FE	Yes	Yes	Yes	Yes	Yes	Yes	Yes	Yes	Yes	Yes	Yes	Yes
GVC export sector excluded	Basic Metals and Fabricated Metal			Coke, Refined Petroleum and Nuclear Fuel			Chemicals and Chemical Products			Electrical and Optical Equipment		
Overall R-squared	0.919	0.889	0.793	0.924	0.896	0.812	0.918	0.887	0.794	0.916	0.884	0.794
Within R-Squared	0.289	0.282	0.279	0.317	0.307	0.308	0.309	0.302	0.299	0.297	0.289	0.284
Between R-squared	0.956	0.925	0.824	0.958	0.929	0.854	0.954	0.923	0.827	0.953	0.920	0.828

*** = significant at 1%, ** = significant at 5%, * = significant at 10%. Robust standard errors are in parentheses.
AD = antidumping, FE = fixed effects, GVC = global value chain, ISIC = International Standard Industry Classification.
Sources: ADB calculations using data from ADB. 2015 ADB Multi-Regional Input–Output Table; Bown (2016); Institute for Research on the International Economy. http://www.cepii.fr/CEPII/en/cepii/cepii.asp (accessed May 2018); United Nations Statistics Division. National Accounts Main Aggregates Database. https://unstats.un.org/unsd/snaama/dnlList.asp (accessed January 2018); World Integrated Trade Solutions. https://wits.worldbank.org/ (accessed February 2018); and methodology by Wang, Wei, and Zhu (2014).

Table 2c.2: System Generalized Method of Moments (All countries)
Dependent variable: Log(Bilateral GVC Exports ISIC 3 level)

Sector Initiated with AD Case / **Variables**	**Agriculture, Hunting, Forestry, and Fishing** (1)	**Wood and Products of Wood and Cork** (2)	**Food, Beverages, and Tobacco** (3)	**Manufacturing, NEC** (4)	**Manufacturing, NEC** (5)	**Pulp, Paper, Printing, and Publishing** (6)	**Basic Metals and Fabricated Metal** (7)
$Log(GVC\ exports)_{t-1}$	0.687***	0.695***	0.394***	0.558***	0.823***	0.496***	0.503**
	(0.188)	(0.163)	(0.132)	(0.135)	(0.114)	(0.142)	(0.245)
Bilateral applied tariff (simple average)	-0.037	-0.025	0.039	-0.072***	-0.056	-0.053***	-0.049
	(0.036)	(0.029)	(0.061)	(0.023)	(0.051)	(0.017)	(0.040)
Industrial output (exporter)	0.348	0.430*	0.998**	0.646**	0.366	0.740***	0.596*
	(0.277)	(0.260)	(0.397)	(0.255)	(0.258)	(0.258)	(0.306)
Industrial output (importer)	0.204	0.166	0.644***	0.183	0.298**	0.193	0.531
	(0.356)	(0.295)	(0.206)	(0.141)	(0.130)	(0.169)	(0.449)
AD case initiated on sector (=1 or 0)	-0.037	-0.497	-0.840**	-0.460**	-0.744*	-0.596*	-0.788*
	(0.401)	(0.415)	(0.357)	(0.233)	(0.413)	(0.317)	(0.402)
Constant	-12.62		-41.02***	-19.11**			
	(15.190)		(15.710)	(8.002)			
No of observations	148	148	88	298	265	298	148
GVC exports sector	Electrical and Optical Equipment		Rubber and Plastics	Basic Metals and Fabricated Metal	Coke, Refined Petroleum, and Nuclear Fuel	Basic Metals and Fabricated Metal	Electrical and Optical Equipment
AR(2) p-value	0.352	0.434	0.877	0.522	0.467	0.239	0.652
Hansen p-value	0.671	0.773	0.812	0.229	0.159	0.424	0.592
No. of instruments	45	43	23	53	53	53	35

*** = significant at 1%, ** = significant at 5%, * = significant at 10%. Robust standard errors are in parentheses.
AD = antidumping, FE = fixed effects, GVC = global value chain, ISIC = International Standard Industry Classification, NEC = not elsewhere classified.
Sources: ADB calculations using data from ADB. 2015 ADB Multi-Regional Input–Output Table; Bown (2016); Institute for Research on the International Economy. http://www.cepii.fr/CEPII/en/cepii/cepii.asp (accessed May 2018); United Nations Statistics Division. National Accounts Main Aggregates Database. https://unstats.un.org/unsd/snaama/dnlList.asp (accessed January 2018); World Integrated Trade Solutions. https://wits.worldbank.org/ (accessed February 2018); and methodology by Wang, Wei, and Zhu (2014).

Foreign Direct Investment

Trends and Patterns of Foreign Direct Investment in Asia

Despite a downturn in global investment, foreign direct investment in Asia—both inward and outward—weakened only slightly.[13]

Asia remained the largest recipient of foreign direct investment (FDI) in 2017, attracting 36.2% of global FDI, up from 27.8% in 2016. The People's Republic of China (PRC) remained the top destination. While the region continues to benefit from inward FDI—helping drive economic growth and rising incomes—it has also cemented its position as a major source of FDI, as Asian firms continue to internationalize both within and outside the region. In 2017, Asia's share of global outward FDI increased to 34.1%, up from 33.6% in 2016. Japan reemerged as top Asian investor, followed by the PRC and Hong Kong, China.

Updates on Global Inward FDI to Asia

Global inward FDI fell sharply in 2017; but inward FDI to Asia weakened just 0.5%—to $517.5 billion.

Based on standard balance of payments (BOP) data, global inward FDI in 2017 fell 23.4%—to $1.4 trillion (Figure 3.1). The decline was mainly driven by a reduction in FDI to developed and transition economies, while there was only a modest growth in developing economies. Lower rates of return on FDI, a slowdown in the expansion of international production, and the uncertain global trade and economic environment may have dampened investments.

Figure 3.1: Total Inward Foreign Direct Investment

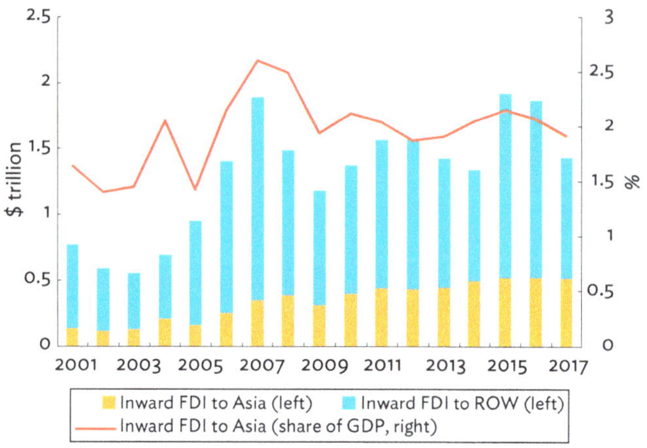

FDI = foreign direct investment.
Sources: ADB calculations using data from Association of Southeast Asian Nations Secretariat. ASEANstats Database. https://www.aseanstats.org/ (accessed July 2018); and United Nations Conference on Trade and Development. World Investment Report 2018 Statistical Annex Tables. http://unctad.org/en/Pages/DIAE/World%20Investment%20Report/Annex-Tables.aspx (accessed June 2018).

Nevertheless, Asia still attracted $517.5 billion in FDI during 2017, just $2.4 billion (0.5%) below the 2016 level. The PRC; Hong Kong, China; Singapore; Australia; and India remained Asia's top FDI recipients (Table 3.1). Indonesia saw an almost sixfold rise in inward FDI—receiving $23.1 billion in 2017, up from $3.9 billion in 2016.

As a share of GDP, however, inward FDI to the region has been on a downward trend since 2007, except for a modest recovery between 2012–2015. It fell to 1.9% of GDP in 2017 (from 2.1% in 2015), slightly higher than the global share of 1.8%. In 2017, inward FDI as a percentage of GDP was the highest in Hong Kong, China (30.6%); Singapore (19.1%); Mongolia (13.1%); Cambodia (12.6%); and Georgia (12.3%).

[13] Asia refers to the 48 Asia and the Pacific members of the Asian Development Bank (ADB) with available data, which includes Japan and Oceania (Australia and New Zealand) in addition to the developing Asian economies.

Table 3.1: Top 10 Global and Asian Foreign Direct Investment Recipients ($ billion)

Global	2017	2016	2012	Asia	2017	2016	2012
United States	275.4	457.1	199.0	China, People's Republic of	136.3	133.7	121.1
China, People's Republic of	136.3	133.7	121.1	Hong Kong, China	104.3	117.4	70.2
Hong Kong, China	104.3	117.4	70.2	Singapore	62.0	77.5	59.8
Brazil	62.7	58.0	76.1	Australia	46.4	47.8	59.6
Singapore	62.0	77.5	59.8	India	39.9	44.5	24.2
Netherlands	58.0	85.8	25.0	Indonesia	23.1	3.9	19.1
France	49.8	35.2	16.1	Korea, Republic of	17.1	12.1	9.5
Australia	46.4	47.8	59.6	Viet Nam	14.1	12.6	8.4
Switzerland	41.0	48.3	29.5	Japan	10.4	11.4	1.7
India	39.9	44.5	24.2	Malaysia	9.5	11.3	9.2

Source: ADB calculations using data from United Nations Conference on Trade and Development. World Investment Report 2018 Statistical Annex Tables. http://unctad.org/en/Pages/DIAE/World%20Investment%20Report/Annex-Tables.aspx (accessed June 2018).

Figure 3.2: Foreign Direct Investment, by Mode of Entry—Asia

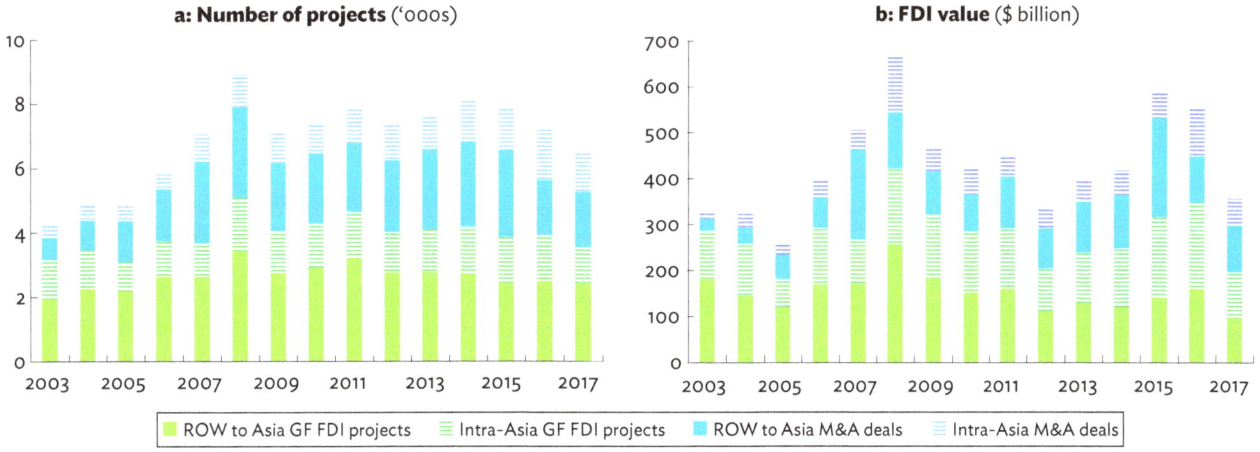

FDI = foreign direct investment, GF = greenfield, M&A = merger and acquisition, ROW = rest of the world.
Sources: ADB calculations using data from Bureau van Dijk. Zephyr M&A Database; and Financial Times. fDi Markets (both accessed June 2018).

While standard BOP data only show a modest decline in inward FDI to the region, firm-level investment activity data—which provide information on mode of entry and ultimate investment ownership—show that both mergers and acquisitions (M&As) and "greenfield" FDI in Asia declined abruptly in 2017 (Figure 3.2).[14] The number of greenfield projects and M&As declined 9.3% compared with 2016 levels, while by nominal value inward greenfield FDI declined 43.5% and M&As 21.9%.

The steeper decline of inward FDI based on firm-level investment suggests that some Asian economies may have acted as a conduit for FDI ultimately directed outside the region. For example, Hong Kong, China accounted for 26.2% of the total decrease by nominal value in inward FDI to Asia based on firm-level investment data (Table 3.2). It received $13.9 billion in 2017 (down 78.7% from 2016)—compared with $104.3 billion as recorded by BOP data (which fell just 11.1%).

[14] Investments can either be "greenfield" (building new assets) or by mergers and acquisitions (acquiring existing ones). For more detailed description of the data, see online Annex 1: http://aric.adb.org/pdf/aeir2018_onlineannex1.pdf

Table 3.2: Top Affected Recipients of Foreign Direct Investment in Asia—Greenfield and Mergers and Acquisitions

Destinations	2017 ($ billion)	2016 ($ billion)	y-o-y change (%)	Share in total decline (%)
Hong Kong, China	13.9	65.3	-78.7	26.2
Kazakhstan	7.1	40.6	-82.5	17.1
India	63.0	87.3	-27.9	12.4
Malaysia	8.0	25.7	-68.9	9.0
Viet Nam	22.6	40.2	-43.9	9.0
Indonesia	12.8	27.4	-53.4	7.5
Australia	37.0	45.2	-18.1	4.2
Myanmar	2.8	10.4	-73.0	3.9
Philippines	5.2	11.6	-54.8	3.2
Thailand	7.3	13.1	-44.0	2.9

y-o-y = year-on-year.
Sources: ADB calculations using data from Bureau van Dijk. Zephyr M&A Database; and Financial Times. fDi Markets (both accessed June 2018).

Inward FDI—as measured by the number of greenfield projects and M&As—did not decline as steeply (9.3%) as the nominal committed value of investments (35.5%) (Table 3.3). The size of the average greenfield FDI project fell sharply—by 37.2%—with smaller investments in the primary and manufacturing sectors. This indicates that the outlook for greenfield investment may not be as bleak in the future. The average value of M&As fell 14.7%, driven by smaller investments in services.

Reversing the historical trend, firm-level greenfield FDI to the region declined mainly in manufacturing (by 36.8%), while M&As dropped in services (by 39.4%).

In 2017, greenfield FDI and M&As in both manufacturing and services were below their 5-year averages (Figure 3.3 a, b). Inward greenfield FDI in manufacturing fell 36.8% between 2016 and 2017, while investments through M&As in services also declined sharply (39.4%). Investments in primary sectors favored M&A more than greenfield with the value of M&As in the sector more than doubling in 2017 to $22.6 billion—half of which was the acquisition of Essar Oil in India for $11.3 billion by Petrol Complex Pte Ltd of Singapore.

In a departure from previous years, the fall in greenfield and M&As was mainly driven by a 46.2% decline—or $134.5 billion—in intra-Asian projects and deals (Figure 3.4). Intra-Asian greenfield FDI fell to $99.7 billion in 2017 (down from $187.8 billion in 2016) affecting mainly manufacturing, while intra-Asian M&As fell to $57.1 billion in 2017 (from $103.6 billion) mostly in services. While the PRC still remained the top source for intra-Asian investments in 2017, its investments in the region fell sharply (70.2%) in 2017 to $31.0 billion, mainly affecting financial services and real estate. Recipient economies most affected by the drop in intra-Asian greenfield investments were India, Viet Nam, Malaysia, and Australia—due to the decline in FDI from the PRC; Taipei,China; Malaysia; and Singapore. The value of intra-Asian M&As in Hong Kong, China fell $50.5 billion in 2017, also mainly due to the drop in the PRC's investments. On the other hand, inward FDI from the rest of the world declined by a relatively moderate 23.6% mainly due to a reduction in greenfield investments (M&As from the rest of the world in fact increased 1.6%). The United States (US) has historically been the largest investor in the region, but the US FDI to Asia fell 36.6% in 2017. As source economies, the PRC and the US together

Table 3.3: Average Project and Deal Size—Asia ($ million)

Period	Greenfield	M&A	Total	Greenfield			M&A			Total		
				MFG	PRI	SRV	MFG	PRI	SRV	MFG	PRI	SRV
2016	88.6	62.7	76.9	110.2	1008.5	33.3	45.7	52.6	73.3	84.8	410.4	53.1
2017	55.7	53.5	54.7	78.3	275.8	29.5	50.1	198.7	46.2	67.6	221.2	38.0

M&A = merger and acquisition, MFG = manufacturing, PRI = primary, SRV = services.
Note: Average project and deal size equals Greenfield project value and M&A deal value in Asia divided by number of projects and deals.
Sources: ADB calculations using data from Bureau van Dijk. Zephyr M&A Database; and Financial Times. fDi Markets (both accessed June 2018).

Figure 3.3: Total Inward Foreign Direct Investment to Asia, by Sector ($ billion)

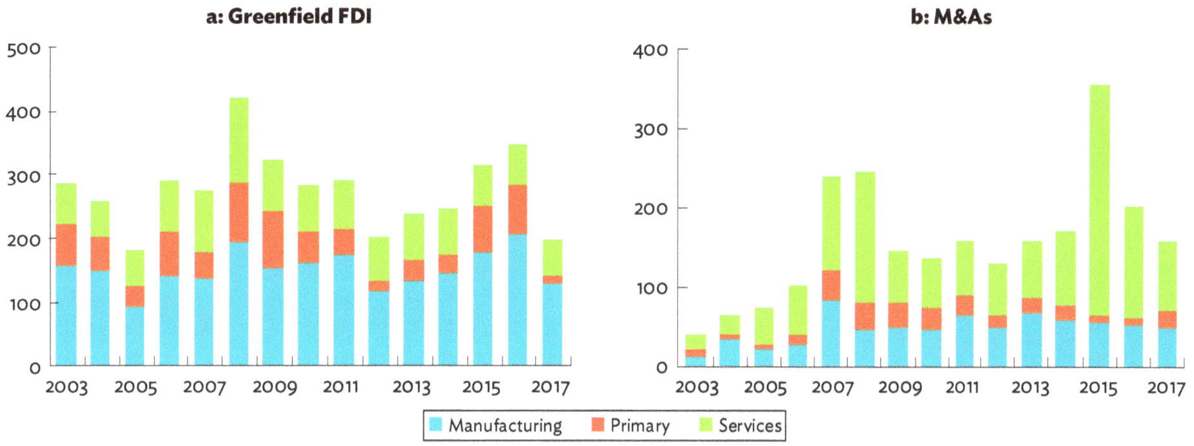

FDI = foreign direct investment, M&A = merger and acquisition.
Sources: ADB calculations using data from Bureau van Dijk. Zephyr M&A Database; and Financial Times. fDi Markets (both accessed June 2018).

Figure 3.4 Intra-Asia Foreign Direct Investment, by Sector ($ billion)

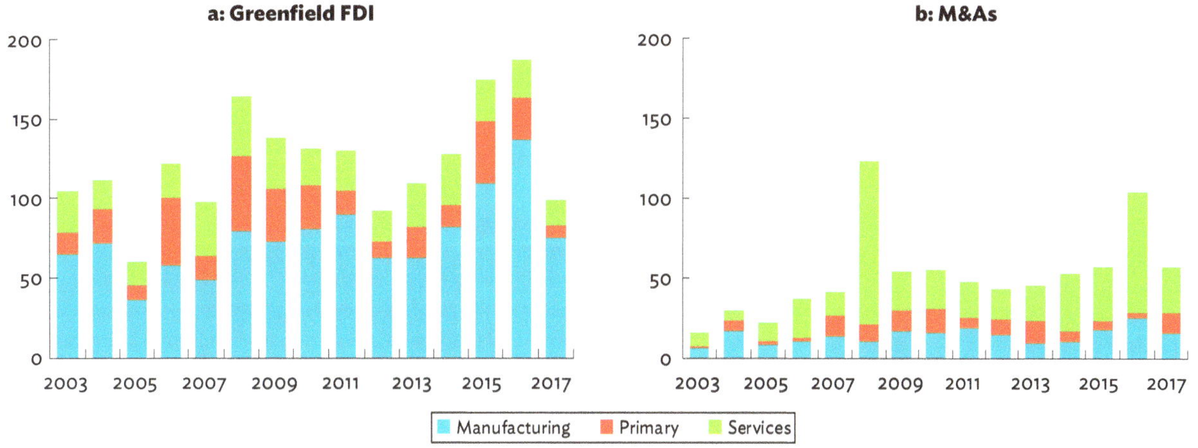

FDI = foreign direct investment, M&A = merger and acquisition.
Sources: ADB calculations using data from Financial Times. fDi Markets; and Bureau van Dijk. Zephyr M&A Database (both accessed June 2018).

accounted for 59.2% of the decline in greenfield FDI and M&As to Asia in 2017 (Table 3.4).

The slowdown in inward greenfield FDI is concerning, as many Asian economies historically have leveraged trade-promoting greenfield FDI for widespread job creation, especially in labor-intensive manufacturing (Box 3.1).

While manufacturing remains important, inward FDI to Asia in services has taken on a larger role in recent years (Box 3.2). FDI inflows in services rose to $140.5 billion in 2017 from $85.9 billion in 2003—equivalent to a 3.6% (compounded) annual average growth rate. Services FDI has steadily accounted for around a third of Asia's total inflows since 2012, and the majority of the region's cross-border M&As since 2015.

Table 3.4 Top Sources of Decline of Foreign Direct Investment in Asia—Greenfield and Mergers and Acquisitions

Source	2017 ($ billion)	2016 ($ billion)	y-o-y change (%)	Share in total decline (%)
China, People's Republic of	31.0	103.9	-70.2	37.1
United States	75.1	118.6	-36.6	22.1
United Kingdom	13.7	29.3	-53.2	8.0
Taipei,China	12.2	26.7	-54.2	7.4
Japan	29.6	37.4	-20.9	4.0
Singapore	24.7	30.7	-19.4	3.0
Hong Kong, China	15.8	16.2	-2.3	0.2
Germany	17.0	14.4	17.5	-1.3
Korea, Republic of	23.2	20.6	12.5	-1.3
Cayman Islands	17.6	14.1	24.5	-1.8

y-o-y = year on year.
Sources: ADB calculations using data from Bureau van Dijk. Zephyr M&A Database; and Financial Times. fDi Markets (both accessed June 2018).

Box 3.1: Greenfield Foreign Direct Investment and Job Creation—Emerging Trends

Greenfield foreign direct investment (FDI) creates jobs, facilitates technology transfer, and is better linked to global value chains (ADB 2016). Between 2003 and 2017, greenfield investments created 29.5 million new jobs globally, 43.6% of which were in Asia (box figures 1a, 1b).

Jobs created by greenfield FDI in Asia peaked in 2008 at 1.2 million and have been slowing overall since (box figure 2a). In 2017, for example, Asia's share of global FDI job creation was well below the most recent 5-year average (43.8%). Greenfield investments to Asia fell 43.5% in 2017, accompanied by a 29.9% drop (0.3 million) in the number of jobs created. Of the 667,039 greenfield jobs created in 2017, almost half were in the region's two mammoth economies—the People's Republic of China (PRC) (153,423 or 23.0% of the total) and India (162,541 or 24.4%). Viet Nam (83,744 or 12.6%), the Philippines (37,098 or 5.6%), and Singapore (30,833 or 4.6%) also received substantial numbers. The largest number of greenfield jobs in Asia came from the United States (US) investments (139,296 new jobs), followed by Japan (86,079), and Germany (59,658). Jobs generated by US investments were mostly in software and information technology (IT) services, Japan's in real estate, and Germany's in transportation. But it was real estate that generated the greatest number of jobs overall in 2017 (87,859), followed by software and IT services (64,845), and electronic components (55,513).

1: Global Greenfield Foreign Direct Investment Jobs Creation

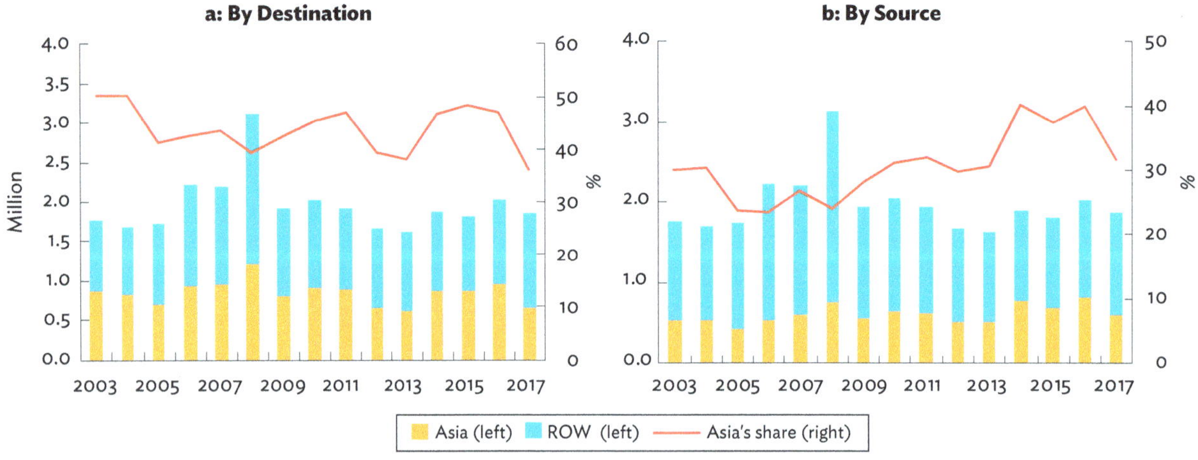

ROW = rest of the world.
Source: ADB calculations using data from Financial Times. fDi Markets (accessed June 2018).

Continued on next page

Box 3.1 *continued*

2: Inward Greenfield Foreign Direct Investment Job Creation in Asia, by Source

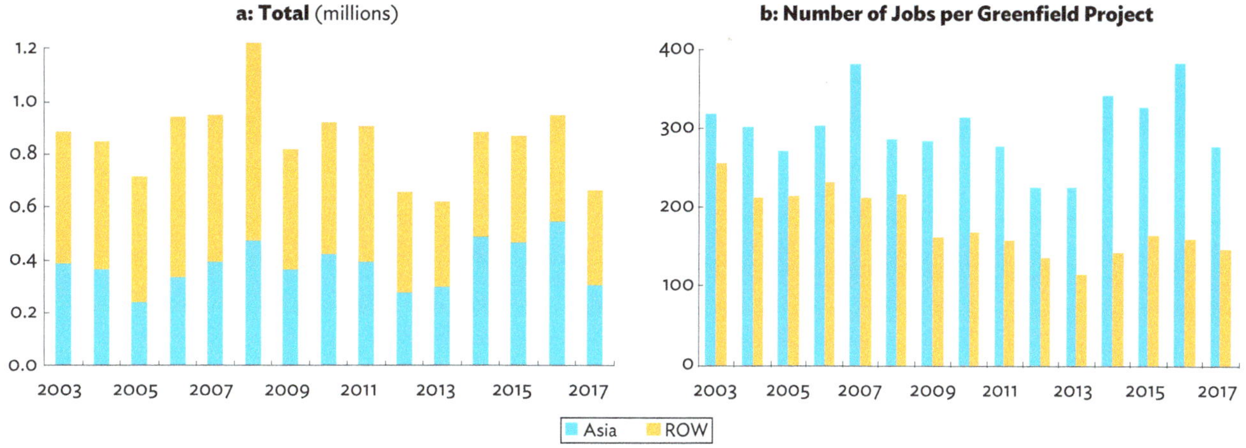

ROW = rest of the world.
Source: ADB calculations using data from Financial Times. fDi Markets (accessed June 2018).

Intraregional investments created almost half (46.2%) the greenfield jobs in 2017—led by Japan (28.0% of intra-Asian greenfield jobs), the PRC (15.0%), and the Republic of Korea (14.2%) with the PRC, Viet Nam, and India collectively receiving 57.4% of total intra-Asian jobs. Intraregional greenfield FDI is also more labor intensive—it creates more jobs per investment project compared with FDI from outside the region. Intraregional investments created 302 jobs per greenfield project in 2003–2017, almost double the average from non-regional investments (178 jobs) (box figure 2b). For example, a Republic of Korea textile company invested in Soc Trang, Viet Nam, creating 8,000 new jobs. An investment in the Philippines by an electronics company based in Taipei,China added 7,500 new jobs.

Manufacturing remains dominant in terms of both number of greenfield jobs and jobs created per project. The share of manufacturing in jobs created by greenfield FDI has been relatively stable (70.5% in 2003–2017, and 70.3% in 2017), while the share of new jobs in services (26.8% in 2003–2017 and 29.0% in 2017) has increased at the expense of jobs created in the primary sector (2.7% in 2003–2017 and 0.7% in 2017) (box figure 3a). In 2017, an average 283 jobs per greenfield project were generated in manufacturing notably in plastics, semiconductors, and automotive original equipment manufacturers (OEM)—each with at least 500 jobs per project. Services created an average 106—at least 100 per project were added in most service industries including transportation, hotels and tourism, communications, leisure and entertainment, financial, and business services—and primary sector created 96 (box figure 3b).

The distribution of new greenfield jobs is moving toward high-technology manufacturing and services. Since 2010, greenfield jobs have shifted from electronic components, automotive OEM, and business services to mostly real estate and software and IT services. Similarly, the highest new job generation has occurred

3: Inward Greenfield Foreign Direct Investment Job Creation in Asia, by Sector

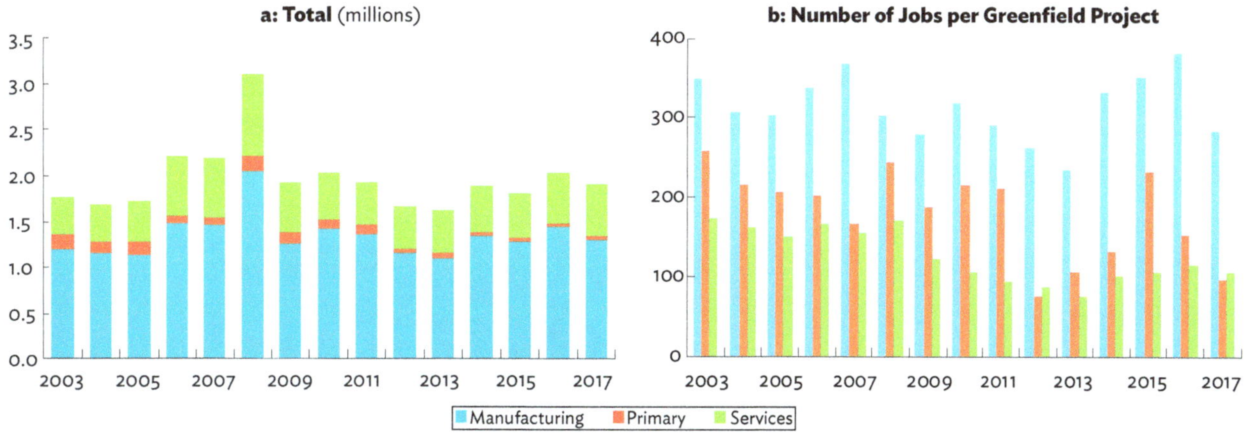

Source: ADB calculations using data from Financial Times. fDi Markets (accessed June 2018).

Continued on next page

Box 3.1 *continued*

in several medium- to high-technology manufacturing and service industries—including leisure and entertainment, plastics, real estate, software and IT services, space and defense, and transportation industries—each with at least 5% (compounded) annual average growth over 2010–2017.

Despite the recent decline in greenfield job creation, the share of jobs created by greenfield FDI to the total change in formal employment in Asia still increased from 3.1% in 2003 to 4.8% in 2017, driven mostly by investments in manufacturing. Notably, greenfield FDI job creation in manufacturing in 2014–2017 accounted for 81.7% of Asia's overall net manufacturing job creation—up 10.1% from the 2009–2013 average. This is in stark contrast to the 87.7% overall decline in net job creation in manufacturing—a symptom of the so called "jobless growth in manufacturing." This has affected many Asian economies recently due to shifts from labor-intensive to capital-intensive industries and the changing nature of work (for example, the impact of automation) (International Labour Organization 2016). However, in services, jobs created by greenfield FDI grew only 5.0% between these two time periods, below the 9.1% job creation in services overall.

While Asia has benefited immensely from FDI, Asian investors have also been a major contributor to global greenfield job creation. From 2003 to 2017, almost a third (30.3%) of jobs generated by greenfield FDI globally originated from Asia (see box figure 1b), led by investments from Japan (31.6% of all jobs from Asian investments), the PRC (13.5%), and the Republic of Korea (12.0%). Jobs created by Asian greenfield investments were mostly in manufacturing industries, particularly in real estate, automotive OEM, and electronic components. Outside Asia, the US received the largest number of jobs from Asian greenfield investments—predominantly in automotive components, automotive OEM, real estate, and software and IT services. These jobs came largely from Japanese investments (13.9% of all greenfield jobs in the US), the PRC (5.6%), the Republic of Korea (4.1%), and India (4.0%). For example, two investments by Japan's Toyota Motors in the automotive OEM industry created 7,000 jobs and one investment by Mitsui & Co in real estate added another 3,000. Other major beneficiaries of jobs from Asia's greenfield investments outside the region include Mexico, the Russian Federation, and the United Kingdom.

Greenfield FDI creates new jobs in both advanced and developing economies. Creating jobs in manufacturing is critical for poverty reduction. However, the current trade conflict and increasing investment restrictions—along with the changing nature of manufacturing away from labor-intensive activities—has created new challenges. Thus, it is important to continue working toward strengthening investment linkages and policies that attract sustainable and job-creating investments.

Source: ADB staff.

Box 3.2: The Internationalization of Services

Trade in services in Asia has been growing rapidly, especially in recent years. The region's trade in services with the world nearly tripled—from $1.2 trillion in 2005 to $2.9 trillion in 2017 (box figure 1). Asian economies are among the major services traders globally, accounting collectively for about a quarter of global services exports and imports between 2005 and 2017.[a] In general, increasing cross-border investment activity has historically contributed to the internationalization of services. Over the years, the spread of manufacturing firms in search of new markets or export platforms has encouraged the internationalization of home-country service suppliers. More recently—and in the wake of pro-competitive regulatory reforms, privatization, and investment liberalization—a growing share of service firms have pursued their own internalization strategies in more open host-country environments (ADB 2009). With the continued fragmentation of services production in conjunction with the proliferation of production networks in services dependent on information and communication technology (ICT), foreign direct investment (FDI) will increasingly play a key role in the internationalization of services.

1: Services Trade in Asia, by Subregion

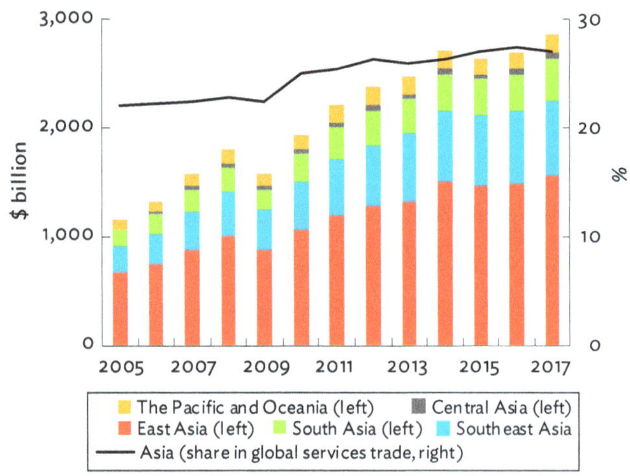

Source: ADB calculations using data from World Trade Organization-United Nations Conference on Trade and Development-International Trade Centre Trade in Services data set. https://www.wto.org/english/res_e/statis_e/daily_update_e/services_annual_dataset.zip (accessed July 2018).

Continued on next page

[a] Within the region, the largest services traders by far have been in East Asia, accounting for 55.2% of Asia's total services trade with the world between 2005 and 2017, with the People's Republic of China (PRC) alone contributing 20.7%.

Box 3.2 *continued*

2: Inward Services Foreign Direct Investment in Asia, by Subregion

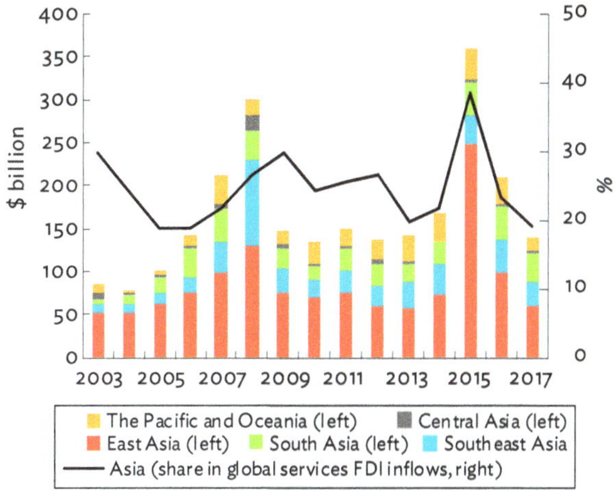

FDI = foreign direct investment, M&A = merger and acquisition.
Sources: ADB calculations using data from Bureau van Dijk. Zephyr M&A Database; Financial Times. fDi Markets (both accessed June 2018).

Globally, services FDI is rising. Based on firm-level investment data (see Footnote 14), global FDI inflows in services more than doubled—from $288.8 billion in 2003 to $736.5 billion in 2017. Asia is among the largest FDI destinations for services, attracting $2.5 trillion (or almost 25%) of global services FDI between 2003 and 2017. Services have also become an increasingly important FDI segment, accounting for nearly 40% ($140.5 billion) of Asia's total inward FDI in 2017, up from 26.1% ($85.9 billion) in 2003 (box figure 2). By far, cross-border mergers and acquisitions (M&As) are the more important mode of FDI entry for services (see Figure 3.2) accounting for 61.5% of total inward services industries investment in 2017 (up from 24.9% in 2003). Within the region, most FDI inflows in services went to East Asia, with $1.3 trillion (51.2%) of cumulative greenfield and M&As in 2003–2017, followed by Southeast Asia ($457.4 billion, 18.2%), South Asia ($389.3 billion, 15.5%), and the Pacific and Oceania ($319.7 billion, 12.7%). While Central Asia has attracted the least ($57.2 billion or 2.3% of Asia's total inward FDI), services FDI inflows to the subregion increased 5.1% in 2017—while services FDI fell in other Asian subregions. In 2017, the People's Republic of China (PRC); India; Singapore; Australia; and Hong Kong, China remained the top recipients of services FDI in Asia, both in terms of global and intraregional flows (Annex Table 3a.1).

About a third of Asia's FDI flows in services during 2003–2017 was intraregional (box figure 3), mainly through M&As, and in communications, financial, real estate, and transportation services. In particular, the PRC (19.3% of total intraregional); Japan (15.2%); Singapore (14.9%); Hong Kong, China (12.7%); and Australia (12.1%) were the major service sector investors within the region. North America (especially the United States) was the second-largest investor in the region, accounting for 27.2%; followed by the European Union (EU) (especially the United Kingdom) at 18.6%. North America's FDI in services to Asia was primarily in communications, financial, and software and information and technology (IT) services, again mostly through M&As. However, EU service sector investments were focused on communications, financial, and transportation services, predominantly through greenfield investments.

By industry, services inflows in financial (30.5%), communications (15.4%), real estate (10.9%), transportation (10.5%), and business (10.4%) accounted for the bulk of the $2.5 trillion total inward investment in services to Asia between 2003 and 2017—mainly through M&As, with the exception of transportation services which received mostly greenfield (Annex Table 3a.2). In 2017, the bulk (83.4%) of Asia's total FDI inflows in services were in business, communications, financial, software and IT, and transportation services. In addition to these, hotels and tourism services attract a significant proportion of intraregional services FDI. In 2017, software and IT services, healthcare, personal services, and other services in the automotive industry more than doubled from their average inflows in 2003–2009. The significant growth in these service industries was mainly driven by high-value M&A deals from within the region and North America.

By and large, as Asia's regional production networks become more sophisticated and capital-intensive, the region is shifting to more advanced and technology-based production. This can be seen as FDI flows increase in industries enabled by ICT and other advanced industries. For example, financial services, business services, healthcare, and alternative/renewable energy each grew at least 7% in 2015–2017, compared with their average levels in 2003–2014. Across many Asian economies,

3: Inward Services Foreign Direct Investment in Asia, by Source
($ billion)

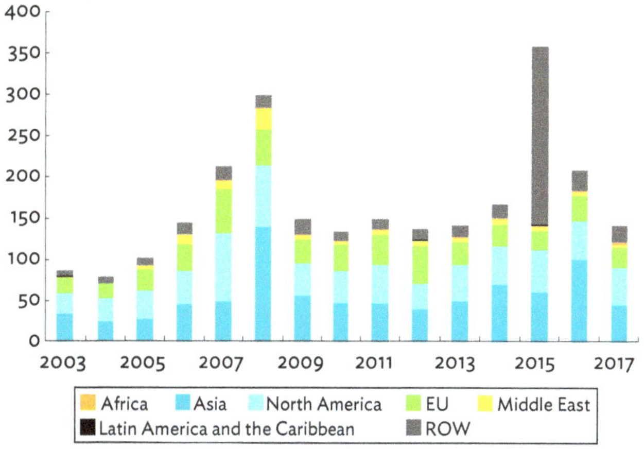

EU = European Union, M&A = merger and acquisition, ROW = rest of the world.
Sources: ADB calculations using data from Bureau van Dijk. Zephyr M&A Database and Financial Times. fDi Markets (both accessed June 2018).

Continued on next page

Box 3.2 *continued*

regulatory reforms in services, the rise in FDI inflows to knowledge-based sectors, and increased public investment in ICT infrastructure are creating an enabling environment for these industries to thrive.

Services contribute significantly to gross domestic product and job creation (ADB 2017). They provide the inputs needed for economies to thrive. Developing countries can benefit from increased services exports as their services industries expand, producing higher growth, more jobs, and greater foreign exchange earnings. Services imports—or the entry of foreign service providers—can also bring about greater competition, international best practices, better skills and technologies, and investment capital. Given that services FDI is associated with the growth and tradability of services (box figure 4), it is important that economies in the region continue to attract services investment. However, significant barriers to services investment remain—survey data show Asian firms in the services are primarily constrained by practices of the informal sector (14.2%), political instability (12.9%), high taxes (12.2%), and access to finance (11.6%).[b] Similarly, institutional quality and the business environment—in turn determined by government policies and regulations—are the most important drivers of FDI in Asia, particularly for M&As and services (ADB 2016). Thus, continued investment liberalization, domestic regulatory reform, improving the quality of institutions and the business environment, and advancing regional integration can help foster sustainable FDI inflows to the region, particularly in services.

4: Total Services Foreign Direct Investment Inflows and Aggregate Services Trade (average 2005–2017)

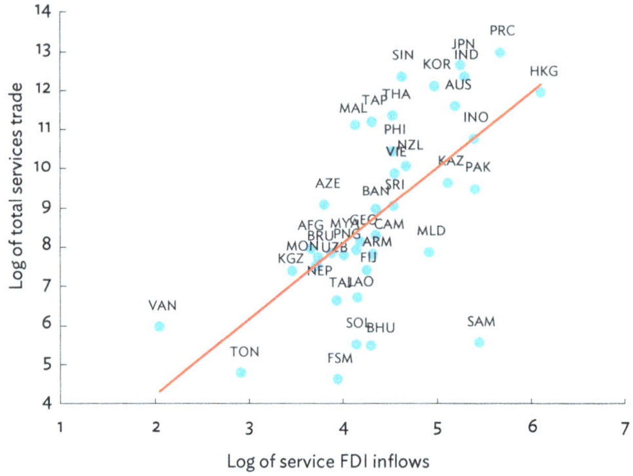

AFG = Afghanistan; ARM = Armenia; AUS = Australia; AZE = Azerbaijan; BAN = Bangladesh; BHU = Bhutan; BRU = Brunei Darussalam; CAM = Cambodia; FDI = foreign direct investment; FIJ = Fiji; FSM = Federated States of Micronesia; GEO = Georgia; HKG = Hong Kong, China; IND = India; INO = Indonesia; JPN = Japan; KAZ = Kazakhstan; KGZ = Kyrgyz Republic; KOR = Republic of Korea; LAO = Lao People's Democratic Republic; MAL = Malaysia; MLD = Maldives; MON = Mongolia; MYA= Myanmar; NEP = Nepal; NZL = New Zealand; PAK = Pakistan; PHI = Philippines; PNG = Papua New Guinea; PRC = People's Republic of China; SAM = Samoa; SIN = Singapore; SOL = Solomon Islands; SRI = Sri Lanka; TAJ = Tajikistan; TAP = Taipei,China; THA = Thailand; TON = Tonga; UZB = Uzbekistan; VAN = Vanuatu; VIE = Viet Nam.

Sources: ADB calculations using data from Financial Times. fDi Markets; and Bureau van Dijk. Zephyr M&A Database (both accessed June 2018); and World Trade Organization-United Nations Conference on Trade and Development-International Trade Centre Trade in Services data set. https://www.wto.org/english/res_e/statis_e/daily_update_e/services_annual_dataset.zip (accessed July 2018).

[b] World Bank. Enterprise Surveys (accessed August 2018).

Source: ADB staff.

Update on Regional Trends

Inward FDI across Asia's subregions fell except for Southeast Asia.

BOP data show inward FDI to Asia moderated slightly to $517.5 billion in 2017 compared with $519.9 billion in 2016. More than half of Asia's inward FDI went to East Asia, while Southeast Asia accounted for 26.1% (Figure 3.5). South Asia and Central Asia each received 9.0% of total inward FDI to Asia, while the share of the Pacific and Oceania remained below 3.0%.

Inward FDI to all Asia subregions declined in 2017—except in Southeast Asia where it grew 12.1%. The subregion attracted $135.2 billion in 2017, $14.5 billion more than 2016. Investment grew throughout much of the subregion. In Indonesia, inflows rose nearly sixfold to $23.1 billion, primarily driven by high value M&A deals in manufacturing, especially in food and tobacco and metals industries. The $1 billion acquisition of Indonesia's Karyadibya Mahardhika Pt by Japan Tobacco Inc, and a $505.7 million deal between FIC Properties Sdn Bhd of Malaysia and Indonesia's Eagle High Plantation Tbk Pt were two prominent deals. FDI inflows to Myanmar, the Philippines, Thailand, and Viet Nam also rose by

Figure 3.5: Global Inward Foreign Direct Investment in Asia, by Subregion ($ billion)

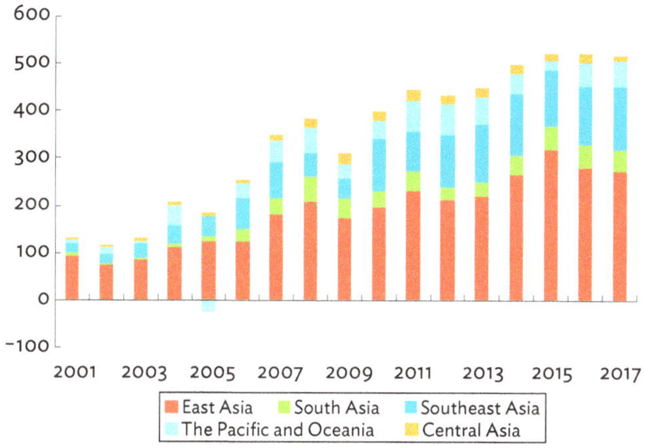

Sources: ADB calculations using data from Association of Southeast Asian Nations Secretariat. ASEANstats Database. https://www.aseanstats.org/ (accessed July 2018); United Nations Conference on Trade and Development. World Investment Report 2018 Statistical Annex Tables. http://unctad.org/en/Pages/DIAE/World%20Investment%20Report/Annex-Tables.aspx (accessed June 2018).

44.9% . PRC companies are increasing their presence in the Association of Southeast Asian Nations (ASEAN) markets—mainly through M&As, such as the $1.1 billion acquisition of Indonesia's PT Tokopedia by the Alibaba Group (UNCTAD 2018).

In 2017, the largest drop in inward FDI by subregion was to Central Asia, decreasing 31.0% to $12.2 billion—mainly due to the 42.8% contraction in FDI to Kazakhstan. Nonetheless, 37.8% of the subregion's inward FDI still went to Kazakhstan ($4.6 billion), 23.4% to Azerbaijan ($2.9 billion), and 18.9% to Turkmenistan ($2.3 billion). Among the top sources of FDI to Central Asia were the PRC, the Netherlands, and the United Kingdom (UK).

Inward FDI to East Asia dropped by 2.4%—to $272.9 billion. FDI to Hong Kong, China declined $13.1 billion, while inflows to the PRC, the Republic of Korea, and Mongolia increased. The $781 million greenfield investment by Singapore's Poh Group for an electricity project and a $200 million deal between the US mining company Milost Global Inc helped Mongolia's inward FDI rise to $1.5 billion.

Inward FDI to South Asia dropped by 7.5% (or by $3.8 billion) to $47 billion, mainly due to lower inflows to India. Still, 85.0% of FDI to the region went to India. The largest increase was in Sri Lanka, which drew $1.4 billion of inward FDI—a 53.3% increase over 2016. A PRC state-owned firm, China Merchants Port, accounted for most of the increase, investing in Sri Lanka's southern Hambantota Port.

The Pacific and Oceania attracted $50.2 billion in FDI, down from $51.0 billion in 2016, with 92.4% going to Australia, 7.1% to New Zealand, and the remainder to Pacific developing member countries. Inward FDI to the Cook Islands, Timor-Leste, Tonga, and Vanuatu all increased more than 10.0% between 2016 and 2017. Papua New Guinea's inward FDI recovered somewhat in 2017, but net FDI remained negative.

Despite the slowdown, intraregional FDI continued to strengthen by both absolute value and as a share of total inward FDI.

Intraregional FDI in Asia rose slightly in 2017, rising to $260.0 billion from $254.7 billion. The intraregional share of inward FDI in 2017 also inched upward—to 50.2% from 49.0% (Figure 3.6). East Asia received 56.1% of the intraregional flows, while 27.2% went to Southeast Asia. While most intraregional FDI occurs within subregions, inter-subregional investment has also been gradually strengthening over time—from 9.2% in 2003 to 18.9% in 2017 (Figure 3.7).

Figure 3.6: Intraregional Foreign Direct Investment Inflows—Asia

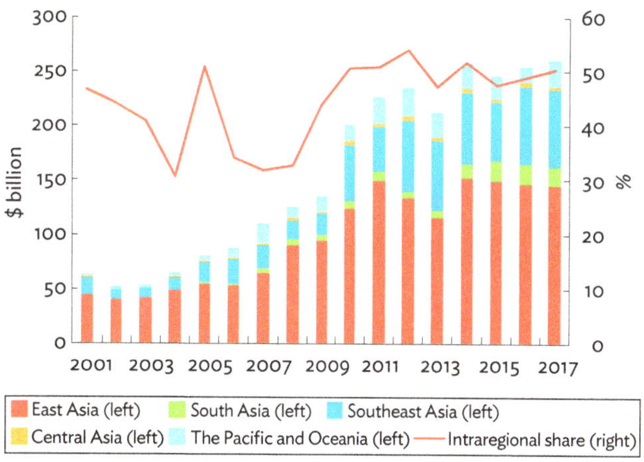

FDI = foreign direct investment.
Note: Based on balance of payments data. Due to limited availability of bilateral FDI data, missing values were imputed with gravity model estimates.
Sources: ADB calculations using data from Association of Southeast Asian Nations Secretariat. ASEANstats Database. https://www.aseanstats.org/ (accessed July 2018); Eurostat. Balance of Payments. http://ec.europa.eu/eurostat/web/balance-of-payments/data/database (accessed June 2018); United Nations Conference on Trade and Development. Bilateral FDI Statistics. http://unctad.org/en/Pages/DIAE/FDI%20Statistics/FDI-Statistics-Bilateral.aspx (accessed June 2018) and World Investment Report 2018 Statistical Annex Tables. http://unctad.org/en/Pages/DIAE/World%20Investment%20Report/Annex-Tables.aspx (accessed June 2018).

Figure 3.7: Foreign Direct Investment Shares in Asia—Intra-subregional, Inter-subregional, and Rest of the World (%)

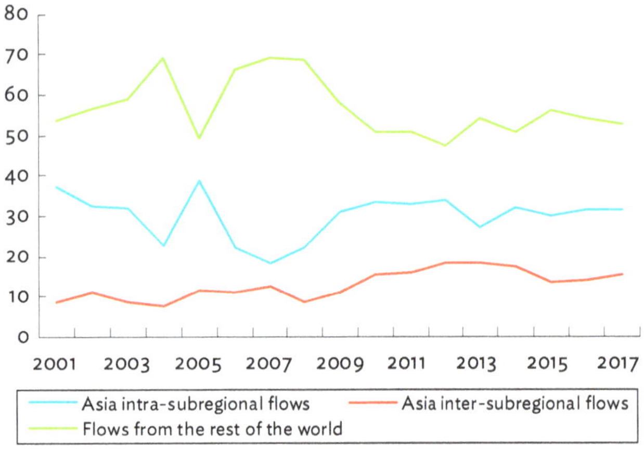

Sources: ADB calculations using data from Association of Southeast Asian Nations Secretariat. ASEANstats Database. https://www.aseanstats.org/ (accessed July 2018); Eurostat. Balance of Payments. http://ec.europa.eu/eurostat/web/balance-of-payments/data/database (accessed June 2018); United Nations Conference on Trade and Development. Bilateral FDI Statistics. http://unctad.org/en/Pages/DIAE/FDI%20Statistics/FDI-Statistics-Bilateral.aspx (accessed June 2018) and World Investment Report 2018 Statistical Annex Tables. http://unctad.org/en/Pages/DIAE/World%20Investment%20Report/Annex-Tables.aspx (accessed June 2018).

Figure 3.8: Global Outward Foreign Direct Investment, by Source ($ trillion)

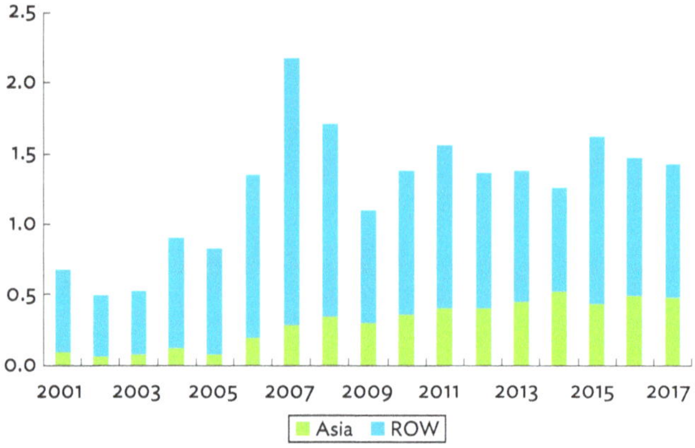

ROW = rest of the world.

Source: ADB calculations using data from United Nations Conference on Trade and Development. World Investment Report 2018 Statistical Annex Tables. http://unctad.org/en/Pages/DIAE/World%20Investment%20Report/Annex-Tables.aspx (accessed June 2018).

Figure 3.9: Asia's Outward Foreign Direct Investment, by Source ($ billion)

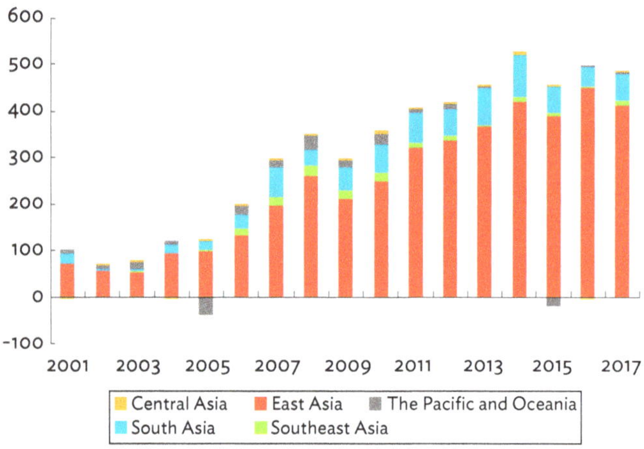

Source: ADB calculations using data from United Nations Conference on Trade and Development. World Investment Report 2018 Statistical Annex Tables. http://unctad.org/en/Pages/DIAE/World%20Investment%20Report/Annex-Tables.aspx (accessed June 2018).

Outward Foreign Direct Investment

Global outward FDI decreased 2.9% in 2017, primarily due to a drop in FDI from developed economies; outward investment from Asia weakened only 1.4%.

Based on BOP data, global outward FDI in 2017 fell 2.9% (Figure 3.8). Outward FDI from developed economies dropped 3.1%—to $1.0 trillion. Asia's outward FDI moderated 1.4%—to $487.9 billion. Of Asia's total, 84.2% by value came from East Asia, 11.3% from Southeast Asia, and 2.4% from South Asia (Figure 3.9).

Based on firm-level investment activity data, Asia's combined greenfield and M&A outward FDI in 2017 fell to $475.6 billion—59.3% via M&As. Over two-thirds of greenfield and M&A outward FDI from Asia was directed outside the region, primarily to the US (27.7% of Asia's FDI to outside the region), Switzerland (14.2%), the UK (10.1%), the Cayman Islands (4.7%), and Germany (4.4%).

Asia's outward greenfield investments remain concentrated in manufacturing, while outward M&As continue to shift to services. The region's greenfield and M&A outward FDI declined across all sectors, with primary sector investments experiencing the greatest contraction, especially through greenfield. The largest industry for Asian outward FDI in 2017 was chemicals (13.0% of the total, or $61.6 billion), which increased more than fivefold, mostly through M&As. The second-largest was coal, oil, and natural gas (8.6% or $41.1 billion), followed by real estate (7.3% or $34.7 billion) and financial services (7.1% or $33.7 billion).

Table 3.5: Top 10 Global and Asian Sources of Foreign Direct Investment ($ billion)

Global	2017	2016	2012	Asia	2017	2016	2012
United States	342.3	280.7	318.2	Japan	160.4	145.2	122.5
Japan	160.4	145.2	122.5	PRC	124.6	196.1	87.8
PRC	124.6	196.1	87.8	Hong Kong, China	82.8	59.7	83.4
United Kingdom	99.6	-22.5	20.7	Korea, Republic of	31.7	30.0	30.6
Hong Kong, China	82.8	59.7	83.4	Singapore	24.7	27.9	20.1
Germany	82.3	51.5	62.2	Thailand	19.3	12.4	10.5
Canada	77.0	73.6	55.9	Taipei,China	11.4	17.9	13.1
British Virgin Islands	70.8	36.7	54.0	India	11.3	5.1	8.5
France	58.1	63.2	35.4	Malaysia	5.8	8.0	17.1
Luxembourg	41.2	44.4	89.8	Australia	4.9	2.3	7.9

PRC = People's Republic of China.
Source: ADB calculations using data from United Nations Conference on Trade and Development. World Investment Report 2018 Statistical Annex Tables. http://unctad.org/en/Pages/DIAE/World%20Investment%20Report/Annex-Tables.aspx (accessed June 2018).

Real estate—the top recipient in 2016—became a less favored target industry for Asian outward FDI.

Japan was Asia's largest outward investor in 2017, and the second-largest globally—up from third in 2016 (Table 3.5). Japanese outward FDI totaled $160.4 billion with 30.6% invested within the region. While financial services was the top recipient industry, the majority of Japanese outward M&As and greenfield investments went to manufacturing. Japanese firms were very active in infusing capital in the region. For example, Japan Tobacco Inc acquired Karyadibya Mahardhika Pt of Indonesia for $1.0 billion, Mitsui Sumitomo Insurance Co Ltd bought a 97.7% ($1.6 billion) stake in Singapore's First Capital Insurance Ltd, and Sumitomo Group built a $2.6 billion coal-fired power plant in Viet Nam. However, the largest outward investment from Japan was by the Asahi Group—through its UK-based Asahi Breweries Ltd Europe—buying Plzensky Prazdroj AS brewery in the Czech Republic for $7.8 billion.

The PRC's outward FDI slowed in 2017 to $124.6 billion, 36.5% below the 2016 level. Firm-level investment data show 88.1% of the drop in the PRC's outward FDI was through greenfield investments, primarily in Egypt, Malaysia, India, and Algeria—mostly in real estate and transportation. The value of the PRC's M&As in Hong Kong, China and the US fell markedly in 2017, possibly due to tightened restrictions on outbound acquisitions.[15] The sharp decline in the PRC's outbound investments was a reversal from the surge in 2016. In 2017, the PRC's outward M&As fell by 5.8% and greenfield investments by 50.9%. The recent trade and investment friction with the US also does not bode well for the near term prospect. Over the years, the US was consistently a top destination for PRC investments (peaking at $27.0 billion in 2016) only to plunge by more than 40% in 2017, mainly in consumer products, consumer electronics and real estate.[16]

While the deepening trade conflict and increasing investment restrictions could slow the PRC's outward FDI to the US, the drop could be offset by increasing the PRC's investments in other destinations. For instance, despite the 70% fall in the PRC's FDI to Asia in 2017, some Asian economies saw a significant increase

[15] Since November 2016, the PRC has tightened scrutiny of outward FDI from companies in the PRC. On 18 August 2017, the National Development Reform Commission (NDRC), Ministry of Commerce, People's Bank of China, and the Ministry of Foreign Affairs formalized the approval process of outward FDI transactions by issuing the *Opinions on Further Guiding and Regulating Outbound Investment.* On 26 December 2017, the NDRC issued Order No. 11, which promulgates the *Administrative Measures for Overseas Investment by Enterprises.* It became effective 1 March 2018.

[16] Similarly, global outbound investments by the US grew at a meager 1.1% to $383.3 billion in 2017. While M&As were 19.2% higher than the previous year, greenfield investments were 26.3% lower. Moreover, while the US investments increased in other parts of the world especially in Africa and Europe, it significantly dropped in Asia at 36.6% (around $43 billion less than the level in 2016), largely owing to the decline in overall investment outflows to major Asian recipient economies including Australia, India, the Republic of Korea, and Singapore—coal, oil, and natural gas accounting for the majority of the fall followed by financial services and transportation. While overall US outward FDI to the PRC increased by 57.8%, greenfield investments fell by 17.6%. The sudden and significant slowdown of US outward investment possibly reflect the impact of its tax reforms (UNCTAD 2018) and escalating and broadening protectionist stance.

in industries such as medical devices, chemicals, metals, and transportation. Kazakhstan, Singapore, Pakistan, the Philippines, the Republic of Korea, New Zealand, and Georgia all at least doubled 2016 investments from the PRC. Moreover, the PRC's FDI outside Asia in fact increased by 7.1%, mainly in chemicals, transportation and industrial machinery and equipment. European economies—such as Switzerland, the UK, Germany, the Netherlands, Italy, Portugal, Sweden, and Serbia—accounted for most of this growth. Some Latin American and Caribbean and African economies also received significantly higher amounts of FDI from the PRC—for example, Nigeria, Kenya, Argentina, Zambia, Chile, and Colombia all saw a more than threefold increase.

Three newly industrialized economies—Hong Kong, China; the Republic of Korea; and Singapore—had combined outward investments of $139.2 billion, up 18.4% since 2016. While inward FDI to Hong Kong, China fell markedly in 2017, outward FDI increased by more than $23.1 billion, primarily from deals such as the $3.0 billion acquisition of Australia's Alinta Energy by Chow Tai Fook Enterprises Ltd.

India, Thailand, and Australia also saw large increases in outward FDI in 2017, with India and Australia doubling 2016 levels and Thailand rising by more than half. India's Tata Motors Ltd, for example, invested $1 billion in Faraday & Future Inc, a US automobile manufacturing company. Firms in India have also made substantial indirect investments as ultimate owners. For example, Intas Pharmaceuticals Ltd invested $739.1 million in Actavis Ireland Ltd, through the UK-based Accord Healthcare Ltd. Overall, India's outward greenfield and M&A investments remain mostly directed to economies outside Asia—especially the US (about a quarter of the total in 2017)—into manufacturing (such as pharmaceuticals) as well as services such as software and information technology. By comparison, Thailand's outward greenfield and M&A investments were largely intraregional (87.5%) and mostly in manufacturing, including building and construction materials and alternative or renewable energy. For instance, Thailand's Siam City Cement PCL acquired a 65.0% stake in Holcim Co Ltd of Viet Nam, worth $535.9 million. Australia's outward FDI also more than doubled in 2017 after declining in 2013–2015, mainly driven by a robust increase in cross-border M&As in the primary (such as minerals) and financial service sectors.

Despite an uncertain global economic policy environment, Asia's continued rise as an outward investor is an encouraging sign for further strengthening of intraregional FDI.

At the firm level, combined greenfield and M&A outward FDI surpassed inward FDI in 2016 by $101.0 billion. The gap widened in 2017 to $118.9 billion. Positive net investments also went to the rest of the world, mostly through M&As and mostly in services and manufacturing (Figure 3.10). In 2017, there was $225.1 billion in outward extraregional Asian M&As. The PRC was the largest source, accounting for 48.1%, with the majority going to developed economies such as Switzerland, the UK, the

Figure 3.10: Asian Outward Foreign Direct Investment to the Rest of the World, by Sector ($ billion)

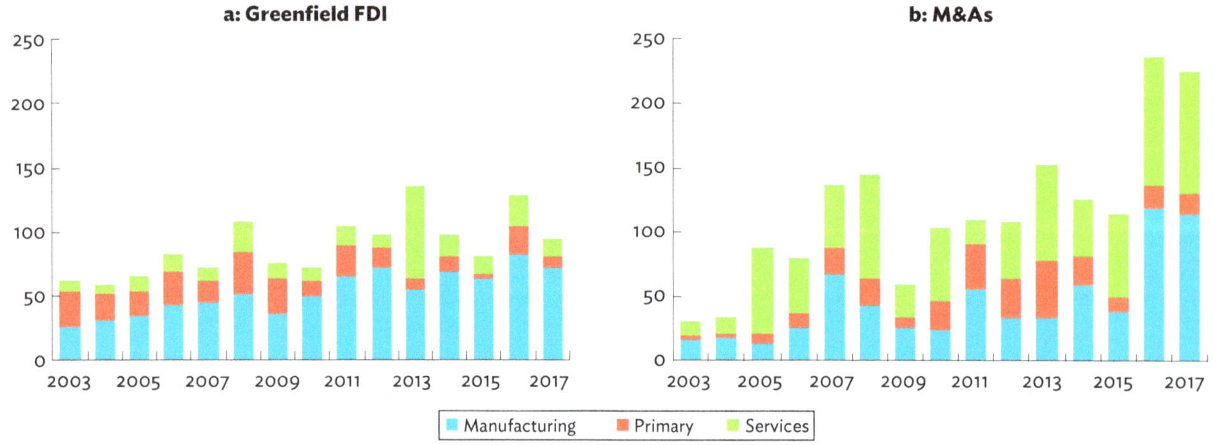

FDI = foreign direct investment, M&A = merger and acquisition.
Sources: ADB calculations using data from Bureau van Dijk. Zephyr M&A Database; and Financial Times. fDi Markets (both accessed June 2018).

Figure 3.11: Total Foreign Direct Investment Flows—Asia ($ billion)

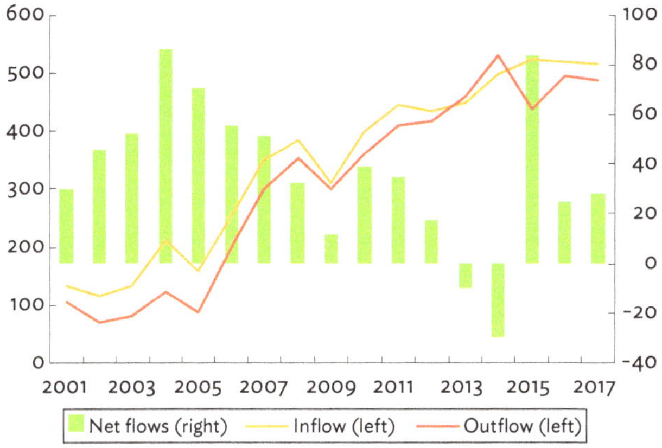

Sources: ADB calculations using data from Association of Southeast Asian Nations Secretariat. ASEANstats Database. https://www.aseanstats.org/ (accessed July 2018); United Nations Conference on Trade and Development. World Investment Report 2018 Statistical Annex Tables. http://unctad.org/en/Pages/DIAE/World%20Investment%20Report/Annex-Tables.aspx (accessed June 2018).

US, Germany, and the Cayman Islands. For greenfield FDI to the rest of the world, the largest Asian sources were the PRC, India, and Japan.

Based on BOP figures, Asia has by and large retained positive net FDI flows since 2001 (Figure 3.11). The region receives the most global FDI, while at the same time being home to some of the biggest investors in the world. The trade conflict between the US and PRC may alter and divert investment patterns. But the prognosis for the region's trade and investment linkages—especially intraregional—remains good. Asia's growing share of global inward FDI, as it attracts more investment in services and higher technology manufacturing—along with Asian multinationals increasingly investing within the region—bodes well for the region's capacity to create good jobs and advance opportunities for more inclusive growth.

References

ADB. 2017. Aid for Trade in Asia and the Pacific: Promoting Connectivity for Inclusive Development. Manila

———. 2016. *Asian Economic Integration Report 2016: What Drives Foreign Direct Investments in Asia and the Pacific?* Manila.

———. 2009. *Trade and Investment in Services: An ADB–ITD Training Module for the Greater Mekong Subregion.* Manila.

Association of Southeast Asian Nations Secretariat. ASEANstats Database. https://www.aseanstats.org/ (accessed July 2018).

Eurostat. Balance of Payments. http://ec.europa.eu/eurostat/web/balance-of-payments/data/database (accessed June 2018).

International Labour Organization. 2016. *World Employment and Social Outlook: Trends 2016.* Geneva.

———. ILOSTAT. http://www.ilo.org/ilostat/faces/oracle/webcenter/portalapp/pagehierarchy/Page3.jspx?MBI_ID=33 (accessed August 2018).

International Monetary Fund. World Economic Outlook April 2018 Database. https://www.imf.org/external/pubs/ft/weo/2018/01/weodata/download.aspx (accessed July 2018).

———. Bilateral FDI Statistics. http://unctad.org/en/Pages/DIAE/FDI%20Statistics/FDI-Statistics-Bilateral.aspx (accessed June 2018).

———. World Investment Report 2018 Statistical Annex Tables. http://unctad.org/en/Pages/DIAE/World%20Investment%20Report/Annex-Tables.aspx (accessed June 2018).

United Nations Conference on Trade and Development (UNCTAD). 2018. *World Investment Report 2018: Investment and New Industrial Policies.* Geneva.

World Bank. Doing Business Database. http://www.doingbusiness.org/ (accessed June 2018).

———. World Development Indicators. http://databank.worldbank.org/data/source/world-development-indicators# (accessed June 2018).

———. Worldwide Governance Indicators. http://info.worldbank.org/governance/wgi/#home (accessed June 2018).

World Trade Organization-United Nations Conference on Trade and Development-International Trade Centre Trade in Services Data set. https://www.wto.org/english/res_e/statis_e/daily_update_e/services_annual_dataset.zip (accessed July 2018).

Annex 3a: Top Destinations and Recipient Industries of Foreign Direct Investment in Services

Table 3a.1: Top 10 Asian Destination Economies of Foreign Direct Investment in Services ($ billion)

Total					Intra-Asia				
	2003–2009	2010–2015	2016	2017		2003–2009	2010–2015	2016	2017
China, People's Republic of	44.2	38.7	27.6	35.9	China, People's Republic of	16.4	13.6	8.0	8.7
India	20.4	21.4	33.1	29.8	India	2.8	5.6	7.7	8.0
Singapore	6.3	9.7	14.4	13.7	Singapore	3.0	3.3	4.9	7.2
Australia	12.4	22.2	24.7	13.5	Australia	2.0	5.4	6.1	3.0
Hong Kong, China	14.2	41.6	59.4	11.5	Hong Kong, China	8.2	5.7	52.1	3.0
Japan	11.5	10.5	3.8	6.7	Malaysia	0.7	1.7	2.7	1.8
Viet Nam	6.4	4.4	2.2	3.7	Thailand	0.9	2.1	2.6	1.7
Korea, Republic of	5.3	4.9	6.2	3.4	Viet Nam	2.8	2.6	1.1	1.6
Malaysia	2.3	3.5	3.8	3.2	Korea, Republic of	0.5	1.0	0.3	1.4
Thailand	2.2	2.8	3.6	2.7	Pakistan	0.7	0.3	0.0	1.3

Sources: ADB calculations using data from Bureau van Dijk. Zephyr M&A Database; and Financial Times. fDi Markets (both accessed June 2018).

Table 3a.2: Top Foreign Direct Investment Recipient Industries in the Services Sector in Asia ($ billion)

Total					Intra-Asia				
	2003–2009	2010–2015	2016	2017		2003–2009	2010–2015	2016	2017
Communications	23.9	23.6	44.2	32.1	Financial Services	20.0	18.3	60.4	11.7
Financial Services	52.2	48.7	79.8	28.7	Communications	9.2	8.4	11.4	8.5
Transportation	15.8	19.3	18.3	19.2	Business Services	1.7	3.3	8.3	7.2
Software and IT services	9.5	12.6	19.1	19.0	Transportation	5.7	4.3	3.6	6.6
Business Services	8.5	26.3	24.5	18.2	Software and IT services	1.6	1.9	6.8	5.4
Hotels and Tourism	13.4	7.0	6.3	6.5	Hotels and Tourism	5.2	3.0	2.7	1.7
Leisure and Entertainment	2.9	2.2	5.0	3.9	Healthcare	0.4	1.5	1.1	0.8
Healthcare	1.5	3.1	3.5	3.1	Warehousing and Storage	3.1	3.5	2.7	0.7
Warehousing and Storage	6.6	6.1	3.9	2.8	Real Estate	5.6	5.8	0.1	0.7
Beverages	0.0	0.0	0.3	2.7	Other Business Services	0.6	1.3	0.9	0.6
All services	153.2	181.3	208.8	140.5	All services	53.6	52.2	99.7	44.8

Sources: ADB calculations using data from Bureau van Dijk. Zephyr M&A Database; and Financial Times. fDi Markets (both accessed June 2018).

4

Financial Integration

Asia's Cross-Border Financial Assets and Liabilities

Asia's cross-border financial linkages continue to grow and strengthen, underpinning the region's growing degree of financial integration, both within and outside the region.[17] Total cross-border asset holdings grew by $3.8 trillion between 2012 and 2017. The largest part of the increase came from equity investment, which increased by $2.2 trillion.

Asia's cross-border asset holdings continued to increase between 2012 and 2017 (Figure 4.1).[18] Assets grew by $3.8 trillion over the period, from $13.2 trillion in 2012 to $17.0 trillion in 2017. The region's cross-border assets continue to be predominantly from outside the region, as assets held outside the region account for more than 75% of total cross-border assets. Meanwhile, the intraregional share has increased for all asset classes except portfolio equity, with the share of intraregional assets increasing slightly from 22.7% in 2012 to 23.7% in 2017. The category of portfolio equity holdings increased its share of total cross-border assets significantly over the past 5 years. In particular, while it was only 17.1% in 2012, it increased to 26.2% in 2017. Over the same period, the share of portfolio debt investment decreased from 30.2% in 2012 to 24.6% in 2017, indicating that

Figure 4.1: Cross-Border Assets—Asia

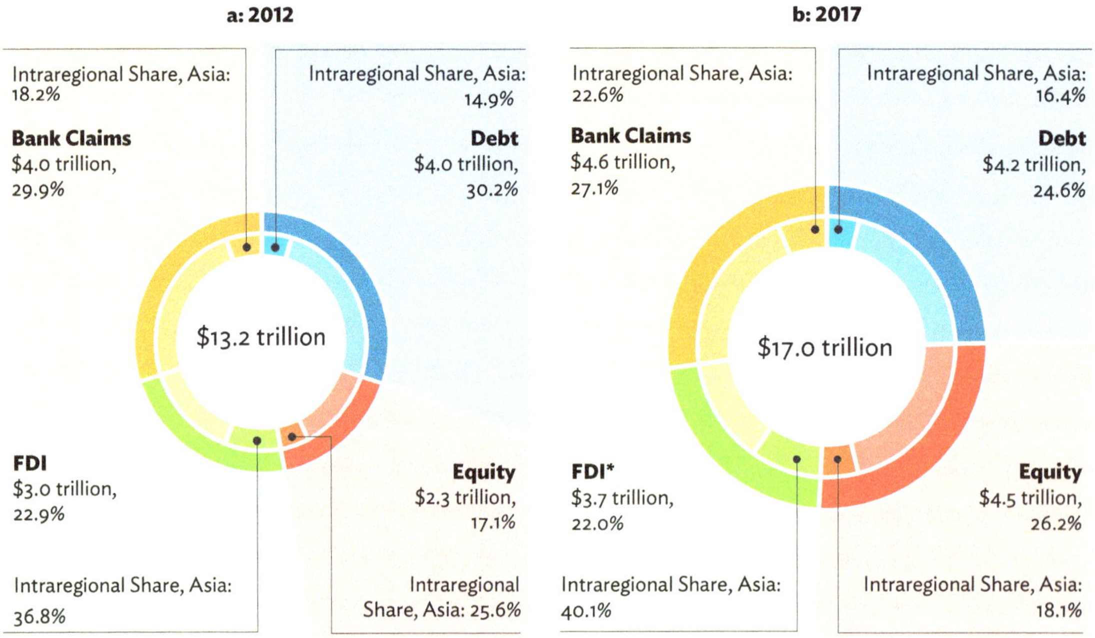

* = data are for 2016, FDI = foreign direct investment.
Notes: FDI assets refer to outward FDI holdings. Bank assets refer to bank claims of Asian economies. Asia includes ADB regional members for which data are available.
Sources: ADB calculations using data from Bank for International Settlements. Locational Banking Statistics. https://www.bis.org/statistics/bankstats.htm (accessed August 2018); International Monetary Fund. Coordinated Portfolio Investment Survey. http://data.imf.org/CPIS (accessed September 2018); and International Monetary Fund. Coordinated Direct Investment Survey. http://data.imf.org/CDIS (accessed February 2018).

17 Asia refers to the 48 Asia and the Pacific members of the Asian Development Bank (ADB), which includes Japan and Oceania (Australia and New Zealand) in addition to the 45 developing Asian economies.

18 Throughout this chapter, Asia's cross-border asset holdings refer to the stock of outbound portfolio debt, portfolio equity, and foreign direct investment (FDI), as well as cross-border bank claims. Asia's cross-border liabilities refer to the stock of inward portfolio debt, portfolio equity, and FDI, as well as cross-border bank liabilities.

Figure 4.2: Cross-Border Liabilities—Asia

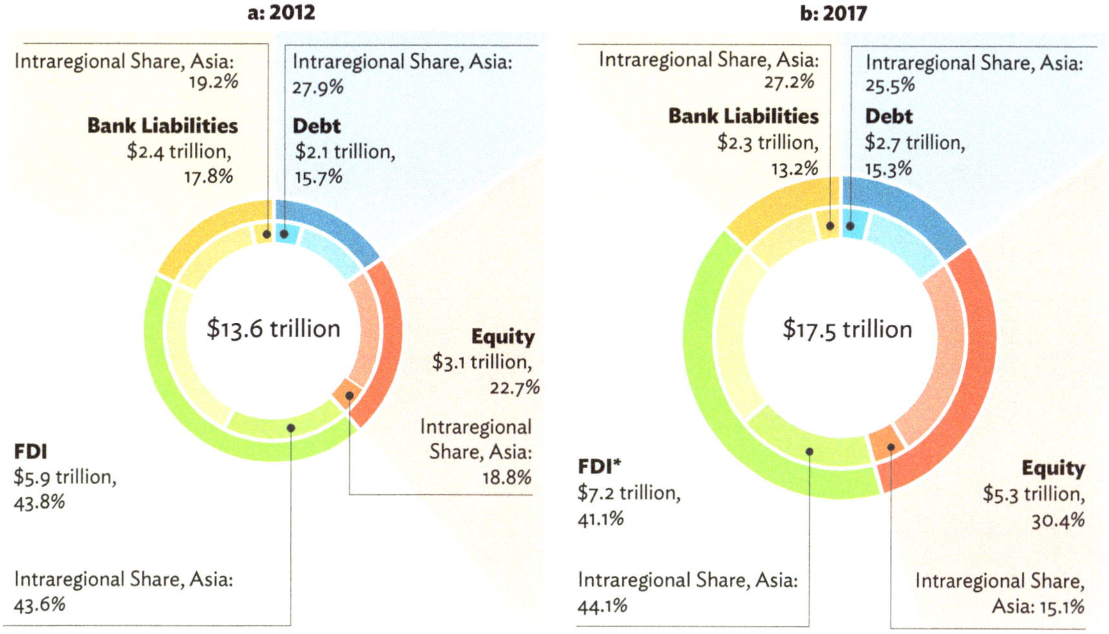

* = data are for 2016, FDI = foreign direct investment.

Notes: FDI assets refer to outward FDI holdings. Bank assets refer to bank claims of Asian economies. Asia includes ADB regional members for which data are available.

Sources: ADB calculations using data from Bank for International Settlements. Locational Banking Statistics. https://www.bis.org/statistics/bankstats.htm (accessed August 2018); International Monetary Fund. Coordinated Portfolio Investment Survey. http://data.imf.org/CPIS (accessed September 2018); and International Monetary Fund. Coordinated Direct Investment Survey. http://data.imf.org/CDIS (accessed February 2018).

the increase in cross-border equity holdings outpaced portfolio debt holdings. Meanwhile, Asia's cross-border bank claims account for 27.1% of Asia's cross-border assets, the largest share in 2017, while the share of Asia's cross-border debt assets was 30.2%, the biggest share in 2012.

Asia's cross-border liabilities increased by $3.9 trillion from 2012 to 2017. Foreign direct investment remains the largest source of cross-border liabilities, with intraregional foreign direct investment increasing both in volume and by share.

Cross-border liabilities also continued to increase, with total liabilities rising by $3.9 trillion, from $13.6 trillion in 2012 to $17.5 trillion in 2017 (Figure 4.2). Foreign direct investment (FDI) accounted for over 40% of total cross-border liabilities for both periods, followed by equity investment, accounting for 30.4% in 2017, up from 22.7% in 2012, a large increase over past years. As with cross-border assets, Asia's cross-border liabilities remain more linked to the rest of the world. Over the past 5 years, the share of liabilities from outside the region rose to 69.8% in 2017 from 68.9% in 2012. The intraregional share of Asia's cross-border liabilities increased for bank lending by 8 percentage points, while the shares of portfolio debt and equity fell between 2012 and 2017.

Inward Portfolio Investment[19]

Portfolio equity investment into Asia reached $5.3 trillion in 2017, far exceeding the region's inward debt investment of $2.7 trillion. Inward portfolio equity investment grew at an average annual rate of 12.1% over the past 5 years, with particularly strong growth in 2017 (32.0%).

[19] Portfolio investment data are based on stock data from the Coordinated Portfolio Investment Survey of the International Monetary Fund. For outward portfolio investment, due to unavailability or lack of comparable data, the following economies were excluded from the calculations: Aruba, the Bahamas, Barbados, Curaçao and Sint Maarten, Liberia, the Netherlands Antilles, Peru, Uruguay, and Vanuatu. The PRC is also excluded due to lack of comparable data for 2001–2014.

Figure 4.3: Inward Portfolio Investment—Asia

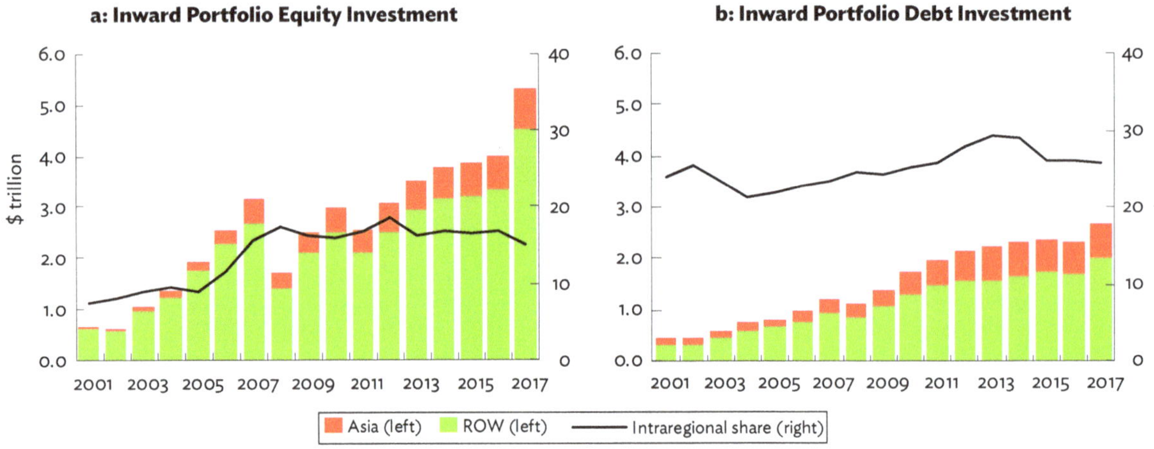

ROW = rest of the world.
Note: Asia includes ADB regional members for which data are available.
Source: ADB calculations using data from International Monetary Fund. Coordinated Portfolio Investment Survey. http://data.imf.org/CPIS (accessed September 2018).

Inward portfolio equity investment reached $5.3 trillion in 2017—with an average annual growth rate of 12.1% over the last 5 years (Figure 4.3a), far outpacing growth in inward portfolio debt investment, which averaged 4.9% over the same period. Favorable equity market conditions in 2017 coupled with global investors' search for higher returns due to subdued return-on-debt in 2017 drove the strong increase. Strengthening global linkages have seen equity investment grow particularly from outside the region, primarily from the United States (US) and the European Union (EU). Consequently, the intraregional share has fallen gradually from 18.8% in 2012 to 15.1% in 2017. Meanwhile, portfolio debt investment into Asia rose to $2.7 trillion in 2017, after slightly decreasing in 2016. The US and the EU remained the primary portfolio debt investors into Asia, while the intraregional share of Asian investors dipped to 25.5% in 2017 from 29.3% in 2013 (Figure 4.3b).

International holdings of Asian portfolio equity assets increased by $1.3 trillion in 2017, exceeding the combined increase of $954.0 billion over the past 4 years.

Inward equity investment increased sharply by $1.3 trillion in 2017 (Figure 4.4a). The majority of the surge came from a rise in US ($606.2 billion) and EU ($368.3 billion) investments, mainly to East Asia,[20] highlighting the region's strong financial linkages with global equity markets. In contrast, inward portfolio debt investment to Asia increased only by $390.4 billion in 2017, mainly due to increased investment from the rest of the world (ROW)[21] ($138.7 billion)—primarily in Japanese debt securities ($78.1 billion)—the US ($127.9 billion), and Asia ($92.6 billion) (Figure 4.4b). Debt investment from the EU also increased, but at a more modest $31.1 billion, compared with other regions.

Ample global liquidity, favorable economic conditions in the region, and investors' appetite for positive equity returns from Asia based on buoyant market performance in 2017 were behind the boost, but the pace will likely moderate in 2018 due to the regional equity markets' relatively tepid performance. There has also been a shift from debt to equity investment. For example, while the EU reduced $22.5 billion of its debt investment in Japan, equity investment in that country rose by $89.7 billion in 2017.

Inward equity investment outstanding from outside the region was $4.5 trillion in 2017 (Table 4.1). The majority came from the US and the EU, concentrating on Japanese equities. In particular, US investment in Japanese equities reached $891.0 billion in 2017,

20 Japan ($285.3 billion), the Republic of Korea ($134.5 billion), and the PRC ($112.3 billion) were among the major beneficiaries of the inward equity investment by the US and the EU in 2017.

21 For this chapter, computations using the rest of the world (ROW) do not include countries in Asia, the EU, and the US.

Figure 4.4: Change in Inward Portfolio Investment—Asia ($ billion)

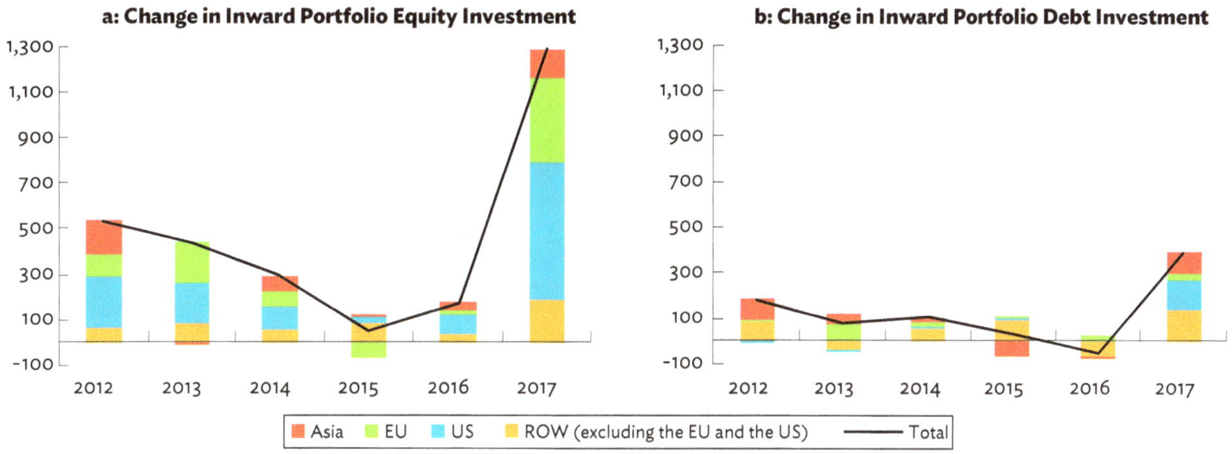

EU = European Union, ROW = rest of the world, US = United States.
Note: Asia includes ADB regional members for which data are available.
Source: ADB calculations using data from International Monetary Fund. Coordinated Portfolio Investment Survey. http://data.imf.org/CPIS (accessed September 2018).

followed by the Republic of Korea ($240.6 billion), Australia ($196.3 billion), and India ($180.5 billion). The EU's equity investment in Japan was $490.8 billion in 2017, followed by the People's Republic of China (PRC) ($151.0 billion); the Republic of Korea ($144.5 billion); Hong Kong, China ($129.7 billion); and India ($119.3 billion).

The top sources of intraregional cross-border equity holdings are regional financial hubs such as Hong Kong, China; Singapore; and Japan, which account for 78.6% of intraregional equity investment. In contrast to investment from outside of the region, intraregional equity investment is focused on the PRC—with Hong Kong, China contributing $225.3 billion. Singapore also largely invests in PRC equities ($84.2 billion), but also

Table 4.1: Sources of Inward Portfolio Equity Investment—Asia ($ billion)

	2017		2012		
	$ billion	**% share**	**$ billion**	**% share**	**
Asia					
Hong Kong, China	262	(4.9%)	204	(6.6%)	▼
Singapore	254	(4.8%)	187	(6.1%)	▼
Japan	116	(2.2%)	73	(2.4%)	▼
Other Asia	172	(3.2%)	115	(3.7%)	▼
Asia's inward portfolio equity investment from Asia	805	(15.1%)	579	(18.8%)	▼
Non-Asia					
United States	2,313	(43.5%)	1,317	(42.8%)	▲
European Union	1,419	(26.7%)	840	(27.3%)	▼
Canada	187	(3.5%)	103	(3.4%)	▲
Other non-Asia	595	(11.2%)	236	(7.7%)	▲
Asia's inward portfolio equity investment from non-Asia	4,514	(84.9%)	2,496	(81.2%)	▲
Asia's total inward portfolio equity investment	**5,319**	**(100.0%)**	**3,075**	**(100.0%)**	

** = direction of change in share, ▼ = decrease, ▲ = increase.
Source: ADB calculations using data from International Monetary Fund. Coordinated Portfolio Investment Survey. http://data.imf.org/CPIS (accessed September 2018).

Table 4.2: Sources of Inward Portfolio Debt Investment—Asia ($ billion)

	2017		2012		
	$ billion	**% share**	**$ billion**	**% share**	**
Asia					
Hong Kong, China	253	(9.4%)	217	(10.2%)	▼
Japan	190	(7.1%)	195	(9.1%)	▼
Singapore	125	(4.7%)	137	(6.4%)	▼
Other Asia	117	(4.4%)	47	(2.2%)	▲
Asia's inward portfolio debt investment from Asia	686	(25.5%)	596	(27.9%)	▼
Non-Asia					
European Union	757	(28.2%)	617	(28.9%)	▼
United States	546	(20.3%)	406	(19.0%)	▲
International Organizations	387	(14.4%)	355	(16.6%)	▼
Other non-Asia	308	(11.5%)	161	(7.5%)	▲
Asia's inward portfolio debt investment from non-Asia	1,998	(74.5%)	1,539	(72.1%)	▲
Asia's total inward portfolio debt investment	**2,684**	**(100.0%)**	**2,134**	**(100.0%)**	

** = direction of change in share, ▼ = decrease, ▲ = increase.
Source: ADB calculations using data from International Monetary Fund. Coordinated Portfolio Investment Survey. http://data.imf.org/CPIS (accessed September 2018).

in Japan ($39.4 billion), India ($30.5 billion), and the Republic of Korea ($25.9 billion).

The majority of Asia's intraregional portfolio debt investment outstanding comes from Hong Kong, China; Japan; and Singapore—accounting for 82.9% of the total of intraregional debt investment (Table 4.2). Yet, the share of other Asian economies in the total intraregional debt investment has been increasing—from 7.8% in 2012 to 17.1% in 2017—driven by increased inward debt investment from Australia and the Republic of Korea. Despite a possible risk of PRC deleveraging, the majority of Hong Kong, China's portfolio debt investment goes to the PRC ($129.5 billion), followed by Japan ($42.7 billion) and Australia ($32.8 billion).

Outside the region, the EU, the US, and international organizations remain leading sources of portfolio debt investment to Asia. In 2017, investors from the EU flocked to Japan (with investment outstanding of $255.2 billion) and Australia ($211.3 billion). Debt investment holdings from the EU also went to Southeast Asian destinations such as Indonesia ($49.4 billion) and Singapore ($42.2 billion).

Outward Portfolio Investment

Asia's appetite for outward portfolio investment—especially in equities outside the region—continues to rise, resulting in a gradually declining intraregional share in outward equity investment over the past years. Asia's outward equity portfolio investment averaged an annual growth rate of 14.9% over the last 5 years, far outstripping debt investment (1.2%), while the intraregional share of outward debt investment increased for the first time in 3 years.

Since the sharp decline in equity investment in 2008 and a slight dip in 2011, buoyant market performance has driven regional investor appetite for equities, which increased over the last decade to reach $4.5 trillion in 2017 from $3.5 trillion in 2016 (Figure 4.5a). The average annual growth rate over the last 5 years has been 14.9%. Asia's portfolio equity investment to the ROW (excluding the EU and the US) led the rise, reaching $1.9 trillion in 2017 from $1.3 trillion a year earlier. Consequently, the intraregional share decreased

Figure 4.5: Outward Portfolio Investment—Asia

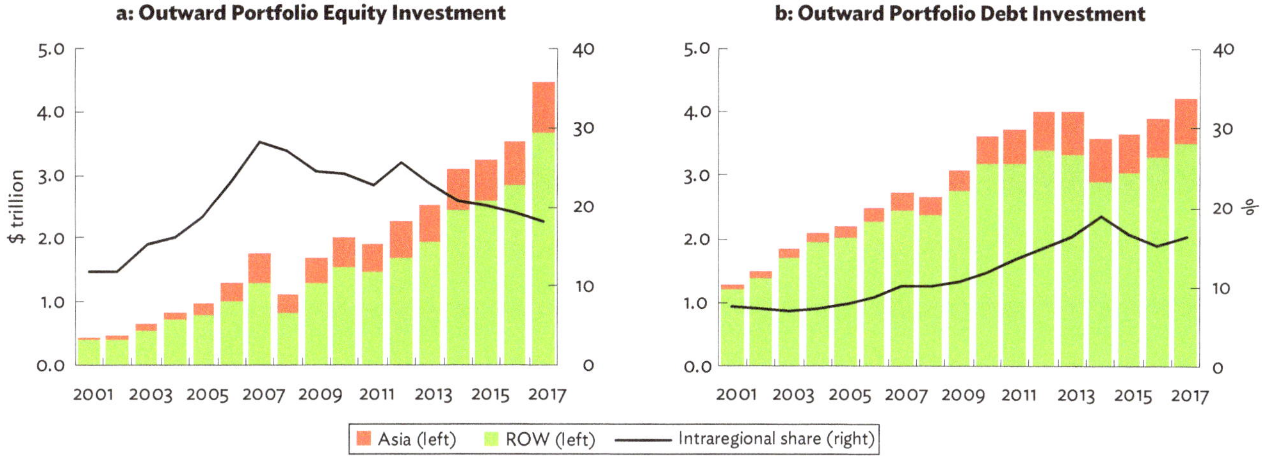

ROW = rest of the world.
Note: Asia includes ADB regional members for which data are available.
Source: ADB calculations using data from International Monetary Fund. Coordinated Portfolio Investment Survey. http://data.imf.org/CPIS (accessed September 2018).

to 18.1%, down from 25.6% in 2012. Meanwhile, Asia's outward portfolio debt investment outstanding reached $4.2 trillion in 2017 from $3.9 trillion in 2016, with a large portion directed toward mature markets such as the US and those in the EU. Asia's intraregional share inched up to 16.4% in 2017 from 15.3% in 2016, the first increase in 3 years (Figure 4.5b).

Buoyant global equity markets, combined with low returns on debt securities, led to a modest increase in outward debt investment outstanding in 2017, while outward equity investment outstanding grew substantially.

Fueled by well-performing equity markets globally, Asia's portfolio equity investment rose by $943.6 billion in 2017, predominantly directed to the ROW ($541.8 billion), the US ($179.3 billion), and the EU ($94.6 billion) (Figure 4.6a). Intraregional investment increased by $127.8 billion. Meanwhile, outward portfolio debt investment increased by $301.8 billion in 2017, driven largely by a rise in Asian holdings of debt securities issued by regional economies ($92.6 billion) and the ROW ($96.2 billion), excluding the EU and the US (Figure 4.6b). Debt investment to the US increased modestly, by $38.0 billion in 2017 as opposed to $175.5 billion in 2016, indicating investor preference for portfolio equity investment over debt.

Figure 4.6: Change in Outward Portfolio Investment—Asia ($ billion)

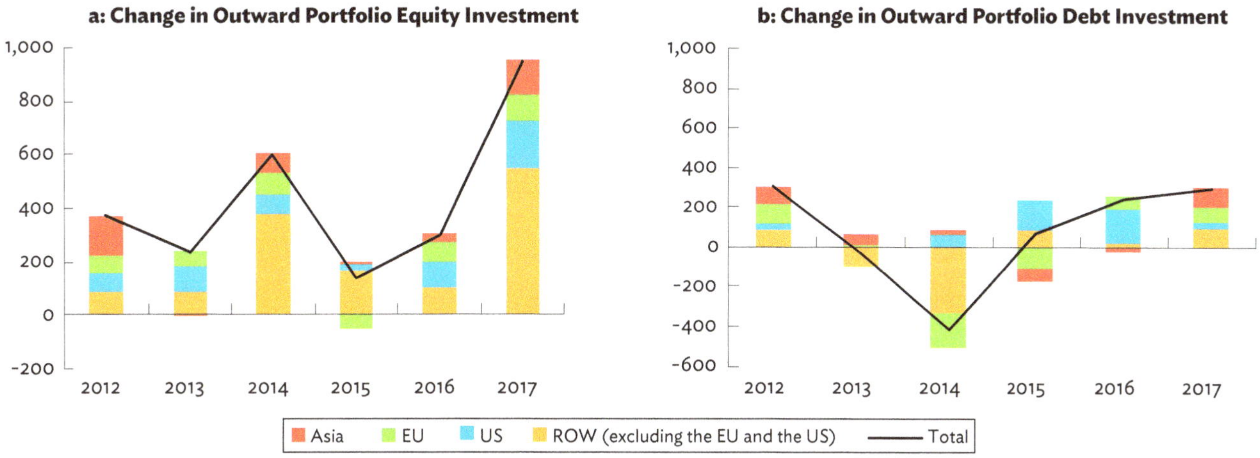

EU = European Union, ROW = rest of the world, US = United States.
Note: Asia includes ADB regional members for which data are available.
Source: ADB calculations using data from International Monetary Fund. Coordinated Portfolio Investment Survey. http://data.imf.org/CPIS (accessed September 2018).

Table 4.3: Destinations of Outward Portfolio Equity Investment—Asia ($ billion)

	2017		2012		
	$ billion	**% share**	**$ billion**	**% share**	**
Asia					
China, People's Republic of	348	(7.8%)	256	(11.3%)	▼
Japan	96	(2.1%)	49	(2.2%)	▼
Australia	71	(1.6%)	60	(2.7%)	▼
Other Asia	290	(6.5%)	213	(9.4%)	▼
Asia's outward portfolio equity investment to Asia	805	(18.1%)	579	(25.6%)	▼
Non-Asia					
Cayman Islands	1,263	(28.3%)	295	(13.1%)	▲
United States	1,105	(24.8%)	635	(28.1%)	▼
European Union	633	(14.2%)	388	(17.2%)	▼
Other non-Asia	651	(14.6%)	364	(16.1%)	▼
Asia's outward portfolio equity investment to non-Asia	3,652	(81.9%)	1,682	(74.4%)	▲
Asia's total outward portfolio equity investment	**4,457**	**(100.0%)**	**2,261**	**(100.0%)**	

** = direction of change in share, ▼ = decrease, ▲ = increase.
Source: ADB calculations using data from International Monetary Fund. Coordinated Portfolio Investment Survey. http://data.imf.org/CPIS (accessed September 2018).

The most preferred portfolio investment destinations outside the region were the Cayman Islands, the EU, and the US. Australia, Japan, and the PRC remained popular destinations for Asia's intraregional outward portfolio investment.

The largest share of intraregional equity investment holdings was with the PRC (43.3% in 2017), highlighting the prominent role PRC equity markets play in the region. Other popular destinations were Japan and Australia (Table 4.3). The three accounted for 64.0% of the total intraregional portfolio equity investment in 2017, with top investors from Hong Kong, China ($225.3 billion to the PRC); Singapore ($39.4 billion to Japan); and Japan ($29.1 billion to Australia).

Outside Asia, the region continues to invest heavily in Cayman Islands, US, and EU equities. Outward portfolio equity holdings in the Cayman Islands quadrupled over the past 5 years, highlighting the fact that it remains an attractive destination, given its reputation as one of the largest offshore financial centers with favorable tax conditions. The top portfolio equity investors in the Cayman Islands are Japan ($646.3 billion outstanding) and Hong Kong, China ($584.8 billion outstanding).

Australia, the PRC, and Japan remained the top three destinations for Asia's intraregional portfolio debt investment in 2017 (Table 4.4). The three accounted for the majority of intraregional debt investment (64.7%), with shares of the PRC and Japan rising. Other notable destinations in 2017 were the Republic of Korea ($49.2 billion outstanding) and Singapore ($43.9 billion outstanding).

The top three destinations for Asia's non-regional debt investment were the US, the EU, and the Cayman Islands. Investment to the US increased by $441.7 billion over the last 5 years, but declined in the EU by $116.3 billion, due to weak yield performance of European bond markets as the result of the massive asset purchase program by the European Central Bank over recent years. Within the EU, France remains the top destination ($251.6 billion), followed by the UK ($207.8 billion) and Germany ($180.2 billion). Other non-Asian markets include Canada ($97.0 billion) and international organizations ($93.5 billion).

Table 4.4: Destinations of Outward Portfolio Debt Investment—Asia ($ billion)

	2017		2012		
	$ billion	**% share**	**$ billion**	**% share**	**
Asia					
Australia	190	(4.5%)	194	(4.9%)	▼
China, People's Republic of	181	(4.3%)	111	(2.8%)	▲
Japan	73	(1.7%)	39	(1.0%)	▲
Other Asia	242	(5.8%)	251	(6.3%)	▼
Asia's outward portfolio debt investment to Asia	686	(16.4%)	596	(14.9%)	▲
Non-Asia					
United States	1,611	(38.5%)	1,170	(29.3%)	▲
European Union	1,069	(25.5%)	1,186	(29.7%)	▼
Cayman Islands	211	(5.0%)	502	(12.6%)	▼
Other non-Asia	612	(14.6%)	544	(13.6%)	▲
Asia's outward portfolio debt investment to non-Asia	3,504	(83.6%)	3,402	(85.1%)	▼
Asia's total outward portfolio debt investment	**4,190**	**(100.0%)**	**3,997**	**(100.0%)**	

** = direction of change in share, ▼ = decrease, ▲ = increase.

Source: ADB calculations using data from International Monetary Fund. Coordinated Portfolio Investment Survey. http://data.imf.org/CPIS (accessed September 2018).

Inter- and Intra-Subregional Portfolio Investment

East Asia remains the most prominent subregion as both source and destination for intraregional portfolio investment, while the Pacific and Oceania continues to be a popular destination for intraregional portfolio debt investment.

Intraregional portfolio equity investment remains concentrated toward East Asia, resulting in a 72.6% share ($584.4 billion) of total intraregional portfolio equity investment (Figure 4.7). The PRC is the main destination in the subregion, accounting for 59.6% of intraregional equity investment to East Asia. Southeast Asia is next largest (11.2%), with a considerable amount of intraregional equity investment directed to financial hub Singapore ($42.4 billion), followed by Indonesia ($15.7 billion), Thailand ($11.6 billion), and Malaysia ($9.4 billion).

East Asia also continues to account for the largest share of intraregional portfolio debt investment (Figure 4.8), largely due to significant investment in the PRC. In 2017, debt investment to East Asia accounted for 48.9% of total intraregional investment outstanding, up by 7.0 percentage points from its 2012 share. Intraregional debt investment into the Pacific and Oceania remained strong at $199.2 billion in 2017, mainly from the high debt investment into Australia. However, the share of the subregion fell from 34.4% in 2012 to 29.1% in 2017. Meanwhile, investment to South Asia decreased by $13.2 billion in 2017.

There was a marked rise in outward debt investment in the Pacific and Oceania, which more than tripled from $13.3 billion in 2012 to $45.5 billion in 2017. Most came from Australia ($36.4 billion in 2017). The majority of investment from the region went to Japan ($18.5 billion), Australia ($6.7 billion), and Singapore ($6.7 billion). Recent progress in integrating Asia's payment and settlement systems in tandem with the boost of intra-subregional trade and tourism may further facilitate intraregional financial integration in the future (Box 4.1).

Figure 4.7: Inter- and Intra-Subregional Portfolio Equity Investment—Asia

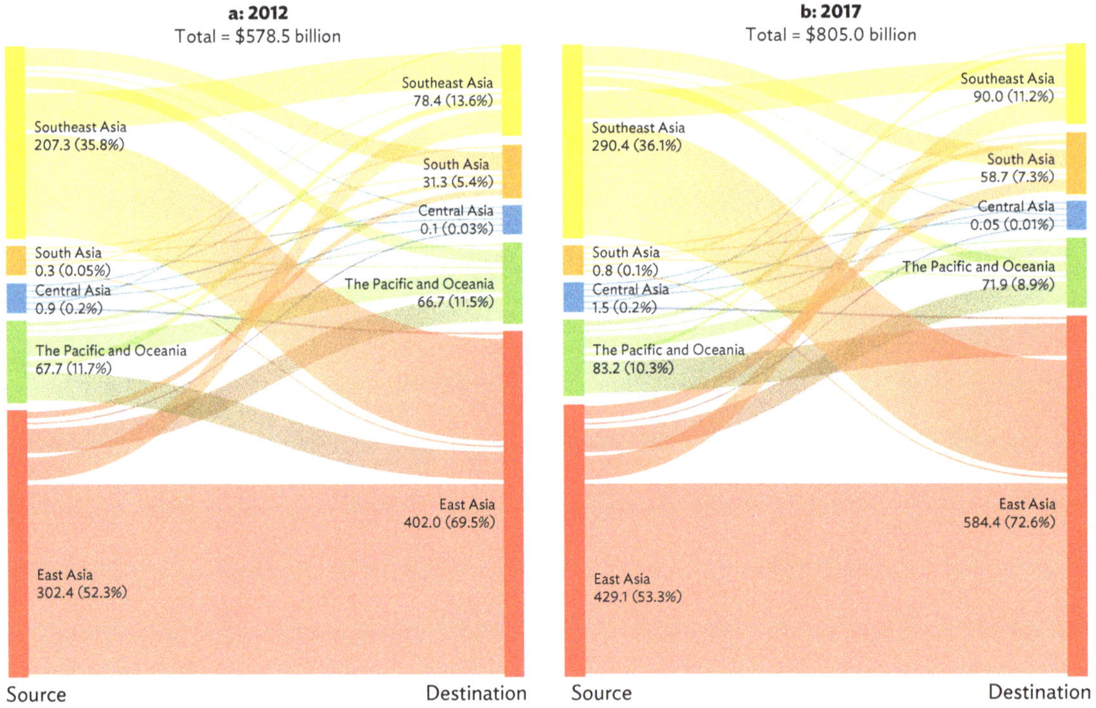

Notes: Numbers in parentheses indicate the percent share of the total. Central Asia includes Kazakhstan. East Asia includes Hong Kong, China; Japan; Mongolia; the People's Republic of China; and the Republic of Korea. The Pacific and Oceania includes Australia, New Zealand, Palau, and Vanuatu. South Asia includes Bangladesh, India, and Pakistan. Southeast Asia includes Indonesia, Malaysia, the Philippines, Singapore, and Thailand. Asia includes Central Asia, East Asia, the Pacific and Oceania, South Asia, and Southeast Asia.
Source: ADB calculations using data from International Monetary Fund. Coordinated Portfolio Investment Survey. http://data.imf.org/CPIS (accessed September 2018).

Box 4.1: Progress in Integrating ASEAN+3 Payment and Settlement Systems for Local Currency Transactions

Intra-subregional trade among members of the Association of Southeast Asian Nations, plus Japan, the People's Republic of China (PRC), and the Republic of Korea (ASEAN+3) continues to grow—accounting for 47% of the group's total trade, comparable to Europe.[a] The high intra-subregional trade share in part stems from the development of sophisticated supply-chain networks within the region. The final destinations of consumption goods used to be primarily the United States (US) and Europe. But today these are shifting more toward Asia—a trend expected to continue as Asia changes from a production base to consumer market.

This is not true for currencies, however. Currencies settled for intraregional transactions remain limited to US dollars (USD). According to the Society for Worldwide Interbank Financial Telecommunication (SWIFT), 85% of intra-ASEAN commercial flows in 2016 was in USD—followed by the Singapore dollar (6%) and Thai baht (3%) (SWIFT 2017). USD dominates ASEAN+3 transactions as well, given the limited share of the Japanese yen (4% of commercial flows as of July 2018) and the PRC renminbi (1%) as international payment currencies (SWIFT 2018).

The gap between rising intraregional trade and low usage of local currencies for transactions would pose a problem should the shortage of USD for trade be aggravated by financial market conditions. Non-US banks have limited access to USD—which is subject to changes in global dollar funding conditions. ASEAN+3 governments can tap the $240 billion Chiang Mai Initiative Multilateralization (CMIM) short-term liquidity safety net in times of emergency, and the established surveillance unit—the ASEAN+3 Macroeconomic Research

Continued on next page

[a] See Statistical Appendix.

Box 4.1 *continued*

Office. However, the available support pales against the value of constantly expanding intraregional trade. Therefore, it is important to further develop, improve, and integrate the region's financial market infrastructure to facilitate cross-border local currency transactions.

To promote local currency use in cross-border payments, the central banks of Indonesia, Malaysia, and Thailand agreed to create local currency settlement frameworks—between Bank Negara Malaysia and the Bank of Thailand (launched March 2016), between Bank Negara Malaysia and Bank Indonesia, and between the Bank of Thailand and Bank Indonesia (both launched December 2017). Under these frameworks, the central banks appoint local banks and grant foreign exchange flexibility in facilitating local currency settlement for bilateral trade of goods and services.

For example, the framework between Bank Negara Malaysia and the Bank of Thailand allows Thai businesses to engage in financing and deposit transactions with appointed banks in Malaysian ringgit more easily and efficiently—and vice versa in Thai baht. The framework allows these banks to offer a range of financial services—including hedging, financing, and deposit-taking. The appointed banks are required to provide direct foreign exchange quotes between the two local currencies involved in buying and selling.

There has also been progress in facilitating cross-border investment transactions in local currency between the PRC and Hong Kong, China. In particular, Stock Connect links the Hong Kong Stock Exchange with the Shanghai (since November 2014) and Shenzhen (since December 2016) stock exchanges. These links were created to allow the PRC and Hong Kong, China investors to trade stocks across markets using the trade and clearing facilities of their respective exchanges. Today, Stock Connect covers over 2,000 eligible stocks listed on the three exchanges. In August 2018, average daily turnover (buy + sell trades) reached CNY20,093 million (northbound) and HKD10,804 million (southbound).[b]

Following the success of Stock Connect, Bond Connect between the PRC and Hong Kong, China was introduced in July 2017. Bond Connect allows overseas investors to invest in PRC domestic bonds without having to apply under the foreign investor quota. While investment remains limited from Hong Kong, China to the PRC (northbound), 425 international institutional investors have joined Bond Connect as of the end of August 2018, with trading volume reaching CNY81 billion in August 2018 (Bond Connect Company 2018).

ASEAN members are also working to improve their retail payment systems and move beyond borders. In Thailand, a new interbank real-time payment system (PromptPay) was launched in January 2017, allowing registered customers to transfer funds through mobile phone—using only the mobile number or national identification number of the recipient, resulting in significantly lower remittance fees. At first the system was only available to individuals, but it eventually expanded in March 2017 to include business-to-business services. As of May 2018, the system attracted more than 40 million users with over 173 million transactions, including THB700 billion ($22 billion) in money transfers (Hornblass 2018). Thai commercial banks started to abolish the current interbank funds transfer fees to encourage customers to move to the more efficient digital banking platform.

Similarly, Singapore's PayNow system (launched in July 2017) allows customers of participating banks to send and receive Singapore dollars almost instantaneously by using their mobile number or Singapore National Registration Identity Card. PayNow began accepting business-to-business transactions in August 2018.

In November 2017, the Bank of Thailand and Monetary Authority of Singapore announced that they were exploring linking PromptPay and PayNow to allow users in both countries to transfer money to each other using mobile phone numbers rather than through the traditional banking network. Malaysia is also considering joining. Strong intra-subregional trade and tourism makes it natural to consider linking retail payment systems—which enhances financial integration and inclusion as well.

Technology plays an important role in enhancing the efficiency of cross-border payment and settlement systems. However, technological advances alone are not a panacea. Understanding relevant regulations and requirements across all network jurisdictions is essential. Also, technologies used must be harmonized and standardized to ensure interoperability when making cross-border transactions. For example, while Quick Response Codes (QR codes) are used in many countries, QR code generation often varies by country- or company-specific circumstances—creating multiple codes at the time of payment. Standardization would reduce vulnerabilities in data security—currently, the lack of an agreed security protocol and experience in sharing security threats could lead to more data breaches. Likewise, standardizing competing blockchain and distributed ledger systems is becoming more urgent. Data in one blockchain system may not be linked with others, while differences in operational requirements may reduce system

Continued on next page

[b] Based on data from Hong Kong Stock Exchange. www.hkex.com.hk (accessed September 2018).

Box 4.1 *continued*

scalability. Even minimum coordination and standardization can benefit all users and reduce future costs.

To promote standardization and harmonization, coordination among stakeholders in all relevant jurisdictions is indispensable. Information sharing and a common understanding of various regulations across jurisdictions are also required. ADB's experience with the ASEAN+3 Bond Market Forum (ABMF)—under the Asian Bond Markets Initiative—is a case in point. The ABMF was established in 2010 as a common platform to foster standardization of market practices and harmonization of regulations relating to cross-border bond transactions across the region. Published bond market guides for ASEAN+3 markets allow public authorities, academics, and market professionals to comprehensively understand and compare markets. The ABMF continues to promote awareness of standardization and international standards to ensure interoperability of payment and settlement infrastructure, thereby advancing financial integration in the region.

Source: ADB.

Figure 4.8: Inter- and Intra-Subregional Portfolio Debt Investment—Asia

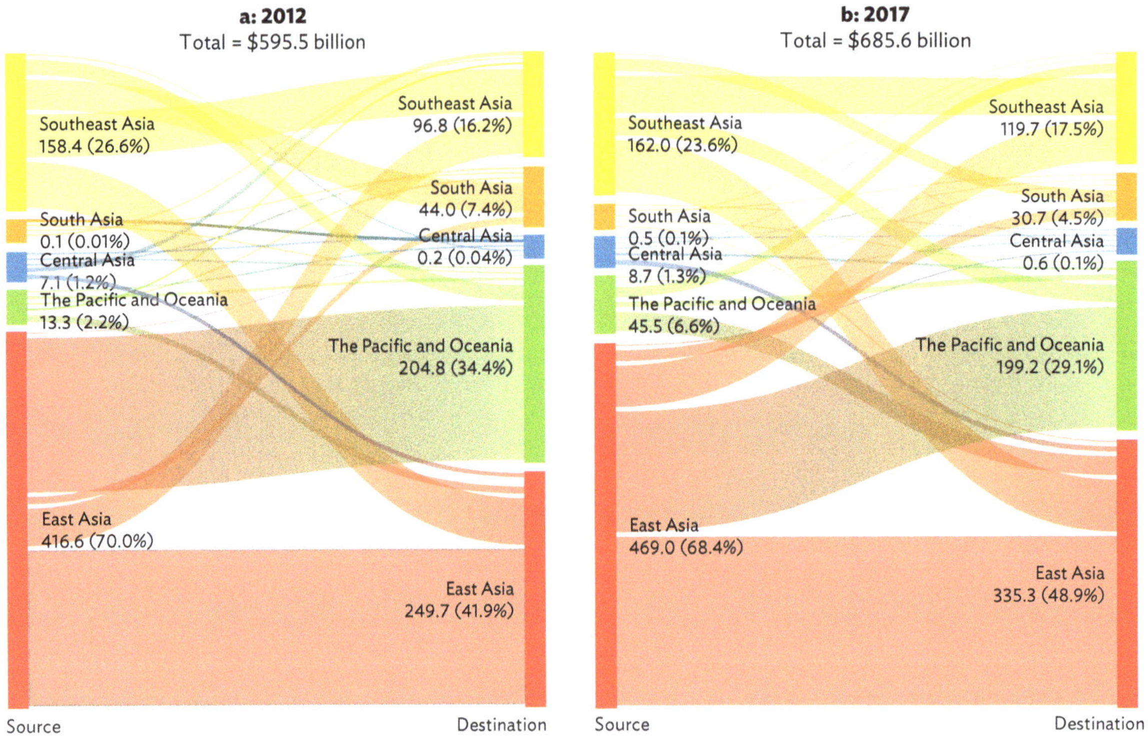

Notes: Numbers in parentheses indicate the percent share of the total. Central Asia includes Kazakhstan. East Asia includes Hong Kong, China; Japan; Mongolia; the People's Republic of China; and the Republic of Korea. The Pacific and Oceania includes Australia, New Zealand, Palau, and Vanuatu. South Asia includes Bangladesh, India, and Pakistan. Southeast Asia includes Indonesia, Malaysia, the Philippines, Singapore, and Thailand. Asia includes Central Asia, East Asia, the Pacific and Oceania, South Asia, and Southeast Asia.

Source: ADB calculations using data from International Monetary Fund. Coordinated Portfolio Investment Survey. http://data.imf.org/CPIS (accessed September 2018).

Bank Holdings[22]

Asia's cross-border bank claims, along with its intraregional share, continued to grow in 2017. Rising intraregional shares of bank claims and bank liabilities point to an increasing role of regional bank lending.

Asia's cross-border bank claims rose to $4.6 trillion in 2017 from $4.4 trillion in 2016 (Figure 4.9a). While the majority of Asia's claims remain on countries outside the region, the share of intraregional bank claims rose to 22.6% in 2017 from 21.4% in 2016. Asia's cross-border bank liabilities slightly decreased from $2.4 trillion in 2016 to $2.3 trillion (Figure 4.9b) in 2017. However, data from the first quarter in 2018 suggest an increase in cross-border bank liabilities, more than equal the 2017 decrease. The region's bank liabilities largely come from outside the region, but the intraregional share of Asia's cross-border bank liabilities rose from 18.8% in 2011 to 27.2% in 2017, suggesting the region's demand for cross-border bank financing is increasingly met regionally.

In tandem with the sizable rise in global international banking activities in 2017, Asia's bank claims within the region and the rest of the world increased during the year.

Asia's bank claims within the region and the rest of the world (ROW) increased strongly in 2017 (Figure 4.10a). The increase was predominantly driven by growing overseas bank lending by Japanese banks—the largest foreign lenders globally—especially to Asia (Hong Kong, China; Australia; and India) and the ROW (particularly the Cayman Islands, Bermuda, and Switzerland).[23] As a result, Japan's cross-border bank claims outstanding rose from $3.4 trillion in 2016 to $3.6 trillion in 2017. Intraregional bank claims rose by $94.1 billion, while bank claims on the ROW rose by $153.3 billion. These helped offset a contraction in Asia's bank claims on the US, which fell by $71.5 billion. In the first quarter of 2018, however, Asia's bank claims on the US rebounded.

Asia's cross-border bank liabilities decreased by $107.9 billion during 2017, mainly due to a drop in

Figure 4.9: Cross-Border Bank Holdings—Asia

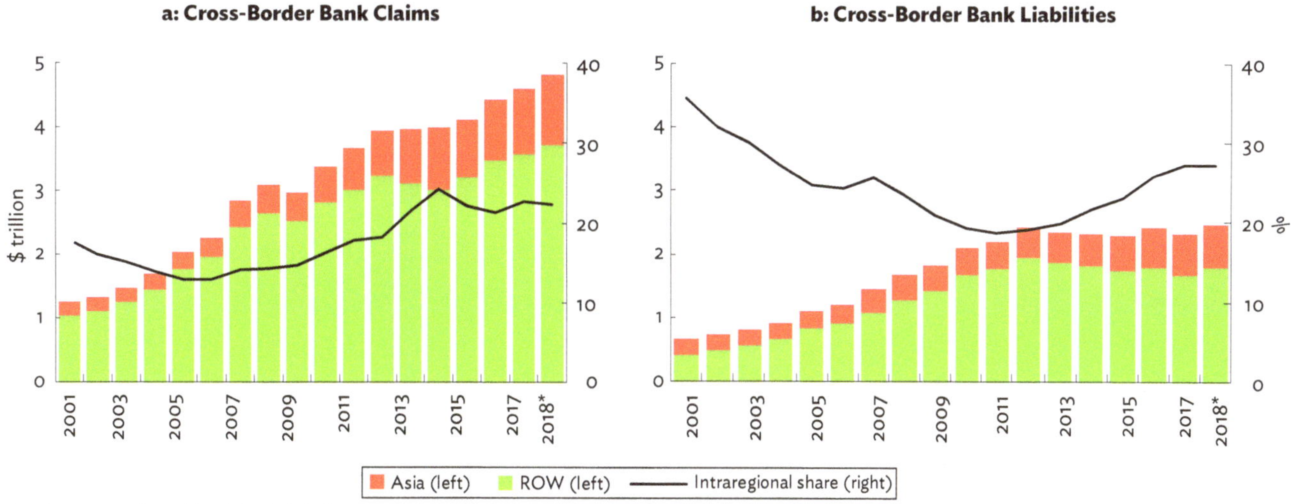

* = data are as of end-March 2018, ROW = rest of the world.

Notes: Asia's reporting economies include Australia; Japan; the Republic of Korea; and Taipei,China. Asian partner economies include ADB regional members for which data are available.

Source: ADB calculations using data from Bank for International Settlements. Locational Banking Statistics. https://www.bis.org/statistics/bankstats.htm (accessed August 2018).

22 Bank holdings are based on the Locational Banking Statistics from the Bank for International Settlements (BIS). Asia's reporting economies include Australia; Japan; the Republic of Korea; and Taipei,China. Meanwhile, Hong Kong, China and the Philippines are excluded due to unavailable or lack of comparable data.

23 See Statistical Release in: BIS. International Banking Statistics at end-December 2017.

Figure 4.10: Cross-Border Bank Holdings—Asia ($ billion)

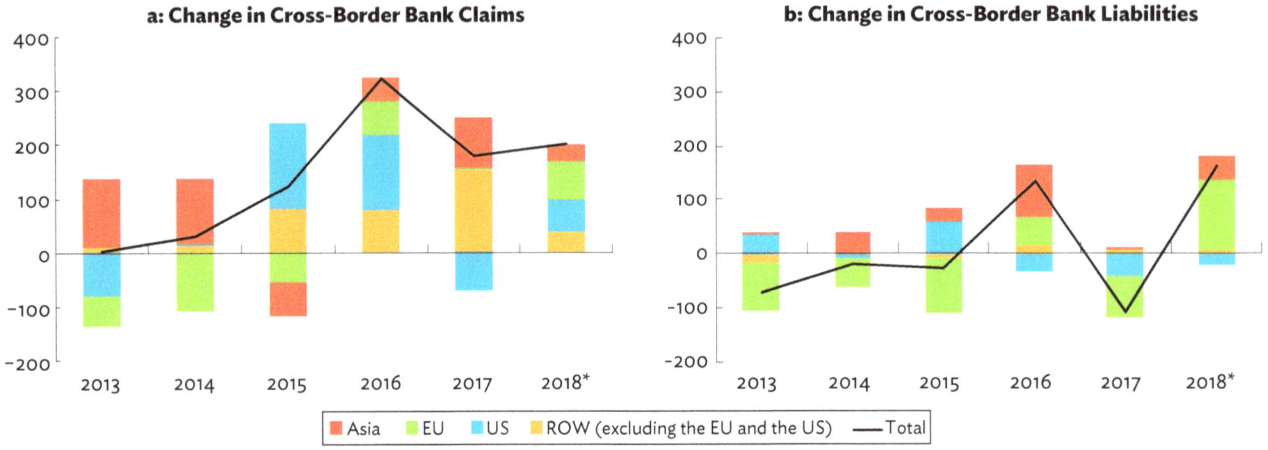

* = data are for the first quarter, EU = European Union, ROW = rest of the world, US = United States.
Notes: Asia's reporting economies include Australia; Japan; the Republic of Korea; and Taipei,China. Asian partner economies include ADB regional members for which data are available.
Source: ADB calculations using data from Bank for International Settlements. Locational Banking Statistics. https://www.bis.org/statistics/bankstats.htm (accessed August 2018).

claims from the EU (by $78.5 billion) and the US (by $42.0 billion) (Figure 4.10b)—in tandem with the progress in the US monetary policy normalization, including the impact on Asian borrower demand and global creditor supply for cross-border dollar lending due to the strengthening of the US dollar. This trend continued in the first quarter of 2018 for the US, while the EU increased its bank lending to the region once more, due to increased bank liabilities with the UK.

Most intraregional bank claims were on Hong Kong, China; the PRC—which have almost tripled over the past 5 years; and Singapore (Table 4.5). Together they accounted for over 60% of Asia's lending within the

Table 4.5: Destination of Cross-Border Bank Claims—Asia ($ billion)

	2017		2012		
	$ billion	**% share**	**$ billion**	**% share**	**
Asia					
Hong Kong, China	229	(5.0%)	147	(3.7%)	▲
China, People's Republic of	225	(4.9%)	80	(2.0%)	▲
Singapore	197	(4.3%)	188	(4.7%)	▼
Other Asia	392	(8.5%)	306	(7.7%)	▲
Asia's cross-border bank claims on Asia	1,043	(22.6%)	720	(18.2%)	▲
Non-Asia					
United States	1,277	(27.7%)	1,129	(28.6%)	▼
European Union	1,193	(25.9%)	1,342	(33.9%)	▼
Cayman Islands	747	(16.2%)	373	(9.4%)	▲
Other non-Asia	351	(7.6%)	390	(9.9%)	▼
Asia's cross-border bank claims on non-Asia	3,569	(77.4%)	3,234	(81.8%)	▼
Asia's total cross-border bank claims	**4,612**	**(100.0%)**	**3,954**	**(100.0%)**	

** = direction of change in share, ▼ = decrease, ▲ = increase.
Source: ADB calculations using data from Bank for International Settlements. Locational Banking Statistics. https://www.bis.org/statistics/bankstats.htm (accessed August 2018).

Table 4.6: Sources of Cross-Border Bank Liabilities—Asia ($ billion)

	2017		2012		
	$ billion	**% share**	**$ billion**	**% share**	**
Asia					
Hong Kong, China	256	(11.1%)	160	(6.7%)	▲
Singapore	135	(5.8%)	133	(5.5%)	▲
China, People's Republic of	75	(3.2%)	27	(1.1%)	▲
Other Asia	164	(7.1%)	142	(5.9%)	▲
Asia's cross-border bank liabilities to Asia	630	(27.2%)	462	(19.2%)	▲
Non-Asia					
European Union	825	(35.6%)	1,083	(44.9%)	▼
United States	680	(29.3%)	673	(27.9%)	▲
Cayman Islands	66	(2.9%)	70	(2.9%)	–
Other non-Asia	118	(5.1%)	123	(5.1%)	–
Asia's cross-border bank liabilities to non-Asia	1,689	(72.8%)	1,950	(80.8%)	▼
Asia's total cross-border bank liabilities	**2,319**	**(100.0%)**	**2,412**	**(100.0%)**	

** = direction of change in share, ▼ = decrease, ▲ = increase, – = no change.
Source: ADB calculations using data from Bank for International Settlements. Locational Banking Statistics. https://www.bis.org/statistics/bankstats.htm (accessed August 2018).

region. Other notable increases in intraregional cross-border bank claims over the last 5 years were on Japan (by $29.2 billion), Thailand (by $15.1 billion), and India (by $13.9 billion). For Hong Kong, China, the largest source of lending was Japan ($142.5 billion), followed by Taipei,China ($39.8 billion) and Australia ($27.4 billion).

The US, the EU, and the Cayman Islands remain top destinations for Asia's non-regional bank claims. Japan remains the largest source of Asian bank lending to the US, accounting for almost 90% ($1.1 trillion). This is only topped globally by the UK, which has the largest bank claims on the US ($1.3 trillion).

Asia's bank claims on the Cayman Islands doubled over the past 5 years, increasing from $373.0 billion in 2012 to $747.0 billion in 2017. The majority of the increase can be attributed to Japan, which almost doubled its claims from $362.1 billion to $700.8 billion. Australia's claims on the Cayman Islands in 2017 were $27.4 billion, 28 times as large as its claims of less than $1 million in 2012.

Hong Kong, China; Singapore; and the PRC are the main sources of intraregional bank liabilities in Asia (Table 4.6). They have increased over the past 5 years along with their share to total bank liabilities. The top sources of bank lending outside the region were the EU, the US, and the Cayman Islands. However, Asia's liabilities decreased significantly to both the EU (by $259.0 billion) and the Cayman Islands ($4.0 billion), while US liabilities increased by $7.0 billion between 2012 and 2017.

Analysis Using Price Indicators

Equity

On average, Asia's equity return correlations with the region and globally remained largely stable as US interest rates continued to normalize. East Asia's correlations with Asia and the world are rising, highlighting the increasing interconnectedness of its financial markets with the region as well as with global markets.

Comparing the post-global financial crisis (GFC) and US monetary policy normalization periods, Asia's equity

Table 4.7: Average Simple Correlation of Stock Price Index Weekly Returns—Asia with Asia and World

Region	Asia				World			
	Pre-GFC Jan 1999–Sep 2007	Post-GFC Jul 2009–Dec 2015	MP Normalization Jan 2016–Aug 2018	**	Pre-GFC Jan 1999–Sep 2007	Post-GFC Jul 2009–Dec 2015	MP Normalization Jan 2016–Aug 2018	**
Central Asia	0.09	0.20	0.16	▼	0.02	0.24	0.15	▼
East Asia	0.35	0.47	0.50	▲	0.42	0.56	0.60	▲
Southeast Asia	0.33	0.41	0.41	-	0.34	0.49	0.45	▼
South Asia	0.14	0.18	0.18	-	0.15	0.18	0.20	▲
Oceania	0.38	0.53	0.48	▼	0.55	0.70	0.56	▼
Asia	**0.28**	**0.36**	**0.36**	-	**0.36**	**0.42**	**0.41**	▼

** = direction of change in simple correlation between post-global financial crisis, and monetary policy normalization periods, ▼ = decrease, ▲ = increase, - = no change, GFC = global financial crisis, MP = monetary policy.

Notes: Central Asia includes Georgia, Kazakhstan, and the Kyrgyz Republic. East Asia includes Hong Kong, China; Japan; Mongolia; the People's Republic of China; the Republic of Korea; and Taipei,China. Southeast Asia includes Indonesia, the Lao People's Democratic Republic, Malaysia, the Philippines, Singapore, Thailand, and Viet Nam. South Asia includes Bangladesh, India, Nepal, Pakistan, and Sri Lanka. Oceania includes Australia and New Zealand. Asia includes Central Asia, East Asia, Oceania, South Asia, and Southeast Asia.

Sources: ADB calculations using data from Bloomberg; CEIC; Haver; International Monetary Fund. World Economic Outlook. https://www.imf.org/external/pubs/ft/weo/2018/01/weodata/index.aspx (accessed September 2018); and Stooq. https://stooq.com/q/?s=^sti (accessed September 2018).

return correlation with the region and the world largely remained constant—and at moderate levels (Table 4.7). Subregionally, there has been a clear upward trend of East Asia's equity return correlation, both within Asia and the world, and across all periods, highlighting a growing integration of East Asia's equity markets, both within Asia and globally. Average correlations of Central Asian equity markets with Asia and the world have decreased recently.

Dynamic conditional correlations of Asian and global equity markets remain high as Asia's equity markets continue to integrate globally.

Equity return dynamic conditional correlations (DCC) between Asia and the world remain higher than the rest, supported by the high equity return DCC between Asia and the EU, and between Asia and the US (Figure 4.11)—underpinning Asia's equity market integration globally. Intra-Asia equity return DCC and between Asia and Japan have also risen during exceptional events—such as the US stock market correction in February 2018, followed by the imposition of US tariffs on imports triggering responses from advanced economies. The Asia–PRC DCC registered a large fall in June 2018, as PRC stock markets continued to fall under pressure as trade tensions between the US and other economies, especially the PRC, continued.

Debt

Contrary to the stable average correlations of Asia's equity market returns, Asia's bond return correlations with global markets have increased substantially.

Recent rate hikes from the US Federal Reserve could have led to increased correlations between Asia's bond markets returns with the world compared with the post-GFC period (from 0.21 to 0.44) (Table 4.8). Except for Australia, the PRC, India, Malaysia, and the Republic of Korea, all other Asian economies have seen increased bond return correlations with Asia during the normalization period as compared with the post-GFC period. Moreover, correlations of all Asian markets have increased with global markets. By correlation level, Singapore currently has the highest correlation with Asia (0.56) and global bond markets (0.64), underlining its important role as one of the region's highly integrated financial centers.

Progress in US monetary policy normalization coincides with a rise in bond return dynamic conditional correlations.

Bond return DCC between Asia and the world, as well as with Asia's selected partner economies rose sharply (except the PRC) in July 2017, as several major central

Figure 4.11: Conditional Correlations of Equity Markets—Asia with Select Economies and Regions

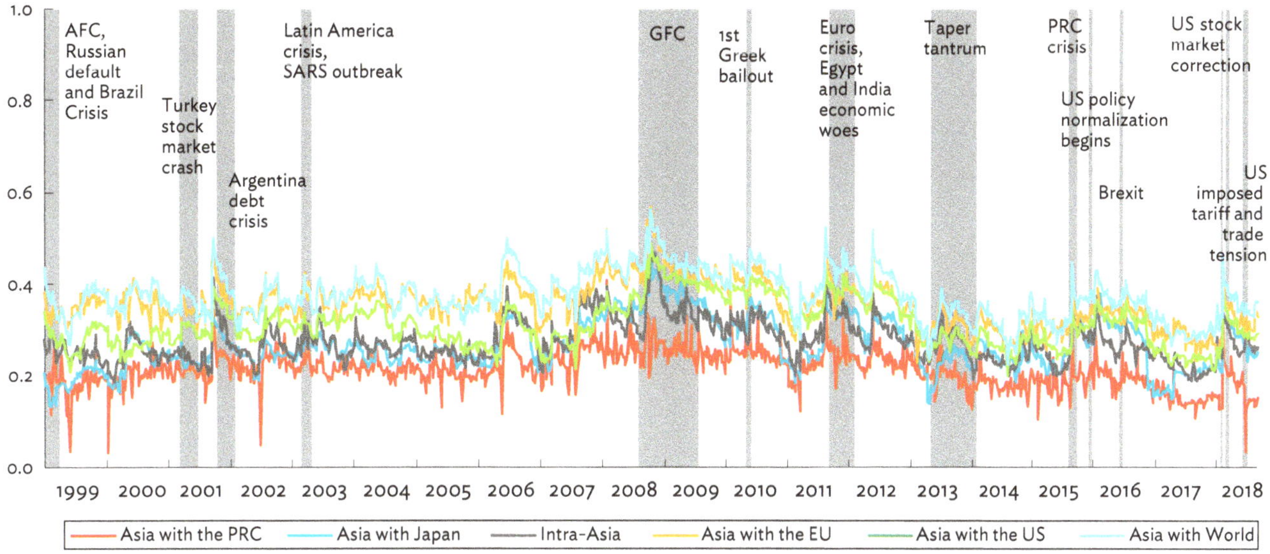

AFC = Asian financial crisis, EU = European Union, GFC = global financial crisis, PRC = People's Republic of China, SARS = severe acute respiratory syndrome, US = United States.

Note: Asia includes Australia; Bangladesh; Georgia; Hong Kong, China; India; Indonesia; Japan; Kazakhstan; the Kyrgyz Republic; the Lao People's Democratic Republic; Malaysia; Mongolia; Nepal; New Zealand; Pakistan; the Philippines; the PRC; the Republic of Korea; Singapore; Sri Lanka; Taipei,China; Thailand; and Viet Nam.

Sources: ADB calculations using data from Bloomberg; CEIC; and Stooq. https://stooq.com/q/?s=^sti (accessed May 2018); and methodology by Hinojales and Park (2010).

Table 4.8: Average Simple Correlation of Weekly Bond Return Index—Asia with Asia and World

	Asia				World			
Economy	**Pre-GFC Jan 2005–Sep 2007**	**Post-GFC Jul 2009–Dec 2015**	**MP Normalization Jan 2016–Aug 2018**	**	**Pre-GFC Jan 2005–Sep 2007**	**Post-GFC Jul 2009–Dec 2015**	**MP Normalization Jan 2016–Aug 2018**	**
Australia	0.38	0.46	0.41	▼	0.41	0.36	0.57	▲
PRC	0.01	0.30	0.21	▼	0.04	0.03	0.18	▲
India	0.06	0.21	0.14	▼	0.23	-0.07	0.07	▲
Indonesia	-0.15	0.23	0.26	▲	0.02	0.25	0.44	▲
Japan	0.19	0.25	0.33	▲	0.28	0.41	0.47	▲
Republic of Korea	0.15	0.47	0.45	▼	0.37	0.23	0.54	▲
Malaysia	0.22	0.44	0.31	▼	0.13	0.15	0.45	▲
Philippines	-	0.21	0.39	▲	-	0.14	0.48	▲
Singapore	0.29	0.49	0.56	▲	0.27	0.44	0.64	▲
Thailand	0.20	0.39	0.47	▲	0.29	0.19	0.53	▲
Asia	**0.16**	**0.34**	**0.35**	▲	**0.23**	**0.21**	**0.44**	▲

** = direction of change in simple correlation between post-global financial crisis and monetary policy normalization periods, ▼ = decrease, ▲ = increase, – = no data available, GFC = global financial crisis, MP = monetary policy, PRC = People's Republic of China.

Notes: Values refer to the average of pair-wise correlations. Weekly returns are computed as the natural logarithm difference between weekly average of daily bond return index for the current week, and the weekly average of the daily bond return index from the previous week. All bond return indexes comprise local currency government-issued bonds.

Sources: ADB calculations using data from Bloomberg; and International Monetary Fund. World Economic Outlook. https://www.imf.org/external/pubs/ft/weo/2018/01/weodata/index.aspx (accessed September 2018).

Figure 4.12: Conditional Correlations of Bond Markets—Asia with Select Economies and Regions

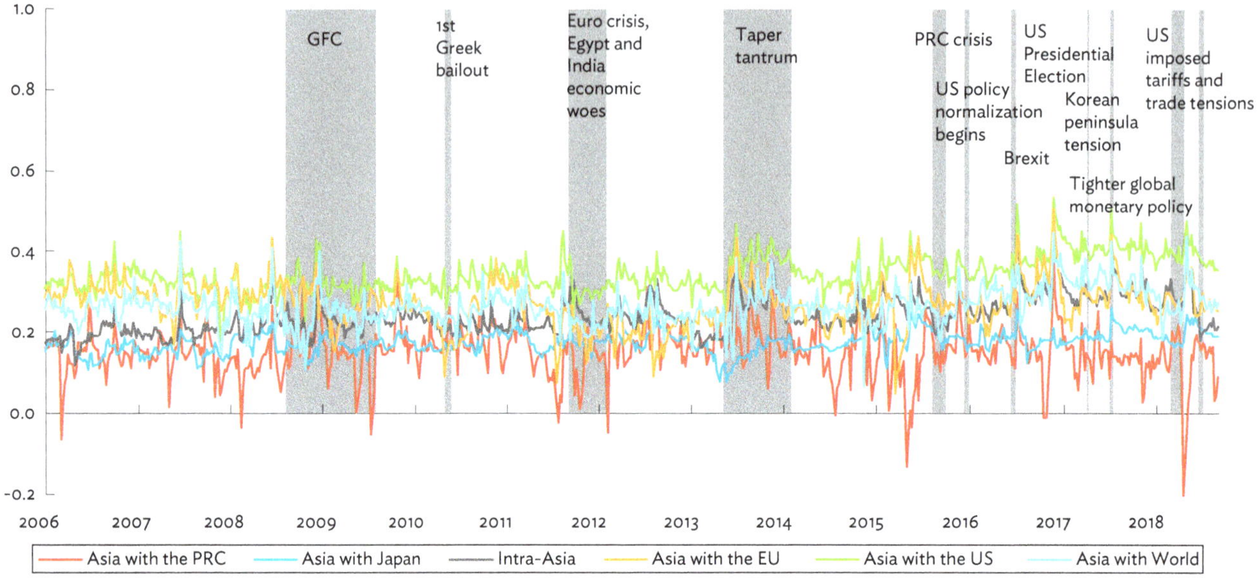

EU = European Union, GFC = global financial crisis, PRC = People's Republic of China, US = United States.
Note: Asia includes Australia, India, Indonesia, Japan, Malaysia, the Philippines, the PRC, the Republic of Korea, Singapore, and Thailand.
Sources: ADB calculations using data from Bloomberg and methodology by Hinojales and Park (2010).

banks surprised markets by releasing non-dovish comments (Figure 4.12). Increases in DCC could also be observed during major episodes such as the 2016 US presidential election, the "Brexit" referendum, and rising trade tensions among major trading partners in 2018. A surprise cut of 100 basis points by the People's Bank of China on the reserve requirement ratio on 17 April 2018 coincided with a sudden drop in bond yields. This in turn could have caused the bond return DCC between Asia and the PRC to drop significantly during the period.

Financial Spillovers

The sensitivity of Asian equity and bond markets to global shocks has risen during monetary policy normalization, highlighting the region's strong degree of integration with global financial markets, as well as reflecting uncertainties surrounding the changes in global financial conditions.

The period of US monetary policy normalization, characterized by US policy rate hikes—and several central banks in emerging markets tightening monetary policy coincides with increased sensitivity to global shocks of Asia's bond and equity markets (Figures 4.13, 4.14).[24] Hence, uncertainties surrounding changing global liquidity conditions lead to this observed increased sensitivity to global shocks. This increasing sensitivity to external shocks is further underscored by elevated exposure to international investors especially from outside the region. Non-regional holdings of Asian portfolio assets grew between 2016 and 2017 from $3.4 trillion to $4.5 trillion in equity and from $1.7 trillion to $2.0 trillion in debt, highlighting a continuation of the integration of the region's financial markets globally.

Thus, the region's policy makers should closely monitor financial risks and market volatilities, while remaining vigilant to safeguard financial stability by strengthening macroeconomic and financial fundamentals, enhancing national and regional economic surveillance, employing appropriate macroprudential measures, reinforcing national and regional financial safety nets, and deepening capital market development. The region should also leverage recent regulatory technology and fintech developments to help promote financial stability and resilience (Box 4.2).

[24] For example, Hong Kong, China (began to raise the policy rates in late 2016) and the Republic of Korea (raised the rates in late 2017). Indonesia, the Philippines, and India raised policy rates multiple times as of September 2018.

Box 4.2: Fostering Financial Stability through Regulatory Technology

Following the 2008/09 global financial crisis, regulatory and compliance requirements imposed upon banks and other financial institutions became more complex, cumbersome, and lengthy. In addition, substantial fines and penalties were introduced for noncompliance. In the United States, considerable post-crisis fines were levied on banks, while annual spending by financial institutions on compliance was estimated at more than $70 billion.[a] Consequently, regulatory fees and the cost of compliance have emerged as principal concerns for the industry.

Technological advances offer a potential means to mitigate these considerable costs. In particular, RegTech—a contraction of "regulatory" and "technology"—has emerged as a promising way to facilitate the adherence of financial institutions to growing compliance and reporting obligations. RegTech includes technology-based systems that facilitate data collection and generate reports conforming to the format and schedules imposed by regulatory bodies. Its applications range from effective processing of "Big Data" to strengthening cybersecurity and the enhancement of macroprudential supervision.

Although RegTech is closely linked to fintech—the utilization of technology in the delivery of financial solutions—the two differ. Fintech encompasses a myriad of emerging platforms, spanning peer-to-peer lending to robo-advice, and encompassing payments and credit scoring. In contrast, the potential of RegTech is not confined to increasing efficiency; it can provide a better tool for rethinking and reshaping the ways in which regulation and finance work. RegTech applications can be as follows:

1. Big Data

Post-crisis regulations require the generation of masses of reports and data. Yet regulators typically lack the capacity to analyze the data received. For instance, suspicious transaction reports are produced as part of anti-money laundering and know-your-customer requirements but are rarely utilized and confined to being used to further prosecution measures after a fraudulent transaction has already taken place. Thus, regulators are unable to curb criminal activity permeating financial systems. RegTech offers a means for analyzing these data sets so that informed and timely decisions can be made and appropriate action taken.

2. Macroprudential policy

This comprises the most promising area for using RegTech. The global financial crisis clearly illustrated the need to put in place early warning systems to stem the buildup of financial vulnerabilities and risks that could possibly lead to new crisis episodes. For instance, Big Data and new data sets can be leveraged to identify alarming patterns—such as financial volatilities. Early identification can help regulators nip emerging problems in the bud and respond proactively, circumventing the problem of learning only after the fact . Ultimately, RegTech should allow for close to real-time monitoring of capital flows, enabling regulators to curb crises before they unfold.

3. Cybersecurity

Cybersecurity is one of the most prominent areas for the application of RegTech, as digital transformation has increased the vulnerability of financial systems to attacks, theft, and fraud. The 2016 Bangladesh central bank cyber-heist underscored the vulnerabilities in existing frameworks as not only data, but money ($81 million), was taken. Proper regulations must be in place to ensure the soundness and security of financial systems.

4. RegTech and regional financial cooperation

To better manage risks, multiple regulatory bodies require institutions to frequently report massive amounts of data. Apart from strengthening national regulatory capacities, possible cooperation among the region's regulators could lead to more streamlined RegTech applications that also address growing financial interconnectedness and help identify cross-border risks. RegTech can be used to support the strengthening of regional cooperation in building appropriate policy and regulatory frameworks, such as the harmonization of regulatory standards or guidelines for digital transformation and data sharing.

[a] A Report on Global RegTech: A $100-Billion Opportunity—Market Overview, Analysis of Incumbents and Startups (April 2016) as cited in Arner, Barberis, and Buckley (2017).

Sources: ADB; and Arner, Barberis, and Buckley (2017).

Figure 4.13: Share of Variance in Local Equity Returns Explained by Global and Regional Shocks (%)

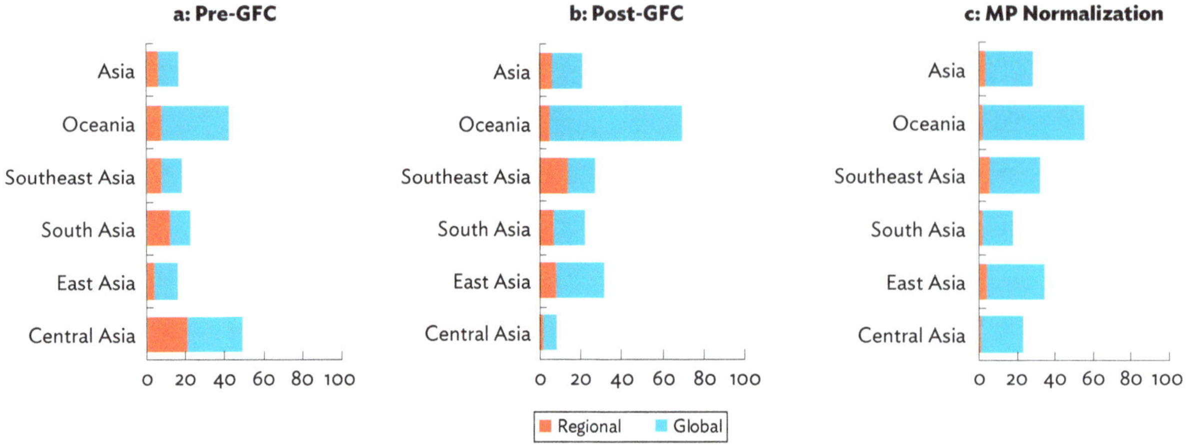

GFC = global financial crisis, MP = monetary policy.
Pre-GFC = January 1999 to September 2007, Post-GFC = July 2009 to December 2015, MP Normalization = January 2016 to August 2018.
Notes: Asia includes Central Asia, East Asia, Oceania, South Asia, and Southeast Asia. Central Asia includes Georgia, Kazakhstan, and the Kyrgyz Republic. East Asia includes Hong Kong, China; Japan; Mongolia; the People's Republic of China; the Republic of Korea; and Taipei,China. Oceania includes Australia and New Zealand. South Asia includes Bangladesh, India, Nepal, Pakistan, and Sri Lanka. Southeast Asia includes Indonesia, the Lao People's Democratic Republic, Malaysia, the Philippines, Singapore, Thailand, and Viet Nam.
Sources: ADB calculations using data from Bloomberg; CEIC; and International Monetary Fund. World Economic Outlook. https://www.imf.org/external/pubs/ft/weo/2018/01/weodata/index.aspx (accessed September 2018); and methodology by Lee and Park (2011).

Figure 4.14: Share of Variance in Local Bond Returns Explained by Global and Regional Shocks (%)

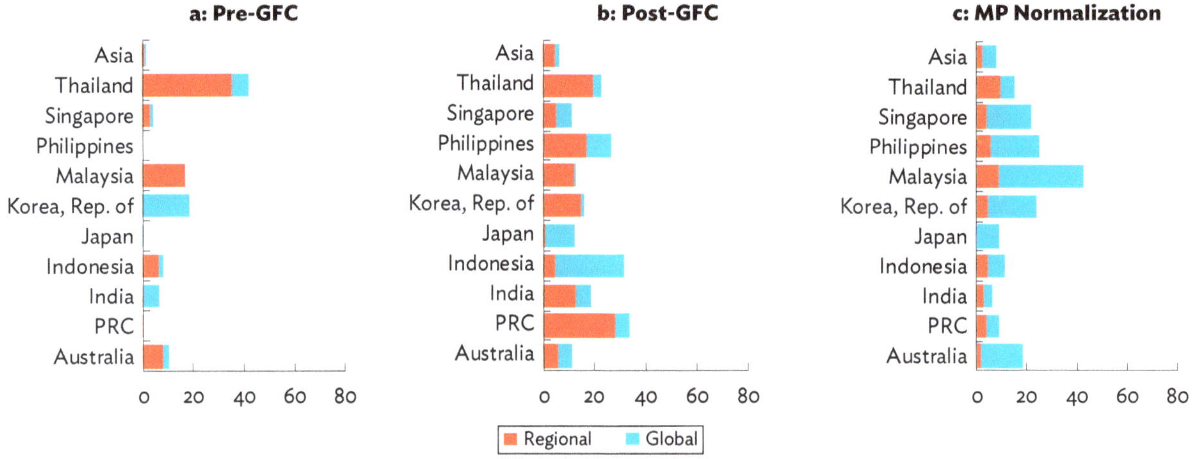

GFC = global financial crisis, MP = monetary policy, PRC = People's Republic of China.
Pre-GFC = January 2005 to September 2007, Post-GFC = July 2009 to December 2015, MP Normalization = January 2016 to August 2018.
Notes: Asia includes Australia, India, Indonesia, Japan, Malaysia, the Philippines, the PRC, the Republic of Korea, Singapore, and Thailand.
Sources: ADB calculations using data from Bloomberg; and International Monetary Fund. World Economic Outlook. https://www.imf.org/external/pubs/ft/weo/2018/01/weodata/index.aspx (accessed September 2018); and methodology by Lee and Park (2011).

Asian bond yields converged both within Asia and with non-Asia in 2016 and 2017, but signs of divergence began to appear in 2018.

Since the 2013 "taper tantrum," intra-Asia 10-year government bond yields in developed Asia and Oceania have continued to converge (Figure 4.15a). In contrast, East Asian yields have been diverging since the beginning of 2017. Unlike for other economies in the subregion, PRC bond yields were rising for most of 2017, triggered by tighter regulations and monetary conditions in the PRC to contain financial risks stemming from elevated levels of debt. But Asia as a whole saw bond yields diverge after the 2013 taper tantrum and slowly converge since the US monetary policy normalization in 2016 and 2017.

Figure 4.15: σ-Convergence of 10-Year Government Bond Yields—Asia

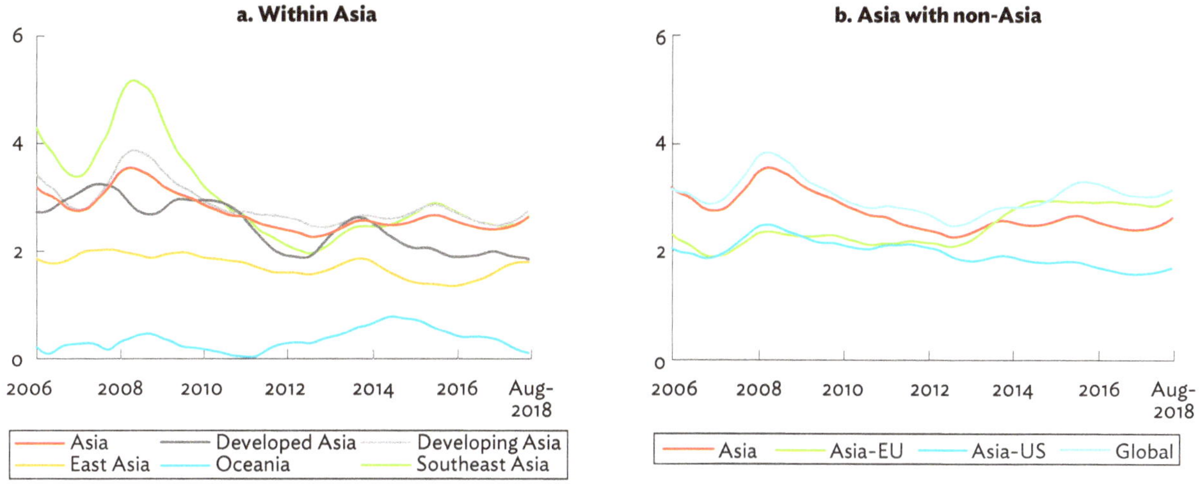

EU = European Union, US = United States.

Notes:

(i) Values refer to the unweighted mean of individual economy's σ-convergence, included in the subregion. Each economy's σ-convergence is the simple mean of all its pairwise standard deviation. Data are filtered using Hodrick-Prescott method.

(ii) East Asia includes Hong Kong, China; Japan; the People's Republic of China; the Republic of Korea; and Taipei,China. Southeast Asia includes Indonesia, Malaysia, the Philippines, Singapore, and Thailand. Oceania includes Australia and New Zealand. Developed Asia includes Japan and Oceania. Developing Asia includes East Asia excluding Japan and Southeast Asia. Asia includes developed Asia and developing Asia. Global includes Asia, Colombia, the EU, Mexico, and the US.

Sources: ADB calculations using data from Bloomberg; CEIC (accessed September 2018); and methodology by Espinoza, Prasad, and Williams (2010); and Park (2013).

Moreover, Asia's local currency bond yields continued to converge more to US bond yields during 2012–2017 (Figure 4.15b). This trend even remains below Asia's intraregional dispersion. The Asia–EU yield dispersion was nearly as narrow as the Asia–US yields until the end of 2012, before Asia's bond yields began to diverge from the EU's. The Asia–EU yield dispersion is even higher than Asia's own σ-convergence since the end of 2014. In 2018, the Asia–US yield dispersion started to rise, reflecting investor sentiment of flight-to-quality assets due to deepening uncertainties and risks driven by global financial market conditions and trade tensions among major trading partners.

References

Arner, D. W., J. Barberis, and R. P. Buckley. 2017. FinTech, RegTech, and the Reconceptualization of Financial Regulation. *Northwestern Journal of International Law and Business*. 37 (3).

Bank for International Settlements. Locational Banking Statistics. https://www.bis.org/statistics/bankstats.htm (accessed August 2018).

———. BIS International Banking Statistics at end-December 2017. https://www.bis.org/statistics/rppb1804.htm (accessed August 2018).

Bond Connect Company. 2018. *Flash Report for Bond Connect August 2018*. http://www.chinabondconnect.com/documents/FlashReportforBondConnect-August2018.pdf

Espinoza, R., A. Prasad, and O. Williams. 2010. Regional Financial Integration in the GCC. *IMF Working Paper*. No. 10/90. Washington, DC: International Monetary Fund (IMF).

Hinojales, M. and C. Y. Park. 2010. Stock Market Integration: Emerging East Asia's Experience. In M. Devereaux, P. Lane, C. Y. Park, and S. J. Wei, eds. *The Dynamics of Asian Financial Integration: Facts and Analytics*. London and New York: Routledge.

Hong Kong Stock Exchange. www.hkex.com.hk (accessed September 2018).

Hornblass, J. J. 2018. Mastercard's PromptPay Hits 40M Users in Thailand (Demo video). 8 May. *Bank Innovation*. https://bankinnovation.net/2018/05/mastercards-promptpay-hits-40m-users-in-thailand-demo-video/

International Monetary Fund (IMF). 2018. *Global Financial Stability Report: A Bumpy Road Ahead*. Washington, DC.

———. Coordinated Direct Investment Survey. http://data.imf.org/CDIS (accessed February 2018).

———. Coordinated Portfolio Investment Survey. http://data.imf.org/CPIS (accessed September 2018).

———. World Economic Outlook 2018 Database. https://www.imf.org/external/pubs/ft/weo/2018/01/weodata/index.aspx (accessed September 2018).

Lee, J. W. and C. Y. Park. 2011. Financial Integration in Emerging Asia: Challenges and Prospects. *Asian Economic Policy Review*. 6 (2). pp. 176–198.

MEDICI. 2016. *A Report on Global RegTech: A $100-Billion Opportunity - Market Overview, Analysis of Incumbents and Startups.* https://gomedici.com/a-report-on-global-regtech-a-100-billion-opportunity-market-overview-analysis-of-incumbents-and-startups/

Park, C. Y. 2013. Asian Capital Market Integration: Theory and Evidence. *ADB Economic Working Paper Series.* No. 351. Manila: Asian Development Bank.

Stooq. Stooq Online. http://stooq.com/q/?s=^sti (accessed September 2018).

SWIFT. 2017. Achieving Financial Integration in the ASEAN Region. *SWIFT Discussion Paper.*

SWIFT. 2018. RMB Tracker August 2018. https://www.swift.com/our-solutions/compliance-and-shared-services/business-intelligence/renminbi/rmb-tracker/document-centre

5

Movement of People

Migration

The stock of international migrants worldwide increased by 4.0% from 247.7 million in 2015 to 257.7 million in 2017 (Figure 5.1).[25] Over the same period, the global stock of migrants from Asia grew by 3.9%—from 83.6 million to 86.9 million. Inward migration to the region grew by 1.4%—from 41.8 million to 42.4 million.[26]

Figure 5.1: International Migrant Stock and Share of Migrants from Asia

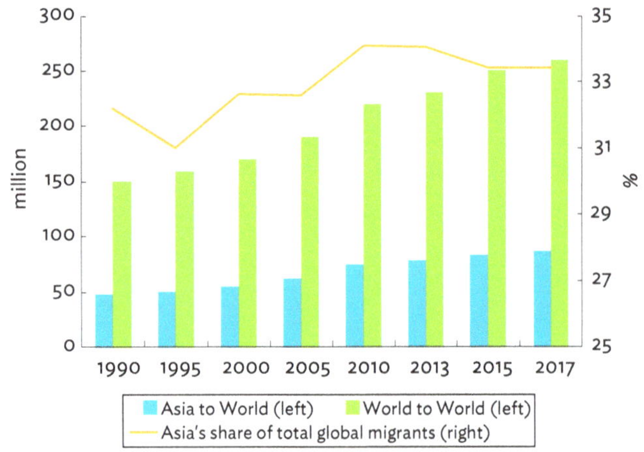

Note: Asia's share of total global migrants is computed as the percentage of migrants from the region (Asia to World) to total global migrants (World to World).
Source: ADB calculations using data from United Nations. Department of Economic and Social Affairs, Population Division. International Migrant Stock: The 2017 Revision. http://www.un.org/en/development/desa/population/migration/data/estimates2/estimates17.shtml (accessed May 2018).

Asia remains the largest source of international migrants.

One in three migrants (33.4%) worldwide comes from Asia. The stock of Asian migrants grew by 79.8% from 1990 to 2017 (from 48.3 million to 86.9 million) (Figure 5.2). European migrants grew by only 28.0% (from 48.1 million to 61.6 million), decreasing its share from 32.1% to 23.7% over the same period. Countries with sustained population growth and an expanding workforce continued to lead outward migration, while rising income levels and improved regulatory efficiency has helped bring down the cost of overseas worker migration. Rapidly aging populations in many developed

Figure 5.2: International Migrants, by Region of Origin (million)

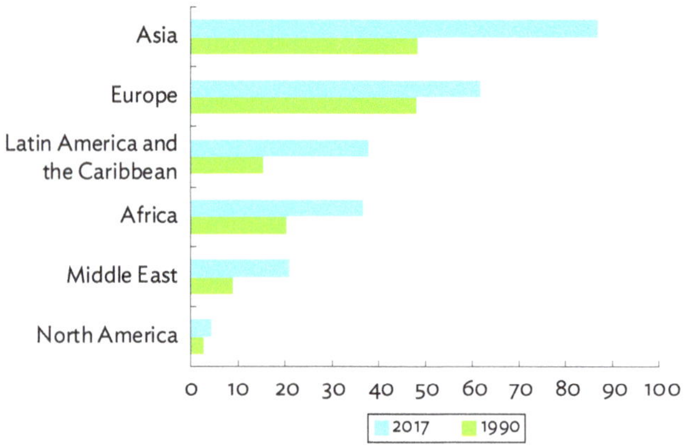

Source: ADB calculations using data from United Nations. Department of Economic and Social Affairs, Population Division. International Migrant Stock: The 2017 Revision. http://www.un.org/en/development/desa/population/migration/data/estimates2/estimates17.shtml (accessed May 2018).

[25] The United Nations (UN) recommendations on statistics of international migration define the "stock of international migrants present in a country" as "the set of persons who have ever changed their country of usual residence, that is to say, persons who have spent at least one year of their lives in a country other than the one in which they live at the time the data are gathered" (UN 1998). International migrant stock consists of persons crossing borders for various reasons—for employment, family reunification, study, and fleeing from conflicts and violence. Some events involve the creation of new borders, generating large numbers of international migrants—as during the 1991 dissolution of the Soviet Union.

[26] Asia refers to the 48 Asia and the Pacific members of the Asian Development Bank (ADB), which includes Japan and Oceania (Australia and New Zealand) in addition to the 45 developing Asian economies. In this chapter, Oceania and the Pacific are treated separately to underscore the distinct pattern and nuances of migration, remittance, and tourism movements in each of these two subregions.

host countries create labor shortages that contribute to rising demand for migrant labor.

Outward migration outpaces inward migration in Asia.

The stock of Asian migrants across the world has grown faster than the number of migrants residing in the region—particularly over the past several years. Migrants to Asia peaked in 2013 at 43.1 million, declining to 41.8 million in 2015, and increasing somewhat in 2017 (Figure 5.3). Major source countries of migrants to Asia are the People's Republic of China (PRC) (5.2 million), the Russian Federation (3.8 million), and Bangladesh (3.7 million) while the major hosts of migrants in Asia are Australia (7.1 million), India (5.2 million), and Kazakhstan (3.6 million). By contrast, outward migration has steadily increased, especially those headed outside Asia. Major host countries for Asian migrants are the United States (US) (12.3 million), Saudi Arabia (8.5 million), and the Russian Federation (6.8 million).

The largest numbers of outward migrants come from India, the PRC, and Bangladesh, while the migration rate is highest in Pacific and Central Asian subregions.

India had the most outward migrants in 2017 (17.0 million), followed by the PRC (10.0 million) and Bangladesh (7.5 million) (Figure 5.4). By subregion, South Asia and Southeast Asia dominate the list. By ratio of total outward migrants to population, the Pacific developing member countries (Pacific DMCs) top the list. Cook Islands outward migrants total 128.0% of the population (22,249 migrants against a population of 17,380),[27] followed by Samoa (59.8%) and Tonga (55.8%) (Figure 5.5). In 2017, 57.3% of migrants from the Pacific DMCs went to Australia and New Zealand. Most Central Asian migrants move to the Russian Federation (63.3%). As expected, the ratios for the world's most populous countries with the largest absolute number of migrants remain very low—India (1.3%) and the PRC (0.7%).

Figure 5.4: Top 10 Sources of Migrants, 2017—Asia (million)

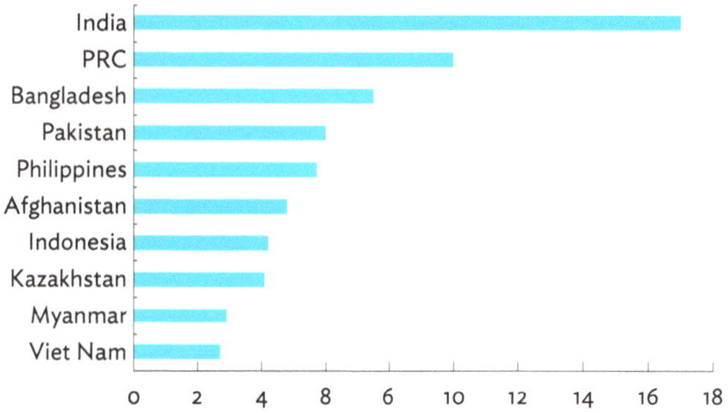

PRC = People's Republic of China.

Source: ADB calculations using data from United Nations. Department of Economic and Social Affairs, Population Division. International Migrant Stock: The 2017 Revision. http://www.un.org/en/development/desa/population/migration/data/estimates2/estimates17.shtml (accessed May 2018).

Figure 5.3: Migration to and from Asia, by Region (million)

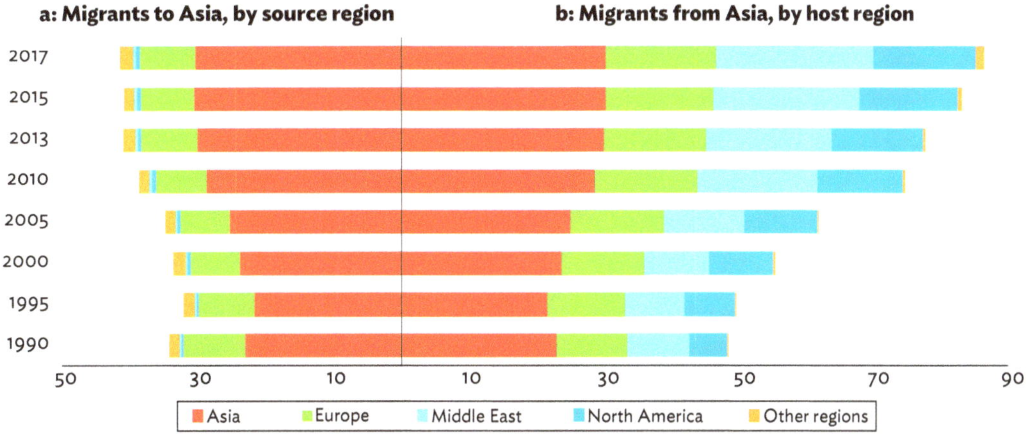

Source: ADB calculations using data from United Nations. Department of Economic and Social Affairs, Population Division. International Migrant Stock: The 2017 Revision. http://www.un.org/en/development/desa/population/migration/data/estimates2/estimates17.shtml (accessed May 2018).

[27] The reason for the high ratio is because Cook Islands nationals are concurrently citizens of New Zealand and they are able to live and work in New Zealand without restriction.

Figure 5.5: Top 10 Ratios of Outward Migrants to Population, 2017—Asia (%)

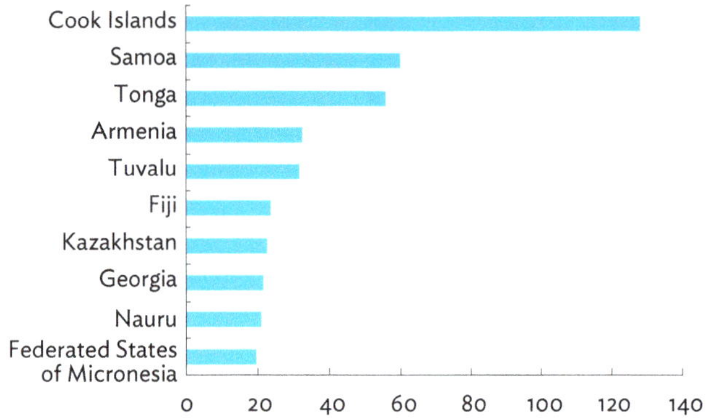

Sources: ADB calculations using data from United Nations. Department of Economic and Social Affairs, Population Division. International Migrant Stock: The 2017 Revision. http://www.un.org/en/development/desa/population/migration/data/estimates2/estimates17.shtml (accessed May 2018); and United Nations, Department of Economic and Social Affairs, Population Division (2017).

Intraregional migration remains important, but it has fallen slightly in recent years.

Intraregional migration remains an important part of international migration from the region, with 33.4% of migrants from Asia staying within the region (Figure 5.6); and 71.3% of all international migrants to Asia originating from within the region. Major host economies for intraregional migration include India (5.0 million); Thailand (3.5 million); Pakistan (3.4 million); Australia (3.2 million); and Hong Kong, China (2.7 million).

Figure 5.6: International Migration Trend—Asia

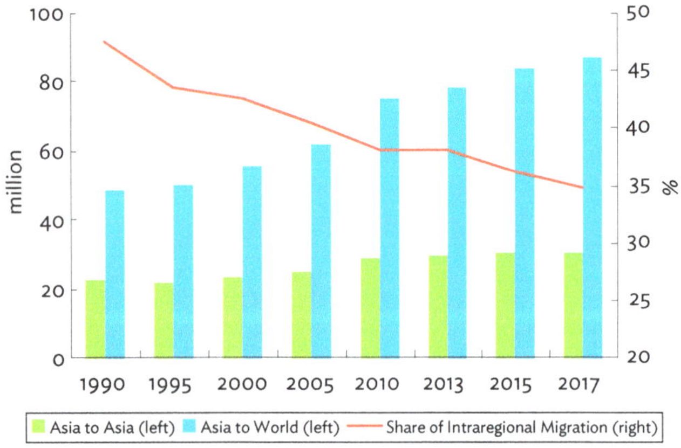

Note: Share of intraregional migration is estimated as percentage of Asia's intraregional migrants (Asia to Asia) to total migrants from Asia (Asia to World).
Source: ADB calculations using data from United Nations. Department of Economic and Social Affairs, Population Division. International Migrant Stock: The 2017 Revision. http://www.un.org/en/development/desa/population/migration/data/estimates2/estimates17.shtml (accessed May 2018).

Intraregional migrants to India largely come from neighboring countries such as Bangladesh (3.1 million), Pakistan (1.1 million), and Nepal (0.5 million). Similarly, Thailand hosted migrants from Myanmar (1.8 million), the Lao People's Democratic Republic (0.9 million), and Cambodia (0.7 million); and to Pakistan largely from either India (1.9 million) or Afghanistan (1.5 million). On the other hand, major sources of intraregional migrants are the PRC (5.2 million), Bangladesh (3.7 million), India (3.3 million), Myanmar (2.4 million), and Indonesia (1.8 million). The proportion of intraregional migration to total outward migration declined over the years—from 47.5% in 1990 to 34.7% in 2017. The absolute number of Asian migrants staying within the region during 2015–2017 also dropped slightly—from 30.24 million to 30.18 million.

By subregion, some 90.4% of Central Asian migrants move outside the region, mostly to the Russian Federation (Figure 5.7). Intraregional migration remains high in the Pacific DMCs (60.7% in 2010, 61.9% in 2017). The share of South Asian migrants residing outside the subregion increased from 64.5% (2010) to 70.6% (2017), primarily due to increased migration to the Middle East.

Figure 5.7: Migration from Asia, by Subregions
(% of total outward migrants)

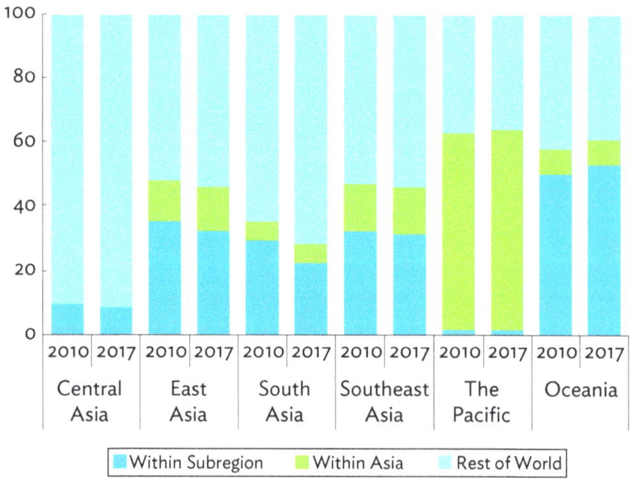

Notes:
(i) Within subregion refers to migrants from subregion *i* as a percentage of migrants from subregion *i* to world.
(ii) Within Asia refers to the migrants from subregion *i* to other Asian subregions as a percentage of migrants from subregion *i* to world.
(iii) Rest of the World refers to migrants from subregion *i* to the rest of the world as a percentage of migrants from subregion *i* to world.
Source: ADB calculations using data from United Nations, Department of Economic and Social Affairs, Population Division. International Migrant Stock: The 2017 Revision. http://www.un.org/en/development/desa/population/migration/data/estimates2/estimates17.shtml (accessed May 2018).

Figure 5.8: International Migrants, Working Age Migrants, and Migrant Workers, 2013

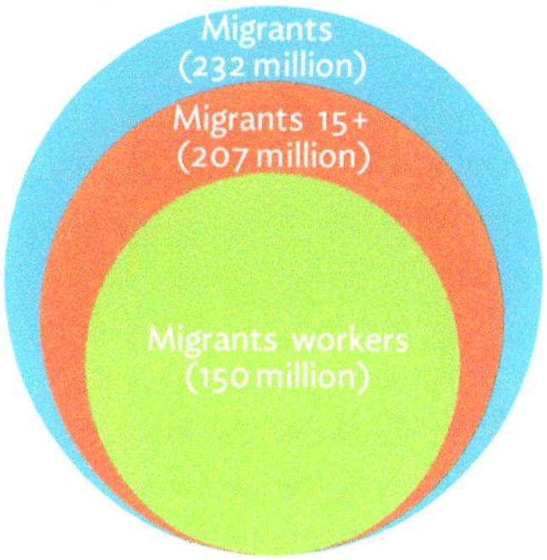

Source: International Labour Organization (2015).

Like Oceania, both East Asia and Southeast Asia retain relatively high mobility within their subregions. Overall, intra-subregional migration declined slightly (except between Australia and New Zealand—50.6% in 2010 to 53.8% in 2017).

Cross-border labor demand drives the movement of people in Asia.

One key driver of the international migration is labor demand, as workers relocate to where they can find higher wages, better benefits, and greater career opportunities.[28] About 89.2% of international migrants globally are over the age of 15, with 72.7% of the migrants[29] entering labor markets in host countries (Figure 5.8).[30] Those proportions are likely higher in Asia as most migration is temporary worker migration to the Middle East and Southeast Asia. Permanent settlement or family reunification that includes nonworking international migrants is highly restricted in these areas.

Departure trends for temporary overseas employment vary among major source countries.

National statistics on annual worker movements give a better sense of the trends in cross-border labor mobility than international migrant stock data (Table 5.1).

Recent trends on the outward migration of workers vary substantially across countries. There have been large increases in Bangladesh, the Philippines, and Viet Nam; while India, Indonesia, Pakistan, Thailand, and Sri Lanka have seen the outflow of workers moderating or declining in recent years. One reason is that several countries actively discourage unskilled workers in vulnerable jobs like manual labor or domestic work.

Also, many source countries have seen sustained growth in job creation. But the rapid expansion in working age population in many of these countries continues to leave substantial workforce supply for overseas jobs. For example, the working age population in Bangladesh and the Philippines has grown more than 7.7% over the past 5 years.

Skilled Asian workers tend to migrate to advanced economies.

The Organisation for Economic Co-operation and Development countries remain the prime destination for skilled workers coming from Asia. The majority move to the US. Since 1997, applicants from Asia received the most H1B visas—a nonimmigrant US visa for professional workers with a bachelor's or master's degree for specified occupations (Figure 5.9). The share of H1B visas granted to applicants from Asia rose from 84.5% in 2013–2015 to at least 90.2% in 2017. The overwhelming majority come from India (about 79.9%) and the PRC (14.2%).

Recently, Japan—with a relatively tiny share of international migrants compared with other advanced economies—has been expanding the list of job categories open to foreign workers (Figure 5.10). Jobs include skilled and unskilled work in nursing and caregiving, household services, and construction. The number of migrant workers in Japan grew an average 13.5% from 2013 to 2017. International migrants granted special and technical skill visas were up by 79.8% (from

[28] Aside from the movement of workers, forced migration also drives the movement of people in the region. For example, the number of Rohingya refugees in Bangladesh rose fourfold between 2015 and 2017—from 231,958 to 932,216—based on United Nations High Commissioner for Refugees (UNHCR) statistics. The UNHCR defines refugees as individuals recognized under the 1951 Convention relating to the Status of Refugees, its 1967 Protocol, the 1969 Organization of African Unity Convention Governing the Specific Aspects of Refugee Problems in Africa, those recognized in accordance with the UNHCR Statute, individuals granted complementary forms of protection, or those enjoying temporary protection. Since 2007, the refugee population also includes people in a refugee-like situation.

[29] "Migrant worker" refers to "all international migrants who are currently employed or are unemployed and seeking employment in their present country of residence" (ILO 2015).

[30] See footnote 25 for the definition of international migrants and other factors driving migration.

Table 5.1: Outflow of Overseas Workers—Selected Asian Countries ('000, growth rate in parentheses)

Economy	2011	2012	2013	2014	2015	2016	2017
Bangladesh	568 (45%)	608 (7%)	409 (-33%)	426 (4%)	556 (31%)	758 (36%)	1,009 (33%)
India	637 (-1%)	746 (17%)	820 (10%)	805 (-2%)	784 (-3%)	521 (-34%)	391 (-25%)
Indonesia	587 (2%)	495 (-16%)	512 (3%)	430 (-16%)	276 (36%)	235 (15%)	262 (12%)
Nepal	355 (21%)	385 (8%)	451 (17%)	520 (15%)	499 (-4%)	404 (-19%)	383 (-5%)
Pakistan	457 (26%)	369 (-19%)	623 (69%)	752 (21%)	947 (26%)	839 (-11%)	466 (-45%)
Philippines	1,319 (17%)	1,435 (9%)	1,469 (2%)	1,431 (-3%)	1,438 (0.5%)	1,670 (16%)	–
Sri Lanka	263 (-2%)	282 (7%)	293 (4%)	301 (3%)	263 (-12%)	243 (-8%)	212 (-13%)
Tajikistan	–	–	–	671	553 (-18%)	517 (-6%)	488 (-6%)
Thailand	148 (3%)	134 (-9%)	131 (-2%)	120 (-8%)	117 (-3%)	114 (-3%)	–
Viet Nam	88 (2%)	80 (-9%)	88 (10%)	107 (22%)	116 (8%)	126 (9%)	135 (7%)

– = not available, ILO = International Labour Organization.

Note: Figures include skilled and unskilled workers requesting clearance for overseas employment from source countries, except India, which only records unskilled migrants.

Sources: Agency on Statistics Under the President of the Republic of Tajikistan. https://www.stat.tj/tj/database-socio-demographic-sector (accessed June 2018); Bangladesh Bank. https://bb.org.bd (accessed June 2018); Bureau of Manpower, Employment, and Training. bmet.org.bd (accessed June 2018); Government of Nepal, Ministry of Labour and Employment (2018); ILO. ILOSTAT. www.ilo.org/ilostat (accessed June 2018); Pakistan Bureau of Emigration and Overseas Employment. https://beoe.gov.pk (accessed June 2018); Philippine Overseas Employment Administration. www.poea.gov.ph; Sri Lanka Bureau of Foreign Employment (2016 and 2017); and Wadhawan (2018).

Figure 5.9: Number of United States H1B Visas Granted, by Region of Migrant Origin ('000)

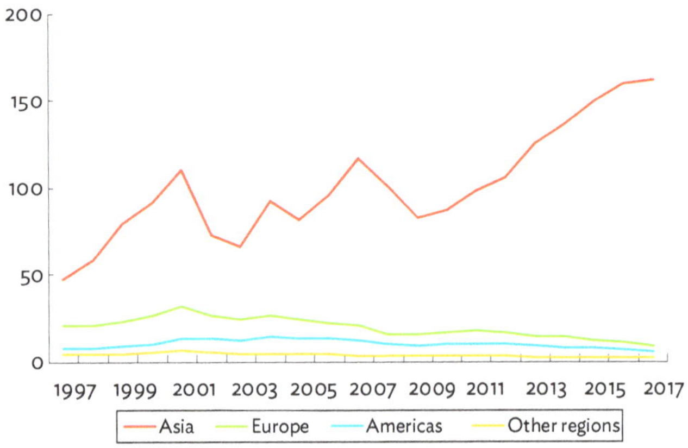

Notes: H1B is a nonimmigrant United States visa for professional workers with a bachelor's or master's degree for specified occupations. It is valid for 3 years and can be extended to a maximum 6 years. Americas include North America and Latin America and the Caribbean.

Source: United States Department of State, Bureau of Consular Affairs. Visa Statistics. https://travel.state.gov/content/travel/en/legal/visa-law0/visa-statistics.html (accessed July 2018).

Figure 5.10: Number of Foreign Workers in Japan, by Visa Type (million)

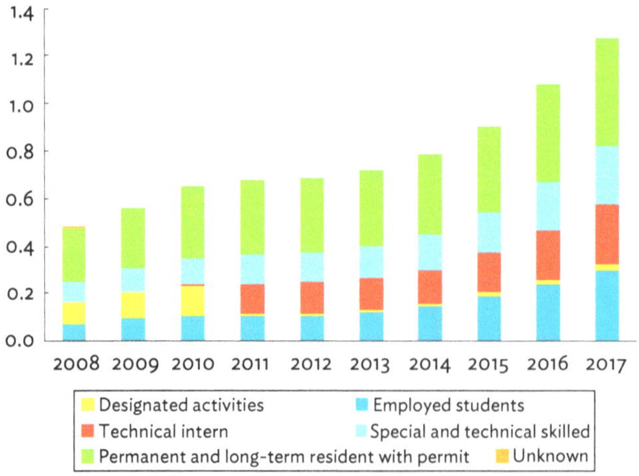

Source: Japan Ministry of Health, Labour, and Welfare. 2018. Status of Notification of "Employment Status of Foreigners" Summary (as of the end of October, Heisei 30). https://www.mhlw.go.jp/file/04-Houdouhappyou-11655000-Shokugyouanteikyokuhakenyukiroudoutaisakubu-Gaikokujinkoyoutaisakuka/44789gr5.pdf

132,571 to 238,412) over the same period. Migrants from Asia accounted for 69.2% of foreign workforce in 2017. The demand for foreign workers will rise due to Japan's aging population. The increase in the support ratio (share of seniors aged 65+ to working age population) is a major reason for the increase in foreign migrant stock from and to Asia (Box 5.1).

Policies in major host countries may be changing, reshaping the pattern of the movement of workers.

Many long-term projections suggest international migration to and from Asia will continue to increase, with many countries continuing to see a growing labor force and others increasing demand for migrant labor

Box 5.1: Demographic Changes and Migration

Using the United Nations' bilateral international migration matrix from 1990 to 2015, the determinants of international movement of people from developing Asia to 30 major host economies were examined.[a] Essential demographic, economic, geographic, and other dyadic variables that push and pull the movement of international migrants from Asia were identified, consistent with existing migration literature (Kim and Cohen 2010, World Bank 2018, and Zaiceva and Zimmermann 2014).

Demographic variables in the empirical exercise included (i) working-age population of origin and destination economies, and (ii) the old-age dependency ratio of the destination economies. Economic variables are (iii) the per capita gross domestic product (GDP) of the origin economies, and (iv) the income gap between host and source economies. Geographic and other dyadic variables include (v) distances between capitals, (vi) contiguity, (vii) official languages, and (viii) colonial relationships.

Our ordinary least squares and fixed-effects estimates suggest that a unit increase in old-age dependency ratio at the host country on average is associated with a 5% increase in migrants in any given bilateral number of international migrants from developing Asia to major host economies. Also, the increase in income level of source country of migrants encourages migration, because it enables families to cover migration costs. Other economic and dyadic variables also contribute to migration. Outward migration from developing Asia most likely gains momentum as the region continues to see incomes rise, while many host countries undergo accelerating population aging.

Drivers of International Migration from Developing Asia
Dependent variable: Log(Bilateral International Migrant Stock)

	OLS	FE
Demographic factors		
Working-age population of origin economies	0.189	0.142
	(0.304)	(0.156)
Working-age population of host economies	1.010***	0.887***
	(0.162)	(0.076)
Old-age dependency ratio of host economies	0.050***	0.051***
	(0.008)	(0.005)
Economic factors		
GDP per capita of origin economies	0.408*	0.256***
	(0.225)	(0.093)
Income gap relative to host economies	0.416**	0.150**
	(0.170)	(0.067)
Geographic and other dyadic variables	**Yes**	**No**
Constant	-0.141	-11.209***
	(5.337)	(3.277)
Number of observations	2,153	2,153
R-squared	0.656	0.502
Number of bilateral routes	–	413

*** = significant at 1%, ** = significant at 5%, * = significant at 10%. Robust standard errors in parentheses.
– = not applicable, FE = fixed effects, GDP = gross domestic product, OLS = ordinary least squares.
Sources: Authors' calculations using data from Institute for Research on the International Economy. http://www.cepii.fr/CEPII/en/cepii/cepii.asp (accessed May 2018); United Nations, Department of Economic and Social Affairs, Population Division (2017); United Nations. Department of Economic and Social Affairs, Population Division. International Migrant Stock: The 2017 Revision. http://www.un.org/en/development/desa/population/migration/data/estimates2/estimates17.shtml (accessed May 2018); and World Bank. World Development Indicators. https://data.worldbank.org/ (accessed May 2018).

[a] The 30 host economies are Armenia; Australia; Bahrain; Canada; France; Germany; Greece; Hong Kong, China; Israel; Italy; Japan; Kuwait; Malaysia; Nepal; the Netherlands; New Zealand; Oman; the People's Republic of China; Qatar; the Republic of Korea; the Russian Federation; Saudi Arabia; Singapore; Spain; Sweden; Thailand; Ukraine; United Arab Emirates; the United Kingdom; and the United States.

Source: Kikkawa and Park (forthcoming).

Figure 5.11: Temporary Skilled Migrant Visas Approved, by Source Region ('000)

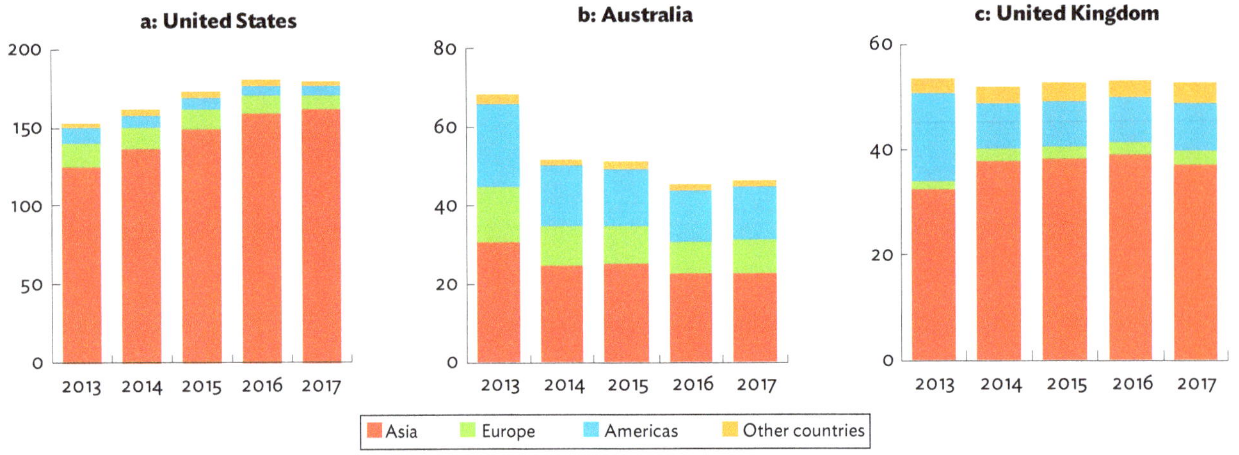

Note: Americas include North America and Latin America and the Caribbean.
Sources: United States Department of State, Bureau of Consular Affairs. Visa Statistics. https://travel.state.gov/content/travel/en/legal/visa-law0/visa-statistics.html; Australian Government, Department of Immigration and Border Protection. Work in Australia–Statistics. https://www.homeaffairs.gov.au/about/reports-publications/research-statistics/statistics/work-in-australia; and United Kingdom Immigration Statistics. https://www.gov.uk/government/publications/immigration-statistics-year-ending-march-2018/list-of-tables (all accessed July 2018).

(Walmsley, Aguilar, and Ahmed 2017). However, policy uncertainties in some major host countries may impact these assessments. The US, for example, has vowed to tighten and reform existing immigration and temporary migration schemes. In February, the US Citizenship Immigration Services agency released a policy memorandum requiring more information about grantees of H1B visas, to ensure that skill shortages truly exist (O'Brien 2018). US approvals in 2017 fell slightly (Figure 5.11a).

Australia is another major host country for migrants from the region. Close to half of skilled workers granted temporary visas come from Asia (Figure 5.11b)—the top three source countries are India, the Philippines, and the PRC.[31] In April 2018, the short-term work visa for skilled workers (457 visa) was abolished, replaced by a temporary skill shortage (TSS) visa—which has a 2-year cap on skilled workers that qualify under its short-term skilled occupation list (Australian Government, Department of Immigration and Border Protection). The number of visa approvals has dropped substantially over the past few years.

The United Kingdom's (UK) "Brexit" from the European Union (EU)—scheduled for March 2019—has reportedly resulted in an exodus of EU professionals from the country. While its intake of skilled migrants from Asia declined 4.9%, the overall drop was 1.4% from 2016 to 2017 (Figure 5.11c).

While some countries have reservations against increasing migrant arrivals, Canada—with its Express Entry program—has been taking advantage of the delays in issuance of green cards in the US. In 2017, it attracted 86,022 top-ranked or highly skilled migrant candidates, more than double 33,782 in 2016 (Kably 2018). The aging workforce in East Asia has also led to a rise in the migrant population. The interplay among immigration policies worldwide may lead to a directional shift in skilled migration flows in the coming years.

Overall, long-term trends show skilled workers from Asia will continue to migrate to developed economies in North America, Europe, and East Asia. Amid policy changes to enhance control over immigration and border issues, creating and implementing labor mobility frameworks and human capital development mechanisms are increasingly important—and are regarded as promising forms of regional cooperation in Asia. In particular, cross-border occupational skill mobility remains limited, with recognition mostly relying

[31] Data are specific to visa subclass 457 primary applicants of the Tier 1 category and intra-company transfers and sportspersons in the Tier 2 category. Primary applicants are defined by the Australian government as people who must satisfy primary criteria under Migration Regulations (Australian Government, Department of Immigration and Border Protection. Work in Australia–Statistics. https://www.homeaffairs.gov.au/about/reports-publications/research-statistics/statistics/work-in-australia [accessed July 2018]).

on host country schemes—except for skills standardized through international or regional agreements. For example, multilateral mutual recognition agreements such as the ASEAN's eight pilot agreements hold much potential to increase skilled labor mobility across borders.

Remittances

Remittances to Asia are growing once again.

After a slight drop in 2016, a record $272.5 billion in remittances were channeled to Asia in 2017, up 6.3% (Figure 5.12).[32] Remittances globally increased by some $39.9 billion to $613.5 billion.

Remittances are an important and stable source of financial inflow to many developing economies in Asia. They are an important source of foreign exchange, especially for economies with limited natural resources. As direct transfers, remittances from overseas workers boost beneficiaries' consumption and savings. And as person-to-person flows, they can better target recipient household needs, raising living standards and family welfare.

Figure 5.12: Financial Flows to Asia, by Type ($ billion)

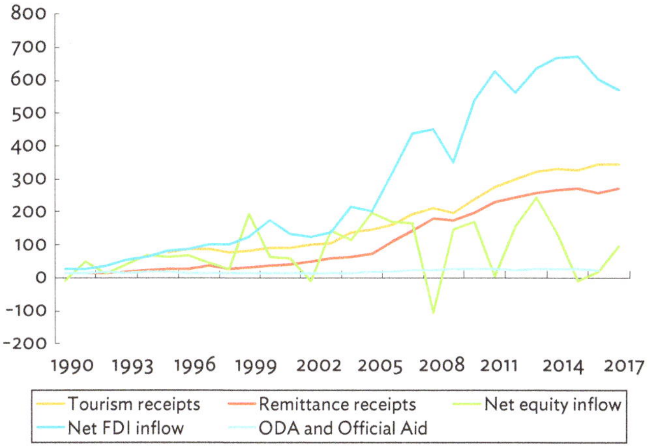

FDI = foreign direct investment, ODA = official development assistance.
Sources: ADB calculations using data from World Bank. World Development Indicators. https://data.worldbank.org/ (accessed September 2018); and Global Knowledge Partnership on Migration and Development (KNOMAD). http://www.knomad.org/data/remittances (accessed May 2018).

Remittances to Asia rose from all regions worldwide.

Remittance inflows increased from all global sources (after falling in 2016) with intraregional transfers growing by $3.7 billion (5.29%) to $75.4 billion (Figure 5.13). Inflows from the Middle East increased $4.2 billion (up 5.2%) from the $80.0 billion remitted in 2016. Remittances from North America reached $69.1 billion (up 7.1%). Inflows from Europe rose to $38.3 billion (up 9.4%).

Figure 5.13: Remittance Inflows to Asia, by Source
(% change, year-on-year)

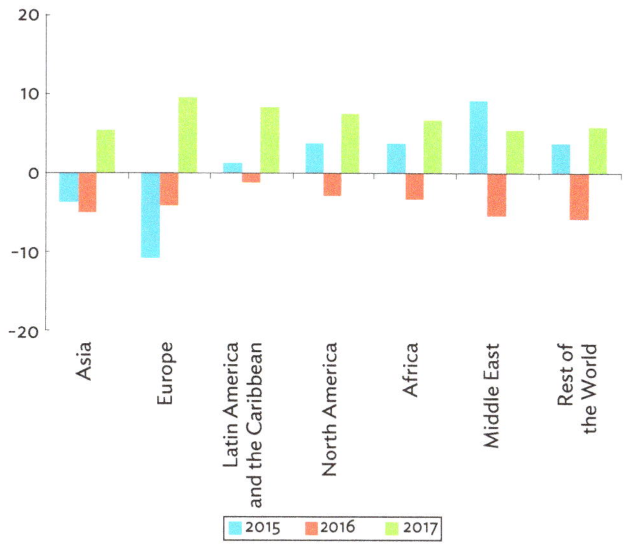

Source: ADB calculations using data from Global Knowledge Partnership on Migration and Development (KNOMAD). http://www.knomad.org/data/remittances (accessed May 2018).

Similarly, remittance flows to all subregions grew in 2017, except for Oceania (Figure 5.14). Remittances to the Pacific grew by 45.6% to $580.4 million, continuing a volatile trend of alternately increasing then decreasing, often dramatically—there were rapid increases to Samoa (up by 272.8%), Tonga (81.9%), and Fiji (6.6%). Remittances to Southeast Asia,

[32] The World Bank defines personal remittances as the sum of personal transfers and compensation of employees. Personal transfers include all current transfers in cash or in kind between resident and nonresident individuals, independent of the source of income of the sender (and regardless of whether the sender receives income from labor, entrepreneurial or property income, social benefits, and any other types of transfers, or disposed assets) and the relationship between the households (regardless of whether they are related or unrelated individuals). Compensation of employees refers to the income of border, seasonal, and other short-term workers who are employed in an economy where they are not resident and of residents employed by nonresident entities.

Figure 5.14: Remittance Inflows to Asia Subregions
(% change, year-on-year)

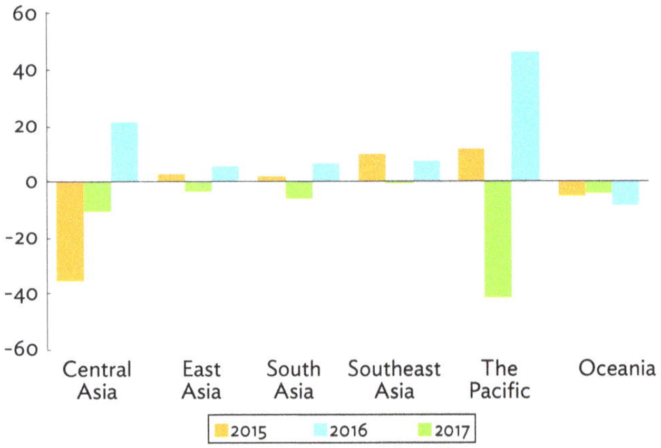

Source: ADB calculations using data from Global Knowledge Partnership on Migration and Development (KNOMAD). http://www.knomad.org/data/remittances (accessed May 2018).

Figure 5.15: Top 10 Remittance Recipients in Asia
($ billion)

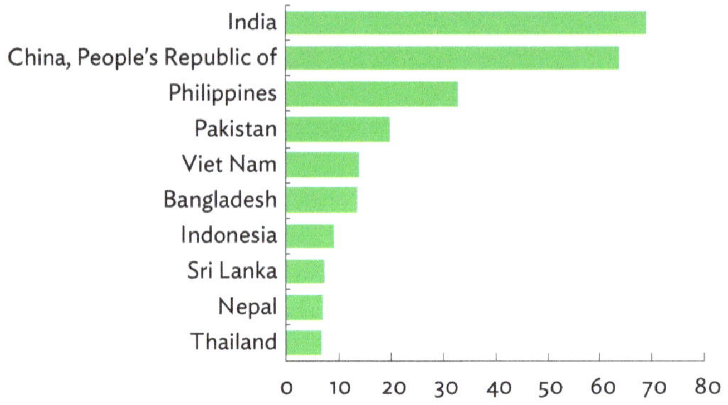

Source: ADB calculations using data from Global Knowledge Partnership on Migration and Development (KNOMAD). http://www.knomad.org/data/remittances (accessed May 2018).

South Asia, and East Asia also recovered, climbing 5.8% to $257.3 billion in total. In Oceania, remittance inflows declined for a fourth consecutive year—down $110.3 million in Australia and $122.7 million in New Zealand. Remittances to Australia were only 78.7% of its peak 2013 level, while those to New Zealand fell for a third consecutive year, but by a much higher 29.2%. The currencies of both countries fluctuated against those of the US and the UK—two major host countries of migrants from Oceania.[33] The high cost of remittance services in the subregion and impact of de-risking on Oceania-based correspondent banks and formal money transfer channels may have driven remitters to use available informal back channels instead.[34]

Remittances are a key income source for several countries.

South Asia, East Asia, and Southeast Asia are the major remittance recipients in Asia. They received, on average, 94.5% of the region's total remittance inflows in 2017—and 91.1% since 2010. In 2017, the top three remittance recipients—India, the PRC, and the Philippines—accounted for roughly 60.8% ($165.6 billion) of all remittances to Asia and 21.7% of remittances globally ($613.5 billion) (Figure 5.15).

Some countries receiving smaller amounts nonetheless depend more on remittances as an income source. For example, remittance inflows are equivalent to some 33.0% of gross domestic product (GDP) in the Kyrgyz Republic, Tonga, and Tajikistan. Remittances to some South Asian countries are also significant components of national income. Nepal's remittances equal 28.4% of GDP in 2017 (Figure 5.16a). Bangladesh, Pakistan, and Sri Lanka relied on remittances for at least proportional to an annual average of 5.0% of GDP since 2010; this has been the trend for these South Asian economies. In Southeast Asia, remittance inflow to the Philippines was equivalent to 10.5% of GDP; in Viet Nam, it was 6.3%. In per capita terms, remittances to Tonga, the Marshall Islands, and Armenia are significant (Figure 5.16b). In the Pacific, remittances not only contribute to output and growth (Brown and Mineshima 2007), but also promote financial development.

The Middle East remains the top source for remittances to Asia.

Around 30.9% of remittances in 2017 came from the Middle East ($84.2 billion), while 27.7% was sourced intraregionally (Figure 5.17). Remittance patterns are fairly proportional to their share of migrants, though they are larger for the Middle East and North America (Figure 5.18). A large proportion of Middle East-bound

33 In 2017, the Australian dollar depreciated 7.8% against the US dollar and appreciated 1.7% against the pound sterling, while the New Zealand dollar depreciated 2.9% against the US dollar and appreciated 6.4% against the British pound.

34 International Finance Corporation (2017) found that as de-risking reduces correspondent banking relationships, it also has a negative effect on money transfer organizations. Fluctuation in the remittance inflow may also be due to change in how remittances are measured (Clemens and McKenzie 2018).

Figure 5.16: Top 10 Remittance-Recipient Economies in Asia, 2017

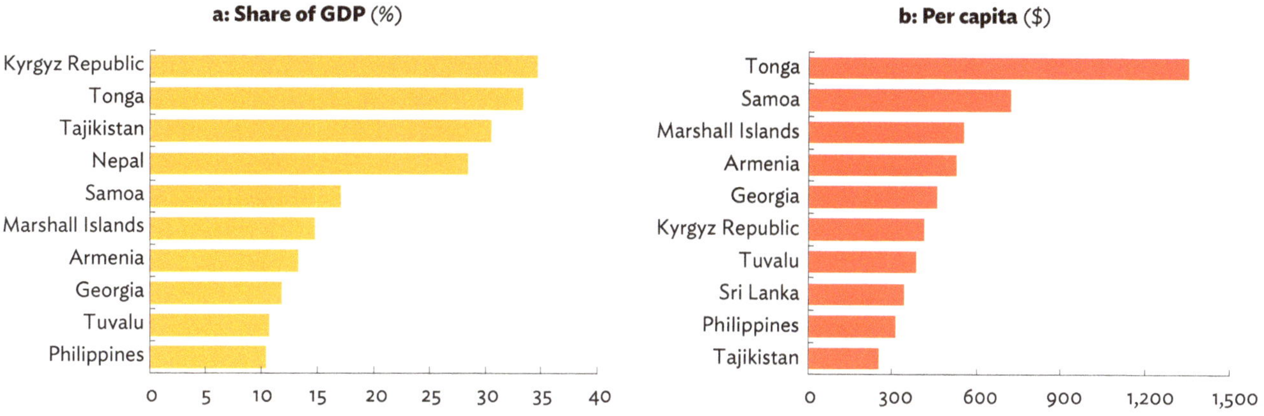

GDP = gross domestic product.
Note: Some countries which recorded substantial remittance inflow (as share of GDP and in per capita terms) in the past years have not made 2017 figures available at the time of publication.
Source: ADB calculations using data from Global Knowledge Partnership on Migration and Development (KNOMAD). http://www.knomad.org/data/remittances (accessed May 2018).

Figure 5.17: Remittance Inflows to Asia, by Source, 2017 (% share)

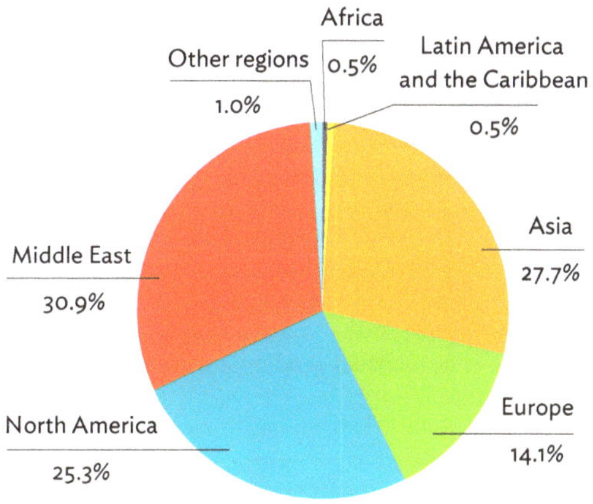

Source: ADB calculations using data from Global Knowledge Partnership on Migration and Development (KNOMAD). http://www.knomad.org/data/remittances (accessed May 2018).

Figure 5.18: Migration from Asia, by Host Region, 2017 (% share)

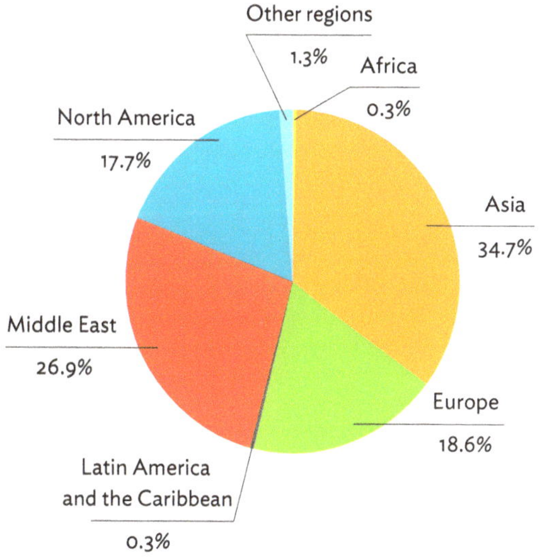

Source: ADB calculations using data from United Nations. Department of Economic and Social Affairs, Population Division. International Migrant Stock: The 2017 Revision. http://www.un.org/en/development/desa/population/migration/data/estimates2/estimates17.shtml (accessed May 2018).

migrants are temporary workers who send most of their earnings back to their immediate families. The relatively larger remittances from North America mirror the large share of skilled migrants earning higher wages, even if they send money to non-immediate family members.

Subregional data show 17.3% of remittances were intra-subregional (Figure 5.19). In the Pacific, Asia was the source of 59.3% of inward remittances. Intra-subregional remittances declined from 2012 to 2017 across all subregions, except for the Pacific. For Central Asia, remittances from outside Asia increased by 28.3%, with most from the Russian Federation. Oceania nearly doubled its remittance shares from within Asia, from 8.6% in 2012 to 17.2% in 2017, while Southeast Asia increased its intraregional remittances by 4.1% over the period.

Figure 5.19: Subregional Remittance Sources in Asia (%)

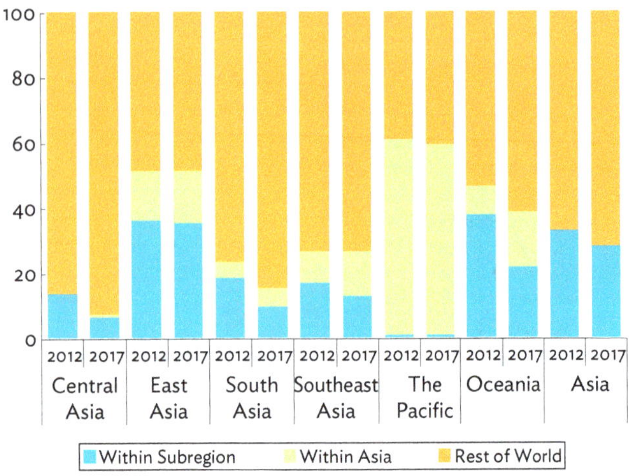

Notes:
(i) Within Subregion refers to remittances within subregion *i* as a percentage of remittances from the world to subregion *i*.
(ii) Within Asia refers to the remittances from other Asian subregions to subregion *i* as a percentage of remittances from the world to subregion *i*.
(iii) Rest of the World refers to the remittances from non-Asian economies to subregion *i* as a percentage of remittances from the world to subregion *i*.
Source: ADB calculations using data from Global Knowledge Partnership on Migration and Development (KNOMAD). http://www.knomad.org/data/remittances (accessed May 2018).

Remittances are projected to grow given the steady economic growth outlook for most host countries.

The Global Knowledge Partnership on Migration and Development (2018) estimates global remittances in 2018 will grow by 4.6%, reaching $641.2 billion. Inflows to Asia should expand by 3.8% to $282.9 billion. However, increasingly restrictive immigration policies in some major host countries pose short- to medium-term downside risks. Nonetheless, demographic changes are expected to drive further migration from countries with growing working-age populations to countries with rapidly aging populations, creating new sources of remittance inflows in the long term.

International Tourism Receipts and the Movement of Tourists

International tourism receipts in Asia grew by 5.3% to a record high $346.0 billion in 2016. Tourism is a main source of income for many Pacific DMCs and Southeast Asian countries.

Global tourism continues to expand and is a key driver of economic development for many countries in the region. International tourism receipts to Asia reached $346.0 billion in 2016, about 24.8% of the global total (Figure 5.20).[35] The two subregions with the largest share of the region's tourism dollars were East Asia (39.7%) and Southeast Asia (35.5%) (Table 5.2). They also accounted for the largest shares of international arrivals. South Asia's tourism receipts continue to rise—tourism receipts increased to $32.3 billion (9.3% of total Asia) in 2016, well above the $5.1 billion (5.7%) in 2000.

By value, Thailand; the PRC; and Hong Kong, China are among the top recipients (Figure 5.21a). Thailand's

Figure 5.20: International Tourism Receipts, by Major Region, 2016

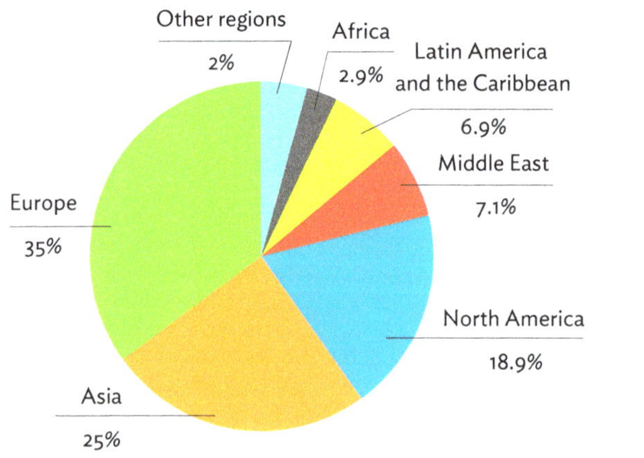

Sources: ADB calculations using data from World Bank. World Development Indicators. https://data.worldbank.org/ (accessed September 2018); and United Nations World Tourism Organization (2018b).

35 The United Nations World Tourism Organization defines international tourism receipts as "expenditures by international inbound visitors, including payments to national carriers for international transport, which may include any other prepayment made for goods or services received in the destination country. They also may include receipts from same-day visitors, except when these are important enough to justify separate classification."

Table 5.2: Tourism Arrivals and Receipts in Asia in 2016, by Subregion

Subregion	International Tourism Receipts ($ million)	Share of Total Tourism Receipts to Asia (%)	International Arrivals (million)	Share of International Tourist Arrivals to Asia (%)
Central Asia	8,556	2.5	19.3	5.1
East Asia	137,267	39.7	220.0	58.1
Oceania	43,893	12.7	11.6	3.1
South Asia	32,306	9.3	12.9	3.4
Southeast Asia	122,766	35.5	113.1	29.9
The Pacific	1,210	0.3	1.6	0.4
Total	**345,998**	**100.0**	**378.5**	**100.0**

Source: ADB calculations using data from World Bank. World Development Indicators. https://data.worldbank.org/ (accessed September 2018); and United Nations World Tourism Organization. Tourism Satellite Accounts. http://statistics.unwto.org (accessed August 2018).

Figure 5.21: Top 10 Recipients of Tourism Receipts (2016)

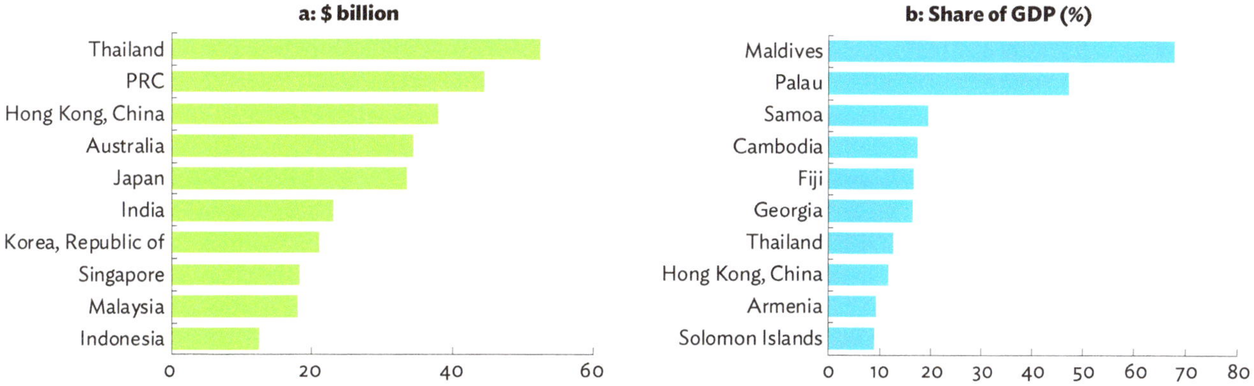

GDP = gross domestic product, PRC = People's Republic of China.

Note: Some economies which recorded substantial tourist receipts (as share of GDP and in per capita terms) in the past years have not made 2016 figures available at the time of publication.

Source: ADB calculations using data from World Bank. World Development Indicators. https://data.worldbank.org/ (accessed September 2018); and United Nations World Tourism Organization (2018b).

"Amazing Thailand" and "Discover Thainess" tourism promotion campaigns successfully attracted new tourists during 2011–2016—with receipts growing at annual average rates of 14.8%. Singapore, which is placed 8th, ranked as the most globally competitive travel and tourism destination among Asian economies (World Economic Forum 2017)—earning $18.4 billion in 2016, up by 11.0% from 2015.[36] Tourism receipts are an essential source of income for several Pacific DMCs and Southeast Asian countries. Maldives tops the list with 68.0% of its GDP derived from tourism followed by Palau (47.3 %) (Figure 5.21b). Samoa earned 19.5% of GDP from tourism and Fiji 16.7%. Cambodia's tourism income was 17.5% of GDP in 2016 and Thailand 12.7%.

The number of international visitors traveling to Asia grew by 9.3% in 2016 to 378.5 million as intraregional tourism continues to expand; but a growing share of Asian tourists is heading to non-Asian destinations.

In 2016, there were 1.2 billion international tourists worldwide, up by 3.7 % from 2015. Arrivals to Asia reached 378.5 million, up by 9.3% over 2015 and well above world year-on-year growth. The share of global arrivals to Asia has grown from 25.6% in 2006 to 30.6% in 2016.

[36] According to the World Economic Forum's Travel and Tourism Competitiveness Report 2017, Singapore ranked 13th among 136 countries, keeping its ranking steady from 11th among 141 countries in 2015. Among the ASEAN economies, it ranked highest.

The growth of intraregional tourism has fueled the increase. Between 2012 and 2016, the number of intraregional Asian tourists grew from 235.0 million to 295.3 million (Figure 5.22). The brisk growth in Asia-bound travel underscores the preference of Asian tourists to travel within the region, thus providing fertile ground for greater regional cooperation in tourism—such as the visa policy harmonization initiative of the Association of Southeast Asian Nations (ASEAN) (Box 5.2). Also, over the past 5 years, Asians traveling outside the region increased by 18.6% (16.1 million) to 102.3 million.

The declining share of intraregional travel is a phenomenon not unique to Asia. In Europe, nearly 90.0% of tourists used to travel within the region, but the share has declined over the past decade to about 83.8% in 2016 (Figure 5.23). Demand for long-haul travel likely increased as tourist markets developed and destination choices diversified.

By destination, in 2000, the most popular for Asian tourists were the PRC (44.7%); Hong Kong, China (4.3%); Thailand (4.3%); Singapore (3.8%); and the Republic of Korea (2.6%) (Table 5.3). The US (3.8%) and the Russian Federation (4.2%) were the only two non-Asian countries among the top 10 destinations. In 2016, the PRC remained the most-visited intraregionally, drawing 108.2 million visitors. Southeast Asia's drive to attract tourists was evident, as Malaysia and Thailand were second and third most favorite destinations, with a total of 48.6 million visitors. Saudi Arabia was among the top five extraregional destinations in both years, largely due to increased flows of Haj pilgrims.

Between 2000 and 2016, the relative shares of the region's visitors to the Middle East and Latin America and the Caribbean doubled, while the share of other regions increased slightly (Figure 5.24). The shares of Europe and North America declined as the intraregional share of Asia rose marginally.

A positive outlook for global economic growth is good for the industry. Outbound tourism is expected to increase further with Asia's expanding middle-income households. The PRC will continue to be targeted as a source for tourists. In 2017, they spent $258.0 billion traveling, nearly twice the tourist expenditures from the US ($37.0 billion) and 37.2% above the combined outbound tourism spending of Germany ($84.0 billion),

Figure 5.22: Number of Asian Tourists, by Major Area of Destination

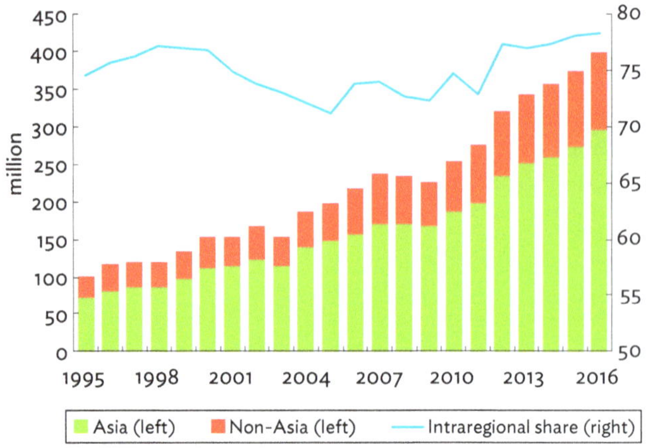

UNWTO = United Nations World Tourism Organization.
Note: 2016 data were calculated using arrivals information from UNWTO Tourism Satellite Accounts.
Source: ADB calculations using data from UNWTO. Tourism Satellite Accounts. http://statistics.unwto.org/ (accessed August 2018).

Figure 5.23: Number of European Tourists, by Major Area of Destination

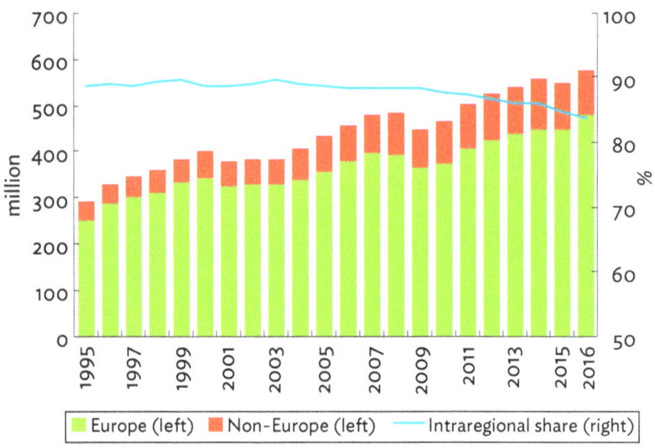

UNWTO = United Nations World Tourism Organization.
Note: 2016 data were calculated using arrivals information from UNWTO Tourism Satellite Accounts.
Source: ADB calculations using data from United Nations World Tourism Organization. Tourism Satellite Accounts. http://statistics.unwto.org/ (accessed August 2018).

the UK ($63.0 billion), and France ($41.0 billion) (UNWTO 2018a). Spending of tourists from the Republic of Korea rose by 9.0% in 2017 from 2016, while Australian spending increased 7.0%.

A growing number of tourists from the region are choosing destinations outside Asia, with Asian's demand for air travel getting a lot of push from the momentum created by the low-cost, low-price model of the budget airlines industry. For example, European travel routes are

Box 5.2: Promoting ASEAN as a Single Tourism Destination—the Unified Visa Policy Scheme

Since the Association of Southeast Asian Nations (ASEAN) Tourism Agreement was signed at the 2001 Brunei Darussalam Summit, the group has worked to promote easy, efficient, and competitive travel across ASEAN.[a] In 2006, the ASEAN Framework Agreement on Visa Exemption was signed, allowing ASEAN nationals visa-free travel to member countries (ASEAN Secretariat 2006). Its impact was rapid—the 11.6 million intra-ASEAN tourists in 2006 increased to 17.3 million in 2010 and doubled to 35.8 million by 2016. ASEAN tourism also has a strong intra-ASEAN component—on average, 43.0% of visitors to ASEAN in 2014–2016 were from other ASEAN countries. However, foreign tourist visa requirements remain restricted to varying degrees.[b] Visa policy is the most essential government policy affecting international tourism and reforms aimed at developing visa standards and procedures generate a policy effect which is closely linked to tourism development. The policy effect comes in the form of increased tourist arrivals—leading to increased tourism receipts and job creation. A study by the World Travel and Tourism Council (2014) estimates that, in the case of ASEAN, the policy effect will lead to an additional 6.0 million–10.0 million international arrivals and additional tourism receipts of around $7.0 billion–$10.0 billion. With arrivals targeted at 123 million by 2020 and 152 million by 2025, ASEAN aims to brand itself as a culturally diverse, cost-competitive 10-country single destination.[c] Thus, officials are working toward creating a unified ASEAN tourism visa—as envisaged in the ASEAN Tourism Strategic Plan (ATSP) 2011–2015 and ATSP 2016–2025—whereby a visa issued to a foreign national in one ASEAN member allows travel across all 10 ASEAN countries (ASEAN Secretariat 2015).

In 2016, Southeast Asia ranked highest in visa openness score by region (Glaesser 2016). ASEAN as a whole has a considerable pull on foreign tourists. But the degree to which each country attracts extra-ASEAN visitors varies substantially. Brunei Darussalam, the Lao People's Democratic Republic (Lao PDR), and Malaysia attract more intra-ASEAN visitors, while 80% of the visitors to the Philippines and Viet Nam come from outside the subregion (box figure).[d]

Annual Average International Tourism Arrivals in ASEAN, 2014–2016

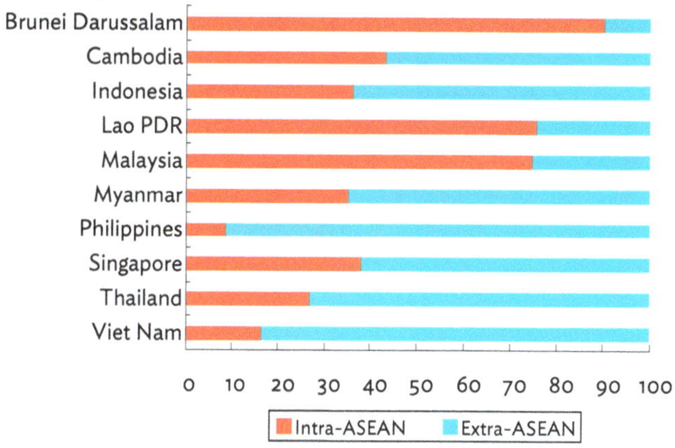

ASEAN = Association of Southeast Asian Nations, Lao PDR = Lao People's Democratic Republic.

Source: ADB calculations using data from ASEAN Secretariat. ASEANstats Data Portal. https://data.aseanstats.org/ (accessed June 2018).

Currently, the visa requirements for individual ASEAN countries vary significantly—which is why creating a unified ASEAN visa scheme is challenging (box table). Laws differ, while some members are more open to international tourism than others. Indonesia and the Philippines are the two strongest supporters of the single visa scheme (Remo 2014)—both are archipelagos and geographically apart from ASEAN's land borders. They are also more dependent on foreign tourism. Between 2014 and 2016, an average 63.8% of tourists to Indonesia came from outside ASEAN, while in the Philippines it reached 91.3%. To build greater

Continued on next page

[a] ASEAN cooperation in tourism was formalized in 1976 following the formation of the Sub-Committee on Tourism under the ASEAN Committee on Trade and Tourism (ASEAN Secretariat 2012).

[b] "Foreign tourist" or "extra-ASEAN tourist" refers to a tourist who is not an ASEAN national.

[c] Estimates by World Travel and Tourism Council.

[d] Philippine immigration bureau estimates indicate that *balikbayans*—Filipinos who have become citizens of other countries—comprised at least 20% of tourist flows in 2013 and 2014. This may also apply to countries with large migrant or diaspora populations abroad.

Box 2.2 ***continued***

Visa Requirements in ASEAN Economies

	Visa Requirements for Tourists from Non-ASEAN Asia, 2016 (number of economies)				
Economy	**VF**	**VOA**	**EV**	**SP**	**VR**
Brunei Darussalam	13	12	3	4	9
Cambodia	2	8	4	4	23
Indonesia	7	9	3	1	19
Lao PDR	2	6	4	1	22
Malaysia	14	13	3	4	7
Myanmar	1	6	2	1	24
Philippines	6	10	4	3	17
Singapore	15	14	2	4	6
Thailand	10	10	3	3	14
Viet Nam	2	7	4	1	21

ASEAN = Association of Southeast Asian Nations, EV = e-visa, Lao PDR = Lao People's Democratic Republic, SP = special permit, VF = visa free, VOA = visa on arrival, VR = visa required.
Source: ADB calculations using data from national sources.

openness, Indonesia now allows visa-free entry for 30 days to citizens from 169 countries, while in the Philippines, 157 economies are allowed visa-free stays up to 30 days. Viet Nam—also visited more by non-ASEAN tourists—grants visa-free entry to only two non-ASEAN Asian countries and requires visas from at least 21 Asian nations outside ASEAN. Given reciprocity in granting or requiring visas, Viet Nam nationals also face visa restrictions from more nations globally compared with its more visa-open ASEAN neighbors—175 nations require a visa from Viet Nam nationals compared with only 38 for Malaysians and 46 for Singaporeans.

While the unified visa scheme for ASEAN remains a challenge, cooperation between some ASEAN members to adopt mechanisms for a common tourist visa is moving forward. One is the Ayeyawady-Chao Phraya-Mekong Economic Cooperation Strategy (ACMECS), a joint development initiative between Cambodia, the Lao PDR, Myanmar, Thailand, and Viet Nam. Thus far, an ACMECS Single Visa is available for Cambodia or Thailand—tourists from 35 non-ASEAN countries can apply for a single visa at either embassy valid for visits to both countries.[e]

Another example is the Mekong Tourism Coordinating Office—established with funding from the governments of Cambodia, the Lao PDR, Myanmar, the PRC, Thailand, and Viet Nam—which aims to "develop and promote the Mekong Region as a single tourism destination" (Mekong Tourism Coordination Office 2017). Although the GMS Tourism Sector Strategy 2016–2025 includes exploring the feasibility of a single GMS tourist visa, it is currently focusing on expanding visa-on-arrival eligibility and making electronic visas more available.

[e] The 35 economies include Australia; Austria; Bahrain; Belgium; Canada; Denmark; Finland; France; Germany; Greece; Hong Kong, China; Iceland; India; Ireland; Israel; Italy; Japan; Luxembourg; the Netherlands; New Zealand; Norway; Oman; Portugal; the People's Republic of China; Qatar; the Republic of Korea; South Africa; Spain; Sweden; Switzerland; Turkey; United Arab Emirates; the United Kingdom; and the United States (ACMECS. http://www.mfa.go.th/acmecs/ [accessed June 2018]).

Source: ADB staff.

Table 5.3: Top Destinations of Tourists from Asia

a: 2016		b: 2000	
Economies	**Number in million** (share of total in parentheses)	**Economies**	**Number in million** (share of total in parentheses)
Within Asia		**Within Asia**	
China, People's Republic of	108.2 (27.2%)	China, People's Republic of	68.4 (44.7%)
Malaysia	24.6 (6.2%)	Hong Kong, China	6.5 (4.3%)
Thailand	24.0 (6.0%)	Thailand	6.5 (4.3%)
Hong Kong, China	23.1 (5.8%)	Singapore	5.8 (3.8%)
Japan	20.8 (5.2%)	Korea, Republic of	4.0 (2.6%)
Outside Asia		**Outside Asia**	
Macau, China	29.9 (7.5%)	Macau, China	9.0 (5.9%)
United States	13.1 (3.3%)	United States	8.3 (3.8%)
Russian Federation	8.9 (2.2%)	Russian Federation	6.4 (4.2%)
Saudi Arabia	5.9 (1.5%)	United Kingdom	2.4 (1.6%)
Turkey	4.3 (1.1%)	Saudi Arabia	1.7 (1.1%)

Sources: ADB calculations using data from United Nations World Tourism Organization (UNWTO). Tourism Satellite Accounts. http://statistics.unwto.org/ (accessed June 2018); and UNWTO (2018b).

Figure 5.24: Regional Destination of Tourists from Asia

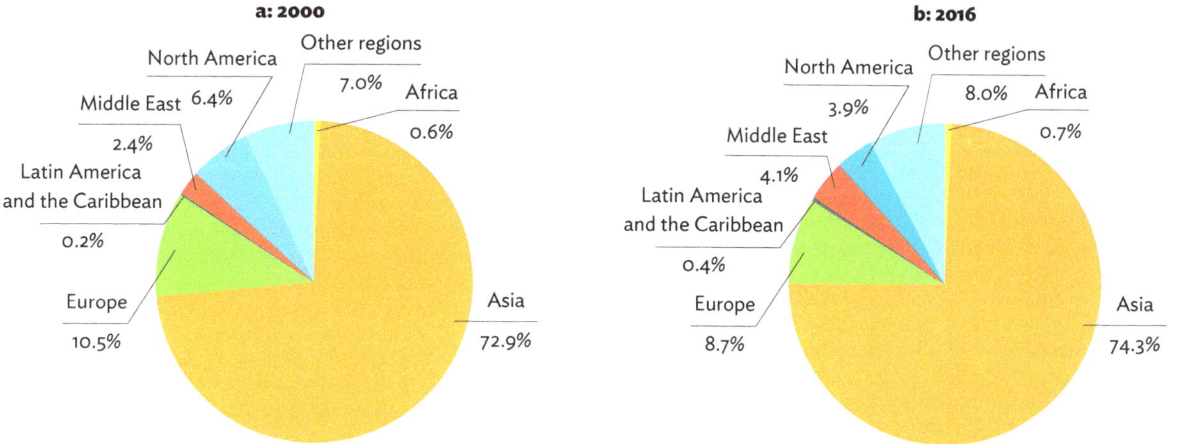

Sources: ADB calculations using data from United Nations World Tourism Organization (UNWTO). Tourism Satellite Accounts. http://statistics.unwto.org/ (accessed June 2018); and UNWTO (2018b).

a growing travel option for PRC tourists—between 2010 and 2015, the number of Europe-bound PRC tourists tripled, with annual growth averaging at least 21.3%. To bolster competitiveness, Asian economies should continue cultivating tourism attractions and diversifying new tourism products to cater to different tourist preferences and offer longer stays within the region. Improving infrastructure to reduce travel time and costs, reducing and harmonizing cross-border formalities, developing human capital for tourism, better engaging private sector businesses and tourism entrepreneurs, and making natural attractions and heritage assets less vulnerable to human-made and climate-caused damage will strengthen the industry and make the region's tourism more relevant and responsive to inclusive, green, and knowledge-based development. For example, current initiatives in the ASEAN Tourism Strategic Plan 2016–2025, the APEC's Tourism Strategic Plan 2015–2019, and the Greater Mekong Subregion Tourism program should be promoted.

References

Agency on Statistics Under the President of the Republic of Tajikistan. https://www.stat.tj/tj/database-socio-demographic-sector (accessed June 2018).

Association of Southeast Asian Nations (ASEAN) Secretariat. 2006. ASEAN Framework Agreement on Visa Exemption. http://agreement.asean.org/media/download/20160831072909.pdf

———. 2012. Plan of Action on ASEAN Cooperation in Tourism. http://asean.org/?static_post=plan-of-action-on-asean-cooperation-in-tourism

———. 2015. *ASEAN Tourism Strategic Plan 2016–2025*. Jakarta.

———. ASEANStatsDataPortal. https://data.aseanstats.org/ (accessed June 2018).

Australian Government, Department of Immigration and Border Protection. Work in Australia–Statistics. https://www.homeaffairs.gov.au/about/reports-publications/research-statistics/statistics/work-in-australia (accessed July 2018).

Ayeyawady–Chao Phraya–Mekong Economic Cooperation Strategy (ACMECS). http://www.mfa.go.th/acmecs/ (accessed June 2018).

Bangladesh Bank. https://bb.org.bd (accessed June 2018).

Bangladesh Bureau of Manpower, Employment, and Training. http://www.bmet.org.bd/BMET/stattisticalDataAction (accessed June 2018).

Brown, C. and A. Mineshima. 2007. Remittances in the Pacific Region. *IMF Working Paper*. WP/07/35. Washington, DC: International Monetary Fund (IMF).

Clemens, M. A. and D. McKenzie. 2018. Why Don't Remittances Appear to Affect Growth? *The Economic Journal*. 128 (612). pp. F179–F209. doi:10.1111/ecoj.12463.

Glaesser, D. 2016. *Visa Openness Report 2016*. Presentation at the International Civil Aviation Organization (ICAO) TRIP Symposium 2016. Montreal. 15–16 November. https://www.icao.int/Meetings/TRIP-Symposium-2016/Documents/Glaesser.pdf

Global Knowledge Partnership for Migration and Development (KNOMAD). 2018. Migration and Remittances: Recent Developments and Outlook. *Migration and Development Brief* 29. April. https://www.knomad.org/sites/default/files/2018-04/Migration%20and%20Development%20Brief%2029.pdf

———. http://www.knomad.org/data/remittances (accessed May 2018).

Government of Nepal, Ministry of Labour and Employment. 2018. *Labour Migration for Employment—A Status Report for Nepal: 2015/2016–2016/2017*. Kathmandu.

International Finance Corporation. 2017. De-Risking and Other Challenges in the Emerging Market Financial Sector. *IFC Insights*. 1 September. Washington, DC.

International Labour Organization (ILO). 2015. *ILO Global Estimates on Migrant Workers: Results and Methodology*. Geneva.

———. ILOSTAT. www.ilo.org/ilostat (accessed June 2018).

Japan Ministry of Health, Labour, and Welfare. 2018. *Status of Notification of "Employment Status of Foreigners" Summary (as of the end of October, Heisei 30)*. https://www.mhlw.go.jp/file/04-Houdouhappyou-11655000-Shokugyouanteikyokuhakenyukiroudoutaisakubu-Gaikokujinkoyoutaisakuka/44789gr5.pdf)

Kably, L. 2018. 200% Rise in Invites to Indians for Canadian Permanent Residency. *The Economic Times*. 15 June. https://economictimes.indiatimes.com/nri/visa-and-immigration/200-rise-in-invites-to-indians-for-canadian-permanent-residency/articleshow/64595673.cms

Kikkawa, A. and C. Y. Park. Forthcoming. *International Migration, Cross-Border Labor Mobility, and Regional Integration in Asia and the Pacific*. Economic Research Institute for Northeast Asia (ERINA).

Kim, K. and J. E. Cohen. 2010. Determinants of International Migration Flows to and from Industrialized Countries: A Panel Data Approach Beyond Gravity. *International Migration Review*. 44 (4). pp. 899–932.

Mekong Tourism Coordination Office. 2017. *Greater Mekong Subregion Tourism Sector Strategy 2016–2025*. https://www.greatermekong.org/sites/default/files/2016_2025_GMS_Tourism_Sector_Strategy.pdf

O'Brien, S. A. 2018. Trump Administration Cracks Down H-1B Visa Abuse. *CNN Tech.* 23 February. http://money.cnn.com/2018/02/23/technology/h1b-visa-abuse/index.html

Pakistan Bureau of Emigration and Overseas Employment. https://beoe.gov.pk/reports-and-statistics (accessed June 2018).

Philippine Overseas Employment Agency. http://www.poea.gov.ph/ofwstat/ofwstat.html (accessed June 2018).

Remo, A. 2014. PH Pushes Single-visa Scheme for ASEAN. *Philippine Daily Inquirer.* 19 May. http://business.inquirer.net/170806/ph-pushes-single-visa-scheme-for-asean

Sri Lanka Bureau of Foreign Employment. 2016. *Different Perspectives of Departure Details.* http://www.slbfe.lk/page.php?LID=1&MID=218

Sri Lanka Bureau of Foreign Employment. 2018. *Annual Statistical of Foreign Employment–2017.* http://www.slbfe.lk/page.php?LID=1&MID=220

United Kingdom Immigration Statistics. https://www.gov.uk/government/publications/immigration-statistics-year-ending-march-2018/list-of-tables (accessed July 2018).

United Nations, Department of Economic and Social Affairs, Statistics Division. 1998. Recommendations on Statistics of International Migration. *Statistical Papers.* Series M, No. 58, Rev. 1. New York.

United Nations, Department of Economic and Social Affairs, Population Division. 2017. *World Population Prospects: The 2017 Revision.* New York.

———. International Migrant Stock: The 2017 Revision. http://www.un.org/en/development/desa/population/migration/data/estimates2/estimates17.shtml (accessed May 2018).

United Nations High Commissioner for Refugees (UNHCR). Population Statistics. http://popstats.unhcr.org/en/overview (accessed August 2018).

United Nations World Tourism Organization (UNWTO). 2018a. Strong Outbound Tourism Demand from Both Traditional and Emerging Markets in 2017. Press release. 23 April. http://media.unwto.org/press-release/2018-04-23/strong-outbound-tourism-demand-both-traditional-and-emerging-markets-2017

———. 2018b. *World Tourism Barometer.* 16 (3). June.

———. Tourism Satellite Accounts. http://statistics.unwto.org/ (accessed August 2018).

United States Department of State, Bureau of Consular Affairs. Visa Statistics. https://travel.state.gov/content/travel/en/legal/visa-law0/visa-statistics.html (accessed July 2018).

Wadhawan, N. 2018. India Labour Migration Update 2018. New Delhi: ILO Decent Work Team for South Asia and Country Office for India.

Walmsley, T., A. Aguilar, and S. Ahmed. 2017. Labour Migration and Economic Growth in East and South-East Asia. *The World Economy.* 40 (1). pp. 116–139. doi: 10.1111/twec.12334.

World Bank. World Development Indicators. https://data.worldbank.org/ (accessed September 2018).

———. 2018. *Moving for Global Prosperity: Global Migration and Labor Markets: Policy Research Report.* Washington, DC.

World Economic Forum. 2017. *Travel and Tourism Competitiveness Report 2017.* Geneva.

World Travel and Tourism Council. 2014. *The Impact of Visa Facilitation in ASEAN Member States.* Madrid.

———. 2018. *Travel and Tourism: Global and Economic Impact and Issues 2018.* London.

Zaiceva, A. and K. F. Zimmermann. 2014. Migration and the Demographic Shift. *IZA Discussion Papers.* No. 8743. Bonn: IZA Institute of Labor Economics.

6

Subregional Cooperation Initiatives

Central and West Asia: Central Asia Regional Economic Cooperation Program[37]

Not long ago, Central and West Asia was a place to transit through when traveling between East Asia and Europe, the Middle East, and North Africa, and between Europe and South Asia. Today, it is vying to become the world's next growth area, linking to global value chains and as an energy supplier to rapidly growing South Asian economies (Table 6.1).

The Central Asia Regional Economic Cooperation (CAREC) program[38] promotes regional economic integration through cooperation, leading to accelerated economic growth and poverty reduction. CAREC, guided by its overarching vision of "Good Neighbors, Good Partners, and Good Prospects," has proven an effective honest broker as it continues to weave its network of transport and economic corridors across Eurasia.

Overview

Central Asia looks to the next decade.

From 6 transport projects in 2001 worth $247 million, by 2017 there were 185 projects valued at $31.6 billion

Table 6.1: Selected Economic Indicators, 2017—CAREC

	Population (million)	**Nominal GDP** ($ billion)	**GDP growth** (%, 2013–2017, average)	**GDP per Capita** (current prices, $)	**Trade Openness** (total trade, % of GDP)
Afghanistan	35.5	20.1	2.9	565	49.4
Azerbaijan	9.8	40.8	1.3	4,151	38.4
China, People's Republic of	1,390.1	12,267.7	7.1	8,825	33.3
Georgia	3.7	15.2	3.7	4,104	45.1
Kazakhstan	18.2	159.4	3.3	8,762	45.1
Kyrgyz Republic	6.3	7.6	5.5	1,208	78.0
Mongolia	3.1	11.5	5.7	3,755	73.5
Pakistan	197.3	304.3	4.3	1,543	24.0
Tajikistan	8.8	7.3	6.8	828	54.6
Turkmenistan	5.7	41.7	7.9	7,298	33.1
Uzbekistan	32.1	73.0	7.4	2,272	26.5
CAREC	**1,710.6**	**12,948.5**	**7.0**	**7,570**	**33.3**

CAREC = Central Asia Regional Economic Cooperation, GDP = gross domestic product.
Note: CAREC's average GDP growth rate is weighted using nominal GDP.
Sources: ADB calculations using data from Asian Development Bank. 2018. *Asian Development Outlook 2018.* Manila; CEIC; International Monetary Fund. Direction of Trade Statistics. http://data.imf.org; and World Bank. World Development Indicators. http://databank.worldbank.org/ (all accessed June 2018).

37 Contributed by Shaista Hussain, Regional Cooperation Specialist, Central and West Asia Department (CWRD); Guoliang Wu, Senior Regional Cooperation Specialist, CWRD; and Ronaldo J. Oblepias, Consultant, CWRD, ADB.

38 The CAREC Program is a partnership of 11 countries—Afghanistan, Azerbaijan, Georgia, Kazakhstan, the Kyrgyz Republic, Mongolia, Pakistan, the People's Republic of China, Tajikistan, Turkmenistan, and Uzbekistan—supported by six multilateral institutions.

Figure 6.1: CAREC Projects, by Funding Source, end of 2017 ($ billion)

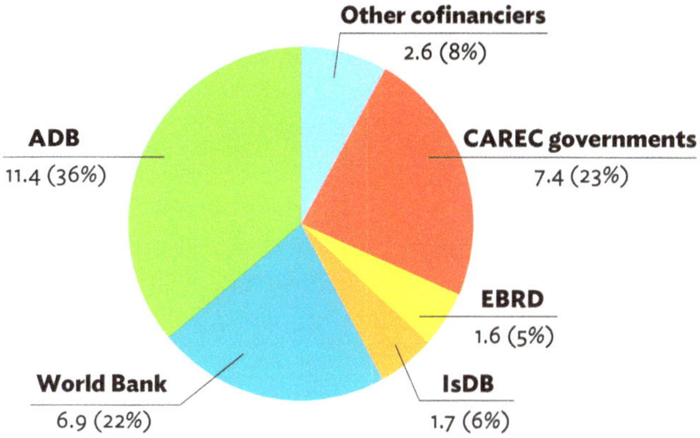

ADB = Asian Development Bank, CAREC = Central Asia Regional Economic Cooperation, EBRD = European Bank for Reconstruction and Development, IsDB = Islamic Development Bank.
Source: ADB. CAREC Program Portfolio.

covering transport, energy, and trade facilitation. Of this, $11.4 billion (36%) was financed by ADB, $7.4 billion (23%) by CAREC governments, and the rest by other donor organizations and cofinanciers (Figure 6.1).

2017 was a landmark year with members formally endorsing CAREC 2030, the program's long-term strategic framework. CAREC 2030 matches members' national development strategies with international development agreements such as the United Nations Sustainable Development Goals (SDGs) and the 21st Conference of the Parties to the United Nations Framework Convention on Climate Change (COP21). While deepening cooperation in the traditional areas of transport, energy, trade, and economic corridor development, it also expands into new areas including financial stability, tourism, agriculture, water, education, and health. It aims to strengthen policy dialogue on regional issues, including through integrating the roles played by the private sector and civil society. It also strives to build an open, inclusive platform to better coordinate and build synergies with international and regional cooperation and other subregional initiatives.

CAREC's infrastructure now better connects countries within the subregion, and with East Asia and South Asia, the Russian Federation, and Europe. Its six multimodal transport corridors spread across the region—shortening distances and the time needed for people and freight to travel. With its large energy reserves, it continues to develop a common market to leverage its resources and attract new leapfrog technology—through cross-border energy connectivity projects and investment forums. CAREC also promotes trade facilitation, through new cross-border physical infrastructure and easing border processing. With much of Central Asia now interconnected by road and rail—and with links to the rest of Asia and Europe—the logical next step is to build seamless air connectivity. CAREC aims to become an aviation hub for both passenger and freight transport.

Performance and Progress over the Past Year

Continuing progress in transport, energy, and trade, CAREC launches a new strategy for a new era.

CAREC's 2017 Dushanbe Declaration, endorsed at its 16th Ministerial Conference in Dushanbe, Tajikistan, stressed that regional cooperation has become even more critical in meeting national development goals given new regional and global challenges.

Responding to members' evolving needs, CAREC 2030 was inspired by aspirations to connect people, policies, and projects for shared and sustainable development. The strategy aims to create an open and inclusive regional cooperation platform and prioritizes five operational clusters for cooperation: (i) economic and financial stability; (ii) trade, tourism, and economic corridors; (iii) infrastructure and connectivity; (iv) agriculture and water; and (v) human development.

CAREC 2030 will also integrate information and communication technology (ICT) across operations to increase productivity and efficiency. Its institutional framework promotes members' and development partners' active, sustained participation in policies and projects, with greater private sector and civil society involvement.

Transport. By the end of 2017, CAREC road and railway projects already surpassed 2020 targets. In 2017, 1,372 kilometers (km) of expressways or national highways were built, upgraded, or improved, bringing the cumulative total to 9,964 km, exceeding the 7,800 km CAREC had targeted for 2020. Work on railways—1,995 km new and 3,433 km improved lines—also surpassed 2020 targets. Kazakhstan's Aktau Port was expanded in 2017, while the Turkmenbashi international seaport and logistics hubs in Turkmenistan and Mongolia are expected to be completed in 2018.

Energy. By 2017, approximately 260,000 km of transmission lines have been installed or upgraded in CAREC countries (excluding the People's Republic of China [PRC] provinces), while generation capacity based on traditional sources reached nearly 15,000 megawatts (MW). Wind power in the CAREC countries (excluding the PRC) reached an estimated 156 MW net capacity producing over 240,000 megawatts per hour (MWh), while the 218 MW of solar net capacity could power nearly 23,000 MWh.

The Central Asia–South Asia Regional Electricity Market Initiative, begun in 2006, remains on track and involves three priority projects: (i) the Turkmenistan–Uzbekistan–Tajikistan–Afghanistan–Pakistan Power Interconnection project; (ii) the Turkmenistan–Afghanistan–Pakistan Power Interconnection project; and (iii) the Turkmenistan–Afghanistan–Pakistan–India Natural Gas Pipeline, to meet growing energy demand in Afghanistan and Pakistan with power imported from Central Asia.

Trade. The CAREC Integrated Trade Agenda 2030 will combine trade policy and facilitation measures to better link CAREC 2030's operational clusters and priorities—such as trade finance and economic corridor development. It will help CAREC members integrate further into the global economy based on three pillars: (i) expanding trade through increased market access, (ii) promoting economic diversification, and (iii) creating stronger institutions for trade. The CAREC Integrated Trade Agenda will be implemented using a pragmatic, phased approach involving 3-year rolling strategic action plans—the first starting 2018–2020.

CAREC's current trade initiatives focus on customs cooperation, modernization of sanitary and phytosanitary (SPS) measures, implementing the World Trade Organization Trade Facilitation Agreement (WTO TFA)—which came into force in February 2017—and boosting private sector participation. For example, the CAREC Federation of Carriers and Freight Forwarders Association is involved in developing harmonized regional standards and best practices on cross-border trade logistics operations. The Regional Improvement of Border Services initiative promotes projects that improve border crossing points, establish national single window systems and facilities, and strengthen project management and supervision capacity—covering the Kyrgyz Republic, Mongolia, Pakistan, and Tajikistan. Under CAREC's integrated trade facilitation approach, ADB is supporting implementation of the Common Agenda for the Modernization of Sanitary and Phytosanitary Measures for Trade (CAST). CAST will (i) create country agencies and a regional body to lead the modernization process; (ii) develop regulations, procedures, and other requirements aligned with international standards; and (iii) improve the capability of border agencies to implement these measures at selected common borders.

Other CAREC Operational Priorities. The Almaty–Bishkek Economic Corridor initiative facilitates the preparation of investment projects and reforms in Almaty, Bishkek, and the surrounding areas. The initiative is (i) developing cross-border agricultural value chains by establishing wholesale markets, collection centers, creating logistical infrastructure and providing export certification; (ii) preparing reforms to ease border-crossing procedures; and (iii) developing regional tourism and marketing.

The CAREC Institute, an intergovernmental organization supporting CAREC through knowledge generation and capacity building, was formally legalized in August 2017.[39] It began drafting its inaugural medium-term strategy and adopted a 2-year rolling operational program. It has already organized a high-level forum for regional think tanks and conducts training workshops for CAREC government officials and private sector representatives.

[39] The intergovernmental agreement requires ratification by at least three countries including the host country for it to enter into force. Four countries—Mongolia, Pakistan, the People's Republic of China, and Uzbekistan—had ratified the agreement by August 2017. By July 2018, Afghanistan, Azerbaijan, the Kyrgyz Republic, and Tajikistan had also ratified the agreement.

Prospects

CAREC 2030 will promote regional approaches to help members achieve the United Nations SDGs.

Most CAREC members are already meeting or are close to meeting several SDGs on poverty reduction, lowering the maternal mortality ratio, full literacy, and access to electricity for all, among others. However, much remains to be done on food security, renewable energy, road safety, and ICT development (ESCAP, ADB, and UNDP 2017; and ADB 2017a).

As mentioned, aligning national strategies and supporting the SDGs and COP21 are core principles of CAREC 2030. National priorities are typically SDG-aligned—for example, promoting inclusive growth, environmental sustainability, economic diversification, improved connectivity, and renewable energy. The importance of health and education, often linked to creation of a knowledge-based economy, is also a recurring theme. Issues related to gender and governance are now explicitly defined in many CAREC member development strategies. Considerations of sustainability and climate resilience will cut across all CAREC investments.

Policy Challenge

CAREC members need to promote economic and financial stability through regional cooperation and integration.

Given their dependence on natural resource exports and remittances from oil-exporting countries, most CAREC members remain vulnerable to external shocks. In theory, countercyclical policies should help, but in practice, many country policies are not countercyclical enough at most—given limited fiscal space, shallow financial markets, and difficulties in assessing whether external shocks are temporary or permanent.

A decade after the 2008/09 global financial crisis, the economic effects are still being felt across CAREC. Just as they began recovering postcrisis, they were hit again by the 2014 plunge in oil prices. While many CAREC members gained much experience on how effective monetary and fiscal measures were in mitigating shocks, they now face the challenge of phasing out fiscal stimulus without harming the continued fragile recovery in the region.

Aside from dialogue on what worked and what did not, regional cooperation also allows countries to work together to avoid crisis contagion across the region. Over time, joint initiatives for economic surveillance, cooperation among central banks and capital market regulators, and emergency liquidity safety nets based on lessons learned from the Chiang Mai Initiative Multilateralization of the Association of Southeast Asian Nations (ASEAN) Plus Three can help prevent and mitigate the impact of shocks or crises.

Southeast Asia: Greater Mekong Subregion Program[40]

Cambodia, Yunnan Province and the Guangxi Zhuang Autonomous Region in the PRC, the Lao People's Democratic Republic (Lao PDR), Myanmar, Thailand, and Viet Nam make up the Greater Mekong Subregion (GMS) Program—an economic partnership guided by a strategy of enhancing connectivity, improving competitiveness, and fostering a sense of community. After 25 years of cooperation, the GMS has created an interconnected, competitive subregion with generally robust economic growth. Through the end of 2017, GMS governments—with multilateral and bilateral development partners—approved 87 investment projects amounting to $20.8 billion. ADB contributed $8.2 billion, while GMS governments have contributed $5.5 billion and other development partners have contributed $7.1 billion. Since its inception, GMS has built, upgraded, or improved over 10,000 km of roads and 500 km of railway lines; built or added 3,000 km of power transmission and distribution lines; and installed 1,570 gigawatt-hours of power generation facilities.

[40] Contributed by the GMS Secretariat, Southeast Asia Department, ADB.

Overview

The GMS Program takes on high priority subregional projects in both hard and soft infrastructure. One strategic priority is economic corridor development, an approach adopted in 1998. Economic corridors are designed to not only help participants improve physical connectivity, facilitate the movement of people, goods, and vehicles across borders, but also to develop border and corridor towns, and promote investment and enterprise development to ensure wider economic benefits to communities around the cross-border transport infrastructure. The economic corridors link GMS capitals and major urban centers to one another and to maritime gateways.

Gross domestic product (GDP) growth remains strong (Table 6.2). Although the subregion's 5-year average GDP growth slowed to 6.1% in 2013–2017 compared with 6.7% in 2012–2016, overall growth remains above the 2017 ASEAN average (5.2%). Trade between GMS members reached $483 billion in 2017. Trade-to-GDP ratios are rising in Cambodia (from 107.3 in 2016 to 126 in 2017) and in Myanmar (from 23.1 in 2016 to 40.0 in 2017). Tourism continues to boom with more than 60 million international tourist arrivals in 2016, 15% of which is intra-GMS tourism, generating $90 billion, creating jobs and boosting incomes. Improved transport connectivity, GMS marketing as a multi-country tourist destination, and rising per capita GDP within Asia have helped power tourism growth.

Table 6.2: Selected Economic Indicators, 2017—Greater Mekong Subregion

	Population (million)[a]	**Nominal GDP** ($ billion)[b]	**GDP Growth** (2013–2017, average, %)[c]	**GDP per Capita** (current prices, $)[d]	**Trade Openness** (total trade, % of GDP)[e]	**FDI Openness** (total FDI Inflows, % of GDP)[f]
Cambodia	16	22	7.1	1,384	126	12.6
Guangxi, PRC	56	302	8.3	5,354	20	0.4
Yunnan, PRC	48	245	9.4	5,095	10	0.4
Lao PDR	7	17	7.3	2,457	27	4.8
Myanmar	53	69	7.2	1,299	40	6.3
Thailand	69	455	2.8	6,495	88	1.7
Viet Nam	96	224	6.2	2,343	202	6.3
GMS	**345**	**1,334**	**6.1**	**3,864**	**75**	**2.4**

FDI = foreign direct investment, GDP = gross domestic product, GMS = Greater Mekong Subregion, Lao PDR = Lao People's Democratic Republic, LCU = local currency unit, PRC = People's Republic of China, UNCOMTRADE = United Nations Commodity Trade Database, UNCTAD = United Nations Conference on Trade and Development.

[a] Population data for Guangxi, PRC is estimated. Data for Cambodia, the Lao PDR, Myanmar, Thailand, and Viet Nam are from World Bank, Word Development Indicators (accessed August 2018). Data for Yunnan, PRC are from CEIC (accessed August 2018).

[b] GDP in LCU data of Cambodia, the Lao PDR, Myanmar, Thailand, and Viet Nam are from World Bank, World Development Indicators (accessed August 2018); GDP in LCU data are converted to market prices $ using Atlas method. Data for Guangxi and Yunnan are from CEIC (accessed April 2018) and converted to market prices $ using the Atlas conversion factor of the PRC.

[c] GDP growth rates of Cambodia, the Lao PDR, Myanmar, Thailand, and Viet Nam are from the *Asian Development Outlook April 2018*. Growth rates of Guangxi and Yunnan are computed from their respective GDP indexes. GDP indexes are from CEIC (accessed August 2018). GMS annual growth rate is weighted using shares in GDP current prices $. Average for 2013–2017 is simple average.

[d] GDP per capita is the ratio of GDP current market prices $ to total population. GMS GDP per capita is the ratio of total GMS GDP at market prices $ to total GMS population.

[e] Trade data of Cambodia, the Lao PDR, Myanmar, Thailand, and Viet Nam are from UNCOMTRADE (accessed August 2018); and all trade data are reporters' data. Trade data of Guangxi and Yunnan are sums of their monthly trade data; monthly data are from CEIC (accessed August 2018). Trade openness is the ratio of total trade (sum of exports to the world and imports from the world) to GDP at market prices $, multiplied by 100. GMS trade openness is the ratio of total GMS exports to the world and imports from the world to GMS GDP at market prices $, multiplied by 100.

[f] FDI inflows data for Guangxi and Yunnan are estimates. Data for Cambodia, the Lao PDR, Myanmar, Thailand, and Viet Nam are from UNCTAD (accessed August 2018). FDI openness is the ratio of total FDI inflows from the world to GDP at market prices $, multiplied by 100. GMS FDI openness is computed as the ratio of total GMS FDI inflows from the world to total GDP at market prices $, multiplied by 100.

Sources: ADB. 2018. *Asian Development Outlook 2018*. Manila; CEIC (accessed April and August 2018); GMS Secretariat calculations; UNCOMTRADE. https://comtrade.un.org/ (accessed August 2018); UNCTAD FDI Statistics. http://unctad.org/en/Pages/Home.aspx (accessed August 2018); and World Bank. World Development Indicators. https://data.worldbank.org/products/wdi (accessed August 2018).

Performance and Progress over the Past Year

GMS continued to strengthen its transport network, established new working groups on urban development and health cooperation, expanded private sector cooperation in e-commerce and agriculture, and deepened support to small and medium-sized enterprises through the Mekong Business Initiative.[41]

In March 2018, at the 6th GMS Leaders' Summit, GMS leaders adopted the Ha Noi Action Plan 2018–2022 (ADB 2018b) and Regional Investment Framework 2022 (ADB 2018c) to guide the implementation of the second half of the GMS Strategic Framework 2012–2022. The Regional Investment Framework 2022 is a $66 billion project pipeline supporting the Ha Noi Action Plan. The plan has four elements: (i) spatially focusing on an economic corridor network that balances internal and external connectivity; (ii) refining GMS program sector strategies and operational priorities; (iii) improving planning, programming, and monitoring and processes; and (iv) enhancing institutional arrangements and partnerships. Transport, tourism, agriculture, and environment sector strategies were updated while the health cooperation strategy is being completed and the current urban development strategy remains valid (ADB 2018d, Mekong Tourism Coordinating Office 2017, ADB 2018e, GMS Environment Operations Center 2017). The project pipeline—227 investment and technical assistance projects in 10 sectors,[42] which will be regularly updated—will be used (i) to strengthen alignment between regional and national planning and programming for GMS projects, and (ii) to attract new project financing.

Cross-Border Transport and Economic Corridor Development. In 2017, transport infrastructure development continued at a fairly rapid pace. Following completion of key transport links the previous 2 years—the Tsubasa Bridge in Neak Loeung, Cambodia, along the Southern Economic Corridor, Lao–Myanmar Friendship Bridge over the Mekong at Xiengkok–Kainglap, PRC–Viet Nam second road bridge over the Beilun River, the road section of the East–West economic corridor (EWEC) in Myanmar from Myawaddy to Kawkareik—several major connectivity infrastructure projects commenced or were ongoing in 2017: (i) the EWEC section from Kawkareik to Eindu in Myanmar; (ii) the second Myanmar–Thailand Bridge over the Moei River; (iii) upgrading of the Phitsanulok to Lom Sak Highway along the EWEC and the Phanom Sarakham to Sa Kaeo highway along the Southern economic corridor; (iv) the PRC–Lao PDR (Boten–Vientiane) Railway; and (v) the PRC–Thailand (Bangkok–Kele) Railway.

The Greater Mekong Railway Association also identified and is assessing the financial viability of nine priority railway links to complete GMS rail connectivity. Three of these links are already under construction: (i) the PRC–Lao PDR (Boten–Vientiane) line; (ii) the Viet Nam–PRC (Hekou–Lao Cai) line; and (iii) the Cambodia–Thailand (Poipet–Aranyaprathet) line.

The GMS Secretariat is also conducting a study to assess the physical condition and economic potential of transport and related infrastructure along its corridors.

Energy. In energy and power connectivity, the GMS countries are continuing to work together to develop more permanent institutional mechanisms to coordinate power sector integration. In the meantime, bilateral power trade between GMS countries also continues to expand, with two GMS projects advancing well: the Ban Hatxan–Pleiku 220 kilovolt (kV) transmission line and the Nabong 500 kV substation. The Regional Power Trade Coordination Committee continues to build the subregion's power interconnections and trade to seamlessly link GMS energy trade. Two working groups cover (i) performance standards and grid codes (WGPG) and (ii) regulatory issues (WGRI). They aim to harmonize regional power trade policy. The WGRI (i) analyzes GMS members' institutional structures,

41 The Mekong Business Initiative is a development partnership between ADB and the Government of Australia to accelerate growth in Cambodia, the Lao PDR, Myanmar, and Viet Nam. Launched in 2015, it is an advisory facility managed by ADB to help catalyze private sector-led sustainable business growth in the emerging ASEAN market through business advocacy, access to finance, and innovation support.

42 The GMS Program covers the following sectors: transport, energy, agriculture, environment, health and other human resources development, urban development, other multisector and border economic zones, tourism, transport and trade facilitation, and information and communication technology.

identifying potential barriers, and proposes member-specific reform agendas; (ii) proposes specific rules and principles for open access and develops an overall methodology for wheeling charge calculations; and (iii) proposes short-term trading rules and balancing mechanisms. The WGPG (i) reviews operational practices of each member relevant to the subregion, (ii) finalizes policies related to power transmission regulations, (iii) works on standardized metering, and (iv) reviews the Governance Code and Connection Code of the GMS grid.

Agriculture. The Second GMS Agriculture Ministers' Meeting was held in September 2017 in Cambodia, a decade since its first meeting. The ministers endorsed a new sector strategy to make the GMS a leading producer of safe and environment-friendly agriculture products through value-chain integration involving smallholders, rural women, and agriculture-based small and medium-sized enterprises (SMEs) (ADB 2018e). The ADB technical assistance on GMS Core Agriculture Support Program II 2011–2020 harmonizes food safety policies to ensure consumers and producers are protected—inclusively and sustainably—which supports the implementation of the strategy. Several projects have been completed: participatory guarantee systems for GMS farmer groups; piloting climate-friendly and gender-responsive farm practices; and applied research/extension work on climate- and environment-friendly agriculture.

Tourism. The ongoing ADB-funded GMS Tourism Infrastructure for Inclusive Growth Project for Cambodia, the Lao PDR, and Viet Nam is helping to accelerate inclusive economic growth along targeted segments of GMS economic corridors by improving tourism-related infrastructure and the environment at cross-border tourism centers. It also strengthens capacity of public and private tourist destination management organizations. Other initiatives of the GMS Tourism Working Group are bilateral and/or in cooperation with other development partners in strengthening human resources, developing sustainable infrastructure, enhancing tourist experience, services, creative marketing and promotion, and facilitating regional travel. A new GMS Tourism Sector Strategy 2016–2025 was completed with ADB technical assistance and endorsed in September 2017. Member consultations aim to establish an intergovernmental Mekong Tourism Coordinating Office. Cooperation on tourism took the theme "Prosper with Purpose" at the innovative Mekong Tourism Forum organized in Luang Prabang, Lao PDR, in June 2017, and in 2018 with the theme "Transforming Travel, Transforming Lives" held in Nakhon Phanom, Thailand.

Health and Other Human Resources Development. A 2016 ADB-funded GMS Health Security Project for Cambodia, the Lao PDR, Myanmar, and Viet Nam is strengthening public health security against communicable diseases such as severe acute respiratory syndrome, avian influenza, and Middle East respiratory syndrome as well as traditional communicable diseases, including drug-resistant malaria, dengue, and antimicrobial-resistant infections. It improves public health security systems and boosts national and regional capacity for disease surveillance and response, risk assessment, case management, and subregional collaboration. The project covers relatively poor border and economic corridor provinces where outbreaks of cross-border communicable disease can occur. It focuses on mobile and migrant populations as well as other vulnerable groups. In 2016, the Working Group on Health Cooperation was created to lead regional health cooperation initiatives and operationalize these through a vetted regional project pipeline. The working group met for the first time in December 2017 and is now preparing the GMS Health Cooperation Strategy.

Capacity-building programs and workshops were also held for government officials in the GMS and other ASEAN-centric subregional programs on a number of topics related to regional cooperation and integration, including health impact assessments in special economic zones, economic corridor development, cross-border power trade, and e-commerce.[43]

Environment. The ADB-supported Core Environment Program Phase II is being completed. In 2017, two major priorities were (i) adopting the Core Environment Program Strategic Framework and Action Plan 2018–2022 (GMS Environment Operations Center 2017);

[43] For example, the Indonesia–Malaysia–Thailand Growth Triangle (IMT-GT) program and Brunei Darussalam–Indonesia–Malaysia–Philippines East ASEAN Growth Area (BIMP-EAGA).

and (ii) consolidating and finalizing program activities, focusing on impact and sustainability. The program continued to support GMS members by (i) providing policy, strategic planning, and institutional support; (ii) applying sound environment management policies and tools; (iii) strengthening transboundary biodiversity landscape monitoring and management; (iv) training on climate change adaptation and disaster preparedness; and (v) attracting greater private sector participation. The 5th Environment Ministers' Meeting in January 2018 endorsed the Strategic Framework and Action Plan, which addresses climate change, leverages green growth opportunities, further decentralizes implementation to GMS members, and gives the GMS Working Group on Environment greater control in governing the program.

Transport and Trade Facilitation. In early 2018, a memorandum of understanding (MOU) was signed by GMS members covering "Early Harvest" implementation of the Cross-Border Transport Facilitation Agreement (CBTA), under which GMS road transport permits will be issued to ease border crossings. Work has also been initiated in updating the CBTA provisions to be at par with current international best practices, expanding the coverage of the routes covered under CBTA, and strengthening private sector transport and logistics services. Through a recently completed regional policy and advisory technical assistance project, partnership between customs administration and the private sector, particularly SMEs, was strengthened, enabling better understanding of and compliance with customs requirements. A time release study will be conducted in selected GMS members to help customs increase efficiency. And SPS arrangements under ADB-assisted projects in Cambodia and the Lao PDR were scaled up.

Urban and Border Area Development. This is a new focus for GMS in helping transform transport corridors into full economic corridors. Total investment from ADB and other development partners is estimated at $2.0 billion, covering the ongoing (i) GMS Corridor Towns Development projects in Cambodia, the Lao PDR, and Viet Nam; (ii) the Guangxi Regional Cooperation and Integration Promotion Investment Program; and (iii) the Cambodia–Lao PDR–Viet Nam Development Triangle Area Border Area Development Project. The Yunnan Lincang Border Economic Cooperation Zone Infrastructure Development and Corridor Towns Development projects (which extend to Myanmar) are expected to be approved in 2018.

Prospects

GMS is focusing more on spatial and multisector planning along with regional development. It will continue to build its economic corridor network by including more border areas, promoting subregional tourism and agriculture value chains, and strengthening domestic and cross-border transport networks.

As mentioned, the next 5 years of the GMS Program will be guided by the Ha Noi Action Plan; the Regional Investment Framework; and sector strategies in agriculture, tourism, the environment, transport, urban development, and health cooperation. All will require greater resource mobilization, including from the private sector, and more synergies with other regional cooperation frameworks. Officials will also begin considering the longer-term vision after the current GMS Strategic Framework (2012–2022).

Policy Challenge

As physical connectivity and economic growth continue to rise, GMS members must leverage new or strengthen existing regional institutions and mechanisms.

Establishing GMS institutions and mechanisms such as the Regional Power Coordination Center, the Mekong Tourism Coordination Office, and the GMS Railway Association can help ensure sustainable development, resource planning, and equitable resource sharing. Cooperative mechanisms like the Working Group on Environment and the Working Group on Health Cooperation have been effective in promoting regional public goods such as climate change and transnational health security. These working groups are also a platform for coordination and resource mobilization with development partners, and as a way for the private sector to join in implanting the Ha Noi Action Plan and Regional Investment Framework.

East Asia: Support for RCI Initiatives under CAREC and GMS Subregional Programs and Knowledge-Sharing Activities[44]

ADB supports regional cooperation and integration (RCI) in East Asia through CAREC and GMS. It also supports knowledge cooperation under the Regional Knowledge Sharing Initiative (RKSI). ADB aims to maximize synergies under new cooperation initiatives led by government stakeholders—as RCI is a strategic priority in ADB's country assistance to both the PRC and Mongolia.

Performance and Progress over the Past Year

ADB continues to support projects in Mongolia and the PRC related to CAREC and GMS.[45]

Under the GMS framework, ADB supports establishing border economic zones (BEZs) as a tool to harness border area development. ADB technical assistance helped facilitate the 2013 MOU between the PRC and Viet Nam prioritizing four paired-border gateways for BEZ development.[46] ADB currently supports the MOU implementation, including a large-scale investment program to develop BEZs in Guangxi Zhuang Autonomous Region (GZAR). The $450 million investment program will improve trade and transport efficiency, cross-border connectivity, and accelerate border area development. Another regional technical assistance project works to help maximize benefits of cross-border trade on both sides of the border.

In addition, a $250 million loan approved in 2017 will help develop and implement the Guangxi Modern Technical and Vocational Education and Training Development Program. From 2017 to 2022, the loan will help establish a technical and vocational education and training (TVET) system to offer graduates better employment opportunities in the GZAR. It will ensure TVET relevance, quality, and inclusiveness, and expand its role in regional economic development by promoting partnership agreements and cross-border training programs between TVET institutions and enterprises in GZAR and ASEAN (initially with Viet Nam).

Under CAREC, ADB supports efforts to improve cross-border trade and economic corridor development. An ADB-supported loan for Regional Upgrades of SPS Measures for Trade (RUST) in Mongolia aims to improve inspection and control systems that will increase agri-food trade and help diversify the economy. Investment focuses on the three *aimags* (first-level administrative subdivisions) of Darkhan-Uul, Dornogovi, and Selenge, and particularly the border crossing points (BCPs) of Altanbulag and Zamyn-Uud—which are part of a CAREC corridor. Work is underway to build or rehabilitate laboratories and equip them with new diagnostic equipment. This will decentralize testing and diagnostic capacity and support early disease detection. The project complements a $40 million loan for Mongolia's regional logistics development, expected to be completed in early 2019. The project develops multimodal facilities for road-to-road, road-to-rail, and rail-to-rail transshipment. It equips these with modern customs and quarantine facilities to connect Mongolia's road and rail links in Zamyn-Uud on the southeast border with the PRC.

Further to improving the Altanbulag and Zamyn-Uud BCPs, a $27 million Regional Improvement of Border Services Project was approved in April 2016. The project aims to reduce trade costs through infrastructure and technology upgrades, improving the automated information systems that support customs operations, cross-agency data sharing and coordination

[44] Contributed by Ying Qian, Dorothea Lazaro, Stephanie Kamal, Edith Joan Nacpil, and Aihua Wu—all from ADB's East Asia Department (EARD)—and Chaoyi Hu (Consultant, RKSI).

[45] EARD provides technical and administrative support for the CAREC trade program and provides direct support for Mongolia's participation in CAREC. It also supports projects in those PRC provinces and autonomous regions involved with CAREC and GMS.

[46] The border gateways are (i) Mong Cai–Dongxing, (ii) Lao Cai–Hekou, (iii) Tra Linh–Longbang, and (iv) Dong Dang–Pingxiang.

to eventually help build a single window system in Mongolia. ADB is also currently working on additional financing to expand the project in two BCPs of Borshoo and Bichigt.

ADB offers a platform for RCI dialogue and South–South knowledge-sharing.

ADB works closely with various institutions to help share South–South knowledge and experience on globalization and RCI. For example, a forum in September 2017 in Hohhot explored avenues of economic growth and regional integration. In December 2017 in Shanghai, the CAREC Institute and the Asia-Pacific Finance and Development Institute organized a series of workshops on public–private partnerships and e-commerce development.

The PRC and ADB established RKSI in 2012 to facilitate the exchange of development-related knowledge among ADB's developing member economies. RKSI draws primarily on the PRC's experience over the past 30 years in promoting and supporting rapid economic growth and social transformation. Currently, RKSI focuses on three themes: (i) inclusive growth, inclusive urbanization, and social transformation; (ii) environment and climate change; and (iii) regional cooperation.

From 2016 to 2018, RKSI organized three training sessions on special economic zones as catalysts for economic corridors, value chains, and production networks. It also jointly organized two annual CAREC Think Tanks Development Forums—on regional knowledge sharing for cross-border trade logistics and facilitation, and a knowledge-sharing workshop on RCI and on cross-border e-commerce. The forums brought together some 500 participants. Through RKSI, ADB also worked closely with (i) Tsinghua University in organizing a lecture series covering development and environment, and (ii) the Asia-Pacific Finance and Development Institute on a semester-long series of lectures on international development, emphasizing challenges, approaches, and case studies based on development projects.

Prospects

ADB supports cross-border economic zone development.

A $250 million loan is being processed for the Yunnan Lincang Border Cooperation Zone Development Project. The project will improve cross-border trade capacity by building logistics parks, border trade markets, and other facilities. It will also upgrade urban environment infrastructure—including municipal roads and water supply, wastewater treatment, and solid waste management facilities in selected border towns. It will provide social infrastructure and services, including hospitals and schools, and strengthen institutional capacity of implementing agencies. The project is expected to improve connectivity between the PRC and Myanmar and support RCI objectives such as control of transboundary diseases, improved cross-border labor mobility, and increased cross-border tourist flows promoted under the GMS program.

A multitranche financing facility for the $490 million Xinjiang Regional Cooperation and Integration Promotion Investment Program is being prepared to support development of cross-border economic zones between the PRC's Xinjiang Uygur Autonomous Region, Kazakhstan, and Mongolia. The investment program will develop essential trade-related facilities and services, support border transport connectivity, and provide support for SMEs in the border areas of Alashankou, Khorgos, Altay, Jeminay, and Qinghe of the Xinjiang Uygur Autonomous Region.

Another multitranche financing facility for the Inner Mongolia Regional Cooperation and Integration Promotion Investment Program is proposed to support the participation of the PRC's Inner Mongolia Autonomous Region (IMAR) in CAREC and other RCI initiatives. It will strengthen cooperation between IMAR and neighboring countries by improving connectivity, increasing cross-border trade and investment, and upgrading infrastructure and social services and people-to-people exchanges in border areas—including Erlian and Manzhouli (PRC) with Mongolia and the Russian Federation, respectively. Of the estimated $1.2 billion investment program, ADB will finance $420 million. To ensure complementarity and create synergies with the IMAR Investment Program, ADB technical assistance will help Mongolia establish a cross-border economic zone between Erlian (PRC) and Zamyn-Uud (Mongolia).

Policy Challenge

Open regionalism and coordination with other subregional initiatives must be maintained.

RCI is a priority in the PRC 13th Five-Year Plan for 2016–2020. In 2015, the PRC announced its Silk Road Economic Belt and 21st Century Maritime Silk Road Initiative—now referred to as the "Belt and Road Initiative"—which aims to promote connectivity and strengthen economic partnerships across Asia, Europe, and Africa in a spirit of open regionalism. Also, the PRC and Mongolia actively participate in other RCI programs—such as the ASEAN–PRC Pan Beibu Gulf Economic Cooperation; the Greater Tumen Initiative led by United Nations Development Programme; and the PRC–Mongolia–Russian Federation Economic Corridor Program. Coordination with other cooperation initiatives could enhance knowledge-sharing, create synergies, and optimize the use of resources toward open regionalism.

South Asia: South Asia Subregional Economic Cooperation[47]

In 2017, the South Asia Subregional Economic Cooperation (SASEC) Program added financing commitments for seven projects valued at $2.5 billion, including $1.3 billion in ADB financing. This brings investments in transport, trade facilitation, energy, and economic corridor development since 2001 to $10.72 billion. Its members—Bangladesh, Bhutan, India, Maldives, Myanmar, Nepal, and Sri Lanka—endorsed a vision of "SASEC Powering Asia in the 21st Century" and fine-tuned its operational plan 2016–2025 (ADB 2017b). Several flagship initiatives were launched, focusing on sustainable expansion of cross-border power trade and the development of new energy sector projects.

Overview

SASEC has consistently focused on building multimodal connectivity to facilitate trade.

In 2001, Bangladesh, Bhutan, India, and Nepal established SASEC to strengthen subregional economic cooperation and address development challenges such as low intraregional trade and persistent poverty (Table 6.3). Maldives and Sri Lanka joined in 2014 followed by Myanmar in 2017, expanding opportunities to improve cross-border connectivity, facilitate intraregional trade, and strengthen regional economic cooperation. ADB is lead financier, secretariat, and development partner, financing investments and technical assistance.

By the end of 2017, 49 ADB-financed projects (worth a total $10.7 billion) had been committed (Figure 6.2), with an additional $72 million in technical assistance grants. Investments in infrastructure connectivity accounted for the largest share (32 projects, $8.5 billion), with power generation, transmission, and cross-border electricity trade second (11 projects, $1.48 billion). Investments in economic corridor development, trade facilitation, and ICT development amounted to $785 million (Figure 6.3). ADB financed almost $6.2 billion in investments ($4.1 billion from ordinary capital resources and $2.1 billion in concessional finance), while SASEC members and cofinanciers contributed over $4.5 billion (Figure 6.4).

The SASEC Operational Plan 2016–2025 (SASEC OP) (ADB 2016a) laid the groundwork for broader investments in multimodal transportation networks along major trade routes with more focus on railway and seaport development, maritime- and land-based trade facilitation, and logistics. This more integrated approach to trade will standardize operations and enhance

[47] Contributed by Rosalind McKenzie, Senior Regional Cooperation Specialist, South Asia Department (SARD); Jesusito Tranquilino, ADB Consultant, SARD; and Leticia de Leon, ADB Consultant, SARD.

Table 6.3: Selected Economic Indicators, 2017—SASEC

	Population (million)	Nominal GDP ($ billion)	GDP Growth (%, 2013–2017, average)	GDP per Capita (current prices, $)	Trade Openness (total trade, % of GDP)
Bangladesh	163.7	249.7	6.6	1,525.8	31.7
Bhutan	0.8	2.4	5.7	2,985.0	88.9
India	1,3316.0	2,572.4	7.1	1,954.7	28.4
Maldives	0.4	4.7	5.6	10,660.1	55.6
Myanmar	53.4	66.5	6.8	1,246.0	43.9
Nepal	29.1	24.5	3.9	843.3	44.2
Sri Lanka	21.4	87.2	4.4	4,065.2	36.6
SASEC	**1,584.8**	**3,007.3**	**7.0**	**1,897.6**	**29.5**

GDP = gross domestic product, IMF = International Monetary Fund, SASEC = South Asia Subregional Economic Cooperation.
Notes: Average GDP growth rates for Maldives and Sri Lanka cover 2014–2017, while Myanmar for 2017. SASEC average GDP growth rate is weighted using nominal GDP. Nominal GDP figures are based on IMF staff estimates.
Sources: ADB. 2018. *Asian Development Outlook 2018*. Manila; International Monetary Fund (IMF). Direction of Trade Statistics. http://data.imf.org; IMF. World Economic Outlook July 2018 Database. http://www.imf.org/external/pubs/ft/weo/2018/01/weodata/index.aspx; and World Bank. DataBank. Population estimates and projections. http://databank.worldbank.org (all accessed May 2018).

Figure 6.2: SASEC Investment, by Sector and Volume ($ million)

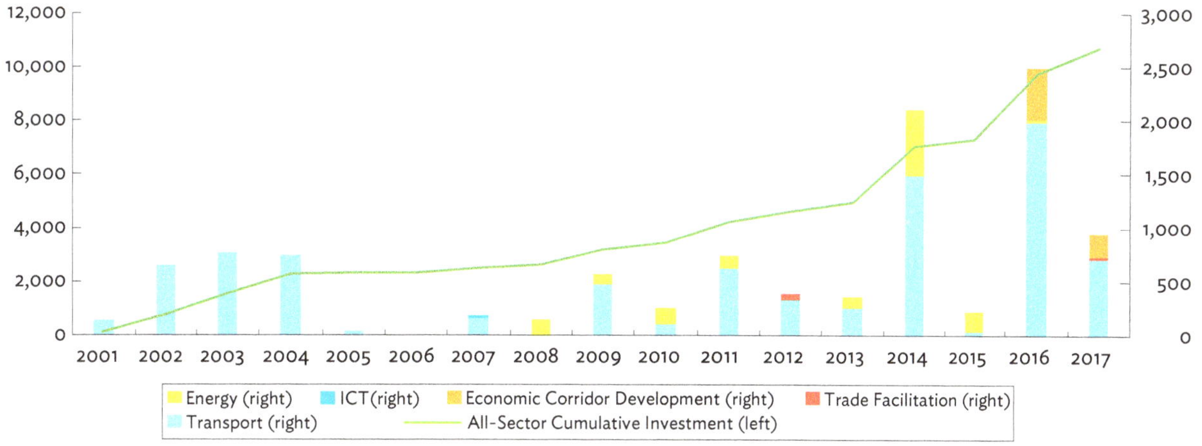

ICT = information and communication technology, SASEC = South Asia Subregional Economic Cooperation.
Source: ADB. SASEC Project Portfolio 2018.

Figure 6.3: SASEC Projects, by Sector, end of 2017

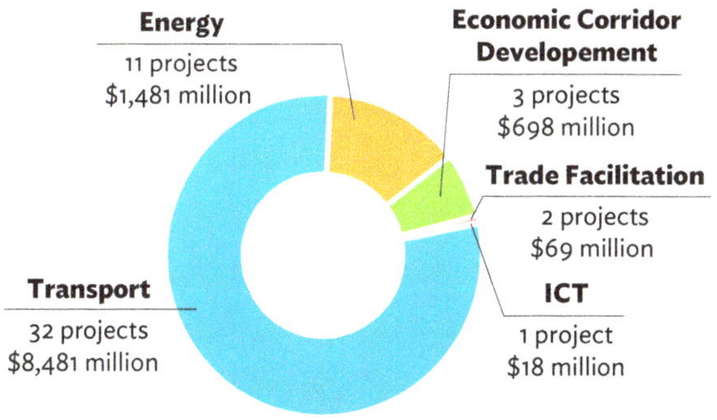

ICT = information and communication technology, SASEC = South Asia Subregional Economic Cooperation.
Source: ADB. SASEC Project Portfolio 2018.

overall trade. Regional power trade is focused on clean energy, master planning, and increased dialogue on pertinent issues. Finally, reinforcing existing value chains and developing new ones through economic corridor development will boost local economies along SASEC transport corridors throughout South Asia.

The SASEC Vision and SASEC OP aim to transform the subregion into a growth engine by seeking ways to leverage resource-based industries, expand and develop new regional value chains, and strengthen gateways and hubs across member economies.

Figure 6.4: SASEC Investment, by Financier ($ million)

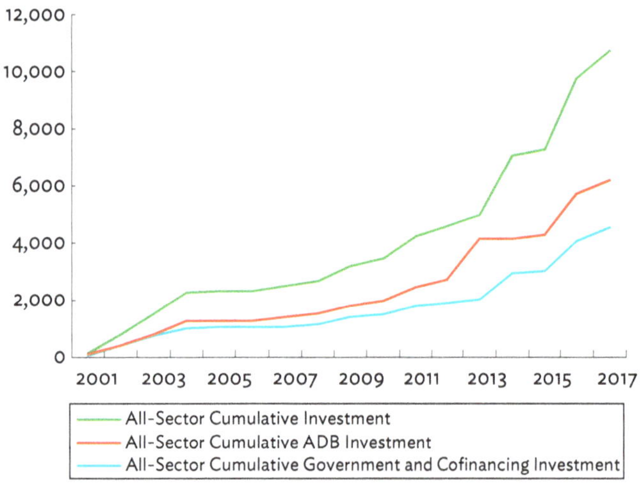

ADB = Asian Development Bank, SASEC = South Asia Subregional Economic Cooperation.
Source: ADB. SASEC Project Portfolio 2018.

Performance and Progress over the Past Year

The SASEC OP is being reviewed to more accurately reflect regional project priorities of the member countries. It will also propose ways to integrate Myanmar, its newest member, into the group as a vital link between South Asia, Southeast Asia, and East Asia.

Transport. Multimodal and cross-border connectivity remains the focus of SASEC transport projects, including the upgrading of national road networks with special attention to challenges faced by landlocked Bhutan and Nepal. Rail corridors will link landlocked areas to ports, facilitating freight traffic and international trade. Airport capacity is also expanding with operations modernized for better safety and service. In 2017, seven SASEC transport projects received $1.77 billion in funding commitments ($787 million from ADB)—including road projects in Bangladesh and Bhutan, and a rail project in Bangladesh.

The Dhaka–Northwest Corridor Road Project, Phase 2-Tranche 1 ($714 million) will improve Bangladesh's second busiest artery and ultimately extend northward to Burimari Land Port, the gateway to India and landlocked Bhutan, while the SASEC Chittagong–Cox's Bazar Railway Project ($300 million) will bring the SASEC–Myanmar rail corridor closer to completion and strengthen international rail linkages. Nepal's SASEC Roads Improvement Project ($257 million) will improve Nepal's international road network and connectivity to India.

Trade Facilitation. The SASEC Trade Facilitation Strategic Framework 2014–2018 (ADB 2014) helps members move toward faster, more efficient, and less costly cross-border trade, as well as compliance with WTO TFA provisions that require harmonization and modernization, among others. Six national diagnostic studies identified trade-restrictive SPS and other technical barriers to trade and recommended ways to improve regulatory and institutional frameworks, along with the relevant infrastructure facilities. A study on coordinated development of border infrastructure at border crossings between Bangladesh, India, and Nepal laid out policy and investment options to narrow connectivity gaps. Electronic cargo tracking systems and motor vehicle agreements are easing transport across the subregion, with electronic cargo tracking system trial runs underway between India and Bangladesh as well as India and Nepal for inland cargo transport and off-border clearances. Motor vehicle agreements between Bangladesh, Bhutan, India, and Nepal are finalizing passenger and cargo protocols in 2018.

Nepal's Customs Reform and Modernization for Trade Facilitation Program ($21 million) will diversify exports and support the continued modernization of the country's WTO TFA obligations and comply with other international standards.

Energy. One of the SASEC Vision flagship initiatives is the SASEC Cross-Border Power Trade Working Group, a regional mechanism to promote power grid interconnection and hydropower development for energy trade. The group identified priority generation and transmission projects to form the backbone of the SASEC power market. It included necessary economic and commercial assessments, institutional and regulatory requirements for regional transmission and generation projects, and programs to share knowledge in renewable energy and energy efficiency. Three ongoing SASEC energy projects ($841 million) are the Nepal Power System Expansion, the Second Bangladesh–India Grid Interconnection, and the Bhutan Second Green Power Development. These will strengthen transmission and generation capacity while enabling greater cross-border power flows.

Other SASEC Vision flagship initiatives launched in 2017 include petroleum/gas pipeline corridors and the development of a liquid petroleum gas transshipment hub. Further studies were suggested on (i) the private sector role in the liquid petroleum gas hub development, and (ii) liquid natural gas demand and investment needs to address supply gaps.

Economic Corridor Development. In early 2017, ADB committed $370 million to develop the Vizag–Chennai Industrial Corridor—the first phase of India's East Coast Economic Corridor. SASEC then decided to expand its economic corridor development plans to Bangladesh, Nepal, and Sri Lanka, identifying multi-sector investment opportunities. A series of seminars shared the findings of these economic corridor development studies, including (i) the Multimodal Logistics Park in Karnataka, India; (ii) Chennai–Kanyakumari Industrial Corridor in India; (iii) Southwest Bangladesh Economic Corridor; and (iv) Colombo–Trincomalee Economic Corridor in Sri Lanka.

Financing was committed for Nepal's Regional Urban Development Project ($150 million) to improve urban services and facilities in the Terai region along the country's southern border with India. Increased competitiveness and economic growth along the project route could spur cross-border trade with India and across the subregion.

Prospects

Initiatives in the energy sector are in full swing and expanding regional trade markets.

SASEC Vision flagship initiatives in energy are beginning to leverage natural resources and address the energy imbalances in South Asia. For example, greater subregional power trade can make better use of available resources for power generation—whether coal, gas, hydropower, or other renewable energy—to meet varying demand and supply patterns and seasonal needs. The recently established SASEC Cross-Border Power Trade Working Group will continue to advance priority hydropower generation and cross-border transmission projects, while using technical assistance to gain expertise on the institutional, regulatory, and commercial aspects of power trading. Another initiative is examining a regional gas value chain with, for example, India and Bangladesh collaborating on oil and gas pipeline transportation. Potential benefits include savings and expanded markets for fuel products. Also, all SASEC members can coordinate and improve liquid natural gas and liquid petroleum gas supply chains through regional hubs and networks with inland and coastal transport corridors. As mentioned, preparatory studies were begun in 2017 to assess regional demand.

Policy Challenges

SASEC demographic dividend is both an opportunity and challenge for subregional development.

A rise in the share of working-age population within SASEC over the next decade—a "demographic dividend"—creates a strong opportunity for faster economic growth in South Asia. It could be driven by strong consumption and investment backed by sound macroeconomic and market-oriented reforms. The SASEC Vision seeks to tap the economic potential from this demographic dividend through more cohesive planning and policy, and program and project coordination. However, several risks could delay or upend the process, including trade tensions and rising protectionism, mounting debt, systemic financial issues, the human capital gap, and climate change, among others.

A major issue facing a rapidly growing labor force is the potential adverse impact of technological innovation on employment, with rising automation leading to job loss. Today's innovations are driving change faster than previous technological revolutions, so SASEC members must prepare for more complex adjustments to mitigate risk. Innovation can highly skew returns and widen inequality. National policies should focus on inclusiveness, social protection, better labor regulations, and education and skill-development systems geared toward adapting to occupational shifts, among others (ADB 2018a).[48]

[48] See *Asian Development Outlook 2018* theme chapter, "How Technology Affects Jobs."

The Pacific: Building Regional Disaster Resilience through Contingent Financing[49]

Regional contingent financing can assist the region in responding to disasters.

The Pacific Disaster Resilience Program establishes a regional contingent financing solution to assist in disaster response. The program supports policies that strengthen prevention and preparedness, and provides quick and flexible financing in the immediate aftermath of disasters that are becoming more frequent across the subregion. Tonga's February 2018 disaster—tropical cyclone Gita—proved the value of contingent finance, and efforts are underway to expand coverage through similar programs across the Pacific.

Overview

Several Pacific countries are exploring innovative measures to further build resilience against disasters. In December 2017, ADB approved the Pacific Disaster Resilience Program, which provides access to contingent finance to participating countries in the immediate aftermath of a disaster. The program uses a regional approach to address disaster risk—covering Samoa, Tonga, and Tuvalu—and builds upon a contingent financing model pioneered in the Cook Islands in 2016 (ADB 2016b, 2017c).

The availability of quick-disbursing finance enables these countries to better support disaster response—from early recovery to eventual reconstruction. In this way, the program fills a gap and supplements other existing disaster risk financing instruments including contingency allocations in annual budgets, national disaster funds, and various forms of insurance.

Disaster Risk in the Pacific. Pacific economies are highly exposed to a range of natural hazards from tropical cyclones, floods, and storm surges to droughts, earthquakes, tsunamis, and volcanic eruptions. The subregion also experiences a disproportionately high share of global disasters relative to its demographic and economic size. The Pacific accounts for only 0.1% of the world population but suffers 2.3% of disasters globally. Of the 10 economies with the highest potential annual losses relative to GDP in the world, 3 are in the Pacific (Figure 6.5). In per capita terms, Pacific economies face the highest disaster risk globally (ADB 2015).

Disaster risk is also growing with climate change. For example, climate change may increase the intensity of extreme weather events, particularly severe cyclones (typhoons). Rising sea levels accelerate erosion and increase the risk of storm surges in cyclone-affected countries, while rising ocean temperatures and ocean acidification are destroying the coral reefs that form natural coastal barriers, also resulting in ecosystem decline. Weak development planning and unmanaged urbanization further exacerbate the impacts of climate change and disasters on the welfare and livelihoods of vulnerable people and communities.

Disasters can set development gains back many years by damaging critical infrastructure, disrupting social services, and diverting resources from development spending toward disaster response and reconstruction (Table 6.4). In the Pacific, where economic growth has been perennially constrained by the twin challenges of small size and remoteness, disasters have further reduced average trend growth in GDP from an estimated potential of up to 3.3% with no disasters to an actual outcome of just 2.6% over 1980–2014 (Cabezon et al. 2015).

Financing Disaster Response

Most Pacific economies have relatively small populations widely dispersed over several islands—many of which are isolated and difficult to reach when disasters strike. These geographic challenges contribute to the relatively

49 Contributed by Paul Curry, Principal Operations Coordination Specialist; Hanna Uusimaa, Climate Change Specialist; and Rommel Rabanal, Senior Economics Officer, Pacific Department. In this section, Pacific economies include the Cook Islands, the Federated States of Micronesia, Fiji, Kiribati, the Marshall Islands, Nauru, Palau, Papua New Guinea, Samoa, Solomon Islands, Timor-Leste, Tonga, Tuvalu, and Vanuatu.

Figure 6.5: Average Annual Losses from Disasters (% of gross domestic product, 2008–2017 averages)

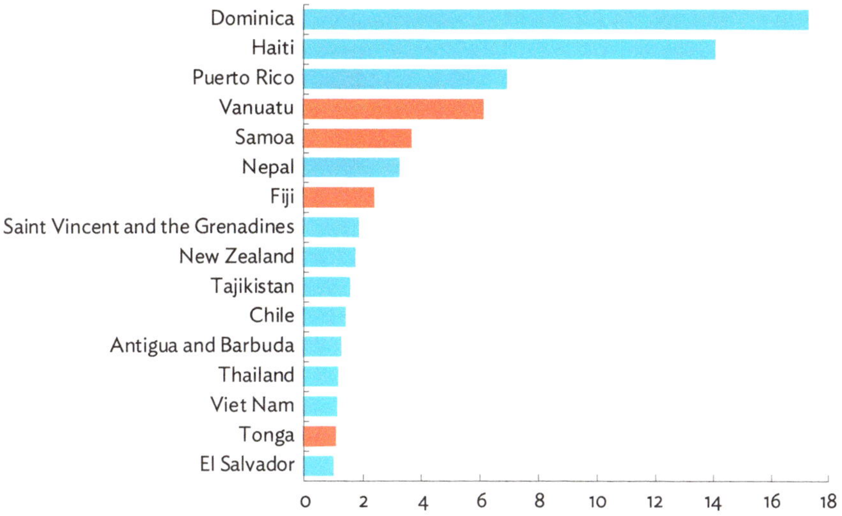

Note: Red bars are for Pacific developing member countries.
Source: EM-DAT: The Emergency Events Database - Universite catholique de Louvain (UCL) - Centre for Research on the Epidemiology of Disasters, D. Guha-Sapir - www.emdat.be, Brussels, Belgium (accessed June 2018).

Table 6.4: Economic Impact of Recent Severe Disasters in the Pacific

Cyclone/Typhoon	Year	Affected countries	Estimated value of total damage and losses ($ million)
Evan	2012	Fiji, Samoa	318.8
Haiyan	2013	Palau	1.2
Ian	2014	Fiji,[a] Tonga	45.4
Ita	2014	Solomon Islands	100.0
Maysak	2015	Federated States of Micronesia	8.5
Pam	2015	Kiribati,[a] Tuvalu, Vanuatu	478.9
Winston	2016	Fiji	108.8
Gita	2018	Tonga	164.0

[a] The value of damages and losses in Fiji and Kiribati are not included in the estimated total.
Sources: Cabezon et al. (2015); and Tonga Ministry of Finance and National Planning.

high cost of disaster response. With their small economic size and limited access to international financial markets, these countries also have limited resources and capacity to invest in disaster risk reduction and facilitate timely post-disaster recovery and reconstruction. Delays in response and recovery in turn exacerbate the indirect economic and social costs of disasters, effectively extending and deepening their impacts at the expense of a government's long-term fiscal position.

No single financing instrument is suited for all types of disasters, which range from frequent, small-scale events to rare catastrophic cataclysms. Thus, a layered approach to disaster risk financing—using a range of tools within a common framework to address different types of risk—is the most cost-effective way to comprehensively finance disaster response. Ideally, a comprehensive disaster risk financing strategy combines mechanisms prepared ahead of time (ex ante)—such as disaster reserves, contingency budgets, and insurance—and those disbursed immediately afterward (ex post), which include post-disaster budget reallocations, borrowing, and international assistance. The precise mix depends on the relative cost-effectiveness of alternative instruments for specific layers of risk in individual country contexts.

A range of potential financing tools is already available across the Pacific—from annual budget allocations that address low-impact, high-frequency events (such as localized flooding) to global bonds that address rare yet highly damaging events (like catastrophic earthquakes). But there remains strong demand for additional instruments to strengthen financial preparedness for disasters, particularly given the rising incidence of disaster events.

Contingent Finance: An Innovative Approach

There is a clear financing gap for medium-layer risks in most Pacific countries. Governments typically set aside contingency budgets and reserves to cover lower-layer risks (up to 3-year cycles), while insurance schemes such as the Pacific Catastrophe Risk Assessment and Financing Initiative and international assistance cover high-layer risks (from 10-year events). However, medium-layer risks involve events that would exhaust annual contingency budgets and reserves, but are too frequent to be covered cost-effectively through insurance (Figure 6.6).

Contingent financing is particularly cost-effective for medium-layer risks. In 2016, ADB piloted contingent financing with the Cook Islands Disaster Resilience Program as a way to provide more timely disaster-response support. A contingent line of financing was established using a policy-based approach, whereby the country's eligibility to draw financing was based on prior actions taken to strengthen policy and institutional arrangements for disaster risk management (DRM). However, actual disbursements are deferred and only triggered after the government declares a state of disaster or emergency after a natural hazard event.

The Pacific Disaster Resilience Program. Building on its Cook Islands experience, ADB designed a Pacific Disaster Resilience Program in 2017 to develop a regional contingent financing approach. The program covers Samoa, Tonga, and Tuvalu. Each suffered recent disasters causing significant damage and losses: (i) cyclone Evan in Samoa (2012), with damage equivalent to about 29% of GDP; (ii) cyclone Ian in Tonga (2014; 11% of GDP); and (iii) cyclone Pam in Tuvalu (2015; 33% of GDP). In the immediate aftermath of these disasters, the response had to be mostly financed from contingency budgets (Samoa and Tonga) and reserve funds (Tonga National Emergency Fund and the Tuvalu Survival Fund).

The Pacific Disaster Resilience Program uses policy matrices that support the development of effective and comprehensive DRM strategies and programs at the country level, and disaster resilience-related policies. These policy actions strengthen the resilience

Figure 6.6: Three Layers of Disaster Risk

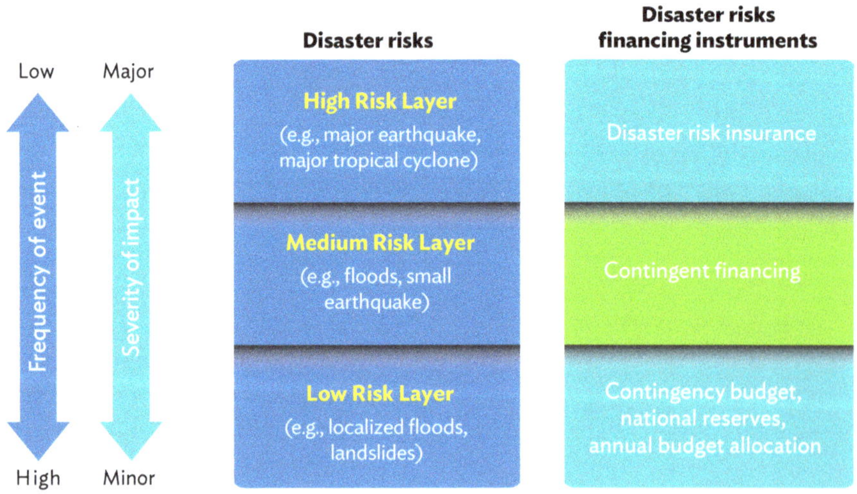

Source: World Bank (2011).

of institutions and communities in participating Pacific economies. Samoa, Tonga, and Tuvalu face similar DRM challenges and therefore benefit from a regional approach under which good practices are shared.

In the event of a declared disaster, governments can withdraw their allocations partially or entirely, depending on their assessment of the disaster's severity and resulting need. Therefore, the program provides a source of financing for response, early recovery, and reconstruction, complementing existing disaster risk financing instruments. It has several unique features: (i) it can make a payment quickly and use funds flexibly with no additional requirements—beyond national public financial management requirements—to track and report expenditures; (ii) the amount that can be released is significant in terms of immediate response needs; (iii) the amount is not dependent on any assessment of loss or measure of the intensity of the natural hazard; and (iv) funds are available for disaster events triggered by any type of natural hazard.

Immediate Proof-of-Concept: Cyclone Gita. On 12 February 2018, Cyclone Gita struck Tonga's main island of Tongatapu and neighboring 'Eua island with sustained winds of up to 230 km (145 miles) per hour. The cyclone damaged homes, government buildings, and infrastructure for basic services, including water supply, sanitation and waste management, electricity, and communications. The Ministry of Finance and National Planning estimated damage at $164 million, equivalent to about 38% of Tonga's annual GDP.

The Pacific Disaster Resilience Program allowed ADB to provide $6 million within days to help fund priority recovery activities. This marked the first time that ADB provided post-disaster funds through contingent financing, allowing the government to respond quickly to evolving needs. The contingent financing successfully supplemented Tonga's available financial resources to fund critical early response and recovery efforts. Recognizing the clear benefits of the program, Tonga has requested for replenishment of their line of contingent finance.

Moving Forward

Given the demonstrated value of contingent financing, ADB is exploring the expansion of its coverage to other Pacific economies. Initial discussions are underway, for example, to establish similar lines of contingent financing for Palau and Solomon Islands.

The Pacific Disaster Resilience Program also includes technical assistance to support and monitor progress toward achieving governments' long-term DRM goals, and to explore options for regional cooperation and collaboration for contingent financing and to potentially develop a permanent regional contingent savings mechanism. These new and innovative approaches can ensure the immediate availability of adequate disaster financing—which will be important cornerstones toward building the Pacific's overall resilience against ever-rising risks to its population's welfare and livelihood.

Improving the Provision of Public Goods through Regional Cooperation

Promoting Regional Public Goods in CAREC through Achievement of Sustainable Development Goals and COP21 Targets

CAREC 2030, the new strategic framework for CAREC, has been formulated in close alignment with the 2030 global development agenda. Achieving the 2030 global development agenda will largely depend on national efforts, but such efforts can be enhanced and complemented by regional cooperation. Coordination problems are more acute at the regional and global levels. CAREC, with its convening power, is facilitating high-level policy dialogue and promoting trust building among member countries on developing regional approaches to the SDGs and COP21 targets. Implementing the global development agenda involves coordination among many stakeholders operating at different levels (government agencies, the private sector, civil society, etc.). By providing a robust mechanism and platform for coordination and cooperation among member countries to discuss common development challenges and evolve joint approaches, CAREC is serving as a platform to unleash the potential of regional cooperation to help its members achieve the goals and targets set out in the global agenda. With support from the CAREC Institute, CAREC will help promote data collection and database creation, strengthen countries' institutional capacity, and facilitate exchange of knowledge, skills, and experience among member countries toward developing effective regional approaches to progress on the global development agenda.

Regional Public Goods in GMS

The GMS Program contributes to regional public goods in Southeast Asia by investing and developing policies that promote regional public health, mitigate climate change, and strengthen cooperation mechanisms. The GMS Health Security Project, for example, is a $114 million ADB loan to improve migrant health and mobile populations in areas where communicable disease is associated with poverty, poor sanitation, and weak health services—covering Cambodia, the Lao PDR, Myanmar, and Viet Nam. In December 2017, the GMS Core Environment Program published a Strategic Framework and Action Plan 2018–2022, designed to "mainstream sound environment management and climate resilience across priority development sectors to enhance the development impact and sustainability of the GMS Program." Finally, as regional public goods increasingly involve collective action, the GMS is strengthening cooperation mechanisms and developing regional institutions—such as the Greater Mekong Railway Association, the Mekong Tourism Coordinating Office, and working groups on environment and health.

Developing Clean Energy Resources as a Regional Public Good in SASEC

As South Asia addresses power supply and demand and increases power trade across the subregion, SASEC remains committed to developing clean energy resources, including low-carbon alternatives and energy efficiency and conservation measures. The SASEC OP anticipates harnessing unutilized hydropower potential, as well as abundant wind and solar power resources for renewable energy. SASEC members also endorsed an energy efficiency road map in 2012 to support energy efficiency policies and reform. Since the early years of SASEC power trade, the focus has been on renewable energy—for example, Bhutan's 2008 $266 million Green Power Development Project, which supported both power exports and rural electrification. It constructed the Dagachhu hydropower plant to export electricity from Bhutan to India—the first certified cross-border Clean Development Mechanism in the world—and increased domestic access to green power at lower prices using export revenues. While remote schools, health clinics, and community facilities in Bhutan benefited from access to green electricity, the project also contributed to inclusive economic growth. Nepal's 2014 $460 million SASEC Power System Expansion Project will likewise build transmission and distribution lines, along with grid substations, and will also install mini-hydroelectric power plants and mini-grid based solar or solar/wind hybrid systems.

References

Asian Development Bank. 2014. *South Asia Subregional Economic Cooperation: Trade Facilitation Strategic Framework 2014–2018*. Manila.

———. 2015. *Pacific Economic Monitor: Midyear Review, July 2015*. Manila.

———. 2016a. *South Asia Subregional Economic Cooperation: Operational Plan 2016–2025*. Manila.

———. 2016b. *Samoa, Tonga, and Tuvalu: Pacific Disaster Resilience Program*. Manila.

———. 2017a. *Key Indicators for Asia and the Pacific 2017*. Manila.

———. 2017b. *SASEC Powering Asia in the 21st Century*. Manila.

———. 2017c. *Cook Islands: Disaster Resilience Program*. Manila.

———. 2018a. *Asian Development Outlook 2018: How Technology Affects Jobs*. Manila.

———. 2018b. *The Ha Noi Action Plan 2018–2022*. Manila.

———. 2018c. *Greater Mekong Subregion Economic Cooperation Program: Overview of the Regional Investment Framework 2022*. Manila.

———. 2018d. *GMS Transport Sector Strategy 2030: Toward a Seamless, Efficient, Reliable, and Sustainable GMS Transport System*. Manila.

———. 2018e. *Strategy for Promoting Safe and Environment Friendly Agro-Based Value Chains in the Greater Mekong Subregion and Siem Reap Action Plan 2018–2022*. Manila.

Cabezon, E., L. Hunter, P. Tumbarello, K. Washimi, and Y. Wu. 2015. Enhancing Macroeconomic Resilience to Natural Disasters and Climate Change in the Small States of the Pacific. *IMF Working Paper Series. WP/15/125.* Washington, DC: International Monetary Fund.

EM-DAT: The Emergency Events Database - Universite catholique de Louvain (UCL) - Centre for Research on the Epidemiology of Disasters, D. Guha-Sapir. Brussels, Belgium. https://www.emdat.be (accessed June 2018).

ESCAP, ADB, and UNDP. 2017. *Asia-Pacific Sustainable Development Goals Outlook*. Bangkok: United Nations.

GMS Environment Operations Center. 2017. *Greater Mekong Subregion Core Environment Program Strategic Framework and Action Plan 2018–2022*. Bangkok.

International Monetary Fund. Direction of Tade Statistics (IMF-DOTS). https://data.imf.org (accessed May 2018).

———. World Economic Outlook database (IMF-WEO). https://www.imf.org/external/pubs/ft/weo/2018/01/weodata/index.aspx (accessed May 2018).

Mekong Tourism Coordinating Office. 2017. *Greater Mekong Subregion Tourism Sector Strategy 2016–2025*. Bangkok.

South Asia Subregional Economic Cooperation. http://www.sasec.asia/

Tonga Ministry of Finance and National Planning.

UN Comtrade Database. https://comtrade.un.org/ (accessed August 2018).

United Nations Conference on Trade and Development (UNCTAD) FDI Statistics. http://unctad.org/en/Pages/DIAE/FDI%20Statistics/FDI-Statistics.aspx (accessed August 2018).

World Bank. 2011. *Pacific Catastrophe Risk Financing Initiative: Catastrophe Risk Assessment and Options for Regional Risk Financing—Phase 1 Report*. Washington, DC.

———. Population Estimates and Projections. https://datacatalog.worldbank.org/dataset/population-estimates-and-projections (accessed May 2018).

———. World Devleopment Indicators. https://data.worldbank.org/products/wdi (accessed August 2018).

7

Toward Optimal Provision of Regional Public Goods in Asia and the Pacific

Introduction

Globalization, along with increasing trade, capital flows, movement of people, and rapid evolution of information and communication technology, is generating more cross-border interdependence, spillovers, and externalities of economic activities and policies. In Asia, regional trade and financial linkages have strengthened significantly over the past 2 decades along with globalization.[50] The evolution of economic growth and development in Asia is therefore characterized by global and regional linkages.

Growing regional economic interdependence and integration has created development challenges that can be most effectively dealt with collectively. Climate change and environmental pressures in the region continue to grow. Increased cross-border flow of agricultural commodities and people raises the potential for the spread of contagious diseases. Financial globalization confers benefits to capital-deficit economies, but also poses risks of financial contagion.

Solutions to these issues are available through the provision of public goods. Public goods play an important role in economic development. For example, investment in social overhead capital often provides important assistance to private capital in building an economy's productive capacity. Such investment may include transportation links, power grids, communication networks, and established property rights—all of which can lay the foundation for infrastructure that sustains development. Extending the benefits beyond one country requires regional perspectives and approaches.

Regional public goods (RPGs) are public goods whose benefits extend beyond a single nation's territory to a well-defined region (Sandler 2013). The case for RPGs embodies the need to harness the opportunities of regional cooperation and integration (RCI) and to take collective action to tackle challenges shared by neighboring economies. Good examples of RPGs include cross-border infrastructure connectivity as well as efforts to deal with transnational issues such as environmental degradation, the spread of infectious diseases, and the promotion of regional financial stability.

Regional efforts can complement national and global efforts. Regional arrangements can encourage collective action to take on transnational challenges. With fewer nations involved, regional arrangements can reduce uncertainty and help increase mutual trust among concerned economies. They can take advantage of spatial and cultural proximity in supplying RPGs collectively. Repeated long-term interactions among a small group of economies in the region can facilitate compliance with international arrangements. Multilateral developments banks (MDBs) can increase RPG provision via reducing knowledge and financing gaps. MDBs play the role of an honest broker and coordinator to enhance mutual trust and facilitate regional cooperation to help regional economies take collective actions to deal with transnational challenges.

While demand for RPGs has increased as RCI has deepened, a major difficulty in providing regional public goods is the tendency for under-provision due to their properties: the absence of a market for these goods means that consumption by people who have not paid for the good cannot necessarily be excluded. Such incentives to "free ride" can lead to a collective action problem (an extension of the well-known "Prisoners' Dilemma") among parties involved and act as a block to adequate supply. Indeed, suboptimal outcomes are the result for all participating countries when each nation acts unilaterally.

[50] Asia refers to the 48 Asia and Pacific members of the Asian Development Bank (ADB), which includes Japan and Oceania (Australia and New Zealand) in addition to the 45 developing Asian economies.

RPGs are a complex concept due to significant ambiguity in both the "regional" and "public goods" components and the following challenges to measurement of RPGs. Unlike the benefits of national and global public goods (GPGs) that can be seen within certain boundaries and are well identified, it is more difficult to determine the spillover effects of RPGs. The scope of benefits may be unclear, and placed somewhere between public goods that are national or global in nature. This makes identification of RPG beneficiaries difficult, which often generates less incentive to invest in public goods that can solve regional market failures.

The types of desirable provision mechanisms also vary by the way individual nations contribute to aggregate RPG provision. For example, while benefits of tropical rain forests are global, a regional action to protect a rain forest that extends over more than one country has a clear comparative advantage. Identifying influential players in preserving the shared resource is the key, and financial and technical assistance for the countries' lacking funds and knowledge capacity would motivate them to provide the RPG.

Accordingly, there are several reasons why the study to enhance conceptual clarity of RPGs is useful to understand RPGs. First, it is important to distinguish RPGs from other classes of public goods and to identify factors that either facilitate or inhibit their provision. Second, RPGs take various forms, each with a distinct set of properties that determine the incentives for provision. Some RPGs are provided effectively by the countries themselves, while others require assistance from regional institutions that have a wider operational experience as well as funding capacity and technical expertise. An understanding of the incentives to provide RPGs is necessary to establish whether scope exists for intervention from multilateral institutions. Third, the study on the concept and issues of RPGs can help analyze the effectiveness of different policies in fostering RPG provision.

Therefore, the next section revisits the concept of RPGs and analyzes issues that impede adequate provision of RPGs in Asia with a view to offering some guidance for a policy framework on how the region can work together toward better RPG provision. In the third section of this chapter, the rising importance of RPG provision is examined as regional cooperation and integration is increasing and the need to take collective action to address complex and transnational development challenges is further required in Asia, and a snapshot of RPG provision is presented using a few measures. In the fourth section, practical approaches to identifying and measuring RPG benefits are also discussed, alongside case studies on provision mechanisms in various sectors and regions such as Europe, Latin America and the Caribbean, and Asia. The last section presents policy considerations by RPG functional areas and a mode of RPG provision to stress the roles of RPG suppliers, in particular the roles of MDBs based on their strengths.

Concepts, Typologies, and Issues in Efficient Provision

Concepts and Typologies of RPGs

RPGs in this chapter refer to "public goods whose benefits extend beyond a single nation's territory to some well-defined region."

The definition of RPGs, adopted from Sandler (2013, 2018a), stem from being "public" and being "regional." The representation of public goods commonly used today stems from Musgrave (1969), who defined them in terms of two "classic" properties.[51] First is nonexcludability, which implies that once a good is provided, everyone will enjoy the benefits of its consumption (that is, benefits cannot be withheld from nonpayers for the good). Second is nonrivalry, that is, one person's consumption does not diminish the consumption opportunities of others (Cornes and Sandler 1996). When a public good satisfies both properties, this is considered as a "pure" public good. The examples of pure public goods include national defense, lighthouse, public health, and public knowledge

[51] The concept of "public goods" came to maturity in the middle of the 20th century, owing largely to the contributions of Paul A. Samuelson and Richard A. Musgrave. In his 1954 seminal paper "The Pure Theory of Public Expenditure," Samuelson laid the foundation for the contemporary theory of these goods by offering the first mathematical definition of public goods.

Table 7.1: A Classification of Goods

	Rival	Nonrival
Excludable	Pure private good	Club good (impure public good)
Nonexcludable	Common-pool resource (impure public good)	Pure public good

Source: Mankiw (2015).

such as official statistics published by government agencies, which are available to all including those who do not pay for their benefits, while their consumption does not diminish the benefits enjoyed by others.

However, most public goods are "impure," meaning that they are partially rivalrous and/or partially excludable. Types of impure public goods include (i) "club goods" which involve some excludability but do not involve rivalry among the group of users, and (ii) "common-pool resources" which involve rivalry but not excludability (Table 7.1).

An example of a club good is a toll road where additional vehicles using the road do not reduce the benefits (up to a maximum road capacity) enjoyed by current users, but they can be excluded if they do not pay the toll. A common pool resource includes a shared fishing ground in a region where one country's catch reduces the fish stock available.[52] In general, partial nonexcludability could easily occur when costs for maintenance need to be charged at minimal levels while partial rivalry could arise when the quality and quantity of RPGs could be worsened when there are a large number of participating countries in a club (Sandler 2013, Cornes and Sandler 1996). Further examples of RPGs are illustrated in Table 7.2.

As much as being "public" may not be easily defined for a certain good, being "regional" is often elusive to appropriately capture the reach of the good's benefits.

Goods can easily change from being public to private and vice versa, subject to policy decisions with legal and institutional setups. For example, a book is a private good, but the words it contains are only private if protected by copyright laws. Knowledge is a public good, but inventions are private only when patented. Without copyright and patent laws, the writers and inventors may not have incentive to provide innovations that produce public benefits. On the other hand, many nonprofit organizations make research and information freely available, making the good public. As such, being public may not be defined by characteristics such as nonrivalry and nonexcludability, but by prevailing social values and the perception of what good should be provided by society through nonmarket mechanisms.

Like being public, being regional is also subject to a geographic definition that in many cases is set through national policy and/or intergovernmental decisions. Limitations are inherent in the definition of "a region" whose boundaries are seldom well-defined (De Lombaerde et al. 2010). A region can be defined variously in geological, geoclimatic, geographic, cultural, or political terms (Sandler 2004). The degree of interconnectedness with other countries can influence the definition of a region. Furthermore, a region's boundaries may change over time (Estevadeordal and Goodman 2017). The size of a political union can grow as more countries join. The expansion of a region implies that the number of potential beneficiaries increases.

While the scope of benefits of RPGs is often used to distinguish the classes of public goods (being either national, regional, or global public goods), it is rather difficult to clearly delineate the boundaries of these benefits between nations or regions in practice.

National public goods (NPGs) such as national security, lighthouses, and national parks, produce public benefits that remain within a national border. GPGs such as the protection of the ozone layer and climate change mitigation can produce benefits worldwide. RPGs such as controlling regionally contained diseases, cross-border infrastructure connectivity, and a regional

[52] Another class of public goods are "joint products," which result in multiple outputs that vary in their degree of publicness (Sandler 2003). Joint products may yield both country-specific benefits and nonexcludable regional benefits. For instance, electricity generated from renewable sources can provide domestic consumers with electricity at a premium (a country-specific benefit) and can reduce pollution in the region by displacing fossil fuel-based electricity sources, which is a regional pure public benefit (Kotchen 2006).

Table 7.2: Examples of Regional Public Goods and Their Benefits/Externalities

Function	Regional Public Goods	Benefits/Externalities
Economic Cooperation and Integration	Bilateral and regional trade agreements	Reduces discriminatory trade restrictions and promotes peace and security
	Prevention of financial contagion	Prevents spread of negative shocks such as excessively volatile exchange rates and equity prices
	Regional liquidity support through regional financial agreements	Promotes regional macroeconomic and financial stability
Human and Social Development	Response to outbreaks of emerging and reemerging diseases	Reduces health-related loss of work hour and labor productivity
	Elimination of communicable diseases	Breaks chain of transmission within region. May serve as stepping stone to global elimination
	Preventing emergence of resistance	Prevents reduction in the region's working-age population who are affected by the virus' resistance to drugs
	Unrestricted knowledge generated from research and development particularly beneficial to the region	Improves the quality of life in the region through technological advances in fields such as medicine and education
	Advisory services and research on agriculture through regional agricultural organizations	Increases agricultural productivity in the countries applying such knowledge
Natural Resources and Environment	Reduction in greenhouse gas emissions and climate change adaptation	Lowers the risk of climate change (such as rising sea level, changing growing seasons, and increased droughts and heatwaves) while adaptation reduces the damages from climate change to particular countries
	Control of air pollution transboundary in nature	Reduces prevalence of diseases related to air pollution as well as occurrence of acid rain
	River basin management	Benefits all riparian states in terms of water sharing, flood control, water quality
	Control of marine pollution and protection of regional seas	Protects marine life and is especially beneficial to coastal states.
	Control of persistent pollutants	Protects human health and the environment
	Control of hazardous waste transport	Benefits countries with weak governance that import wastes
	Marine fisheries management	Increases sustainable yields and prevents collapse of stocks
	Food security and resource management through regional cooperation	Promotes consistent supply of food and other agricultural products, as well as conservation of their sources
Connectivity	Cross-border transport and ICT infrastructure and national infrastructure that involves cross-border dimensions	Expands trade opportunities and promotes freer movement of commodities and inputs
	Trade facilitation such as customs reform and national single window	Facilitates international trade, faster movement of perishable goods
Peace and Security	Nonproliferation of nuclear weapons	Provides a security to all countries in the region and beyond
	Prohibition on nuclear testing	Limits development of new weapons, and therefore a technological arms race
	Prevention of terrorism	Promotes influx of investments and tourists, as well as stable business environment
	Preventing state failure	Promotes market stability and investor confidence
Governance	Nonproprietary technical standards	Encourages adapting best practices for increased productivity and growth
	Harmonized standards and higher quality education through regional cooperation	Promotes regionwide labor productive gain due to wider access to quality education
	Harmonization of intellectual property rules	Increases knowledge production at the margin; it would also redistribute rents to past research and development

ICT = information and communication technology.
Source: ADB based on Barrett (2018a, 2018b).

Figure 7.1: Classes of Public Goods, by Scope of Benefits

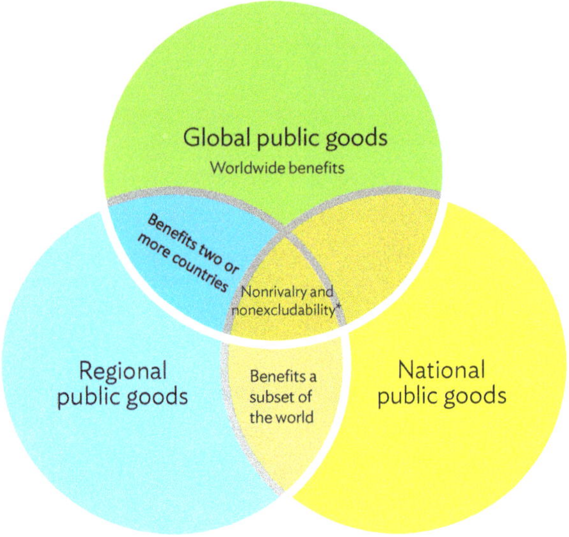

* It is possible for the public good to be partially rival and/or partially excludable, in which case it would be an impure public good.
Source: Fredriksson and Wolff (2018).

Table 7.3: Definition of Regional Public Goods—Multilateral Development Banks and the Literature

MDB / Literature	RPG Definition
Asian Development Bank	A benefit shared by two or more countries in a region
African Development Bank	Goods or services whose benefits are shared by a group of countries in the same region in a nonrival and nonexcludable way
Sandler (2013, 2018a)	RPGs are public goods whose benefits extend beyond a single nation's territory to some well-defined region.

MDB = multilateral development bank, RPG = regional public good.
Sources: ADB (2006), AfDB (2013).

disaster warning system, lie in between national and global public goods in the scope of benefits (Figure 7.1). However, NPGs are becoming increasingly interlinked and challenging the domain of regional and global public goods. For example, national defense, commonly considered an NPG, may have cross-country spillovers if it affects the likelihood of conflict between countries within a region. Reducing air or water pollution can be considered an example of an NPG and RPG, since a country doing so provides benefits of cleaner air or water domestically and to its neighbors, but such benefits may not necessarily have global reach. Most GPGs are indeed more regional in nature than global, as many public goods are at least on some level excludable and only to some degree nonrival, confining the benefits to a certain geographic scope.

Overall, some concepts of being "public" and "regional" are used together to define RPGs by most RPG suppliers including MDBs.

For example, the Asian Development Bank (ADB) defines an RPG as "a benefit shared by two or more countries in a region" under its strategy for regional economic cooperation and integration (ADB 2006). The operational definition of RPGs used by the Inter-American Development Bank (IDB) is "goods, services, or resources that are produced and consumed collectively by the public sector and, if appropriate, the private, nonprofit sector in a minimum of three borrowing member countries of the IDB" (Tres et al. 2014). The African Development Bank (AfDB) defined RPGs as goods or services whose benefits are shared by countries in the same region in a nonrival and nonexcludable way (AfDB 2015) (Table 7.3).

Issues in Efficient Provision of RPGs

This subsection touches upon four key properties of determining RPG provision. Those four key properties help determine countries' incentives to contribute to RPG provision and the scope for collective action, including the degrees of (i) nonexcludability; (ii) nonrivalry; (iii) aggregation technology (that is, how individual contributions add up to make the socially available level of the public good); and (iv) the scope of benefits (Figure 7.2). The effectiveness of provision mechanisms mainly depends on these properties, and potential interventions should therefore be tailored accordingly.

For instance, in response to bottlenecks in road transport network where it is nonrival and excludable and the role of a country with the poorest transport network is the most influential, multilateral institutions can provide capacity building and funds if the country lacks knowledge and financial resources. Efficiency of the RPG provision mechanism may also depend on

Figure 7.2: An Overview of the Regional Public Good Provision Process

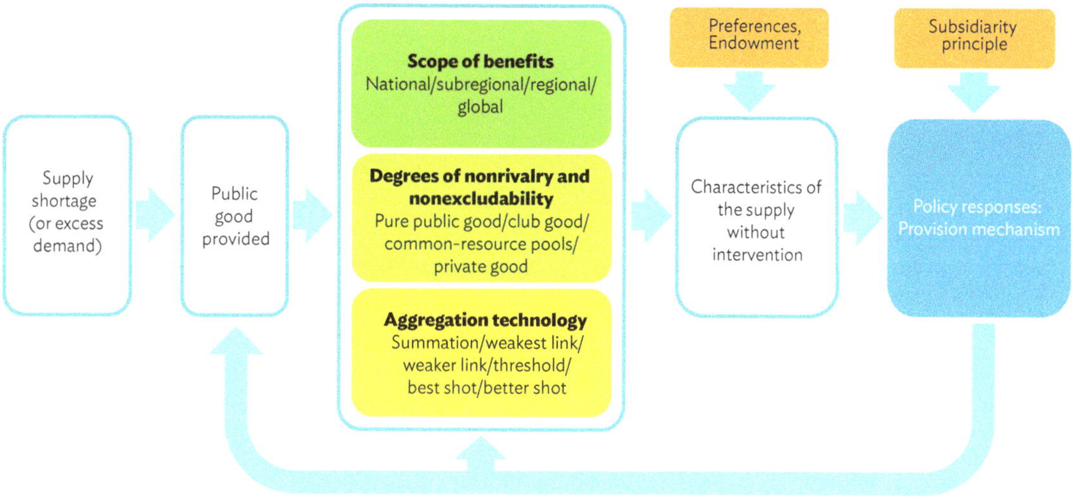

Source: ADB based on Sandler (2018a, 2018b).

country-specific endowment and preferences as well as whether the subsidiarity principle can hold; i.e., if the scope of benefits is matched to the jurisdiction of the RPG supplier.[53]

MARKET FAILURES

The two properties of public goods, making it extremely difficult to exclude consumption by others once provided (termed "nonexcludability") and making it extremely difficult for one party's consumption of a good to diminish consumption by others (termed "nonrivalry"), give rise to market failures that may require policy interventions to facilitate provision.

Nonexcludability means that it is costly to prevent nonpaying parties from consumption of a good's benefits. In this context, the incentive to contribute to the provision of nonexcludable RPGs would be weak due to the free-riding problem (see Box 7.1 for a game theoretic approach to the free-riding problem). Market failures are also caused by nonrivalry of benefits which implies the marginal cost of extending consumption to another user is zero (Hardin 1997). An efficient allocation of nonrival RPGs requires a price of the public good equal to the marginal cost which is zero. However, charging a price above zero for nonrival RPGs is allocatively inefficient, since this implies charging additional users for enjoying the benefits from the good even if it costs nothing to include them. The inefficiency can be reduced if governments tax its consumption and redistribute the revenue. However, citizens' valuations of the good are often unknown and difficult to estimate in practice. Further, imposing a tax at a transnational level may require a supranational authority, which may not exist (Arce M and Sandler 2002).

"Impure" public goods are less undersupplied or overused because of limited exclusion and partial rivalry compared to "pure" public goods.

The inefficiency associated with impure public goods is less extreme than that of pure public goods if some exclusion is practiced to account for consumption-related incremental costs such as user charges (Sandler 2013). Club goods such as highway networks are subject to congestion; in this case toll charges can enhance efficiency by internalizing negative spillovers of congestion via identifying a price mechanism such as charging toll fees. If there is no price mechanism to

53 The subsidiarity principle indicates that allocative efficiency is achieved when an institution's jurisdiction precisely matches the benefit range of the public good (Olson 1969; Sandler 2004, 2006).

Box 7.1: Game Theoretic Approach in Public Goods Provision: The Linear Public Goods Game

Suppose that there are N countries, and that each country must decide whether to contribute to the public good. Country i ($i=1, 2, ..., N$) chooses to provide the good ($q_i=1$) or not to provide it ($q_i=0$) with the objective of maximizing its payoff unilaterally, denoted π_i, taking as given the provision choices of all other countries in the region. The provision of a regional (linear) public good can be viewed as a "game" in the sense that, the outcome any country i is able to realize depends not only on what country i does but also on what the other county does.

The simplest representation of payoffs is for a linear public good:

$$\pi_i = bQ - cq_i, \text{ where } Q = q_i + Q_{-i} = q_i + \sum_{j=1, j\neq i}^{N} q_j$$

where Q is the aggregate provision by all countries, q_i the amount provided by country i, Q_{-i} the amount supplied by all countries except country i, b is a benefit for one more unit of provision, and c is a cost for one more unit of provision.

It can be shown that every country will supply the good if $b>c$. However, every country will want not to supply the good if $c>b$, i.e., "not provide" becomes a dominant strategy, which leads to the Nash equilibrium where no country can gain by changing what it is doing, given what all the other countries are doing.

Alternatively, all countries in the region can act collectively to choose provision levels $q_1, q_2, ..., q_N$ so as to maximize the collective payoffs, denoted Π, assuming that an agreement to cooperate among players is binding:

$$\Pi = \sum_{j=1}^{N} \pi_j = (bN - c)Q$$

It can be shown that that every country contributes to the public good if $bN>c$ and not to supply it if $c>bN$. This solution describes the full cooperative outcome of the linear public goods game.

The first row in the table below shows the conditions under which countries have neither unilateral nor collective incentives to supply the public good. The next row shows the conditions that apply when countries have unilateral incentives to supply the public good, and this is also the best possible outcome for the entire region. Finally, the last row shows the conditions under which the region does best when every country supplies the public good, but no country within the region has an incentive to supply the public good unilaterally. It describes provision of the public good as the "Prisoners' Dilemma" game.

Solutions in the Linear Public Goods Game

Condition	Nash Equilibrium	Full Cooperative Outcome	Interpretation
$c>bN$	$q_i^{NE} = 0$	$q_i^{FC} = 0$	The good is not provided and should not be provided.
$b>c$	$q_i^{NE} = 1$	$q_i^{FC} = 1$	The good is provided and should be provided.
$bN>c>b$	$q_i^{NE} = 0$	$q_i^{FC} = 1$	The good is not provided, but should be provided (Prisoners' Dilemma).

Source: Barrett (2018a).

internalize negative spillovers, then impure public goods are overused.

AGGREGATION TECHNOLOGIES

Understanding how individual nation's contribution adds to the overall provision of RPGs (so called "aggregation technology") can help RPG suppliers, including nations and MDBs alike, take the most appropriate modes of provision to avoid collective action problem.[54]

Aggregation technology may include, for example, "summation," "weighted sum," "weakest link and weaker link," "threshold," and "best and better shot" (Table 7.4).

Summation. A summation aggregator indicates that the level of the public good is determined by the sum of all contributors' provision. This type of public goods is exposed to the strongest free-riding incentive. In reducing greenhouse gas emissions, for example, the overall reduction would be equal to the sum of the decrease in each country's emission level. However, a noncontributing country can easily enjoy the benefits of climate change mitigation by relying on the efforts of other countries. Such free-riding problem can result in the aggregate reduction much less than needed. As such, regional and subregional institutions can fund RPGs with the summation technology through loans or grants. Efforts to fund RPGs can be bolstered by charitable foundations, partnerships, or nongovernment organizations.

Weighted sum. For a weighted-sum aggregator, each contributor's provision can be assigned an empirically determined weight when determining the overall level of the public good. Weighted-sum aggregators have less free-riding incentives as countries are informed about how they impact total provision. Examples include the reduction of acid rain or river pollution, for which a country's relative location affects its ability to clean up the pollutant. In an acid-rain scenario, downwind countries are the main recipients of depositions and are, therefore, motivated to reach agreement with other countries to control sulfur and nitrogen emissions. When regional and subregional institutions take a lead to bolster countries' actions, scientific monitoring data allow these institutions to distribute their resources among countries, where these resources can have the greatest effect based on spatial and other factors.[55]

Weakest link and weaker link. For a weakest-link aggregator, the smallest contribution determines the aggregate level of RPG provision. Weakest-link aggregation for instance is associated with actions that curb the spread of an infectious disease. Disease outbreaks are most likely to occur in those countries with the poorest disease-controlling capacity. Policy intervention would be efficient when it is directed to the most vulnerable economies in need for funding and capacity building. If all countries in a region have the same endowments and preferences, weakest-link public goods present less efficiency concerns; that is, resources are unlikely to be wasted as each country's provision is likely to match the smallest contribution. When endowments differ and poorer countries cannot afford to contribute, necessary assistance can be provided by regional and subregional institutions in the form of grants and capacity building.

A less extreme form of weakest link is weaker link, where the smallest contribution has the greatest influence on the aggregate level of RPG provision, followed by the second smallest contribution, and so on (Cornes 1993, Cornes and Sandler 1996, Sandler 1992). For example, maintaining regional financial stability is the typical weakest- or weaker-link RPG, whose level is disproportionately determined by one or more countries with the most vulnerable financial institutions and the poorest financial practices. When endowments differ by country, shoring-up efforts are still needed by regional and subregional institutions.

54 One of the earliest papers on the aggregation technology of public goods is Jack Hirshleifer's 1983 article "From Weakest-Link to Best-Shot: The Voluntary Provision of Public Goods," where it was called a "social composition function." Afterwards, this concept was discussed by Harrison and Hirshleifer (1989), Cornes (1993), and Cornes and Sandler (1996). Formally, the term aggregation technology then appeared in latter works such as Conybeare, Murdoch, and Sandler (1994); and Sandler (1998). See Cornes and Sandler (1996) for mathematical expressions of aggregation technology.

55 The Convention on Long-Range Transboundary Air Pollution program and the Acid Deposition Monitoring Network are intended to ascertain the weights based on the monitored dispersion of pollutants from the source to the recipient countries (Chung 2017).

Table 7.4: Selected Aggregator Technologies—Characteristics and Recommendations

Technology	Illustration	Characteristics of the Technology and Recommendations
Summation $Q = \sum_{i=1}^{n} q_i$ curbing greenhouse gas emissions	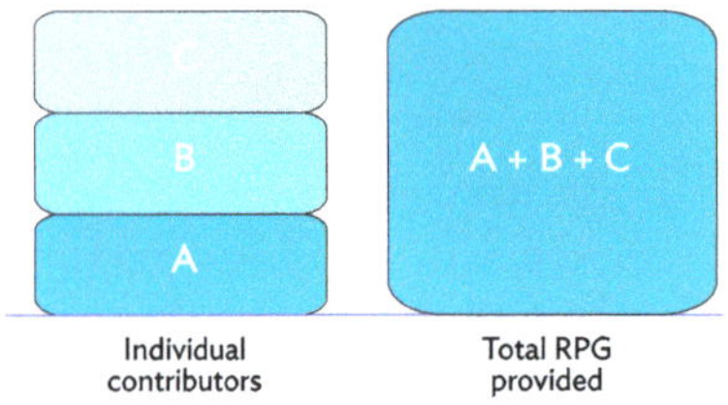 	*Characteristics:* • Free-riding tendency due to the presence of countries relying on the efforts of others • Prisoners' Dilemma tends to arise *Recommendations:* • Regional institutions can provide funding (grants, loans) • Other institutions can bolster the support
Weighted sum $Q = \sum_{i=1}^{n} \alpha_i q_i$ reducing acid rain or river pollution	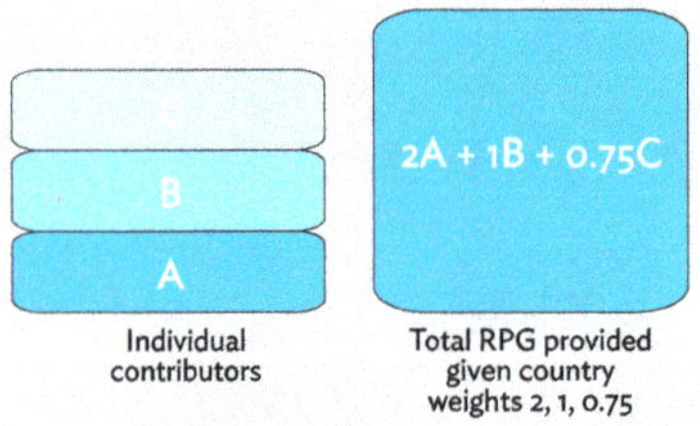 	*Characteristics:* • Less of a free-riding tendency • Countries with larger impacts are incentivized to act *Recommendations:* • Regional institutions can provide information on countries' impacts • Institute monitoring • Distribute resources according to countries' impact
Weakest link $Q = \min\{q_1, \ldots, q_n\}$ reducing the spread of an infectious disease	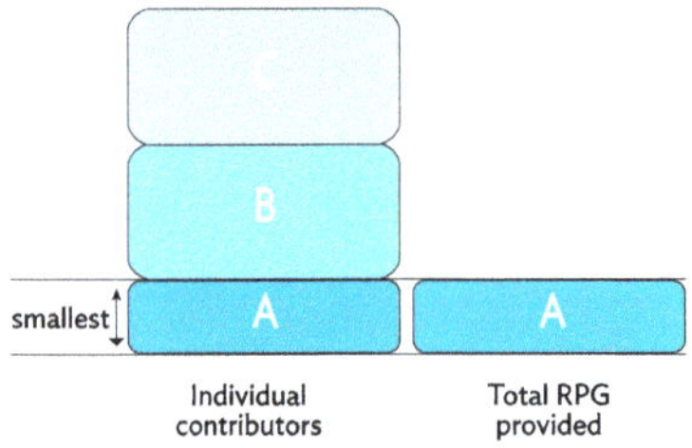 	*Characteristics:* • Efficient if all countries have the same endowments and preferences • Problem arises when poorer countries cannot afford to contribute *Recommendations:* • Capacity building is the key • Regional institutions can shore up weakest-link countries through grants
Threshold $Q = \sum_{i=1}^{n} q_i \geq \bar{Q}$; otherwise 0 malaria elimination	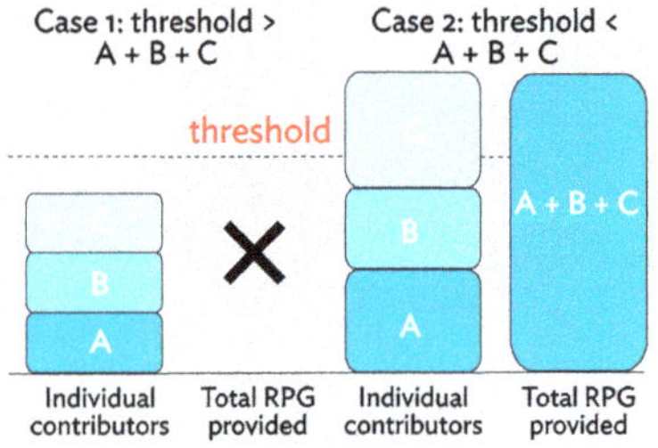 	*Characteristics:* • A higher threshold provides a greater incentive to act • Coordination problem in reaching the threshold *Recommendations:* • Regional institutions can design thresholds • Motivate (reward) countries to be part of the threshold contributors • Global institutions can assist
Best shot $Q = \max\{q_1, \ldots, q_n\}$ Development of vaccines/Best practices and measures to contain financial contagion	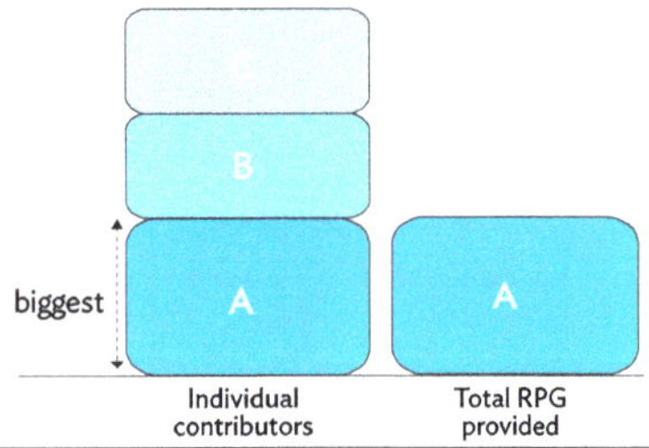 	*Characteristics:* • Hegemony fosters provision • Coordination may be difficult for multiple best shooters • It becomes an issue when a region is devoid of a best shooter *Recommendations:* • Loans are appropriate to assist best-shooter countries • Regional institutions can pool actions for large-scale best-shot RPGs

RPG = regional public good.
Note: Q is overall amount of the public good available for consumption, q_i is a contribution of country i, α_i is a weight, and $\bar{Q}$ is a threshold.
Source: ADB based on Sandler (2018a).

Threshold. The threshold aggregator requires provision of the public good to meet or exceed a certain level before benefits are generated. Threshold RPGs offer greater incentive than summation RPGs to act until the threshold is obtained. A higher threshold provides more incentives to provide toward efficient outcome. For example, in eliminating infectious diseases such as malaria in a region, countries may take possible measures independently and/or collectively to ensure that the required level of aggregate efforts is reached. Regional and subregional institutions can identify or design a threshold so that more efficient provision is achieved.[56] These institutions can also pool efforts by contributing funds of their own and reaching out to other institutions.

Best shot and better shot. For best-shot public goods, the largest contribution determines the available level of RPG. For example, the development of vaccines would have the best chance of success if the most technologically advanced country takes the lead. Loans are appropriate to assist best-shooter countries. At the regional level, the issue becomes a coordination issue when there are many potential best-shooter countries because only a single capable country needs to provide the best-shot RPGs. Regional institutions can serve to coordinate and prioritize actions among the leader countries. If the best-shooter country is not available, then regional institutions can pool actions or coordinate action among subregions. For large-scale best-shot RPGs, funds from global institutions or other multilateral institutions can be solicited.

Better-shot public goods are a softer version of best shot, for which the largest contribution has the biggest marginal influence on the overall provision, followed by the second-largest contribution, and so on. Governance and institutions often involve developing best practices, which are typical examples of better- or best-shot RPGs. More practical examples include regulatory practices, banking practices, and benchmarking data (Berg and Horrall 2008). Better-shot public goods require less need for hegemony, pooling of actions, and outside intervention than the best shot case of many potential best shooter economies. Since more than one country is willing to provide, there is less need to coordinate or concentrate provision activity.

THE SCOPE OF RPG BENEFITS AND THE SUBSIDIARITY PRINCIPLE

The subsidiarity principle indicates that allocative efficiency is achieved when an institution's jurisdiction precisely matches the benefit range of the public good.

If the public good's range of spillover benefits is greater than the institution's jurisdiction whose members supply the public good, provision decisions will fail to account for some benefit recipients, resulting in under-provision (Sandler 2004, 2006). On the other hand, if the range of spillover benefits is smaller than the institution's jurisdiction, over-provision is anticipated as non-recipients cover some of the good's provision cost. Therefore, the subsidiarity implies that global public goods should be provided or assisted by global institutions, while RPGs should be provided or assisted by regional institutions.

A blind application of the subsidiarity principle, however, may be undesirable due to economies of scale and spillovers associated with RPG provision.

Adherence to the appropriate jurisdictional arrangement can boost efficiency, reduce transaction costs, and promote institutional evolution and innovation (Table 7.5). On the other hand, economies of scale may justify an RPG-providing jurisdiction whose domain exceeds that of a good's spillover range if the reduced unit costs offset any inefficiency losses. For example, in peacekeeping missions, the United Nations can achieve scale economies which may not be achievable at the regional or subregional levels. Similarly, economies of scope refer to cost-savings when two or more RPGs are supplied by the same institution regardless of heterogeneous benefit recipients. Tailoring jurisdictions to these spillover ranges would result in a proliferation of jurisdictions, which is costly to support. In practice, when the requisite regional institution or jurisdiction is absent, the next nearest (smaller or larger) jurisdiction can assume the role.

56 Other design principles that promote optimal supply for a threshold RPG is to allow for cost sharing or refundability if the threshold is not reached (Sandler 2004).

Table 7.5: Supporting and Detracting Factors for Regional Subsidiarity

Supporting Factors	Detracting Factors
• Bolsters efficiency by matching recipients' marginal gains with marginal provision costs • Curtails tax spillovers to non-beneficiaries, thereby fostering efficiency • Limits transaction costs by augmenting repeated interactions, reducing asymmetric information, and curtailing the number of participants • Promotes the evolution of regional institutions based on shared culture, experiences, challenges, norms, and values • Fosters intraregional institutional innovations • Focuses on participants with the most at stake	• Economies of scale favor larger jurisdictions than RPG's spillover range • Economies of scope support providing two or more RPGs whose spillover ranges do not coincide • Economies of learning may require oversized jurisdictions to augment the cumulative RPG provision • Requisite subsidiarity-based institution (jurisdiction) may not exist • Too costly to tailor jurisdictions to each subregional public good owing to the proliferation of jurisdictions • Aggregator technologies (e.g., best shot, better shot, and threshold) may favor pooling efforts beyond requisite jurisdiction • Aggregator technologies (e.g., weakest link and weaker link) may require that participants bolster capacity beyond the spillover range of the public good • Requisite financing may require a jurisdiction beyond the good's range of benefit spillovers

RPG = regional public good.
Source: Sandler (2018a).

OTHER FACTORS TO CONSIDER IN RPG PROVISION

The provision of RPGs can be also affected by region-specific circumstances and conditions.

First, some regions may lack a dominant country and consequently leadership in providing RPGs. This issue may be less severe on a global level, as developed countries may either lead by example by providing the global public goods (GPGs) themselves or encourage other countries to also contribute to provision (Arce M and Sandler 2002). Second, regions may be prone to rivalries and local disagreements that reduce the scope for collaboration (Collier et al. 2003, Sandler 2013). Third, donors have traditionally relied on global and national institutions, as opposed to regional institutions, to provide public goods (Sandler 2013). Regional institutions that are often in the best position to promote the provision of RPGs may therefore be weaker in terms of reputation, experience, and capacity (Sandler 2006).

On the other hand, factors such as a smaller number of participants and proximities in geography and culture can facilitate RPG supply relative to GPGs.

Cooperation is more likely to succeed if the size of the group is small and thus, coercion between members is strong (Olson 1965). Countries within a region are located close to each other and may be culturally similar (Estevadeordal and Goodman 2017). As such, they are more likely to regularly interact and may therefore have strong incentives to abide by agreements (Sandler 2006). These can give more scope for collective action than for GPGs by reducing the costs of cooperation or enforcing agreements to provide RPGs.

Regional Public Goods in Asia

Regional Cooperation and Integration and RPGs

Asia's demand for RPGs has been rising as the region is being more interconnected.

Asia has progressed rapidly on regional economic integration over the past few decades, driven by, in particular, trade and investment and the expansion of regional value chain. Asia's intraregional trade share has grown, from 53.2% in 2001 to about 57.8% in 2017, while 68%[57] of Asia's total exports participated in the global value chain in 2017. Foreign direct investment inflows within Asia have risen in the same steady manner, from about \$61.8 billion in 2001 to \$260.0 billion in 2017, with intraregional share increasing from 46.6% to 50.2%

[57] This is measured by the share of value-added contents of gross exports used for further processing through cross-border production networks.

during the same period. Intraregional share of portfolio equity (debt) rose from 11.7% (7.7%) in 2001 to 18.1% (16.4%) as of December 2017. Migration within the region similarly climbed, from about 23.6 million in 2000 to 30.2 million in 2017.

Increasing regional and global integration creates risks that can go beyond national borders and cross generations. The global financial crisis of a decade ago reversed years of development in many countries, while economies and financial systems continue to be vulnerable to the risk of financial contagion. Following the 1997/98 Asian financial crisis, Asian countries recognized the need for a regional mechanism to avert crises, mitigate financial contagion risks, and improve regional policy dialogue and cooperation to deal with potential policy spillovers (Huh and Park 2017). Other regional challenges have emerged in various sectors, including environment and climate change, health and disease, energy, trade, and transport facilitation.

Collective action is required to address increasingly complex and transnational development challenges. However, various obstacles to cooperation, such as diverging national interests, exist.

Climate change affects countries unevenly, and scientific uncertainty about its impacts contributes to divergent interests and incentives to act. Reforms in the global financial system are made difficult when countries do not agree to more stringent standards to protect their national banking systems. Information asymmetries such as insufficient information about corruption or local authorities' implementation also hamper donors' willingness to contribute, while limited resources and capacity make it difficult for low-income countries to reform different economic sectors. Centered on the common goal, knowledge sharing and dissemination as well as support for capacity building can help narrow information gaps and reduce the uncertainty of cooperation failure (Ötker-Robe 2014). When incentives are not aligned, an incremental approach may be useful because it helps communicate the benefits of collective action.

Regional cooperation can promote RPG provision that complements national efforts to advance national welfare.

With fewer nations involved than in global agreements, regional arrangements can complement global frameworks and help effectively provide global public goods such as malaria control and elimination. Regional arrangements can reduce uncertainty and take advantage of spatial and cultural proximity. Past and ongoing interactions among a small group of regional economies facilitates compliance of regional arrangements (Sandler 2006).

Greater provision of RPGs via regional arrangements can promote regional cooperation and integration (RCI). The experience of the European monetary union, for instance, shows the benefits of regional collective actions and how regional institutions can help move the process along, including through proper sequencing from a common currency to regional full regulatory and supervisory integration (Box 7.2). A regional labor mobility framework and a human capital development mechanism are increasingly promising forms of RPGs for aging Asia because they facilitate migration from labor-surplus to labor-deficit countries (Box 7.3).

MDBs can help promote RCI through the provision of RPGs as they have substantial regional expertise in knowledge, finance, and coordinating country efforts.

MDBs can help to reduce knowledge gaps to demonstrate the benefits of regional projects and boost cooperation among member countries in reaching regional agreements. National capacities can be harnessed into higher regional standards and benefit from economies of scale, while financial resources can be mobilized to help low-income countries develop capacity and implement RPG projects. MDBs also reduce the costs of coordination among governments, lifting efforts to tackle common development issues. MDBs play an important role in achieving the Sustainable Development Goals (SDGs) where a systematic link between RPGs and those goals can be established (Box 7.4).[58]

[58] The Sustainable Development Goals (SDGs) represent a global agenda with 17 goals to end poverty, protect the planet, and ensure prosperity for all. The goals were adopted as part of the 2030 Agenda for Sustainable Development adopted by 191 member states of the United Nations in September 2016. (United Nations. About the Sustainable Development Goals. https://www.un.org/sustainabledevelopment/sustainable-development-goals/ [accessed September 2018]).

Box 7.2: Financial Stability in Europe

Europe's historical quest for exchange rate stability lies at the root of the European monetary integration process. An urgent push toward integration came with the crisis of the Bretton Woods international monetary arrangements, which collapsed in 1971 with the suspension of dollar convertibility. Exchange rates were a particular concern to countries that were very open and traded a lot with each other. Moreover, exchange rate volatility would have increased the cost of administering the European Common Agricultural Policy (CAP) (McNamara 1998, Eichengreen 2007).

The Maastricht Treaty, ratified in 1992, laid out a set of convergence criteria for prospective members to meet to join the monetary union.[a] In May 1998, 11 countries met these and formed the nucleus of the monetary union, which then expanded to today's 19 members. On 1 January 1999, the euro was introduced and the Eurosystem—the European Central Bank (ECB) and the central banks of European Economic and Monetary Union (EMU) countries—took responsibility for monetary policy in the euro area.

The monetary union, however, still suffered the typical weakness of fixed exchange rate systems—i.e., that no institution could force central banks to intervene to support the currencies of other countries. The single currency had a huge impact on financial flows within the euro area. The convergence of short- and long-term yields, coupled with persistent differences in inflation rates, led to marked divergence in real interest rates. In the so-called "South" (or "Periphery") of the euro area, interest rates dropped to historic lows. With access to a euro area-wide (as opposed to country-wide) markets for funds, this led to a boom of private indebtedness and the development of large current account imbalances within the monetary union. The volatility underlying the capital flow movements became clear during the euro crisis in 2011, when capital flows suddenly stopped and reversed, revealing an underlying structural economic divergence that was hardly sustainable.

The crisis also revealed that the euro area lacked tools to prevent macroeconomic imbalances and financial imbalances—i.e., strict and uniform micro-prudential banking supervision (Claeys 2017). Efforts at regulatory harmonization left supervision to an exclusively national level: even monetary unification in 1999 was not accompanied by the establishment of supranational institutions for financial supervision and resolution, even though there was a logic for it (Folkerts-Landau and Garber 1992; Schoenmaker 1997; Darvas, Schoenmaker, and Véron 2016).

In 2009, the report from the "de Larosière group" appointed by the European Commission concluded that the supervisory framework needed to be strengthened and recommended the creation of three European supervisory authorities: European Banking Authority, European Securities and Markets Authority, and European Insurance and Occupational Pensions Authority. This also recommended that a European Systemic Risk Board be established to monitor macroprudential risk (but without active macroprudential powers). These initiatives were meant to ensure closer cooperation and better exchange of information between national supervisors and to shape the further development of a "single rulebook" applicable to all the European Union countries.

The bolder institutional development was the establishment of the European banking union for euro area countries, triggered by the self-reinforcing negative feedback loops between banks and issuers of sovereign debt that characterized the euro crisis. The existence of national supervision and resolution for banks that, in the euro area, tended to be overexposed to government bonds created a correlation between banking and sovereign debt crises, which in the context of a monetary union triggered a balance of payment crisis (Merler and Pisani-Ferry 2012). The European Council of 28–29 June 2012 agreed to shift bank supervisory authority from the national to the European level, delegating it to the Single Supervisory Mechanism within the ECB. Overall, national supervisors would have little incentive to internalize the cross-border effects of their domestic decisions, and could be prone to capture by their local political systems. A supranational supervisor like the ECB is better placed to oversee the transnational dimension of domestic policy and identify potential risks for the euro area.

[a] The inflation rate should be no more than 1.5% higher than the average of the inflation rates in the three European Union (EU) states with the lowest inflation. Government deficit should be no more than 3% of GDP. Public debt should be no more than 60% of GDP. Exchange rate should be within a ±15% range from an unchanged central rate stable interest rates. The 10-year government bonds shall be no more than 2% higher than the average of similar 10-year government bond yields in the three EU states with the lowest inflation.

Source: Fredriksson et al. (2018).

Box 7.3: Cross-Border Labor Mobility and Human Capital Development in Aging Asia

In Asia, aging societies in some countries and a growing workforce in others provide an opportunity for labor mobility. Advanced economies in the region are facing aging populations as their working-age population (ages 15–64) declines. According to the United Nations, by 2030, the workforce is expected to contract by 10.4% in Hong Kong, China; 10.3% in the Republic of Korea; and 8.7% in Japan. In contrast, most countries in the region will expect significant increases in their working-age populations by 2030, ranging from 6.8% (Viet Nam) to 33.0% (Papua New Guinea). Kang and Magoncia (2016) project that labor migration from surplus countries is more than sufficient (i.e., a net surplus of around 443 million by 2050) to cover the needs of host (aged and aging) countries.

Projected Percentage Change in Population Ages 15-64 between 2017 and 2030

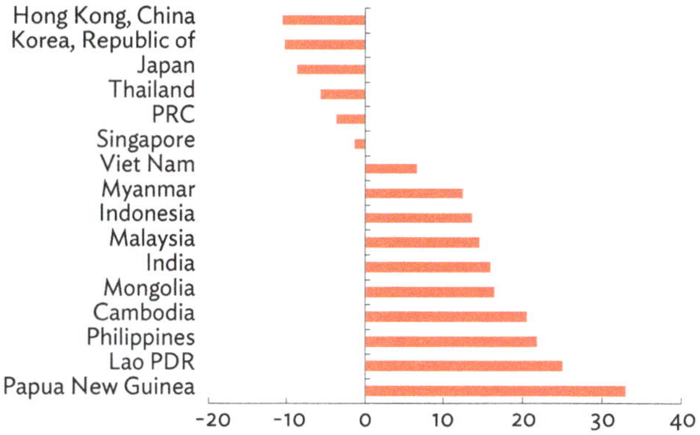

Lao PDR = Lao People's Democratic Republic, PRC = People's Republic of China.
Source: ADB calculations using data from the United Nations, Department of Economic and Social Affairs, Population Division. International Migrant Stock: The 2017 Revision. http://www.un.org/en/development/desa/population/migration/data/estimates2/estimates17.shtml (accessed May 2018).

The benefits gained from both trade and labor mobility liberalization far exceed the anticipated gains from removing barriers to trade or capital flows (Clemens 2011). The estimated global gains are as large as $3.4 trillion (Hamilton and Whalley 1984) and up to $1.97 trillion a year even without full migration in 2004 (Moses and Letnes 2004). In terms of efficiency gains, Iregui (2003) notes that eliminating global restrictions could result in gains from 15% to 67% of the world's gross domestic product (GDP). Moses and Letnes (2004) also show that a 10% increase in international migration corresponds to an efficiency gain of about $774 billion.

However, Asia remains a region of large net emigration, where the number of Asians moving to destinations such as the Middle East, North America, and Europe far exceeds those moving within Asian countries. The share of intraregional movement of people in Asia has declined, from 47.5% in 1990 to 34.7% in 2017. Preference for non-Asian destinations is becoming more apparent as educational attainment rises at a fast pace. Tertiary educated migrants from Thailand to Organisation for Economic Co-operation and Development (OECD) countries more than doubled from 2000–2011 to 2010–2011, followed by Brunei Darussalam (a 74.3% increase), the Philippines (73.8%), and Myanmar (67.2%) (Batalova, Shymonyak, and Sugiyarto 2017).

Creating and implementing a labor mobility framework and a human capital development mechanism can help countries in the region to improve portability of skills, increase job opportunities, and reduce costs of migration.

Portability of occupational skills across national borders often remains limited, and recognition mostly relies on host country schemes. As such, the Mutual Recognition of Skills within the Association of Southeast Asian Nations (ASEAN) have great potential to catalyze labor mobility across borders. Labor facilitation can move beyond mutual recognition agreements by introducing more active policies to facilitate movement across a wider array of skills. Where skills are portable, they are often not linked to job opportunities and are not widely known to professional organizations.

In addition, multilateral arrangements for cross-border labor mobility such as in harmonized skills and qualification recognition schemes reduce the costs of migration. Hredzak and Yuhua (2011), for instance, found that travel costs for Asia-Pacific Economic Cooperation (APEC) business cardholders were reduced by 38% (over a 12-month period from 2010 to 2011), while visa application time improved by 43.3% and immigration processing by 52.4%. The program also brought a 27.8% saving on visa application fees. Moreover, multilateral frameworks on skills recognition and enhanced mobility provide greater flexibility to workers and firms than bilateral processes.

Transparency should also be improved to mitigate exploitation. High migration costs arise from multiple layers of recruitments where workers compete to "buy" limited vacancies. Household workers and agricultural workers can find themselves in highly exploitive work environments. Recipient employers signing cooperation agreements with sourcing agencies abroad can help but monitoring costs can be high if done bilaterally. Implementing a regional framework to set a standard on labor mobility scheme will eliminate duplicate efforts.

Source: Kikkawa (2018).

Box 7.4: The Role of Regional Public Goods in Achieving Sustainable Development

Regional public goods (RPGs) can be found relevant for all 17 Sustainable Development Goals (SDGs). Under "zero poverty" or SDG 1 for instance, target 1.5 seeks to build the resilience of the poor and reduce vulnerability to climate-related extreme events and other economic, social, and environmental shocks and disasters. Climate risk insurance mechanisms will help mitigate these risks, while investment in dams or irrigation to reduce drought risk will generate greater productivity. RPGs are also relevant in the health sector. In the Association of Southeast Asian Nations (ASEAN), the Rational Use of Medicines program was identified as a priority under the ASEAN work plan on pharmaceutical development for 2011–2015. It was a timely initiative to address aging populations, emerging communicable and noncommunicable diseases, increasing income and health literacy, and demands for new medicines and other health technologies (ASEAN 2017). RPGs in other sectors can also contribute to a wider range of SDGs.

Sustainable Development Goals and Regional Public Goods

Sustainable Development Goal	Examples of Related Regional Public Goods in Asia
No poverty, climate action (Goal #1, #13)	Climate risk financing strategies in the Greater Mekong Subregion
Food security and sustainable agriculture and land management (Goal #2, #15)	Regional research institutions on agriculture, ASEAN+3 Emergency Rice Reserve
Health and well-being (Goal #3)	Regional cooperation in health, the Rational Use of Medicines program
Equitable quality education (Goal #4)	Harmonizing standards in education in ASEAN Economic Community
Gender equality, reduced inequalities (Goal #5, #10)	Integrating small and medium-sized enterprises and women in employment, trade, and microfinance
Sustainable management of water and sanitation (Goal #6)	Water management in the Ganges Brahmaputra Meghana and Indus basins

Continued on next page

Box 7.4 *continued*

Sustainable Development Goals and Regional Public Goods *continued*

Sustainable Development Goal	Examples of Related Regional Public Goods in Asia
Access to sustainable energy (Goal #7)	Cross-border energy trading in South Asia
Decent work and economic growth; industry, infrastructure, and innovation (Goal #8, #9)	Investments in cross-border infrastructure (transport, ICT, trade facilitation)
Sustainable and inclusive cities (Goal #11)	Clean Air Asia initiative
Sustainable production, management of marine resources (Goal #12, #14)	Regional cooperation in granting fishing licenses in the Pacific
Strong institutions, partnerships (Goal #16, #17)	Capacity-building programs in national and regional institutions

ASEAN = Association of Southeast Asian Nations, ICT = information and communication technology.
Sources: ADB. ADB's Focus on Regional Cooperation and Integration. https://www.adb.org/themes/regional-cooperation/main (accessed September 2018); and United Nations. Sustainable Development Knowledge Platform. https://sustainabledevelopment.un.org/ (accessed September 2018).

Source: ADB.

Table 7.6: Regional Public Goods and Regional Cooperation and Integration Projects by Multilateral Development Banks

MDB	RPG and RCI
Asian Development Bank	• Promotion of RPGs is required to foster RCI. • ADB will expand and diversify support to (i) mitigate financial and disaster risks, (ii) improve cross-border health security, (iii) assist DMCs to manage shared natural resources, and (iv) assist countries to implement COP21 commitments and similar agreements with regional impact
African Development Bank	• RPGs are part of the regional integration pillar on regional infrastructure development • RPG operations should be in line with the strategic objectives: inclusive growth (including inclusive access to infrastructure) and the transition to green growth

COP21 = 21st Conference of the Parties, DMC = developing member country, MDB = multilateral development bank, RCI = regional cooperation and integration, RPG = regional public good.
Sources: ADB (2016b, 2018b); AfDB (2013, 2015).

To foster RCI, MDBs including ADB are paying more attention to environment, health, and infrastructure as priority areas for RPG provision.

ADB's Strategy 2030, for example, aims to increase support for RPGs and collective actions to mitigate cross-border risks from climate change, pollution, energy and water security, and communicable and infectious diseases (ADB 2018b). ADB supports subregional programs that offer platforms to address cross-border issues and to implement projects. MDBs, as facilitators of partnerships, promote dialogue and collaboration among diverse partners and stakeholders. It is clear that the agenda to promote RCI incorporates RPG considerations in other MDBs such as the African Development Bank where environment, health, and infrastructure are common areas in their assistance for RPG provisions (Table 7.6). The IDB's RPG Initiative is one of several key instruments that it uses for fostering RCI.[59]

Trends of RPG Provision by Sector and RCI Projects

INTERNATIONAL COOPERATION IN RPGs

Two measures can be regarded as proxies for the RPG provision such as official development assistance and international treaties.

Liu and Kahn (2017) suggested the two following measures as proxies for the RPG provision. The official development assistance (ODA) measures the provision of bilateral or multilateral aid from the donor-recipient perspective, whereas international treaties represent the efforts of countries to provide RPGs through cooperative arrangements (see Box 7.5 for data and methodology). ODA beneficiaries are mainly developing countries, while the benefits of international treaties accrue to both developed and developing countries. It is more common for regional and global public goods to be supplied by agreements/treaties aimed at supplying a particular public good or to address a common problem.

[59] Additional information on the IDB's RPG Initiative can be found at IDB. Regional Public Goods. https://www.iadb.org/en/sector/trade/regional-public-goods/home

Box 7.5: Regional Public Good-Related Official Development Assistance and International Treaties—Data and Methodology

The data for the official development assistance (ODA) are taken from the Creditor Reporting System (CRS) of the Organisation for Economic Co-operation and Development (OECD). This database provides information on ODA from 1995 to 2016, including information on the amount, donor, recipient, sector, and the type of aid. The analysis here includes ODA grants and ODA loans as defined in the OECD-CRS database. ODA for debt relief is not included in the data. Following te Velde, Morrissey, and Hewitt (2002); Reisen, Soto, and Weithöner (2004); and Cepparulo and Giuriato (2009), selected ODA sectors are considered proxies for RPGs (box table).

Some of the limitations on the ODA data as proxies for RPG provision are as follows: (i) RPG-promoting national projects self-funded by individual countries are not included, and (ii) the data do not include nonmeasurable efforts to promote RPGs, such as informal coordination efforts and knowledge dissemination by regional institutions.

For the data of international treaties, following Liu and Kahn (2017), the number of treaties is considered a proxy for inputs to promote RPGs. The treaty data are from the IDB RPG cooperation database based on United Nations, World Intellectual Property Organization, and World Trade Organization data for 1945–2017. Six major functional areas are examined: (i) natural resources and environment, (ii) economic cooperation and integration, (iii) human and social development, (iv) governance and institutions, (v) peace and security, and (vi) connectivity.

Classification of Regional Public Goods Sectors in the Official Development Assistance Statistics

Education		
11181: education research		
Health		
12110: health policy/management	12182: medical resources	12250: infectious diseases control
12181: medical education/training	12191: medical services	12281: health education
Population Policies/Programs and Reproductive Health		
13010: population policy	13040: STD control	13081: personnel development for population and reproductive health
13030: family planning		
Water Supply and Sanitation		
14010: water resources policy	14020: supply and sanitation	14050: waste management
14015: water resources protection	14040: river development	14081: education/training
Government and Civil Society		
15110: economic policy		
Other Social Infrastructure and Services		
16361: narcotics control		
Transport and Storage		
21010: policy/management	21040: water transport	21061: storage
21020: road transport	21050: air transport	21081: education/training
21030: rail transport		
Communications		
22010: communication policy	22020: telecommunications	22030: media
Energy		
23030: power generation	23067: solar energy	23070: biomass
23065: hydro plants	23068: wind power	23081: energy education
23066: geothermal energy	23069: ocean power	23082: energy resources

Continued on next page

Box 7.5 *continued*

Classification of Regional Public Goods Sectors in the Official Development Assistance Statistics *continued*

Banking and Financial Services		
24010: financial policy	24020: monetary institutions	
Agriculture, Forestry, Fishing		
31165: agri alternative	31192: protection and pest control	31282: forestry resources
31182: agri resources	31210: forestry policy	31310: fishing policy
31183: agri research	31220: forestery development	31320: fishery development
31184: livestock research	31261: fuel wood/charcoal	31382: fishery resources
Industry, Mining, Construction		
32181: technological research and development		
Trade Policies and Regulation		
33110: trade policy		
General Environmental Protection		
41010: environmental policy	41031: bio diversity	41081: environmental education
41020: bio sphere	41040: site preservation	41082: environmental research
41030: bio diversity	41050: flood prevention	
Other Multisector		
43040: rural development	43050: non-agri alternative	

RPG = regional public good, STD = sexually transmitted disease.
Sources: ADB based on Cepparulo and Giuriato (2009); Reisen, Soto, and Weithöner (2004); and te Velde, Morrissey, and Hewitt (2002).

Sources: ADB based on Cepparulo and Giuriato (2009); Inter-American Development Bank. Regional public good cooperation database based on United Nations, World Intellectual Property Organization, and World Trade Organization data (accessed August 2018); Liu and Kahn (2017); Reisen, Soto, and Weithöner (2004); and te Velde, Morrissey, and Hewitt (2002).

International ODA for developing Asian countries appear to be economically motivated and are largely focused on enhancing connectivity in the region.

Among the ODA sectors considered to have cross-border benefits (defined as RPG-related ODA), aid for infrastructure including transport and energy, accounts for more than half of total ODA for recipients in Asia. The total RPG-related ODA increased rapidly until 2009, then in recent years settled within a range of $70 billion to $80 billion, while its share against total ODA has remained steady over the past decade, at around 30% to 40% (Figure 7.3).

Connectivity is ranked second in cooperative arrangements for RPGs measured by the number of international treaties, following economic cooperation and integration.

The data show that most international treaties in Asia fall under the area of economic cooperation and integration which includes bilateral/multilateral trade agreements and bilateral investment treaties (Figure 7.4). This trend has continued since 1945, with the focus on economic cooperation and integration much more reinforced than other functional areas of RPGs. Connectivity has been another prominent area.

Figure 7.3: Regional Public Good-Related Official Development Assistance

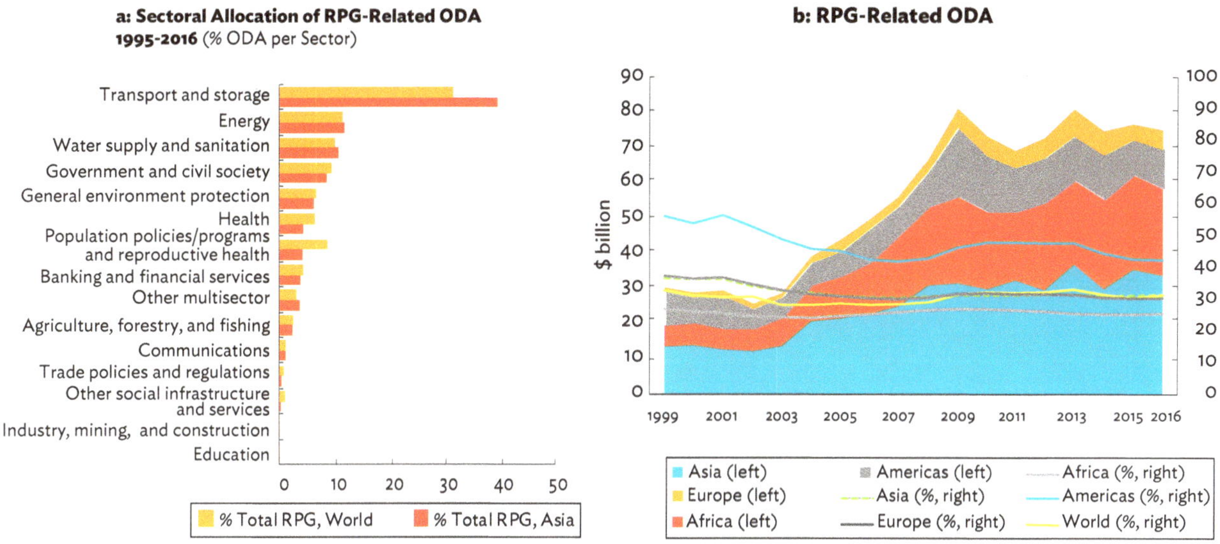

CRS = Creditor Reporting System, ODA = official development assistance, RPG = regional public good.

Notes: See Box 7.5 for the list of CRS subsectors that were considered as RPGs. The figures include ODA grants and ODA loans; ODA for debt relief is not included. The lines on the right chart are 5-year moving averages.

Sources: ADB calculations using data from the Organisation for Economic Co-operation and Development. CRS database. https://stats.oecd.org/index.aspx?DataSetCode=CRS1 (accessed July 2018); Cepparulo and Giuriato (2009); Resien, Soto, and Weithöner (2004); and te Velde, Morrissey, and Hewitt (2002).

Figure 7.4: Number of Regional Public Good-Related International Treaties

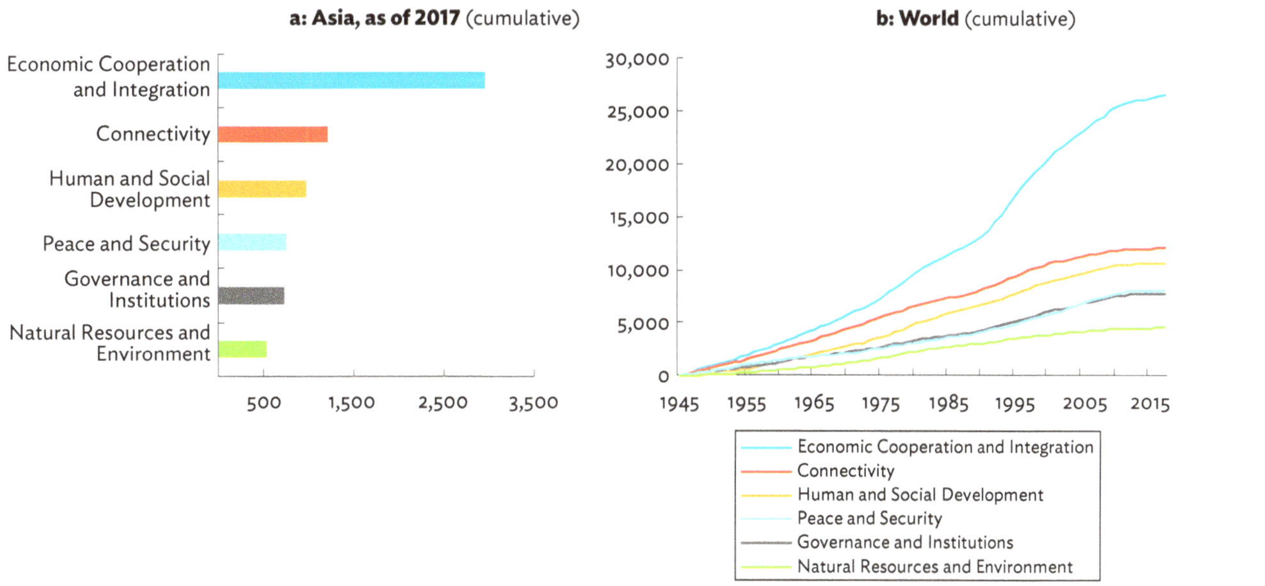

Note: Includes both bilateral and multilateral treaties.

Source: Inter-American Development Bank. Regional public good cooperation database based on United Nations, World Intellectual Property Organization, and World Trade Organization data (accessed August 2018).

MULTILATERAL DEVELOPMENT BANKS' ROLE IN REGIONAL PUBLIC GOOD PROVISION

ADB's RCI Projects and RPGs

Through RCI or regional projects, ADB has been facilitating the provision of RPGs in Asia.

ADB's RCI or regional projects can be either (i) a single-country project such as a national sector project helping implement a multicountry sector agreement, or (ii) a multicountry regional project such as formal joint commitments, actions, and/or resource allocations between at least two countries.[60] Aiming to foster regional cooperation and integration in the region, investing in RPGs and collective action offer support to (i) mitigate financial and disaster risks, (ii) improve cross-border health security, (iii) assist ADB developing member countries in managing shared natural resources, and (iv) help countries implement the 21st Conference of the Parties (COP21) commitments[61] and similar agreements with regional impact (ADB 2016, 2018b). The RPG concept is also used to describe an economic rationale to address market or nonmarket failures when conducting economic analyses for projects (ADB 2017b).

ADB's regional projects come in the form of loans, grants, and technical assistance. ADB aims for 30% of projects to be composed of RCI operations (ADB 2008). During 2010–2017, the share of RCI projects ranged from 18% to 28% of total operations. By sector, around 80% of RCI projects are focused on enhancing connectivity through transport and energy infrastructure (Figure 7.5).

Figure 7.5: ADB Regional Projects

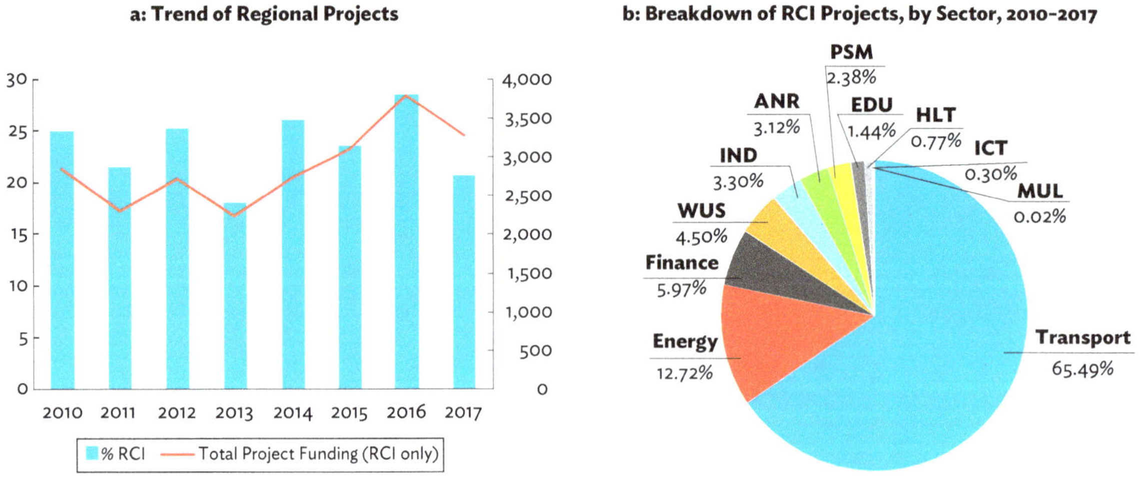

ANR = agriculture, natural resources, and rural development; EDU = education; HLT = health; ICT = information and communication technology; IND = industry and trade; MUL = multisector; PSM = public sector management; RCI = regional cooperation and integration, WUS = water and other urban infrastructure and services.
Source: ADB Internal Projects Database (accessed May 2018).

[60] See ADB (2016) for a comprehensive list of requirements to be classified as RCI projects.

[61] The Conference of the Parties (COP) is the supreme decision-making body of the United Nations Framework Convention on Climate Change (UNFCCC). The 21st session of the Conference of the Parties (COP21), also known as the 2015 Paris Climate Conference, aim to achieve a legally binding and universal agreement on climate to keep global warming below 2°C. Find out more about COP21. http://www.cop21paris.org/about/cop21 [accessed September 2018]).

IDB's Regional Public Goods Initiative

Latin American and Caribbean countries face common development challenges and opportunities that can be addressed more effectively and efficiently at a regional level through collective action.

Among several regional instruments of the IDB to promote regional integration and cooperation is its grant ordinary capital program Regional Public Goods Initiative, created in 2004.[62] Examples of collective action to address development challenges include regional regulation to reduce water pollution in a multinational sea, lake, or watershed, and a common risk management and preparedness strategy in a seismic region. On the other hand, examples of development opportunities include a joint export promotion scheme by small economies to target overseas markets, and a regional arrangement of small countries to purchase medicines at lower prices and at higher quality or creating a single public procurement procedure in the Caribbean.

The objective of the RPG Initiative is to support the generation of RPGs that have a high potential development impact in the IDB's borrowing member countries.

The RPG Initiative provides nonreimbursable grant resources for proposals that have been selected through a competitive process following an annual call for proposals. The proposal must be demand-driven and endorsed by a minimum of three and exceptionally two of the IDB's borrowing member countries, with the proposed good to be produced through collective action. Partner countries and institutions decide together their goal, how to achieve it, including their work plan, the agenda and the mechanisms of their governance and regional cooperation. The IDB plays several roles such as honest-broker, convener, and financier; offers technical support; and identifies global good practices that may benefit the RPG project. Another key feature of the initiative is its thematic focus.[63]

The IDB's RPG Initiative has financed so far more than 160 projects totaling more than $110 million since its launch.

On average, 13–15 projects are selected for financing each year. The initiative focuses on RPGs that have the potential to generate significant shared benefits and positive spillover effects in terms of scope (benefits extend beyond the originally targeted sector in each country) and/or scale (benefits extend beyond the original group of countries).

Measurement Issues and Case Studies on Provision Mechanisms

Measurement of RPGs

RPGs can be measured as either inputs to promote the RPGs or their benefits (outputs).

Given the broad scope of RPGs and its ambiguity in concept, there are no universally accepted data sources and methodologies for their measurement. However, two general approaches to quantitative measuring of RPGs (e.g., regional financial stability) can be considered, depending on the view of input (e.g., regional financial agreements) versus output (e.g., benefits of stable financial markets) (Figure 7.6).

[62] In 2003, the joint volume *Regional Public Goods: From Theory to Practice* was published in the context of early research collaboration between the ADB and IDB on the subject (Frantz, Nguyen, and Estevadeordal 2003).

[63] The initiative is open to the promotion of RPGs in any area, in which the IDB is active. However, alignment with the IDB's goals, objectives, and priorities is a selection criterion. Proposals that address cross-cutting issues of the Update to the Institutional Strategy 2016–2019 will be evaluated positively (gender equality and diversity; climate change and environmental sustainability; and institutional capacity and the rule of law).

Figure 7.6: Two Ways of Measuring Regional Public Goods

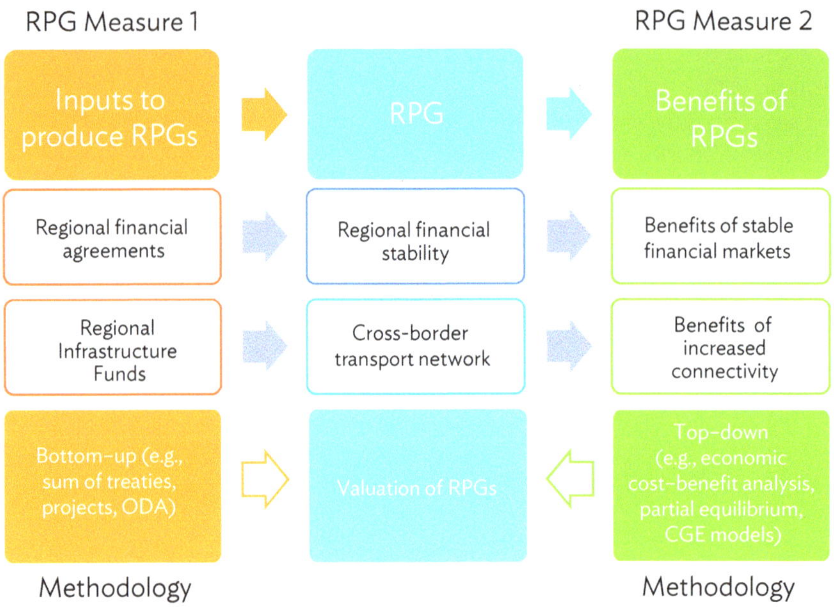

CGE = computable general equilibrium, ODA = official development assistance, RPG = regional public good.
Source: ADB based on Liu and Kahn (2017).

The first is the bottom-up approach, where the inputs used to produce/promote/preserve RPGs are taken as proxy for their value. For example, the amount of ODA to developing countries that is expected to have cross-border benefits can be considered as the RPG supply by aid donors (Raffer 1999; te Velde, Morrissey, and Hewitt 2002; Reisen, Soto, and Weithöner 2004; Birdsall 2005; Cepparulo and Giuriato 2009). Another example includes the number of international treaties that countries signed for creating RPGs such as regional trade and investment agreements (Liu and Kahn 2017).[64]

The second is the top-down approach, where the benefits of RPGs including cross-border spillovers are measured. This methodology can involve analysis of partial equilibrium and computable general equilibrium models using country- and industry-level data. At the project level, economic cost-benefit analyses based on net present value and internal rate of return (Adhikari and Weiss 2004) can also fall under this category. More discussion of the cost-benefit analyses for regional projects by sector follows in the next section.

Valuation of RPG Projects: Cost-Benefit Analysis

For regional projects involving more than one country, the presence of positive spillover implies that the sum of individual contributions is smaller than the overall regional benefits.

In the cost-benefit analysis, the total regional benefits for the group of participating countries is represented by the regional economic net present value (ENPV). The net present value approach suggests that if there is no budget constraint, investment in regional projects should be made up to the point at which an additional investment yields an ENPV of zero at a discount rate, which reflects the collective social time preference in the region.[65] Where a budget is fixed, investment should be made up to the point that the budget is exhausted with projects with a positive ENPV.

[64] The "International Cooperation in RPGs" subsection of this chapter illustrates the application of the bottom-up approach.

[65] Refer to Appendix 18 of ADB (2017c) for more discussion of the social discount rate.

Table 7.7: Channels of Regional Spillover Benefits

Channel	Description
Additional funding and technology transfer through foreign direct investment	New project financed within a regional framework may bring in foreign funding from official or private capital flows that individual economies would otherwise receive.
Additional trade through improved transport and communications	Net benefit of these trade flows not picked up in the national analysis of the project will constitute a regional spillover created by the project.
Economies of scale and efficiency gains from regional specialization	Reduction in unit costs of production through specialization as a result of production for a larger regional market; regional efficiency is improved through a higher consumer surplus.
Agglomeration and network effects through the development of cross-border economic corridors	Increased proximity of producers to urban centers in a neighboring country through economic corridors can enhance productivity by the exchange of ideas, inputs, technology, and skilled workers.
Mitigation of cross-border environmental and public health risks	More efficient to control these risks acting collectively as inaction on one side of a border can undermine efforts taken on the other side.

Source: ADB (2017c).

The proper valuation of regional benefits commonly requires identification of spillover channels, induced benefits through the channels, and beneficiaries while there are also sector-specific considerations.

Regional projects (e.g., cross-border road network) need to identify induced benefits (e.g., increased cross-border trade and movement of people) as well as direct benefits (e.g., increased traffic). These benefits can also be measured savings from averting free-riding by comparing the sum of savings from unilateral projects with the cost savings from a regional project with cross-border spillovers. For regional benefits valuation, it is essential to identify regional spillover channels such as agglomeration and network effects of cross-border economic corridors (Table 7.7).

Some sector-specific considerations including issues and challenges in calculating spillover benefits of regional projects are discussed below.

Energy. For cross-border energy trade, it is necessary to establish whether a power project creates either exports to a regional partner or enables power imports from the region. If it is an export project, the willingness to pay for power in the importing country should be estimated. For energy transmission projects, the existence of surplus capacity in the exporting country should be assessed. If there is surplus capacity, the operating and distribution cost of moving the power to the point of export should be estimated. Any regional benefits in the form of consumer and producer surpluses in the neighboring country must be added to national benefits in the full analysis of the project.

Transport. A key issue for regional transport projects is how accurately generated traffic and the induced trade and production created by the cross-border dimension can be estimated. All road transport projects must tackle the difficulty of separating traffic from diverted traffic and generated traffic that results directly from the new project. A regional dimension arises because traffic can be generated not just because of a reduction in fares and vehicle and time costs, but also because obstacles to cross-border trade, in the form of lengthy customs procedures, have been removed. It is also possible that the reduction in economic distance between production centers in different countries creates cross-border agglomeration effects leading to benefits in terms of higher productivity growth in the linked locations.

Trade Facilitation. Regional benefits of trade facilitation can be expected through the impact of lower transit time on international cross-border trade flows. However, prediction of the extent to which export or import volumes will increase is extremely difficult. The main regional effect will be in creating an operating environment, where it is perceived that transit procedures are no longer an obstacle to trade with neighboring countries. This can encourage investment in export activities on both sides of a border. This type of induced trade effect will also be difficult to capture at the project level and will not be picked up in trade elasticity estimates. Alternatively, economy-wide impacts of trade facilitation are often measured using econometric and general equilibrium models (see Box 7.6 for economy-wide impacts of trade facilitation through infrastructure).

Box 7.6: Empirical Assessment of Spillover Benefits of Trade Facilitation through Infrastructure

Approach 1: A Reduced-Form Model Using Spatial Econometric Methods

Both direct and indirect (or cross-border spillover) impacts of infrastructure can be estimated using spatial econometric methods (See Annex 7a for the data, methodology, and model). In the model, a production function based on Calderón, Moral-Benito, and Servén (2015) is extended to include the infrastructure stock of neighboring countries to explain an own-country's output. While most studies have employed this method to the analysis of subnational economy spillovers, the approach used here explicitly applies to cross-country infrastructure panel data separately (i) for transport (i.e., road and rail) and energy, and (ii) for information and communication technology (ICT) infrastructure (i.e., telephone, mobile, and broadband).

The results show that all transport and energy infrastructure are found to have significant economic impacts on own economies, while rail infrastructure have impacts on neighboring countries as well (box table 1). The finding on spillover effects of rail infrastructure supports the key role of other countries' transport infrastructure on a country's own economy. The quality of trading partners' infrastructure is often highlighted as one of the major determinants that facilitate bilateral trade (see Grigoriou [2007], for example). Human capital also shows positive cross-border spillover effects on growth under the ICT model, while its direct impact on growth is robust across the board.

Among the three types in the ICT infrastructure, broadband shows not only positive direct impact on output, but also indirect impact. This implies that increased internet access can lift not only the investing country's economic growth, but also other neighboring economies.

Approach 2: A Structural Model Using a Computable General Equilibrium Model

Using a static computable general equilibrium (CGE) model, three types of channels are defined to evaluate the impact of infrastructure shocks by assuming that the infrastructure gap in the region estimated in ADB (2017a) is to be met (See Annex 7a for data, methodology, and model). The long-term output impacts of infrastructure investments in Asia are examined through three channels: (i) domestic industries where these investments are made, (ii) domestic spillovers on other industries, and (iii) cross-border spillovers on countries outside Asia (box figure).

The first channel represents the long-run impact of a production increase driven by productivity growth in the affected domestic infrastructure-related industries. Next,

1: Impact of Infrastructure: Spatial Econometric Model Results

1% increase in: (+1yr for human capital)	%∆Output		1% increase in: (+1yr for human capital)	%∆Output	
	Own country	Neighbors		Own country	Neighbors
Non-TRE infra	(0.03)	-	Non-ICT infra	(0.03)	-
Human capital	(0.09–0.14)	(0.13–0.26)	Human capital	(0.10–0.13)	-
TRE: Roads	(0.10–0.11)	-	ICT: Telephone	-	-
TRE: Rails	(0.15–0.17)	(0.46)[a]	ICT: Mobile	-	-
TRE: Energy	(0.20–0.22)	-	ICT: Broadband	(0.02–0.03)[b]	(0.03–0.11)

%∆ = percent change, - = no significant effect, ICT = information and communication technology, TRE = transport and energy, yr = year.
[a] For inverse distance weight matrix only.
[b] For exponential decay weight matrix and square of inverse distance matrix with a cutoff only.
Notes: Based on the spatial panel models including the non-infrastructure variable. See Annex 7a for the details on the spatial econometric models.
Source: Kim et al. (2018).

Continued on next page

Box 7.6 *continued*

Three Channels of Infrastructure Investment Shocks

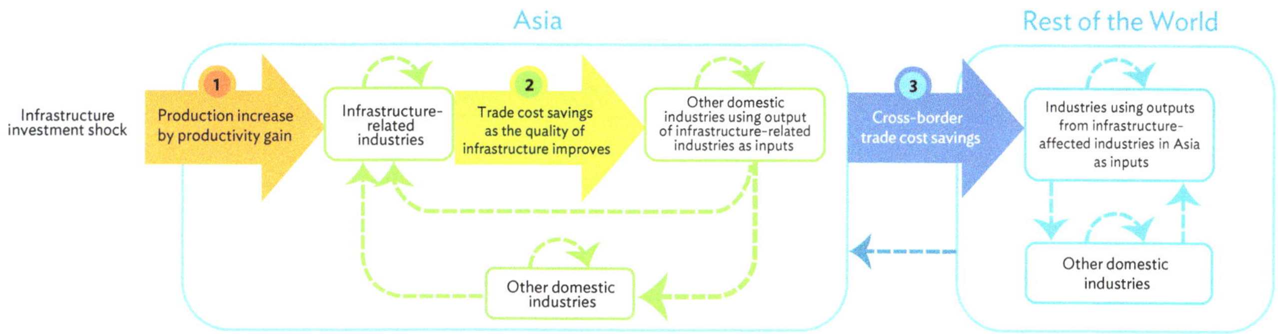

Note: The dotted lines represent indirect impacts due to inter-industry linkages by way of domestic and international input–output relationship.
Source: ADB based on Lee (2018).

the infrastructure investments would also reduce the trade costs (e.g., cost savings from the bottlenecks overcome as infrastructure improves) in other domestic industries using the goods and services produced in the infrastructure industries as intermediate inputs. These benefits are transmitted to other industries sequentially and repeatedly through domestic forward and backward linkages. Finally, the last channel accounts for cross-border spillover effects; i.e., the trade cost savings by foreign industries connected through the global supply chain.

Infrastructure shocks in Asia are expected to stimulate economic growth in the region itself as well as other regions. Simulation results suggest that the output impact of infrastructure investments significantly intensifies in non-Asian regions as well as in the own region when domestic and cross-border spillovers are accounted, besides productivity shock (box table 2). The results imply that Cambodia, the Lao People's Democratic Republic, Myanmar, and Viet Nam (the CLMV countries referred to in box table 2) benefit the most from meeting the infrastructure gaps, followed by other developing Asia and ASEAN4 countries, while these investments benefit other regions too. The results suggest that strengthening the forward linkages of infrastructure with foreign industries would enhance the potential cross-border spillover benefits among trading partners.

2: Impact of Infrastructure on Output: Computable General Equilibrium Model Results

Country/region	**Infrastructure shocks** (gap as %GDP) **used in the model** (2016-2020)	**% change in GDP at 2014 prices due to Spillovers from infrastructure shocks**
PRC*	0.5	4.92
ASEAN4*	3.8	5.33
CLMV*	3.3	11.98
Other developing Asia*	4.6	7.39
Japan	-	0.25
Korea, Rep. of	-	0.30
Other developed Asia	-	0.38
United States	-	0.10
European Union	-	0.07
Rest of the World	-	0.07

* = countries with infrastructure investment shocks (25 countries); ASEAN4 = Indonesia, Malaysia, the Philippines, and Thailand; CLMV = Cambodia, the Lao People's Democratic Republic, Myanmar, and Viet Nam; GDP = gross domestic product; PRC = People's Republic of China.
Notes: Spillovers include (i) the impact of productivity shocks in affected infrastructure industries in Asia, (ii) domestic spillovers on other non-infrastructure industries in Asia, and (iii) cross-border spillovers. See Annex 7a for the details on the CGE model and country breakdown.
Sources: Lee (2018) and ADB (2017a).

Sources: Kim et al. (2018) and Lee (2018).

Health. Analysis of regional health projects requires either a demonstration that a regional approach offers a cost-effective alternative to separate national projects or that a regional approach offers higher benefits, if these can be quantified satisfactorily in economic terms. Health impacts on morbidity and mortality are typically quantified as disability-adjusted life years (DALYs) which can be interpreted as the number of years lost due to disability and premature death (see Box 7.7 for a regional health project using the DALY). An economic rate of return analysis requires that the DALYs saved be given a monetary value per unit to create a benefit value. Cost-effectiveness analysis compares the cost per DALY saved with project costs.

Environment. Environmental valuation may involve transferring values for environmental effects from one site to another and applying these transferred values in a particular appraisal. For example, regional watershed management projects may create various environmental benefits such as soil conservation and improved forest cover through both on-site and off-site effects. On-site benefits from soil conservation include incremental agricultural production and the net income from this is the normal measure of economic value. Such production and income effects on farmers in particular countries can also be allocated in a similar fashion. However, other off-site impacts such as water quality, flood levels, or siltation affected by eroded soil from one site will be more difficult to assess if they are distributed among several countries sharing a river basin.

Education. Regional education projects involve cooperation from higher education and research institutes to spread the fixed costs of university teaching and research across several countries. The "human capital" approach values education on the basis of the higher productivity that additional years of education or research expenditure create. Higher productivity in turn is approximated by the incremental life-time earnings

Box 7.7: Case Study—Calculating Regional Spillovers of the Greater Mekong Subregion Health Security Project

The Greater Mekong Subregion (GMS) Health Security Project is a $132 million project launched in 2016 to assist Cambodia, the Lao People's Democratic Republic (Lao PDR), Myanmar, and Viet Nam to strengthen their health systems for the control of communicable diseases. The project is implemented in the border areas of each country, where the risk of transmission between countries is highest. The original economic analysis in the GMS Security Project shows the returns from the project to each of the four countries but does not separate a distinct regional effect (ADB 2016a). A separate recalculation based on different assumptions shows how a distinct regional effect can be identified.

The project defines three project outputs: (i) improved regional cooperation and disease control in the border areas, (ii) strengthened national disease surveillance and outbreak response systems, and (iii) improvement of laboratory services and hospital infection prevention and control.

Regional benefits from improved regional cooperation and disease control in the border areas

The health effects of the project on a set of infectious diseases (HIV, tuberculosis, dengue, and helminth) are expressed in terms of disability-adjusted life years (DALYs). The improvement in disease incidence due to the project is estimated by assuming that the gap between health status in the border areas and the national average will be reduced due to the project by 10% annually over the project's 10-year life. Total DALYs from each of the four diseases without the project are taken from the World Health Organization's Burden of Disease data. An estimate is made of the difference in health status between border areas and the national average.[a]

Continued on next page

[a] This is done by comparing urban and rural areas in each country using an estimate of health conditions in rural areas as a proxy for the health status in border areas.

Box 7.7 *continued*

Total benefits in the border area for country k (B_{djk}) should be calculated as:[b]

$$B_{djk} = (DALY_{jkbwo} - DALY_{jkw}) * POP_{bk}$$

where $DALY_{jkbwo}$ is DALY per 1,000 from disease j in country k in border areas without the project, $DALY_{jkw}$ is the national incidence of disease from j in k with the project and POP_{bk} is the population in border areas in country k (in 1,000s). As the data are not available to make this estimate, the original values for benefits are retained on the assumption that had this alternative approach been applied it would have created the same estimate in DALYs saved. Using these estimates for DALYs saved from output 1 and the estimated border average income figures gives the benefit figures by country.

As an infectious disease can travel readily across borders, particularly as in this case across land borders, it is a reasonable assumption that most if not all the disease incidence reduction in the border area assumed in the calculations would not occur without complementary prevention and control measures in neighboring countries. Thus, the benefits from output 1 of the project are considered regional benefits arising from cooperation and coordination of health systems.

National benefits from strengthened national disease surveillance and outbreak response systems

The benefits of output 2 are less directly regional in that they arise from improved community and hospital level practices. Benefits are estimated as a reduction in the incidence of epidemics assumed to be attributable to improved surveillance combined with the estimated cost of epidemics. The calculation is at an aggregate level not distinguishing between types of disease outbreak.[c] Further, it does not appear to take account of the activities of the project under output 1 in reducing the probability of a disease outbreak. These are treated as national benefits because the impact of complementary measures in neighboring countries was already allowed for in the calculation of benefits from output 1.

National benefits from improvement of laboratory services and hospital infection prevention and control

Benefits from improved laboratory testing and hospital practices are estimated on the basis of costs saved. They include the reduced cost of dengue infections due to improved laboratory testing, and the reduction in inpatient costs due to shorter hospital stays. The benefits to the border areas are estimated as a proportion of the savings for overall national benefits, with the proportion determined by their population share. Saving in hospital costs due to shortening patient stays are calculated from the starting point of the total national inpatient hospital cost (millions of bed days × the cost per bed day). A saving of 5% is then attributed to the project and this national saving is allocated to border areas on the basis of the population share. As allowance has been made for the feedback effect from output 1, these are treated as national benefits independent from the actions of neighboring countries.

The strong regional effect—with over half of benefits dependent on complementary actions in neighboring countries—is to be expected for this type of regional public good project. For each country, in the recalculation, regional benefits or spillovers are 61% of gross benefits for Cambodia, 80% for the Lao PDR, 30% for Myanmar, 46% for Viet Nam, and 54% for the total project (box table). The results show low project returns in Myanmar and very high returns in the Lao PDR.[d] This would support the case for special financial support to the government of Myanmar to ensure that the project, which creates cross-border benefits for others, is continued despite its low return to the country itself.

Continued on next page

[b] In the original economic analysis, benefits are taken to be a saving in DALYs from each disease set at 10% of the disease incidence created by a difference in health status between the national average and the border areas. These benefits (B_{djk}) are estimated for disease j in country k as

$$B_{djk} = (DALY_{jkwo} * H_k * 0.10) * POP_{bk}/POP_{totk}$$

where $DALY_{jkwo}$ is the total disease burden in DALYs (per 1,000) in country k created by disease j without the project (which rises annually with population growth), H_k is the composite health status index used to adjust the national average data to reflect conditions in the border areas, POP_{bk} is the population in border areas (districts) in country k (in 1,000s) and POP_{totk} is total population in k (in 1,000s). This calculation assumes that benefits in border districts can be calculated from a notional national benefit measured by the term in brackets, which is then allocated to the border areas in proportion to their share of population.

[c] Other parameters in the original analysis are retained. These are the cost of epidemics as a proportion of GDP (3%), the impact of surveillance and response activities in reducing the risk of an epidemic (10%), and the effectiveness of the project output 2 in improving surveillance and responses (5%).

[d] If 9% represents the cost of capital in Myanmar and benefits are captured accurately then with an economic internal rate of return of 5% this project would not be accepted.

Box 7.7 *continued*

Benefit of the Greater Mekong Subregion Health Security Project (present value, $ million)

Country	Total Benefits (A)	Regional Benefits	Costs (B)	ENPV (A-B)	EIRR (%)
Myanmar	10.78	3.27 (30%)	12.10	−1.32	5
Viet Nam	78.87	35.98 (46%)	76.41	2.46	10
Lao PDR	27.07	21.67 (80%)	11.75	15.32	58
Cambodia	29.35	17.94 (61%)	21.01	8.34	22
Total	**146.07**	**78.82 (54%)**	**121.27**	**24.80**	**15**

EIRR = economic internal rate of return, ENPV = economic net present value, Lao PDR = Lao People's Democratic Republic.
Note: Discount rate is 9%.
Source: Weiss (2017).

that can accrue from the education project. These external benefits can also be the changes in innovation, health, and social attitudes that arise in a better-educated society. Such effects are, however, rarely incorporated into national analyses of economic benefits of education and thus, it is unrealistic to expect that they can be estimated in a meaningful way on a regional basis. As such, for education projects, a simple modification of existing practice can be used to approximate regional as opposed to national benefits.

Case Studies: Provision Mechanisms

EUROPEAN CASES

Integrated energy market

The integration of national energy markets has been led by regional institutions through strengthening cooperation among national regulators and harmonizing national market rules.

For over 60 years, the European Union (EU) countries have coordinated their national energy policies to guarantee their citizens access to energy at reasonable and stable prices, to maintain industrial competitiveness, to promote sustainable development, and to ensure security of energy supply.[66] Although significant progress has been made to harmonize rules, more cross-border interconnection capacity is required to achieve a fully integrated energy market. In 2015, the European Commission presented its strategy for establishing an "Energy Union," with the goal of improving Europe's energy security, sustainability and competitiveness. Attaining a fully integrated energy market was highlighted as among the prerequisites to realizing the union.

A fully integrated energy market requires a common legislative framework (the "software") and cross-border infrastructure investments such as gas pipelines and electricity cables (the "hardware").

On the software side, the EU has made significant progress. Between 1996 and 2009, it adopted three major legislative packages to harmonize regulation across energy markets in Europe and liberalize the internal energy market. The most recent one, the Third Internal Energy Market Package, is seen as a key step toward laying a legislative foundation for a joint energy market.

However, progress has been slower on the hardware side. Electricity markets have generally developed either on a national level or through regional pools within the EU. Similarly, gas flows have typically developed on a

66 The integration of the energy markets (i.e., electricity and gas) can be considered a regional club good. The benefits are excludable to nonmembers. They are partially rival for members as the addition of another country to a network may increase administrative and transaction costs.

bilateral basis, through agreements between supplier and consumer countries. These agreements have been motivated by a supply-demand rationale rather than efforts to create an integrated gas market in Europe. Overall, therefore, the European electricity and gas markets remain largely fragmented.

In addition to ongoing support for cross-border infrastructure projects, the Connecting Europe Facility was established in 2013 to further bridge the infrastructure gap.

The European Investment Bank (EIB) has provided financial support for the EU energy projects, including for cross-border infrastructure. The bank is tasked with borrowing on capital markets and lending at favorable terms to projects that support the EU objectives. Among the sectors the EIB has financed since 1959, energy is the third largest, amounting to €195 billion, following credit lines and transport.[67] The Connecting Europe Facility (CEF) was created in 2013 as an EU funding instrument to direct investment in key cross-border infrastructure projects related to energy, transport, and information and communication technology.[68] The CEF budget amounts to €30.4 billion for 2014–2020, of which €5.4 billion is allocated to energy projects.[69] Of that, €4.7 billion is available in grants that support the development of so-called EU Projects of Common Interests.

Substantial efficiency gains from the interconnected energy market are expected due to increased competition and cross-border energy trade.

First, the integration can increase competition among energy suppliers, and thus lead to better usage of inputs and reductions in firm costs. Second, the cross-border trade of electricity can lead to efficiency gains from, among other things, the benefits of exchanging differences in resource endowments across countries (e.g., trading intermittent wind power for dispatchable hydropower) and the ability to maintain a more diversified generation mix. The efficiency gains are found to increase more rapidly as countries expand their capacity of renewables (Zachmann 2013).

Energy market integration in Europe illustrates regional policy implementation based on the weakest-link and best-shot technologies.

Providing financial assistance for energy infrastructure through the EIB and CEF can be considered a weakest-link RPG as the assistance focuses on strengthening the energy infrastructure of the member countries with the lowest level of energy market integration. Harmonization of market rules in the EU has best-shot aggregation technology characteristics as the United Kingdom started energy market reform which then became the main driver for further development in Europe (Karan and Kazdağli 2011).

Mitigating Overpricing in International Mobile Roaming

There have been concerns that the prices of international mobile roaming in Europe are unreasonably higher than the price of domestic telecommunications services.

Before 2007, the wholesale charges for roaming voice calls placed in Europe averaged approximately €1 per minute, even though the cost to provide the service was just a few cents.[70] To the home network, the tariff payment made to an unaffiliated visited network in a different country is a real cost—the underlying cost to the visited network of providing the service is irrelevant to the home network. The wholesale payment of

67 See European Investment Bank. Breakdown by Sector. http://www.eib.org/en/projects/loan/sectors/index.htm?from=1959&to=2018 (accessed September 2018).

68 Specifically, the funding is directed toward investment in the Trans-European Transport Networks (TENT), Trans-European Energy Networks (TEN-E), and Broadband and ICT (European Commission. Connecting Europe Facility. https://ec.europa.eu/transport/themes/infrastructure/ten-t-guidelines/project-funding/cef_en [accessed September 2018]).

69 As of September 2018, the remaining €24.1 billion was allocated to projects in transport, and €1.04 billion to telecommunications.

70 Wholesale charges for roaming (the inter-operator tariff) are the fees that the home network pays the visited (or foreign) network for their roaming subscribers using the visited network (GSMA 2012).

€1 consequently resulted in average retail prices for roaming voice calls placed in Europe of about €1.30, corresponding to a retail margin of about 25%–30% (Stumpf 2001).

The EU initially tried to address the high price of international mobile roaming with ex ante regulation based on competition law principles in each member state, but this approach had limitations due to the transnational nature of the markets for roaming services.

Addressing the excessively high prices of international roaming proved to be difficult as they resulted from rational profit-taking by different networks in two different countries. The incentives of the home network and the visited network are often not aligned. Furthermore, they are regulated by different national authorities whose interests may also not be in step.

The adoption of an EU-wide approach in 2007 reduced the wholesale and retail prices, and thus led to an increase in the consumption of roaming services.

In 2007, an EU-wide regulation was introduced, and was subsequently amended in 2009, 2012, and 2015.[71] In each case, both wholesale inter-operator charges and retail prices were progressively reduced. The measures effectively led to increased consumption of roaming services—far more for data than for voice calls. An analysis conducted in preparation for the 2012 revisions to the EU Roaming Regulation suggests that the societal costs over 2012–2014 in the absence of the roaming regulation would have been substantial, leading to a net loss of €13.6 billion in social welfare (European Commission 2011).

CASES IN LATIN AMERICA AND THE CARIBBEAN[72]

IDB RPG Projects in Latin America and the Caribbean

The Interoperability of Foreign Trade Single Windows project aimed to address the lack of harmonization among national Foreign Trade Single Window platforms in the Pacific Alliance.[73]

This trade facilitation project launched in 2014 called to implement a digital platform to enable the members of the alliance to interoperate and exchange real-time information such as phytosanitary, zoosanitary, and origin certificates. About 7,000 certificates have been exchanged since 2016, and the interoperability platform has contributed to reduce both the time required to process phytosanitary certificates by importers and the time spent at the border by perishable goods subject to phytosanitary clearance.

The Learning in 21st Century Schools project aims to generate data, guidelines, and standards at the regional level that countries can use to upgrade and modernize their educational infrastructure.

This ongoing project has so far yielded a regional comparative inventory of school construction standards and regional norms for maintenance, as well as best practices for school design and construction that withstand disasters.[74] The project also included the implementation of a school census tool in order to collect data for education investment policy making. Recommendations for community involvement and school designs that foster security and an environment conducive to higher learning have also been included.

[71] This covered the 28 EU member states and three European Economic Area countries: Norway, Iceland, and Liechtenstein.

[72] This section was drawn from the presentation by IDB at the ADB–ADB Institute conference on Toward Optimal Provision of Regional Public Goods in Asia and the Pacific held in Tokyo on 10–11 May 2018 (Estevadeordal 2018).

[73] The Pacific Alliance is a Latin American trading bloc consisting of South American neighbors Chile, Colombia, and Peru; and non-neighbor Mexico.

[74] Thirteen countries are participating in the Learning in 21st Century Schools: Argentina, Barbados, Chile, Colombia, Costa Rica, Dominican Republic, Guatemala, Honduras, Mexico, Peru, Paraguay, Trinidad and Tobago, and Uruguay.

The Central American Protocol for Procurement and Quality Control of Medicines sought to improve access to quality pharmaceuticals for public hospitals at better prices by supporting the creation of a regional pharmaceutical market in Central America.

The project aimed to set up a coordinated regulatory framework for medicine procurement through a joint price negotiation process in order to provide the subregion with common regulation, procedures, and quality control standards for the medications used in public hospitals. The IDB ended its financial support for this RPG in 2012, and the Central American countries and their regional institutions, led by the Council of Ministers of Health of Central America, have continued to benefit from lower prices and higher-quality medicines through annual tendering processes. This RPG resulted in the successful implementation of a regional arrangement of small countries to collectively procure medicines at lower prices and at higher quality (Box 7.8 lists IDB's lessons for successful RPG projects).

Box 7.8: Inter-American Development Bank—Lessons for Successful Regional Public Good Projects

The regional public good (RPG) operations of the Inter-American Development Bank (IDB) aim to perform development interventions within the framework of the Management for Development Results as well as to extract lessons learned on why projects work and what institutional arrangements make projects successful.[a] Part of the challenge of implementation is that while RPG projects are regional in nature, they are implemented at the national level. Moreover, the time needed to see the impact of an RPG project is greater than national projects. RPG projects, especially those on less tangible outcomes, such as multinational dialogues, may find it harder to identify a causal link between outputs and expected outcomes while facing omitted variable bias problems during evaluation (Nores and Kennedy 2017).

The experience of the Latin America and the Caribbean highlights new patterns of cooperation and illustrates the importance of innovative approaches to evaluation. Trade cooperation has been shown to be an effective first step for developing regional cooperation in other sectors such as transport, connectivity, finance, climate, and health. Moreover, new patterns of cooperation such as the Pacific Alliance are based on mutual interests rather than geographic proximity and allow a broader form of cooperation for the provision of RPGs. Finally, the issue of evaluation of the outcome of cooperation has been raised as the impact of regional bodies such as the South–South Cooperation is more knowledge-based and institutional-intensive and therefore more challenging to gauge.

IDB's experience also gives rise to key factors for successful RPG projects: (i) aligned and sustained political will is key for executing RPGs; (ii) technical focal points in RPG with closer ties to policy makers may be more effective in promoting reform toward national implementation; and (iii) RPGs should support different moments of the policy cycle from identification, design, and regulatory convergence to national implementation.[b]

The Regional Public Goods Initiative is promoting an evaluation effort in order to find and estimate the impact of RPG project, and extract lessons for other regional cooperation projects. The importance of an RPG evaluation agenda lies in the fact that rigorous evaluation (and its results) would allow to take evidence-based decisions and refocus the RPG Initiative as a relevant instrument for regional development.

RPG projects can have different approaches during the monitoring and evaluation process. A first approach can be placed on interactions, products, and networks that an RPG project creates during its implementation. Second, the spotlight can be placed on whether countries adopt the project on a national level or find some internal barriers to do so. Then, the target is to measure the results of the implementation of the project, in a tangible and rigorous way. Furthermore, an impact evaluation and a cost–benefit analysis can be conducted to estimate the effect and extract lessons about the success or failure of RPG projects.

[a] Management for Development Results (MfDR) is a style of Public Administration which emphasizes the maximization of public value via management tools that complement each other in a collective and coordinated manner to generate the social changes sought in the objectives of government policies. (IDB. What is Management for Development Results (MfDR)? https://www.iadb.org/en/mfdr [accessed September 2018]).

[b] These factors have implications for the IDB's operations. Projects, for instance, average 36 months to reduce the likelihood of changes in national administrations that may jeopardize timely execution; commitment letters and counterpart resources are required while relevant actors are included into the governance structure; and some flexibility is included to finance second phases or existing national projects that want to converge.

Source: ADB based on Estevadeordal (2018).

ASIAN CASES

Early warnings of disasters

The Boxing Day tsunami of 2004 clearly shows the need for a region-wide disaster warning system which is generally underprovided.

More than 230,000 people were killed in the Boxing Day tsunami of 2004 , which originated with the earthquake off of the west coast of Sumatra, Indonesia, where the number of deaths is around 130,000. Had an early warning system been in place at that time, many thousands of lives would have been saved. For example, the tsunami hit Sri Lanka about 2 hours after the initial earthquake, with the epicenter about 1,600 kilometers away. In Sri Lanka alone, more than 30,000 people died.[75]

The "early warning" includes detection of an impending disaster and the reporting of this knowledge. Detection is an RPG if the information is disseminated throughout the region without restriction. Investment in a system for detection and reporting, and its ongoing maintenance, is critical to whether knowledge of an impending disaster is reported.

A collective approach to establishing and maintaining integrated early warning systems for disasters would be more beneficial.

First, the cost of an integrated system would be lower than the aggregate cost of separate systems of equal coverage, not least because an integrated system can avoid duplicative components. Second, an integrated early warning system will generally be more effective than a collection of separate systems, as it will enable full coordination of the deployment of detection equipment and provide every member in the system with a complete reading of the signals, especially as some detection facilities will be under the jurisdiction of other member countries.[76] Detection of the earthquake coupled with detection of the tsunami's path is critical information since waves can be very high in the countries distant from the epicenter of the earthquake.

Once the integrated system is in place, the member countries may have less incentive to maintain the system as the tsunamis of the scale of the Boxing Day 2004 are extremely rare. However, neglect of maintenance could lead to a system failure. One way to help operate the system all the time is to integrate it with a larger system more regularly used for similar hazards such as storm surges (Alverson 2005).[77] Just as tsunamis can be triggered by underwater earthquakes, so storm surges can be caused by tropical cyclones located far from shore. Many of the same investments, like tide gauges, that detect a tsunami can also detect storm surges associated with tropical cyclones.

Regional public good of detection and reporting and the national public good of communication and trained response are strong complements.

The Indian Ocean Tsunami Warning and Mitigation System (IOTWMS) was launched in 2011. Under this arrangement, three tsunami service providers (TSPs) of Australia, India, and Indonesia are responsible for issuing warnings to member states (Intergovernmental Coordination Group/IOTWMS 2017). Figure 7. 7 shows the increase in investment for detection that has been made since the Boxing Day tsunami, and their locations. Seismometers detect seismic waves that point to the creation of a tsunami. Sea-level gauges and tsunameters confirm the existence of a tsunami. Multiple sites of detection make prediction of a tsunami's path more precise.

[75] Compared with the Pacific Tsunami Warning System founded in 1949, a system was not in place in Asia maybe because tsunamis are more common in the Pacific, and a higher frequency of occurrence clearly increases the benefits of having an early warning system. Another reason may be that countries in the Pacific are more accustomed to cooperating and/or that one or two countries, such as the United States and Japan, are willing and able to take the lead in establishing such a system.

[76] Seismometers are generally located on land whereas sea-level gauges are within the exclusive economic zones of coastal states.

[77] Tropical cyclones can be as destructive as tsunamis. For example, cyclone Nargis killed over 130,000 people in Myanmar in 2008. Tropical cyclones occur much more frequently than tsunamis. One regional system for tropical cyclones is the United Nations Economic and Social Commission for Asia and the Pacific (ESCAP)/World Meteorological Organization (WMO) Typhoon Committee, which covers storms in the Western Pacific. Another is the ESCAP/WMO Panel on Tropical Cyclones, responsible for the Bay of Bengal and the Arabian Sea.

Figure 7.7: Placement of Indian Ocean Tsunami Detection Equipment, 2004 and 2014

a: Broadband Seismometer

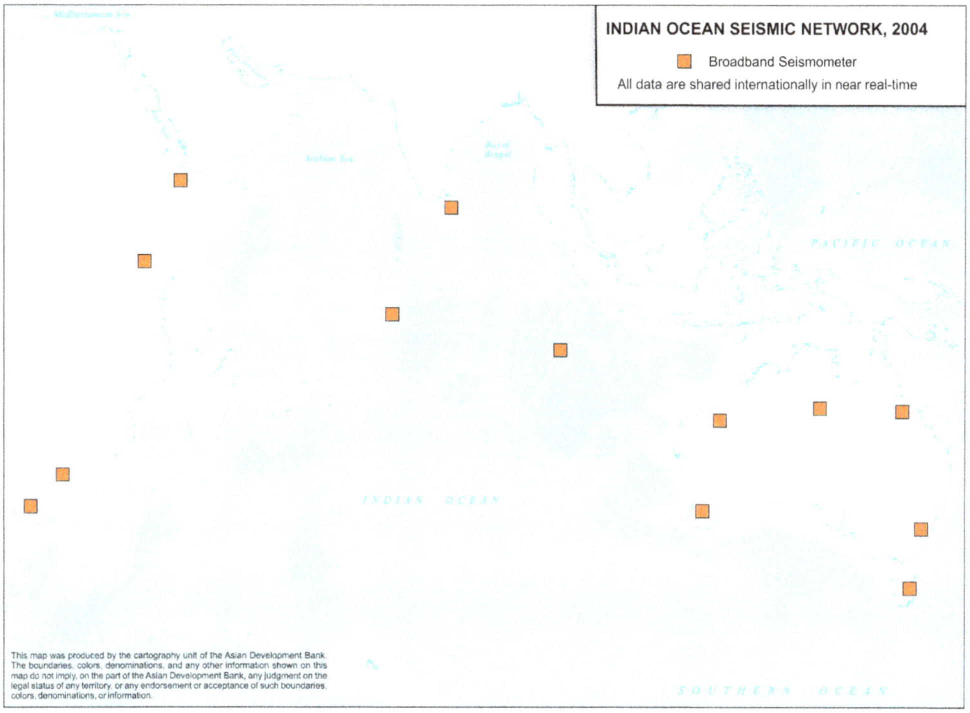
INDIAN OCEAN SEISMIC NETWORK, 2004
Broadband Seismometer
All data are shared internationally in near real-time
This map was produced by the cartography unit of the Asian Development Bank. The boundaries, colors, denominations, and any other information shown on this map do not imply, on the part of the Asian Development Bank, any judgment on the legal status of any territory, or any endorsement or acceptance of such boundaries, colors, denominations, or information.

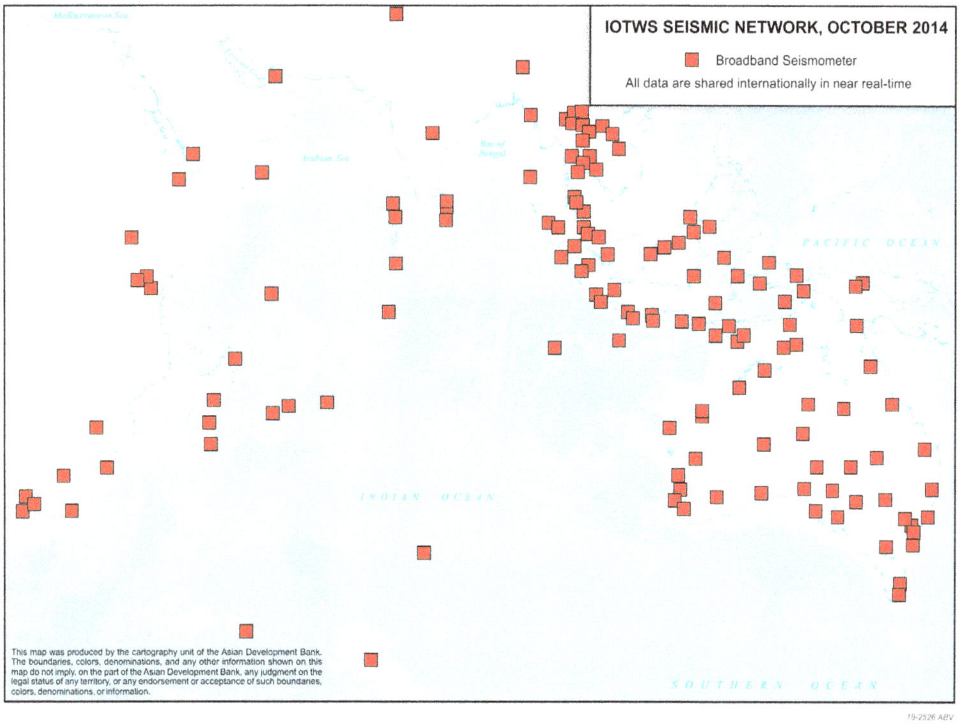
IOTWS SEISMIC NETWORK, OCTOBER 2014
Broadband Seismometer
All data are shared internationally in near real-time
This map was produced by the cartography unit of the Asian Development Bank. The boundaries, colors, denominations, and any other information shown on this map do not imply, on the part of the Asian Development Bank, any judgment on the legal status of any territory, or any endorsement or acceptance of such boundaries, colors, denominations, or information.

Figure 7.7 *continued*

b: Coastal Sea Level Gauges

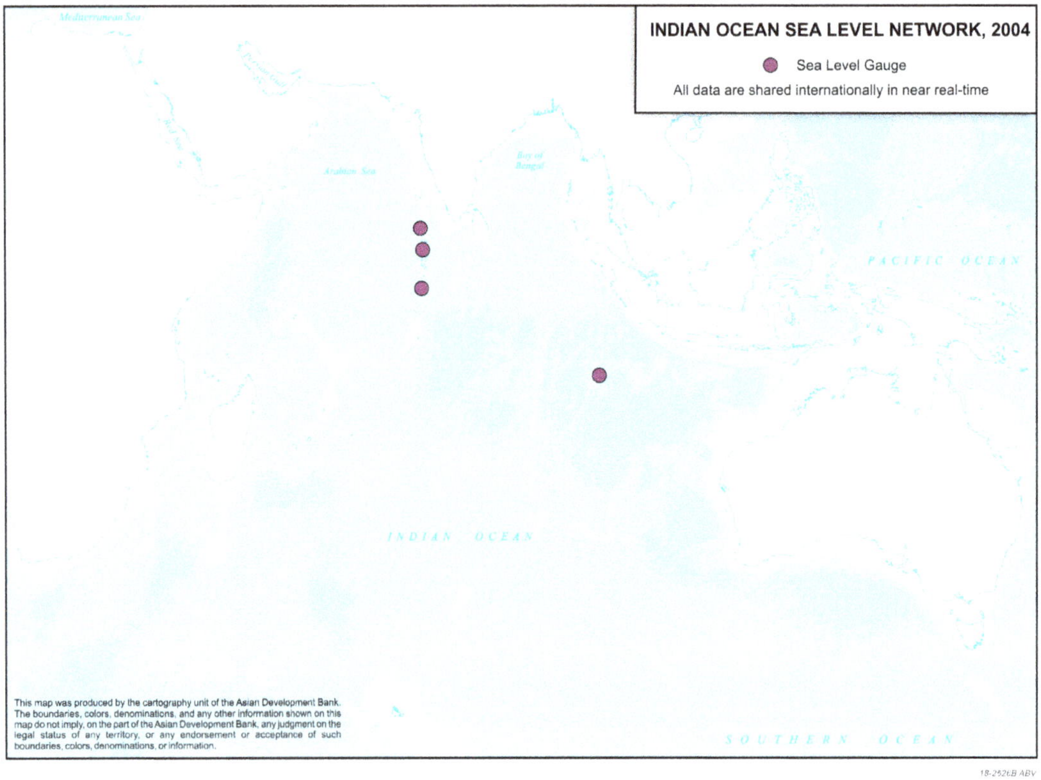
INDIAN OCEAN SEA LEVEL NETWORK, 2004
Sea Level Gauge
All data are shared internationally in near real-time
PACIFIC OCEAN
INDIAN OCEAN
SOUTHERN OCEAN
This map was produced by the cartography unit of the Asian Development Bank. The boundaries, colors, denominations, and any other information shown on this map do not imply, on the part of the Asian Development Bank, any judgment on the legal status of any territory, or any endorsement or acceptance of such boundaries, colors, denominations, or information.

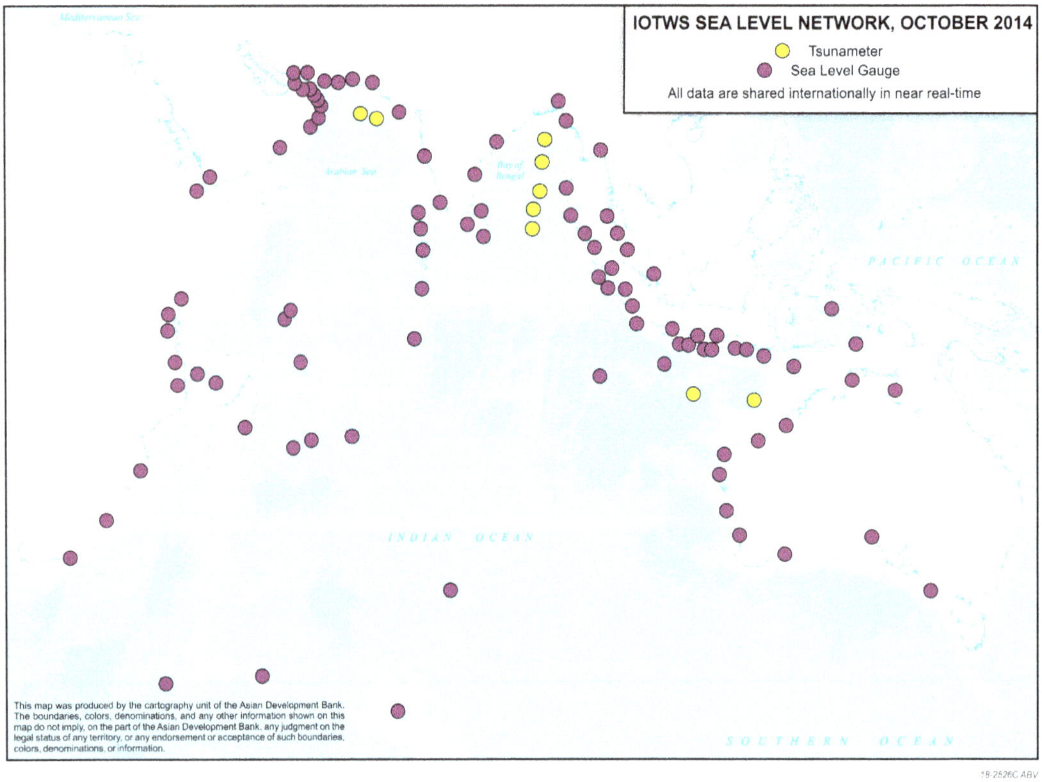
IOTWS SEA LEVEL NETWORK, OCTOBER 2014
Tsunameter
Sea Level Gauge
All data are shared internationally in near real-time
PACIFIC OCEAN
INDIAN OCEAN
SOUTHERN OCEAN
This map was produced by the cartography unit of the Asian Development Bank. The boundaries, colors, denominations, and any other information shown on this map do not imply, on the part of the Asian Development Bank, any judgment on the legal status of any territory, or any endorsement or acceptance of such boundaries, colors, denominations, or information.

IOTWMS = Indian Ocean Tsunami Warning and Mitigation System.
Source: ADB approximation based on the Intergovernmental Oceanographic Commission of United Nations Educational, Scientific and Cultural Organization (2015).

It is essential to have an international reporting system through official channels, involving one state reporting to others or a multilateral organization reporting to its member states. Another part of the system involves states communicating early warnings to communities at risk. It also involves states ensuring that such communities, having been given this information, know how to respond. Communication and trained response are national public goods (NPGs). The benefits from communicating warnings increase both with the timeliness and accuracy of the warnings and the ability and inclinations of communities to respond.

The provision of early warning systems for disasters highlights the role of better-shot and weakest-link technologies as well as the interplay of national and regional provision of a public good.

While detection and reporting at a regional level are led by a few countries with commitment and advanced technologies, communication and trained responses are more national in scope. A regional early warning system is of little value if countries lack the ability to communicate such warnings and respond to the threats to coastal communities. Therefore, regional institutions can shore up the weakest-link economies with financing and capacity building to enhance their communication and trained responses.

Regional fisheries management

Current property rights arrangements for the oceans give every state a right to fish on the high seas.

Coastal states have exclusive jurisdiction over fisheries out to a distance of up to 370 kilometers from shore. Fisheries located entirely within the exclusive economic zone (EEZ) may be managed efficiently, by the coastal state regulating access as a "sole owner." Overfishing is a problem only where the coastal state lacks either the ability or an interest in regulating access. However, an open access fishery on the high seas gives rise to the "tragedy of the commons" (Hardin 1968). Overfishing is likely to occur as every country exploiting the resource will have an incentive to increase its harvest and similarly, countries that had not exploited the resource previously will have an incentive to enter the fishery.[78]

A shared fishery requires aggregate efforts to balance exploitation and preservation to prevent the tragedy of the commons.

The rents earned from open access fisheries are substantially reduced as more rent-seeking countries enter to fish. As long as the number of countries fishing in an open-access fishery is regulated at a certain level, every country exploiting the resource can continue to earn positive rents. However, in the case of highly migratory tuna fishery, under the current property rights arrangements on the high seas, it is not possible to limit fishing to just a few countries. This is the principal challenge to an international regime for managing a fishery: deterring states that are in the fishery from fishing excessively, while at the same time deterring states that are not in the fishery from entering it.

The Western and Central Pacific Ocean which hosts the world's largest tuna fishery is managed by two regional institutions: the Western and Central Pacific Fisheries Commission and the Pacific Islands Forum Fisheries Agency.

The main agreement that applies to this fishery is the Convention for the Conservation and Management of Highly Migratory Fish Stocks in the Western and Central Pacific Ocean, which came into force in 2004. This agreement established the Western and Central Pacific Fisheries Commission, the organization responsible for managing this regional fishery. Another major organization to serve a similar purpose is the Pacific Islands Forum Fisheries Agency, which came into force in 1979 and was established by the South Pacific Fisheries Agency Convention. As a subgroup to the agency, the

78 The cost of overfishing is indeed enormous. According to a recent World Bank (2017) study, overfishing reduced the aggregate net benefit of exploitation of the world's fisheries by $83 billion in 2012. Two-thirds of this loss is borne by Asia.

Parties to the Nauru Agreement (PNA) controls the world's largest sustainable purse seine tuna fishery.[79]

Two measures were adopted to prevent overfishing in the Western and Central Pacific Ocean: closure of high-seas areas that border the EEZs, and a vessel day scheme that involves limiting the total number of days to fish.

The ban, adopted by the PNA in 2008, applies to high-sea "pockets" (areas A and B in Figure 7.8). Compliance with the ban is monitored by the requirement that all licensed vessels fishing in the EEZs of PNA member states carry radio transponders which reveal their coordinates at all times. In this ocean, it is not profitable to fish only within these high-seas pockets, and so the states with expansive EEZs can allow fishing within their waters but conditional on vessels not fishing within these high-seas pockets. In other oceans, a ban on high-seas fishing could not be orchestrated as easily.

A first best solution would be putting a fishery under the exclusive control of a sole owner, involving a multiple of parties implementing the full cooperative outcome. Closing these high-sea pockets could easily be a good

Figure 7.8: High-Seas Areas Closed to Fishing by the Parties to Nauru Agreement

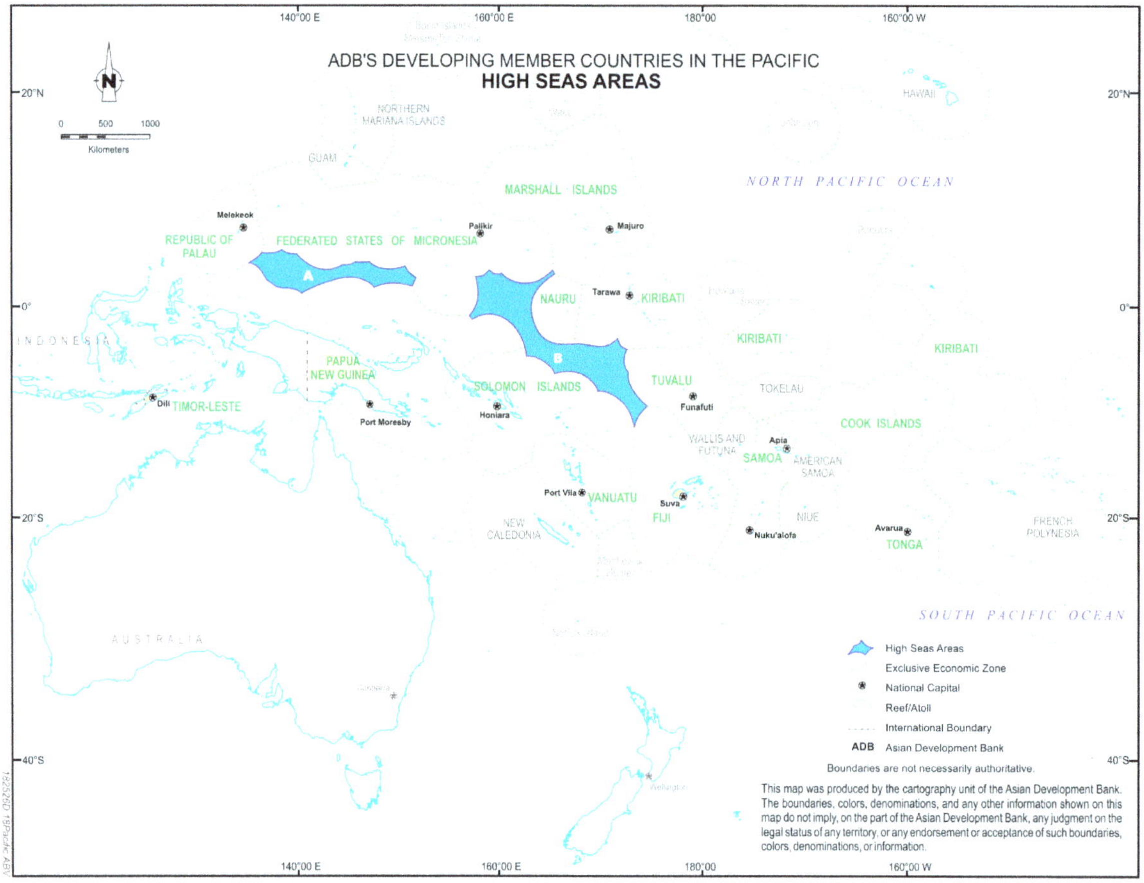

Note: Areas A and B are the sea pockets with the ban on fishing for the members of the Parties of Nauru Agreement as of August 2018.
Source: ADB approximation based on Western and Central Pacific Fisheries Commission (2016).

[79] The Pacific Islands Forum Fisheries Agency (FFA) has 17 Pacific Island members: Australia, the Cook Islands, the Federated States of Micronesia, Fiji, Kiribati, the Marshall Islands, Nauru, New Zealand, Niue, Palau, Papua New Guinea, Samoa, Solomon Islands, Tokelau, Tonga, Tuvalu, and Vanuatu. FFA is an advisory body providing expertise, technical assistance and other support to its members who make sovereign decisions about their tuna resources and participate in regional decision making on tuna management through agencies such as the Western and Central Pacific Fisheries Commission (Pacific Islands Forum Fisheries Agency. Welcome to the Pacific Islands Forum Fisheries Agency. https://www.ffa.int/about [accessed September 2018]).

move for PNA members, as it increases their control over the fishery. However, the restrictions may also increase the cost of fishing. Comprehensive management of the entire territory would likely improve matters.

The vessel day scheme, adopted by the PNA in 2012, sets a total number of days in which vessels may fish within PNA waters, a value chosen to satisfy the overall conservation and management objectives determined by the Western and Central Pacific Fisheries Commission. The current approach contrasts with the previous system, under which vessel numbers were fixed, with the allocations going directly to the vessels rather than the PNA members (Yeeting et al. 2016).

However, under the vessel day scheme, the problem of overfishing still remained due to adoption of new technologies like fish-aggregating devices and the use of larger vessels.

Purse seiners increased their catch of bigeye tuna, causing this species to be overfished. A limit on harvests would be more effective, but also harder to implement due to greater difficulties in monitoring catches as opposed to vessel days. Moreover, it does not tackle the incentives for other fisheries commission members to free ride by setting higher limits in their waters. At the same time, the new scheme increased access fees as a share of the total value of landed fish, rising from 3% to 6% under the old system to 14% under the new scheme (Yeeting et al. 2016).

Malaria control and elimination

Malaria "elimination" is an extreme version of "control." This is a pure public good with a threshold aggregation technology.

"Control" is a public health intervention that reduces the number of cases of malaria in a well-defined area for a certain period. However, it does not necessarily bring the incidence down to zero at any point. "Elimination," on the other hand, is an extreme form of control that reduces the number of cases of malaria to *zero*. Control is normally assumed to be undertaken at the national level. Elimination is a national or regional public good.[80]

In particular, malaria elimination is a threshold public good. To eliminate malaria, the life cycle of the parasite must be broken, which means that infections in mosquitoes and humans must be reduced to zero. This can be done by various means, including the application of larvicides in mosquito breeding sites, indoor spraying of walls with insecticide, the use of insecticide-treated bed nets, and the use of antimalarial drugs. To eliminate malaria, these means must be used in tandem and in sufficient volume to drive transmission to zero. Any less than the sufficient amount will lead to persistence of the disease, while any more would result to wasted resources.

Malaria elimination in Sri Lanka has been a success.

In 1935, there were over 1.5 million cases of malaria in the country, resulting in 80,000 deaths. As part of the global effort to eradicate malaria in the 1950s, Sri Lanka reduced the case count to just 17 in 1963. However, after that, malaria rebounded. By 1970, 1 million cases were recorded, with the epidemic remaining at a high level in the following decades (1980s–1990s).[81] The number of malaria cases began to decline from 1999 onwards (Abeyasinghe et al. 2012). In 2016, Sri Lanka was certified by the World Health Organization (WHO) to have eliminated malaria, following 3 years in which no cases were observed. Although Sri Lanka has one advantage over some other countries, its relative isolation, Sri Lanka will need to institute effective surveillance and treatment of discovered cases to guard against the risks of reintroduction (Galappaththy, Fernando, and Abeyasinghe 2013).

80 Once the parasite is removed from a locale, residents need not fear becoming infected, nor do they have to guard against infection. No one in living where malaria was eliminated can be excluded from enjoying this benefit, and nor does any such person's enjoyment of this good affect anyone else's enjoyment.

81 See World Health Organization. Sri Lanka Defeats Malaria and Reaches Zero Cases. http://www.searo.who.int/srilanka/areas/malaria/sri-lanka-defeats-malaria/en/ (accessed September 2018).

Malaria elimination also requires regional arrangements, and providing poor countries with financing and capacity building can facilitate the elimination process.

Control and elimination in more continental areas is a different matter. The flow of malaria (carried both by infected mosquitoes and infected humans) can be so great that it may never pay or even be feasible for a country to eliminate malaria unilaterally. In these situations, a regional approach is needed.

At the 2014 East Asia Summit, 18 leaders declared the goal of eliminating malaria from the region by 2030.[82] Elimination of this scale would be a true RPG. In a continental context, it may not pay any country in a region to eliminate malaria within its borders unilaterally, and yet it may pay all countries in the region to work together to eliminate malaria. In this case, provision of the public good is likely to succeed as it mainly requires coordination: once each country is assured that others in the region will eliminate malaria, each has an incentive to eliminate malaria.

When the poorest countries in a region lack the incentive or the capability or resources to eliminate malaria within their borders, external support through capacity building and funding will be effective.[83] Such an example is the Regional Malaria and Other Communicable Disease Threats Trust Fund, set up by ADB in 2013 "to support developing member countries to develop multi-country, cross-border, and multisector responses to urgent malaria and other communicable disease issues" (ADB 2015) (see Box 7.9 for the social dimensions of malaria control and the role of MDBs).

Malaria elimination in Asia will have consequences for countries outside the region.

While fewer than 5,000 people—most of them adult males—die of malaria every year in this region, over 400,000 children die of malaria in Africa (WHO 2015). The Greater Mekong Subregion (GMS) has long been a crucible for antimalarial drug resistance (Roberts 2016).[84] If resistance were eliminated there, malaria would be much less likely to develop globally, providing a benefit to the whole world, sub-Saharan Africa especially. In this regard, the Strategy for Malaria Elimination in the GMS (2015–2030), which was endorsed by the World Health Assembly in May 2015, aims to supply this global public good by eliminating malaria throughout the GMS by 2030, at an estimated cost of about $3 billion (WHO 2015).

Cooperative Management of the Mekong River Basin

River basin management is often referred to as an RPG because efficient management of a river basin would benefit all the counties sharing the river.

The Mekong River is shared by six countries and crosses some of the poorest parts of Asia. It starts in the Tibetan highlands of the People's Republic of China (PRC), flows through Yunnan Province, and then into Myanmar, the Lao People's Democratic Republic (Lao PDR), Thailand, Cambodia, and Viet Nam. The Mekong River serves different purposes for different countries. The PRC and the Lao PDR primarily regard the river as a resource for hydropower development and navigation. Thailand values it for irrigation, Cambodia for fisheries, and Viet Nam for agriculture (Pham Do and Dinar 2014). Collective action needs to reconcile not only the river's many alternative uses, but also the interests of the different states as regards these uses.

82 ADB members include Brunei Darussalam, Cambodia, India, Indonesia, the Lao PDR, Malaysia, Myanmar, the People's Republic of China, the Philippines, Singapore, the Republic of Korea, Thailand, and Viet Nam (APLMA 2014).

83 A key component of success in eradicating smallpox was also financing and the provision of technical assistance in poor countries. The same is true of the ongoing efforts to eradicate polio and Guinea worm.

84 Resistance to cholorquine emerged here in the 1950s. Resistance to sulfadoxine-pyrimethamine surfaced here in the 1960s. Mefloquine-resistant strains emerged in the 1970s. In 2008 and 2009, resistance to artemisinin was detected in the same area. Later still, resistance to piperaquine, a drug often used in combination with artemisinin, acquired resistance here.

Box 7.9: The Social Dimensions of Malaria Control and the Role of Multilateral Development Banks

Lack of coordination and cooperation can cause a social dilemma in controlling or eliminating malaria, which suggests the importance of facilitating roles of multilateral development banks (MDBs) in regional public good (RPG) provision in the health sector. Lack of cooperation among neighboring communities in cleaning shared mosquito larval breeding areas such as swamps can be viewed as an outcome of the "Prisoners' Dilemma" in malaria control. Although cleaning the areas would offer both communities the highest aggregate payoffs, a community may expect the other to act first, and both may end up not cleaning the site.[a] In Mauritius, for example, cooperation between villages in the projects to clean Anopheles mosquito breeding sites was lacking even as health workers had given out public service reminders (World Health Organization 2012). The Prisoners' Dilemma in malaria control may be attributed to (i) a lack of cross-community and cross-border arrangements, (ii) the absence of a mechanism for cross-border information sharing on health-related benefits and costs, and (iii) an insufficient political commitment.

Further, Shiroishi (2018) has observed that coordination failure in malaria control in the Greater Mekong Subregion tends to be compounded by (i) a large number of seasonal migrant workers, such as those engaged on private rubber plantations,[b] whom public health agencies struggle to reach; (ii) ethnic minorities in remote areas having different sociocultural backgrounds and languages from most of the population; (iii) the low incomes and education attainment of migrants and rural people in border areas; and (vi) substandard health care and difficult access to people in remote border areas.

Addressing threats to regional health issues needs to first understand the multisectoral nature of the issue and requires integrated approaches and a common set of technical expertise and skills. The control of communicable diseases like malaria is not confined to the human health sector. It requires multisectoral and integrated approaches with significant support from all relevant areas, such as agriculture (particularly animal health and food safety), finance, environment, trade, transport, tourism, urbanization, and climate change. As such, the "One Health" approach,[c] which calls for multisectoral and transdisciplinary cooperation is seen as important in addressing key health security issues such as zoonosis control and antimicrobial resistance, which are increasingly significant threats to human health and economic development in Asia.

MDBs are in a unique and competitive position to contribute to controlling cross-border communicable diseases, including malaria. With substantive operation experiences across multiple sectors, MDBs have a huge potential to establish and implement an integrated health approach in collaboration with governments and relevant agencies. Building on their coordination and cooperation capacity, MDBs can effectively support various regional forums and subregional strategies with effective use of policy dialogues and advocacy with developing member countries and relevant stake holders, including the private sector.

[a] Under the following payoffs, not cleaning the larval breeding sites are the dominant strategies for both village 1 and 2. This results in the Nash equilibrium, where both villages do not clear (Malhotra 2012).

		Community 2	
		Clean (C)	Not Clean (NC)
Community 1	C	1, 1	0, 2
	NC	2, 0	0, 0

[b] The Greater Mekong Subregion accounted for almost a half of global rubber production in 2014 (Golbon, Cotter, and Sauerborn 2018).

[c] One Health is defined as "a collaborative, multisectoral, and transdisciplinary approach—working at the local, regional, national, and global levels—with the goal of achieving optimal health outcomes recognizing the interconnection between people, animals, plants, and their shared environment" (United States Centers for Disease Control and Prevention. History. https://www.cdc.gov/onehealth/basics/history/index.html [accessed September 2018]). Its development was formally recommended in 2007 at the International Ministerial Conference on Avian and Pandemic Influenza.

Source: ADB based on Shiroishi (2018).

A fruitful approach is for the parties to agree on the best use of the river basin taken as a whole, and for claims to individual rights to be addressed using the side-payments and cost-sharing arrangements.

A review of experience in transboundary river basin management worldwide shows that the bargains reached depend on the circumstances (Dinar 2006). When a river forms a border between two states, the costs of joint development are typically shared equally, with no need for side payments. When one state is upstream and another downstream, side payments are typical, but which state pays depends on relative income levels. When an upstream state wishes to develop its portion of a river to the detriment of its downstream neighbor, the upstream state tends to make a payment to the downstream state when the upstream state is richer than the downstream state. When the upstream state is poorer than the downstream state, the downstream state may pay the upstream state to modify its plans.

One of the difficulties for collective action is that the allocation of property rights is often disputed.

Upstream states have an obvious geographic advantage and may claim a right to develop "their" resources as they please. However, international law also recognizes that downstream states have a right not to be harmed by upstream development. Generally speaking, international law favors "equitable utilization" of transboundary rivers, but how this outcome is determined is for the parties themselves to negotiate (Barrett 2003). Side payments are a fairly simple matter when property rights are not in dispute. However, when property rights are disputed, side-payments may not suffice to secure an efficient outcome.

Management of the Mekong River basin has more room for improvement by strengthening cooperation and partnerships between related organizations.

In the Mekong River basin, the lower basin countries, the Lao PDR, Thailand, Cambodia, and Viet Nam, cooperate through the Mekong River Commission, while the upstream countries, the PRC and Myanmar, do not participate but are "dialogue partners." Even among lower basin countries, the commission has struggled to address a dispute over use (Pham Do and Dinar 2014). As such, the GMS Economic Cooperation Program, established with ADB assistance in 1992, might be a more appropriate institution for managing the river basin in partnership with the Mekong River Commission. It can serve as a forum for linking a broader set of issues relevant to regional sustainable development since its membership includes all the states in the GMS.

Conclusions and Policy Considerations

Globalization, economic integration, resource mobility, and technology spillovers have created greater interdependence of economies in the region, and demand for RPGs that can address transnational challenges and benefit a region as a whole. When provided adequately, RPGs can effectively bridge the gap between national and global public goods and hence contribute to achieving the Sustainable Development Goals. Infrastructure connectivity can facilitate international trade, increase employment and incomes both domestically and across borders. Transnational impacts on agriculture and food supplies due to climate change and environmental pressures require collective responses. More open trade regimes and increased labor mobility have potential to spread contagious diseases that can be tackled through regional cooperation in multiple areas such as health, trade, transport, and tourism.

RPGs produce spillover benefits that extend beyond borders. However, along with the often-unclear scope of benefits, their nature of being "public" gives a rise to market failures. Collective action for RPG provision can be difficult to achieve without a regional institution or framework that can coordinate provision across countries. Supply may also hinge on the willingness of countries to cooperate. Individual members in the group acting in their private interests may fail to achieve an optimal outcome for the group. Therefore, policy interventions are required to ensure the provision of adequate level of RPGs.

Policy considerations to encourage RPG provision and address collective action problems are suggested as follows. Proposals include the need to improve understanding of RPGs and better assess the spillover effects of RPGs so that RPGs can receive the policy attention and support for adequate provision. Since different types of RPGs require different responses to address collective action problems, some policy suggestions by RPG type are also discussed. Finally, roles for national governments, MDBs, and other institutions are proposed.

Enhance Understanding of RPGs and Measuring the Benefits of RPGs

Challenges in dealing with coordination problems prevent RPGs from receiving enough policy attention and support.

Even with shared interests and benefits, parties may fail to cooperate over concerns about free-riding or the expected benefits of free-riding themselves. The parties may therefore withdraw efforts in producing a collective good, or they fail to exercise restraint in utilizing a common resource (Olivier 2018). Political economy considerations also matter, where entrenched interests compete with the national objectives. Various coordination challenges are expressed at regional, national, and local levels. Greater recognition is needed that development is also a multilayered collective action problem, with various coordination challenges that prevent governments from acting consistently as "principals" in dynamic development processes (Booth 2012, Olivier 2018). Recognizing such challenges can guide institutional reform for greater effectiveness, however difficult that may be.

It is important to develop better measures to estimate the spillover benefits of RPGs while making more efforts to identify potential beneficiary countries who are yet to be included in the group of RPG suppliers.

Increased understanding of the shared benefits can help close knowledge gaps and create an incentive for cooperation (Figure 7.9). The perception of free-riding and lack of understanding of specific benefits enjoyed by each individual country deter developing countries from making their contributions toward RPGs. Greater effort should be made to identify and value shared regional benefits in addition to more information about clear benefits for each individual country.[85]

In this regard, a guideline for valuation of regional projects should be based on the principle that benefit valuations for a regional project are not the same as

Figure 7.9: Improving Understanding of the Nature and Benefits of Regional Public Goods

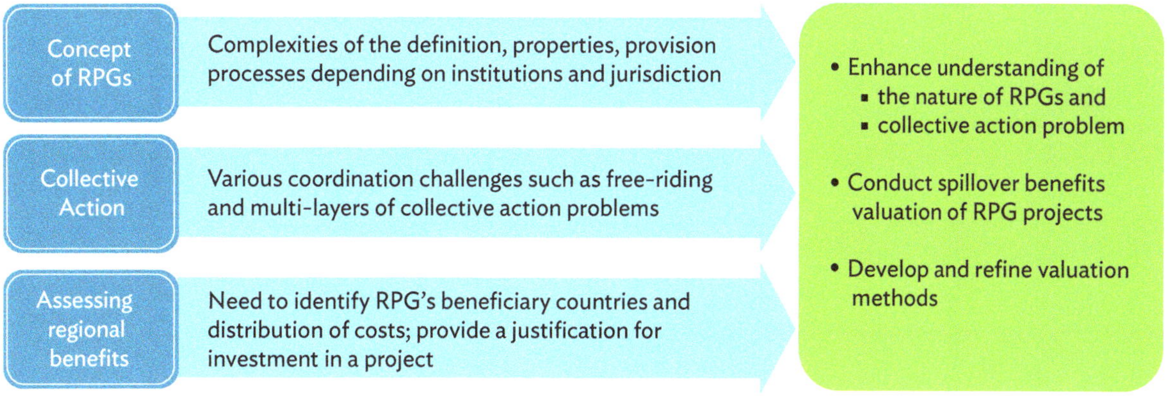

Concept of RPGs
Complexities of the definition, properties, provision processes depending on institutions and jurisdiction
Collective Action
Various coordination challenges such as free-riding and multi-layers of collective action problems
Assessing regional benefits
Need to identify RPG's beneficiary countries and distribution of costs; provide a justification for investment in a project
• Enhance understanding of
▪ the nature of RPGs and
▪ collective action problem
• Conduct spillover benefits valuation of RPG projects
• Develop and refine valuation methods

RPG = regional public good.
Source: ADB.

86 For example, to evaluate economic rationale, viability, and efficiency, ADB's Operations Manual (B.2.; ADB 2017b) require a project to conduct an economic analysis. Specifically, the Guidelines for the Economic Analysis (para 172; ADB 2017c) state that "Economic analysis of regional cooperation projects requires the calculation of the returns for both the regional and individual countries. The regional economic net present value (ENPV) gives the total change in welfare for the group of participating countries, which must be equal to the sum of the national ENPVs." It also says that "The principles of benefit valuation from the national case apply to regional cooperation projects." However, the guidelines do not specify how regional benefits should be calculated.

those for a national case. Compared with a national project, a regional project has more layers of benefits shared across countries, such as induced foreign direct investment, trade, cross-border financial flows, and integrated markets. If possible, their spillover benefits need to be both identified and evaluated at the concept stage. A cost–benefit analysis may be complemented by alternative approaches such as partial/general equilibrium models accounting for spillover effects. Since there is no consensus on the best methods of measuring RPG benefits, a guideline that sets out the criteria for regional projects and potential methodologies for measurement along with the development of an RPG database would help providers and beneficiaries alike. Continued efforts to test the guideline against projects will help further refine the guideline.

Policy Lessons from Case Studies

Regional experiences highlight the important roles of regional institutions in facilitating regional cooperation and coordination, and promoting collective action in providing adequate level of RPGs.

European experiences show the provision of RPGs can be led and coordinated by regional institutions, including common legislation and regulations. For example, the EU tries to achieve a fully integrated energy system for the region to ensure energy security such as stable energy supply and affordable prices. The experience illustrates that the EU-wide legislation together with cooperation of national energy regulators made significant contributions to the progress toward an integrated energy system.

The experience of Latin America and the Caribbean illustrates the importance of sequencing and innovations for collective action to promote regional cooperation and facilitate RPG provision.

For many countries in Latin America and the Caribbean, trade integration has been a common policy priority. Therefore, pursuing trade integration provides an effective first step to foster provision in other related RPG sectors such as cross-border infrastructure. Also helpful in promoting collective action was the adoption of an innovative approach to form a new group for economic cooperation such as the Pacific Alliance based on mutual interests rather than geographic proximity.

Experiences in Asia stress the need for a regional approach to tackling common issues that can complement national and global efforts.

For example, the development of the early warning system for tsunamis across the Indian Ocean has improved detection and reporting of disasters significantly, which was complemented by national efforts such as communication and trained responses. Like malaria control in the Greater Mekong Subregion, a stronger regional response could also improve the effectiveness in the prevention of communicable disease outbreaks both regionally and globally.

Policy Considerations by RPG Type Based on Aggregation Technology

There is no one-size-fits-all mechanism for RPG provision, but different aggregation technologies suggest a useful framework to guide how to promote RPG provision depending on their types.

Grants are usually recommended for shoring up the weakest-link nations, which are in many cases less developed low-income countries, such as in providing quarantine and surveillance to contain contagious diseases or boosting liquidity in troubled financial systems. Best-shot arrangements are desirable when advanced economies supply RPGs that require large capital outlays or specialized technical skills. Designing and implementing best practices, such as in building bond markets and sound financial systems, or finding a cure for communicable diseases, may be led by one country or a small number of countries with sufficient capacity and successful experiences.

Policy considerations specific to the type of RPGs are suggested for (i) natural resources and environment, (ii) economic cooperation and integration, (iii) human and social development, (iv) governance and institutions, (v) peace and security, and (vi) connectivity (see Table 7.8 for summary).

Table 7.8: Policy Considerations by Functional Area of Regional Public Goods

Functional Areas	Aggregator	Regional Institutions	Policy Considerations
Natural Resources and Environment Addressing water pollution, curbing acid rain, commons management, reducing greenhouse gases	Summation, weighted sum	Acid Deposition Monitoring Network in East Asia; Long-Range Transboundary Air Pollution in Northeast Asia; Pacific Island Renewable Energy Investment Program	• Setting up pollution monitors and identification of emitter and recipients requires funding at the regional and subregional levels • Grants can be used to fund poor countries' contribution to the natural disaster monitoring system • For assistance after a natural disaster (a summation technology), rich countries, charitable foundation, and nongovernment organizations have roles to play • Multilateral institutions and networks should bolster regional actions to address GPGs
Economic Cooperation and Integration Free trade agreements, fostering foreign direct investment, maintaining financial stability, promoting macroeconomic stability, fostering regional growth	Summation, weakest link, best shot	Greater Mekong Subregion (GMS) Program; South Asian Association of Regional Cooperation; Association of Southeast Asian Nations (ASEAN); Central Asia Regional Economic Cooperation; Free Trade Area of the Asia-Pacific; South Asia Free Trade Area; Chiang Mai Initiative Multilateralization	• In terms of maintaining regional financial stability, sound financial practices (best-shot RPGs) including well-established bond markets, emergency liquidity pools, or agreements with multilateral institutions can enhance resiliency to the regional financial system • In the case of poor countries, grants would be appropriate for constant surveillance to spot liquidity and other difficulties that could infect neighboring countries' banking systems (weakest-link RPGs)
Human and Social Development Education, health, knowledge creation, culture, furthering science	Weakest link, weaker link, best shot, better shot	GMS Health Security Project; International Rice Research Institute; ASEAN Quality Assurance Framework	• Regional and subregional institutions have a greater role to play for weakest-link health RPGs, such as quarantine and surveillance efforts to contain potential global impact of contagious diseases • Grants are needed to bolster the actions of poor weakest-link countries • Regional and global health efforts should be complementary and reinforcing
Governance and Institutions Regulatory practices, regional collectives, rule of law, banking practices, benchmarking data, capacity building, policy harmonization, surveillance	Best shot, better shot, threshold, weakest link	Economic Review and Policy Dialogue; South Asian Telecommunication Regulators Council; ASEAN+3 Macroeconomic Research Office	• To promote the best practices, regional institutions' capacity-building efforts would be recommended particularly for those weakest-link countries • To apply the very best practices, the region should look to the entire world, especially the most successful industrial countries, and borrow practices that have worked
Peace and Security Peacekeeping, crisis management, limiting weapon proliferation, managing refugee flows, territorial dispute resolution, alliance, curbing drug trafficking, controlling terrorism, limiting corruption	Best shot, better shot, threshold, weakest link	No regionwide Asia-Pacific alliance. Some non-aggression pacts (e.g., India and Pakistan and the People's Republic of China and Pakistan); Alliances with the United States and ASEAN.	• An alliance structure that links the region would allow for more rapid responses to conflict exigencies • Actions to shore up unstable regimes must be undertaken, ideally at the subregional level that richer subregions (e.g., East Asia) are able to address
Connectivity Transportation network, infrastructure, customs control, communication network, energy network, air-traffic control	Weakest link, weaker link, threshold	Border economic zone development; East Asia and Pacific Infrastructure Regulatory Forum; South Asia Forum for Infrastructure Regulation; Turkmenistan–Uzbekistan–Tajikistan–Afghanistan–Pakistan Power Interconnection Framework; GMS Cross-Border Transport Facilitation Agreement	• Connectivity action should first be at the subregional level, followed by regional efforts to link the subregions • When congestion tolls are used to internalize the associated crowding costs, the toll proceeds can be used to finance the club and achieve an efficient solution • Equity concerns can be addressed by regional or subregional institutions through funding the user charges or tolls of poor countries

GPGs = global public goods, RPG = regional public good.
Source: ADB's policy considerations based on Sandler (2018a, 2018b).

Natural resources and environment. This area is generally associated with summation and weighted-sum aggregators. Weighted sum is most applicable to acid rain, water pollution, and other transboundary air and water emissions that affect an entire region and beyond. Thus, it is necessary to know the origin and the recipient countries of the pollutants so that appropriate treaties can be enacted and enforced. Gathering this information requires pollution monitors across a network of locations, with funding at both the regional and subregional levels. A regional institution can then come up with an overall grid for the entire spillover area so that all relevant emitters and recipients are included.[87]

Economic cooperation and integration. Summation and weakest-link aggregators are commonly found in this area. All regional countries must put their financial system on a sound basis, which includes constant surveillance to identify liquidity shortages and other problems that could become systemic and infect neighboring countries' banking systems. This requires assistance via grants to advance financial development in weakest-link (poor) countries. Best-shot aggregators also play a role in economic cooperation. Coming up with sound financial practices that not only limit financial instability but also put into motion ways of ameliorating emerging crises is a best-shot RPG that has spillovers worldwide.

Human and social development. The best shot and weakest link are the most relevant aggregation technologies. Health is a best-shot public good that is created typically by best-endowed and best-staffed research teams—those generally found in the richest countries. Preference for strong public health motivates rich countries to provide the best-shot RPG through their own funds or from loans or aid to groups such as WHO, the Centers for Disease Control, or the Pasteur Institute. For weakest-link health RPGs such as quarantine and surveillance efforts, regional and subregional institutions (e.g., GMS, SASEC, and CAREC) can play a much greater role. Grants are needed to bolster the actions of weakest-link countries.

Governance and institutions. This is an area primarily categorized by best-shot, better-shot, and threshold aggregators. Instituting appropriate regulatory practices, regional collectives, rule of law, benchmarking data, and banking practices are best- or better-shot RPGs. A region would want to apply best practices that make governance effective and further commerce, the functioning of markets, and civil and political freedoms. A weakest-link component is also present because a country that fails to follow best practices can produce negative externalities or consequences on countries that do adhere to them. To promote best practices, regional institutions' capacity-building efforts are recommended, particularly for the weakest-link countries.

Peace and security. This area is primarily driven by best-shot, better-shot, and weakest-link aggregators. Peacekeeping efforts and managing refugee flows, for example, are best-shot or better-shot RPGs led by one or more nations. An alliance structure that links the region would allow for more rapid responses to conflict exigencies. Unstable regimes in a weakest-link country can spread conflicts that can hurt growth in neighboring states. Actions to shore up unstable regimes must therefore be addressed.

Connectivity. Enhancing connectivity is mainly driven by weakest- or weaker-link aggregators, since one substandard piece in an infrastructure grid can limit its entire functionality. To forestall such a consequence and to eliminate choke points or linkage failures, oversight and support must be provided at the regional level. Accordingly, grants to shore up these weakest-link challenged countries are needed.

Roles of RPG Suppliers—Nations, MDBs, and Others

Nations need to build the basic capacity—through the provision of national public goods—to be able to contribute RPGs.

A country that is unable to supply national public goods (NPGs) is unlikely to be able to contribute to the supply of RPGs, at least without external assistance. NPGs are important complements to RPGs. Education

[87] For example, the United Nations Environmental Program (UNEP) can assist as it has done throughout Europe in terms of monitoring sulfur, nitrogen, volatile organic compounds, and other pollutants. Such efforts by the UNEP resulted in effective transboundary air pollution treaties (e.g., Helsinki Protocol, Sofia Protocol, Oslo Protocol, and Geneva Protocol) concerning these substances.

at the country level for instance is essential to take advantage of knowledge shared across a region. The detection and reporting components of a tsunami warning system are best provided as an RPG only when supported by the NPGs of communication and trained responses. Elimination of malaria at the national level is a cornerstone of regional and global elimination of the disease.

Developing economies are generally well aware of the substantial benefits of RPGs, but view it difficult to contribute RPG provision.[88] Collective action can be promoted if national development priorities align with the need for RPGs.

Difficulties in balancing national and regional interests may lead to the view of RPGs as less important in development priorities. The perception of unequal RPG benefits may also discourage countries to contribute. Shortages of financial resources and capacity are another challenge for developing economies in providing RPGs. If national development priorities align with RPGs, developing economies would be much more willing to contribute. For example, when a group of countries share better infrastructure connectivity as their respective national development policies, coordinating more cross-border infrastructure investment can be easily facilitated. As such, the region can benefit from having a mechanism in place to share information on national development priorities and the benefits of RPGs among regional stakeholders. MDBs can also support regional governments in developing their national development strategies to better accommodate regional and subregional policies and priorities.

MDBs can help increase RPG provision via reducing knowledge and financing gaps as well as playing the role of an honest broker to enhance mutual trust and facilitate regional cooperation for the provision of RPGs.

MDBs, including ADB, have been active in RPG provision either directly funding or providing financial support. In addition, they can help facilitate RPG provision of their member economies by strengthening knowledge and information sharing on the benefits and the costs of provision. The strengths of MDBs also build on effective coordination and their role as an honest broker with their accumulated social capital from member countries and their communities in the long run (Box 7.10). Their in-depth knowledge and experiences in multiple countries and sectors allow a more holistic and integrated approach to address regional and subregional development challenges and hence promote regional cooperation for RPG provision that can complement national efforts.

Maintaining an adequate level of RPG and strengthening the maintenance capacities of the participating countries are as crucial as RPG provision itself. An MDB can help in this area too. In the 1960s, for instance, in response to two major tsunamis in the Pacific, the Intergovernmental Oceanographic Commission of the United Nations Educational, Scientific and Cultural Organization (UNESCO) and its member states set up a warning system. By 2004, three of its six seafloor pressure sensors were out of commission, and there was very little funding for maintenance (Alverson 2005). Preventive maintenance for infrastructure can save costs of building new infrastructure (Pacific Infrastructure Advisory Centre 2013).

Collaboration and coordination among regional and subregional institutions can also help boost RPG provision further by complementing each other's different institutional roles and scopes of RPG provision.

Regional institutions including MDBs can coordinate actions among subregional institutions while making sure that the goals and practices of subregional public goods provision are aligned with those of RPG provision (Figure 7.10). Similarly, global institutions can coordinate and support actions among regional institutions. A host of other institutions such networks, partnerships, charitable foundations, and nongovernment organizations can provide additional RPG support to countries lacking knowledge and financial capabilities.

[88] The views from the developing countries' perspectives draw from the discussion at the conference on *Toward Optimal Provision of Regional Public Goods in Asia and the Pacific* which was held on 10–11 May 2018 in Tokyo, Japan. The conference highlights are available in ADB (2018a).

Box 7.10: The Theory of Repeated Games and Roles of Multilateral Development Banks in Regional Public Good Provision

Socially optimal resource allocation may not be guaranteed by the free market. There are situations where individually rational decisions based on conflicting self-interests may lead to persistently inefficient social outcomes, also seen in the Prisoners' Dilemma. Public goods, regardless of global or regional, have been modelled as the Prisoners' Dilemma game. One way to avoid such socially undesirable outcomes is through repeated interactions. The theory of infinitely repeated games shows that cooperation can be a dominant strategy of all players (i.e., a Nash equilibrium) for sufficiently patient players.[a] A major contribution of game theory is the recognition that repeated interactions allow credible punishments or rewards that can lead to self-enforcing cooperation, that is, cooperation without external means to enforce cooperative behaviors among players (Dal Bó and Fréchette 2017). As such, repeated (ongoing) interaction explains cooperative behavior even as the decision to cooperate is against self-interest in the short run.

The classic example is the repeated Prisoners' Dilemma. Following Levin (2006) and Gibbons (1992), given two players $i = 1, 2$ and options "Contribute" and "Not Contribute" for each player, a payoff matrix can be set as follows:

		Player 2	
		Contribute (C)	Not Contribute (NC)
	C	1, 1	-1, 2
Player 1	NC	2, -1	0, 0

If the game is played once, the unique pure-strategy Nash equilibrium is (NC, NC), where each player acting rationally contributes nothing. However, if players 1 and 2 play the game repeatedly at time $t = 0, 1, 2 \ldots \infty$, player i's average payoff for the entire repeated game would be:

$$(1 - \delta) \sum_{t=0}^{\infty} \delta^t \pi_t$$

where π_t is the payoff at time t and δ is a subjective discount factor ($0 \leq \delta < 1$), with $\delta < 1$ means that the players value today's consumption more than tomorrow's. Suppose that the players begin the infinitely repeated game by using such strategies that one continues to contribute as long as the other contributes as well. Otherwise, neither player will contribute. Under such strategies, when player i chooses to contribute in every period, the average payoff for player i is $(1-\delta)(1+\delta+\delta^2+\cdots)=1$. If player i chooses not to contribute today, the average payoff for player i would be $(1-\delta)(2+\delta \cdot 0+\delta^2 \cdot 0+\cdots)=(1-\delta)2$. Therefore, he (or she) will contribute as long as $1 \geq (1-\delta)2$, or $\delta \geq ½$. That is, as long as each player is sufficiently patient (hence putting sufficient weight on the future), cooperation would be a preferred strategy for both players in every round (a sub-game perfect equilibrium) and both players contribute for the entire repeated games.

The theory implies that repeated interactions can reduce the players' opportunistic behaviors, leading them to enter into cooperative agreements and sustain them over time. Behavioral changes instigated by recognizing continuous interactions in the future with the same players, so-called "the shadow of the future" could lead to voluntarily self-enforcing commitments.[b] For example, continued summit meetings (Putnam 1984) and regional forums can be seen as venues for repeated interactions, building relationship, and cooperation without the need for third party enforcement. Similarly, multilateral development banks (MDBs) can create such venues for their member economies and provide the platform for repeated long-term relationships. In addition, MDBs can facilitate each country's voluntary contributions toward regional public goods by building up mutual, informal trust relationship or "social capital" among member economies to recognize shared benefits and mitigate free riding incentives.[c]

Nevertheless, actual applications of infinitely repeated games may be challenging in real international and regional cooperation scenes due to potential changes in nations' political situations and actors. Changes in domestic conditions such as leadership turnovers and the resulting changes in preference and ideology may pose a risk to continued cooperation (Mattes, Leeds, and Carrol 2015). Therefore, MDBs can play a critical role in providing platform for long-term cooperation among countries.

[a] The Folk Theorem says that any individually rational outcome can arise as a Nash equilibrium in infinitely repeated games with sufficiently little discounting (Fudenberg and Maskin 1986). That is, players in repeated games must consider the reactions of the others, where the fear of retaliation may lead to outcomes that otherwise would not occur. Repeated games (or interactions) thus can potentially build trust and promote contribution. This may contrast with one-shot games where noncontribution results as an equilibrium. The latter however is also a feasible set under the Folk Theorem.

[b] Axelord (1984) used the term "the shadow of the future" for the first time to argue that "mutual cooperation can be stable if the future is sufficiently important relative to the present. This is because the players can use an implicit threat of retaliation against the other's defection—if the interaction will last long enough to make the threat effective."

[c] Social capital is defined as informal institutions based on social relationships, networks, and associations that create shared knowledge, mutual trust, social norms, and unwritten rules (Durlauf and Fafchampls 2004). Social capital plays an important role in pushing up growth (Barro 1991). In particular, the relationship of trust to growth is largely observed in poorer countries that may be due to their underdeveloped financial sectors, weak property rights, and inefficient contract enforcement (Knack and Keefer 1997). When social capital is low, it can be built up by "artifacts" such as infrastructure and institutions (Aoyagi, Sawada, and Shoji 2014; and Tabellini 2005).

Sources: ADB based on Axelord (1984); Aoyagi, Sawada, and Shoji (2014); Dal B6 and Fréchette (2017); Durlauf and Fafchampls (2004); Fudenberg and Maskin (1986); Gibbons (1992); Knack and Keefer (1997); Levin (2006); Mattes, Leeds, and Carrol (2015); Putnam (1984); and Tabellini (2005).

Figure 7.10: Roles of Institutions in the Provision of the Regional Public Goods

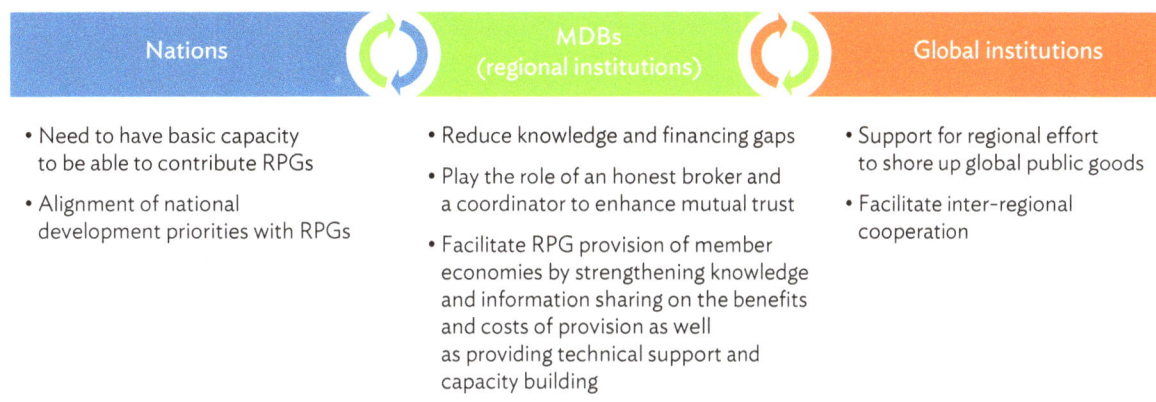

Nations

- Need to have basic capacity to be able to contribute RPGs
- Alignment of national development priorities with RPGs

MDBs (regional institutions)

- Reduce knowledge and financing gaps
- Play the role of an honest broker and a coordinator to enhance mutual trust
- Facilitate RPG provision of member economies by strengthening knowledge and information sharing on the benefits and costs of provision as well as providing technical support and capacity building

Global institutions

- Support for regional effort to shore up global public goods
- Facilitate inter-regional cooperation

MDB = multilateral development bank, RPG = regional public good.
Source: ADB.

Background Papers

Barrett, S. 2018a. Regional Public Goods: Conceptual Foundations. Background paper for the *Asian Economic Integration Report 2018* Theme Chapter on "Toward Optimal Provision of Regional Public Goods in Asia and the Pacific." Manuscript.

———. 2018b. Regional Public Goods: Case Studies in Asia-Pacific. Background paper for the *Asian Economic Integration Report 2018* Theme Chapter on "Toward Optimal Provision of Regional Public Goods in Asia and the Pacific." Manuscript.

Fredriksson, G., J. Marcus, S. Merler, S. Tagliapietra, and G. Wolff. 2018. An Empirical Analysis and Case Studies of RPG Provision in Europe. Background paper for the *Asian Economic Integration Report 2018* Theme Chapter on "Toward Optimal Provision of Regional Public Goods in Asia and the Pacific." Manuscript.

Fredriksson, G. and G. Wolff. 2018. A Conceptual Framework on Regional Public Goods. Background paper for the *Asian Economic Integration Report 2018* Theme Chapter on "Toward Optimal Provision of Regional Public Goods in Asia and the Pacific." Manuscript

Kikkawa, A. 2018. Strengthening Regional Cooperation on Human Capital Development and Cross-border Labor Mobility in Aging Asia. Background note for the *Asian Economic Integration Report 2018* Theme Chapter on "Toward Optimal Provision of Regional Public Goods in Asia and the Pacific." Manuscript.

Kim, K., J. Lee, M. Albis, and R. Ang. 2018. Benefits and Spillover Effects of Infrastructure: A Spatial Econometric Approach. Background paper for the *Asian Economic Integration Report 2018* Theme Chapter on "Toward Optimal Provision of Regional Public Goods in Asia and the Pacific." Manuscript.

Lee, C. 2018. Measuring the Economic Impacts of Cross-Border Infrastructure and Technology: CGE Analysis. Background paper for the *Asian Economic Integration Report 2018* Theme Chapter on "Toward Optimal Provision of Regional Public Goods in Asia and the Pacific." Manuscript.

Sandler, T. 2018a. Regional Public Goods and Their Technologies of Aggregation. Background paper for the *Asian Economic Integration Report 2018* Theme Chapter on "Toward Optimal Provision of Regional Public Goods in Asia and the Pacific." Manuscript.

———. 2018b. Functional Areas, Aggregator Technologies, and Policy Recommendations. Background note for the *Asian Economic Integration Report 2018* Theme Chapter on "Toward Optimal Provision of Regional Public Goods in Asia and the Pacific." Manuscript.

Shiroishi, Y. 2018. Some Points on Regional Public Goods in Health and Relevant Sectors. Background note for the *Asian Economic Integration Report 2018* Theme Chapter on "Toward Optimal Provision of Regional Public Goods in Asia and the Pacific." Manuscript.

Weiss, J. 2017. Benefit Valuation for Regional Public Goods and Regional Projects. Background paper for the *Asian Economic Integration Report 2018* Theme Chapter on "Toward Optimal Provision of Regional Public Goods in Asia and the Pacific." Manuscript.

References

Abeyasinghe, R., G. Galappaththy, C. Gueye, J. Kahn, and R. Feachem. 2012. Malaria Control and Elimination in Sri Lanka: Documenting Progress and Success Factors in a Conflict Setting. *PLoS ONE*. 7 (8).

Adhikari, R. and J. Weiss. 2004. A Methodological Framework for the Economic Analysis of Sub-Regional Projects. In A. Estevadeordal, B. Frantz, and T. R. Nguyen, eds. *Regional Public Goods: From Theory to Practice*. Inter-American Development Bank (IDB) and ADB. Washington, DC: IDB.

African Development Bank Group (AfDB). 2013. *Strategy for 2013–2022: At the Center of Africa's Transformation*. Cote d'Ivoire.

———. 2015. *Regional Integration Policy and Strategy 2014–2023. Integrating Africa: Creating the Next Global Market*. Cote d'Ivoire.

Alverson, K. 2005. Watching Over the World's Oceans. *Nature*. 434 (7029). pp. 19–20.

Aoyagi, K., Y. Sawada, and M. Shoji. 2014. Does Infrastructure Facilitate Social Capital Accumulation? Evidence from Natural and Artefactual Field Experiments in a Developing Country. *JICA-RI Working Paper*. 65. Tokyo: Japan International Cooperation Agency Research Institute.

Arce M, D. and T. Sandler. 2002. *Regional Public Goods: Typologies, Provision, Financing, and Development Assistance*. Stockholm: Expert Group on Development Issues.

Asia Pacific Leaders Malaria Alliance (APLMA). 2014. *Chairman's Statement of 9th East Asia Summit (9th EAS)*. http://aplma.org/upload/resource/Meeting/9th_EAS_chairman_statement.pdf

Asian Development Bank (ADB). 2006. *Regional Cooperation and Integration Strategy*. Manila.

———. 2008. *Strategy 2020: The Long-term Strategic Framework of the Asian Development Bank 2008–2020*. Manila.

———. 2015. *Malaria Elimination: An Entry Point for Strengthening Health Systems and Regional Health Security, and a Public Health Best-Buy*. Manila.

———. 2016a. *Economic and Financial Analysis in the Greater Mekong Subregion Health Security Project: Report and Recommendation of the President*. Manila.

———. 2016b. *Operational Plan for Regional Cooperation and Integration, 2016–2020*. Manila.

———. 2017a. *Meeting Asia's Infrastructure Needs*. Manila.

———. 2017b. *Operations Manual*. Manila.

———. 2017c. *Guidelines for the Economic Analysis of Projects*. Manila.

———. 2018a. *Toward Optimal Provision of Regional Public Goods in Asia and the Pacific: Conference Highlights*. Manila.

———. 2018b. *Strategy 2030: Achieving a Prosperous, Inclusive, Resilient, and Sustainable Asia and the Pacific*. Manila.

———. ADB's Focus on Regional Cooperation and Integration (RCI). https://www.adb.org/themes/regional-cooperation/main (accessed September 2018).

Association of Southeast Asian Nations (ASEAN). 2017. *Rational Use of Medicines in the ASEAN Region*. Jakarta.

Axelrod, R. 1984. *The Evolution of Cooperation*. New York: Basic Books, Inc., Publishers.

Barret, S. 2003. *Environment and Statecraft: The Strategy of Environmental Treaty-Making*. Oxford: Oxford University Press.

Barro, R. 1991. Economic Growth in a Cross Section of Countries. *Quarterly Journal of Economics*. 106 (2). pp. 407–443.

Barro, R. J. and J.W. Lee. 2013. A New Data Set of Educational Attainment in the World, 1950–2010. *Journal of Development Economics*. 104. pp. 184–98.

Batalova, J., A. Shymonyak, and G. Sugiyarto. 2017. *Firing up Regional Brain Networks: The Promise of Brain Circulation in the ASEAN Economic Community*. Mandaluyong: ADB.

Berg, S. V. and J. Horrall. 2008. Networks of Regulatory Agencies as Regional Public Goods: Improving Infrastructure Performance. *Review of International Organizations*. 3 (2). pp. 179–200.

Birdsall, N. 2005. Underfunded Regionalism in the Developing World. In I. Kaul and P. Conceição, eds. *The New Public Finance: Responding to Global Challenges*. New York: Oxford University Press.

Booth, D. 2012. *Development as a Collective Action Problem: Addressing the Real Challenges of African Governance*. London: Africa Power and Politics Programme, Overseas Development Institute.

Calderón, C., E. Moral-Benito, and L. Servén. 2015. Is Infrastructure Capital Productive? A Dynamic Heterogeneous Approach. *Journal of Applied Econometrics*. 30 (2). pp. 177–98.

Cepparulo, A. and L. Giuriato. 2009. Aid Financing of Global Public Goods: An Update. *MPRA Paper*. 22625. Munich: University Library of Munich.

Chung, S. Y. 2017. Building Regional Environmental Governance: Northeast Asia's Unique Path to Sustainable Development. In A. Estevadeordal and L. W. Goodman, eds. *21st-Century Cooperation, Regional Public Goods, and Sustainable Development*. London and New York: Routledge.

Claeys, G. 2017. The Missing Pieces of the Euro Architecture. *Policy Contribution*. 2017/28. Brussels: Bruegel.

Clemens, M. 2011. Economics and Emigration: Trillion-Dollar Bills on the Sidewalk? *CGD Working Paper*. 264. Washington, DC: Center for Global Development.

Collier, P., V. Elliott, H. Hegre, A. Hoeffler, M. Reynal-Querol, and N. Sambanis. 2003. *Breaking the Conflict Trap: Civil War and Development Policy*. Washington, DC: World Bank and Oxford University Press.

Conybeare, J. A., J. C. Murdoch, and T. Sandler. 1994. Alternative Collective-Goods Models of Military Alliances: Theory and Empirics. *Economic Inquiry*. 32 (4). pp. 525–542.

Cornes, R. 1993. Dyke Maintenance and Other Stories: Some Neglected Types of Public Goods. *Quarterly Journal of Economics*. 108 (1). pp. 259–271.

Cornes, R. and T. Sandler. 1996. *The Theory of Externalities, Public Goods, and Club Goods*. Cambridge: Cambridge University Press.

Corong, E. L., T. W. Hertel, R. McDougall, R., M.E. Tsigas, and D. Mensbrugghe. 2017. The Standard GTAP Model, Version 7. *Journal of Global Economic Analysis*. 2 (1). pp. 1–119.

Dal Bó, P. and G. R. Fréchette. 2018. On the Determinants of Cooperation in Infinitely Repeated Games: A Survey. *Journal of Economic Literature*. 56 (1): pp. 60–114.

Darvas, Z., D. Schoenmaker, and N. Véron. 2016. Reform of the European Union Financial Supervisory and Regulatory Architecture and its Implications for Asia. *ADBI Working Paper Series*. 615. Tokyo: ADB Institute.

De Lombaerde, P., F. Söderbaum, L. Van Langenhove, and F. Baert. 2010. The Problem of Comparison in Comparative Regionalism. *Review of International Studies*. 36 (3). pp. 731–53.

Dinar, S. 2006. Assessing Side-Payment and Cost-Sharing Patterns in International Water Agreements: The Geographic and Economic Connection. *Political Geography*. 25. pp. 412–437.

Durlauf, S. N. and M. Fafchamps. 2004. Social Capital. *The Centre for The Study of African Economies Working Paper Series*. 214. Berkeley: The Berkeley Economic Press.

Eichengreen, B. J. 2007. *The European Economy Since 1945: Coordinated Capitalism and Beyond*. Princeton: Princeton University Press.

Estevadeordal, A. 2018. Regional Public Goods: Lessons from Latin America. Presentation at the ADB-ADB Institute Conference on Toward Optimal Provision of Regional Public Goods in Asia and the Pacific. 10–11 May. Tokyo.

Estevadeordal, A. and L. W. Goodman, eds. 2017. *21st-Century Cooperation, Regional Public Goods, and Sustainable Development*. London and New York: Routledge.

European Commission. 2011. *Impact Assessment of Policy Options in Relation to the Commission's Review of the Functioning of Regulation (EC) No 544/2009 of the European Parliament and of the Council of 18 June 2009 on Roaming on Public Mobile Telephone Networks within the Community*. https://eur-lex.europa.eu/legal-content/EN/TXT/PDF/?uri=CELEX:52011SC0870&from=EN

———. Connecting Europe Facility. https://ec.europa.eu/transport/themes/infrastructure/ten-t-guidelines/project-funding/cef_en (accessed September 2018).

European Investment Bank. Breakdown by Sector. http://www.eib.org/en/projects/loan/sectors/index.htm?from=1959&to=2018 (accessed September 2018).

Folkerts-Landau, D. and P. Garber. 1992. The European Central Bank: A Bank or a Monetary Policy Rule? *NBER Working Paper*. 4016. Cambridge, MA: National Bureau of Economics Research.

Franz, B., T. R. Nguyen, and A. Estevadeordal, eds. 2003. *Regional Public Goods: From Theory to Practice*. Washington, DC: Inter-American Development Bank.

Fudenberg, D. and E. Maskin. 1986. The Folk Theorem in Repeated Games with Discounting or with Incomplete Information. *Econometrica*. 54 (3). pp. 533–554.

Galappaththy, G. N. L., S. D. Fernado, and R. R. Abeyasinghe. 2013. Imported Malaria: A Possible Threat to the Elimination of Malaria from Sri Lanka? *Tropical Medicine and International Health*. 18 (6). pp. 761-768.

Gibbons, R. 1992. *Game Theory for Applied Economists.* Princeton, New Jersey: Princeton University Press.

Golbon, R., M. Cotter, and J. Sauerborn. 2018. Climate Change Impact Assessment on the Potential Rubber Cultivating Area in the Greater Mekong Subregion. *Environmental Research Letters*. 13 (8). pp. 1–16.

Grigoriou, C. 2007. Landlockedness, Infrastructure, and Trade: New Estimates for Central Asian Countries. *Policy Research Working Papers*. 4335. Washington, DC: World Bank.

GSM Association (GSMA). 2012. *Mobile SMS and Data Roaming Explained*. https://www.gsma.com/aboutus/wp-content/uploads/2012/03/smsdataroamingexplained.pdf

Hamilton, B. and J. Whalley. 1984. Efficiency and Distributional Implications of Global Restrictions on Labour Mobility: Calculations and Policy Implications. *Journal of Development Economies*. 14 (1). pp. 61–75.

Hardin, G. 1968. The Tragedy of the Commons. *Science*. 162. (3859) pp. 1243–48.

Hardin, R. 1997. Economic Theories of the State. In D. C. Mueller, ed. *Perspectives on Public Choice: A Handbook*. New York: Cambridge University Press.

Harrison, G. W. and J. Hirshleifer. 1989. An Experimental Evaluation of Weakest Link/Best Shot Models of Public Goods. *Journal of Political Economy*. 97 (1). pp. 201–225.

Hirshleifer, J. 1983. From Weakest-link to Best-shot: The Voluntary Provision of Public Goods. *Public Choice*. 41 (3). pp. 371–386.

Hredzak, T. and B. Yuhua. 2011. *Reducing Business Travel Costs: The Success of APEC's Business Mobility Initiatives*. Singapore: Asia-Pacific Economic Cooperation (APEC).

Huh, H. S., and C. Y. Park. 2017. Asia-Pacific Regional Integration Index: Construction, Interpretation, and Comparison. *ADB Economic Working Paper Series*. 511. Manila: ADB.

Inter-American Development Bank (IDB). What is Management for Development Results (MfDR)? https://www.iadb.org/en/mfdr (accessed September 2018).

Intergovernmental Coordination Group for the Indian Ocean Tsunami Warning and Mitigation System (ICG/IOTWMS). 2017.

Intergovernmental Oceanographic Commission of United Nations Educational, Scientific and Cultural Organization (IOC/UNESCO). 2015. *Indian Ocean Tsunami Warning and Mitigation System (IOTWMS) 2005–2015*. Paris.

Iregui, A. 2003. Efficiency Gains from the Elimination of Global Restrictions on Labour Mobility: An Analysis Using a Multiregional CGE Model. *Discussion Papers*. 27. Helsinki: UNU-WIDER.

Kang, J. and G. V. Magoncia. 2016. How to Fill the Working-age Population Gap in Asia: A Population Accounting Approach. *ADB Economics Working Paper Series*. 499. Manila: ADB.

Karan, M. B. and H. Kazdağli. 2011. The Development of Energy Markets in Europe. In A. Dorsman, W. Westerman, M. B. Karan, and Ö Arslan, eds. *Financial Aspects in Energy*. Berlin: Springer.

Knack S. and P. Keefer. 1997. Does Social Capital Have an Economic Payoff? A Cross-Country Investigation. *The Quarterly Journal of Economics*. 112 (4). pp. 1251–1288.

Kotchen, M. J. 2006. Green Markets and Private Provision of Public Goods. *Journal of Political Economy*. 114 (4). pp. 816–34.

Levin, J. 2006. *Repeated Games I: Perfect Monitoring*. Manuscript.

Liu, T. and T. Kahn. 2017. Regional Public Goods Cooperation: An Inductive Approach to Measuring Regional Public Goods. In A. Estevadeordal and L. W. Goodman, eds. *21st Century Cooperation: Regional Public Goods, Global Governance, and Sustainable Development*. New York and London: Routledge.

Malhotra, V. 2012. Role of Game Theory in Public Health. *Online Journal of Health and Allied Sciences*. 11 (2). pp. 1–2.

Mankiw, N. G. 2015. *Principles of Economics*. 7th ed. Stamford, CT: Cengage Learning.

Mattes, M., B. Leeds, and R. Carrol. 2015. Leadership Turnover and Foreign Policy Change: Societal Interests, Domestic Institutions, and Voting in the United Nations. *International Studies Quarterly*. 59 (2). pp. 280–290.

McNamara, K. 1998. *The Currency of Ideas.* Ithaca: Cornell University Press.

Merler, S., and J. Pisani-Ferry. 2012. Who's Afraid of Sovereign Bonds? *Policy Contribution.* 2012/02. Brussels: Bruegel.

Moses, J. and B. Letnes. 2004. The Economic Costs to International Labor Restrictions: Revisiting the Empirical Discussion. *World Development.* 32 (10). pp. 1609–1626.

Musgrave, R. A. 1969. Provision for Social Goods. In J. Margolis, and H. Guitton, eds. *Public Economics: An analysis of Public Production and Consumption and their Relations to the Private Sectors.* London: Macmillan.

Nores, L. G. and P. B. Kennedy. 2017. Why Evaluate the Regional Cooperation Projects? *Beyond Borders: Integration and Trade.* 3 October. https://blogs.iadb.org/integration-trade/2017/10/03/evaluate-regional-cooperation-projects/

Olivier, T. 2018. How Do Institutions Address Collective-Action Problems? Bridging and Bonding in Institutional Design. *Political Research Quarterly.*

Olson, M. 1965. *The Logic of Collective Action: Public Goods and the Theory of Groups.* Cambridge, MA: Harvard University Press.

———. 1969. The Principle of 'Fiscal Equivalence': The Division of Responsibilities among Different Levels of Government. *American Economic Review.* 59 (2). pp. 478–487.

Organisation for Economic Co-operation and Development. Creditor Reporting System Database. https://stats.oecd.org/index.aspx?DataSetCode=CRS1 (accessed July 2018).

Ötker-Robe, I. 2014. Global Risks and Collective Action Failures: What Can the International Community Do? *IMF Working Paper.* 195. Washington, DC: International Monetary Fund.

Pacific Infrastructure Advisory Centre (PIAC). 2013. *Infrastructure Maintenance in the Pacific: Challenging the Build-Neglect-Rebuild Paradigm.* Sydney: PIAC.

Pacific Islands Forum Fisheries Agency. Welcome to the Pacific Islands Forum Fisheries Agency. https://www.ffa.int/about (accessed September 2018).

Pham Do, K. H. and A. Dinar. 2014. The Role of Issue Linkage in Managing Cooperating Basins: The Case of the Mekong. *Natural Resource Modeling.* 27 (4). pp. 492–518.

Putnam, R.D. and N. Bayne. 1984. *Hanging Together: The Seven-Power Summits.* London and Cambridge, MA: Heinemann and Harvard University Press.

Raffer, K. 1999. ODA and Global Public Goods: A Trend Analysis of Past and Present Spending Patterns. *Office of Development Studies Background Paper.* New York: United Nations Development Programme.

Reisen, H., M. Soto, and T. Weithöner. 2004. Financing Global and Regional Public Goods through ODA: Analysis and Evidence from the OECD Creditor Reporting System. *OECD Development Centre Working Paper.* 232. Paris: Organisation for Economic Co-operation and Development.

Roberts, L. 2016. Malaria Wars. *Science.* 352 (6284). pp. 398–405.

Samuelson, P. A. 1954. The Pure Theory of Public Expenditure. *Review of Economics and Statistics.* 36 (4). pp. 387–389.

Sandler, T. 1992. *Collective Action: Theory and Applications.* Ann Arbor: University of Michigan Press.

———. 1998. Global and Regional Public Goods: A Prognosis for Collective Action. *Fiscal Studies.* 19 (3). pp. 221–247.

———. 2003. Assessing the Optimal Provision of Public Goods: In Search of the Holy Grail. In I. Kaul, P. Conceicao, K. Le Goulven, and R. U. Mendoza, eds. *Providing Global Public Goods: Managing Globalization.* New York: Oxford University Press.

———. 2004. *Global Collective Action.* Cambridge: Cambridge University Press.

———. 2006. Regional Public Goods and International Organizations. *The Review of International Organizations.* 1 (1). pp. 5–25.

———. 2013. Public Goods and Regional Cooperation for Development: A New Look. *Integration and Trade Journal.* 17 (1). pp. 13–24.

Schoenmaker, D. 1997. Banking Supervision and Lender of Last Resort in EMU. In M. Andenas, L. Gormley, C. Hadjiemmanuil, and I. Harden, eds. *European Economic and Monetary Union: The Institutional Framework.* London: Kluwer International.

Stumpf, U. 2001. Prospects for Improving Competition in Mobile Roaming. Background paper for the Telecommunications Policy Research Conference. 27–29 October. Alexandria, VA.

Tabellini, G. 2005. "Culture and Institutions: Economic Development in the Regions of Europe." *CESifo Group Working Paper*. 1492. Munich: Center for Economic Studies.

te Velde, D. W., O. Morrissey, and A. Hewitt. 2002. Allocating Aid to International Public Goods. In M. Ferroni and A. Mody, eds. *International Public Goods: Incentives, Measurement, and Financing*. Dordrecht: Kluwer Academic Publishers.

Tres, J., K. Wollrad, L. García, R. Pascual, and M. Shearer. 2014. *Regional Public Goods: An Innovative Approach to South-South Cooperation*. Washington, DC: Inter-American Development Bank.

United Nations Framework on Climate Change (UNFCCC). Find out more about COP21. http://www.cop21paris.org/about/cop21 (accessed September 2018).

United Nations. About the Sustainable Development Goals. https://www.un.org/sustainabledevelopment/sustainable-development-goals/ (accessed September 2018).

———. Sustainable Development Knowledge Platform. https://sustainabledevelopment.un.org/ (accessed September 2018).

United Nations, Department of Economic and Social Affairs, Population Division. International Migrant Stock: The 2017 Revision. http://www.un.org/en/development/desa/population/migration/data/estimates2/estimates17.shtml (accessed May 2018).

United States Centers for Disease Control and Prevention. History. https://www.cdc.gov/onehealth/basics/history/index.html (accessed September 2018).

University of Groningen. The Database Penn World Table version 9.0. https://www.rug.nl/ggdc/productivity/pwt/ (accessed September 2018).

Western and Central Pacific Fisheries Commission (WCPFC). 2016. *Proposal for CMM for the Special Management of Certain High Seas Areas*. https://www.wcpfc.int/node/28456

World Bank. 2017. *The Sunken Billions Revisited: Progress and Challenges in Global Marine Fisheries*. Washington, DC.

———. World Development Indicators. https://datacatalog.worldbank.org/dataset/world-development-indicators

World Health Organization. 2012. *Preventing Reintroduction in Mauritius*. Geneva.

———. 2015. *World Malaria Report 2014*. Geneva.

———. Sri Lanka Defeats Malaria and Reaches Zero Cases. http://www.searo.who.int/srilanka/areas/malaria/sri-lanka-defeats-malaria/en/ (accessed September 2018).

Yeeting, A. D., S. R. Bush, V. Ram-Bidesi, and M. Bailey. 2016. Implications of New Economic Policy Instruments for Tuna Management in the Western and Central Pacific. *Marine Policy*. 63. pp. 45–52.

Zachmann, G. 2013. *Electricity Without Borders: A Plan to Make the Internal Market Work*. Brussels.

Annex 7a: Measuring Regional Benefits of Infrastructure: Data, Methodology, and Model

A reduced-form model using spatial econometric methods (Kim et al. 2018)

The variables were primarily taken from the data set in Calderón, Moral-Benito, and Servén (2015), spanning from 1960 to 2000, and extended up to 2014. Two new information and communication technology (ICT) infrastructure variables—mobile and fixed broadband subscriptions—were added. The final data set has a panel data for 78 countries covering 1960 to 2014 except for mobile and broadband subscriptions, which are available from 1995 to 2014.[1]

Six types of infrastructure variables were used separately under two broader categories for analysis:

[1] The final data set includes 15 countries in Asia: East Asia—the People's Republic of China, Japan, the Republic of Korea; South Asia—Bangladesh, India, Nepal, Sri Lanka; Southeast Asia—Indonesia, Malaysia, the Philippines, Singapore, Thailand; Central and West Asia—Pakistan; Oceania— Australia, New Zealand.

- Transport and energy (TRE) infrastructure variables: length of total roads (in kilometers) from the World Road Statistics, length of rails (in route-kilometers) from the International Road Federation, and electricity generating capacity (in millions of kilowatts) from the United States Energy Information Administration; and

- ICT infrastructure variables: fixed-telephone subscriptions from the International Telecommunication Union (ITU), mobile-cellular telephone subscriptions from the ITU, and fixed broadband subscriptions from the World Banks' World Development Indicators (WDI).

The dependent variable, per capita income, was computed by dividing the output-side real GDP at chained purchasing power parity (in millions of 2011 $) by the population. Both variables are from the Penn World Table 9.0 (PWT). The data for capital stock at constant 2011 national prices are also from the PWT. For the variable for human capital, average years of secondary schooling by country obtained from Barro and Lee (2013) was used.

The total capital stock variable includes all asset classes of gross fixed capital formation in the public and private industrial sectors of the national accounts: residential and nonresidential buildings, machinery and equipment, and civil engineering work. This raises an issue of double counting if infrastructure stock variables are included together with the total capital stock as explanatory variables. Therefore, an effort was made to extract non-infrastructure capital stock from the total capital stock using a statistical method; i.e., regressing total capital stock on infrastructure variables, and using the residuals as a proxy for non-infrastructure variable. The original data sources include many missing values for less developed countries. These omissions prevented the running of the spatial panel model due to missing information on neighbors. Thus, the data were collapsed from an annual frequency to a 5-year frequency by averaging non-missing values only.

Based on the Cobb–Douglas production function following Calderón, Moral-Benito, and Servén (2015), the spatial Durbin model (SDM) was implemented to account for the spatial spillover effect in the production function of country given by the equation:

$$y_{it} = \beta_0 + \beta_1 k_{it} + \beta_2 h_{it} + z_{it}\eta + \sum_{j=1}^{n} w_{ij} x_j' \theta + \rho \sum_{j=1}^{n} w_{ij} y_{jt} + \mu_i + \gamma_t + \epsilon_{it}$$

where y_{it} is the log of per capita real output for country $i=\{1,...,n\}$ at time t, k_{it} is the log of per capita non-infrastructure capital stock, h_{it} is human capital, z_{it} is a vector of log of infrastructure variables, μ_i is the unobserved country effect, γ_t is the time fixed effect, ε_{it} is a random fluctuation, and β_0, β_1, β_2, and η are elasticities. x is a vector of other countries' infrastructure variables with its corresponding coefficient vector θ. w_{ij} is an entry of a spatial weight matrix, W_{nxn}.

The definition of a neighborhood depends on the spatial weight matrix W. Four weight matrices with rows standardized were used: (i) exponential decay $W_1=\{\exp(-0.01*1/d_{ij})\}$ where d_{ij} is the geographic distance between country i and j, (ii) inverse of distance $W_2=\{1/d_{ij}\}$, and (iii) inverse of square of distance $W_3=\{1/d_{ij}^2\}$, all with a 25th percentile cutoff; i.e., the neighbors of a particular country are only the closest 25% of all countries in terms of distance. Countries with distance beyond the cutoff have a weight of zero. And lastly to account for economic distances among countries, a trade flow matrix was also used. That is, W_4={total goods trade beween countries i and j} with the rows standardized.

A structural model using a computable general equilibrium model (Lee 2018)

The computable general equilibrium (CGE) analysis is conducted using the Global Trade Analysis Project (GTAP) model. The GTAP model can be described as a global, comparative static, general equilibrium model which hinges on an input–output accounting framework. First, it is global in a sense that all countries are represented in the model. Second, being a comparative static model, analysis using the GTAP model indicates being able to compare "base" and "policy cases" of the global economy—either at a fixed point or with respect to two periods (one serving as the base, and the other as the policy case). Finally, the GTAP model as a general equilibrium model means, as opposed to a partial equilibrium model, that all sectors in the model economy interact to endogenously determine supply, demand,

Global Trade Analysis Project Model: Sectoral and Regional Breakdown

a: Sectoral Breakdown

	GTAP Industry	**Infrastructure Sectors in ADB** (2017a)
1	Agriculture	
2	Mining	
3	Textile and clothing	
4	Chemical	
5	Metal	
6	Vehicles	
7	Electronic products	Mobile
8	Other manufacturing	
9	Electricity and gas	Electricity
10	Water and sewage	Water
11	Construction	
12	Trade	
13	Transport-land	Rail, Road
14	Transport-sea	Seaport
15	Transport-air	Airport
16	Communications	Broadband, Telephone
17	Financial services	
18	Other business services	
19	Public services	Sanitation
20	Other services	

b: Regional Breakdown

1	People's Republic of China*		
2	Japan		
3	Republic of Korea		
4	ASEAN4		Indonesia*, Malaysia*, Philippines*, Thailand*
5	CLMV		Cambodia*, Lao PDR, Myanmar*, Viet Nam*
6	Other developed Asia	ASEAN developed	Brunei Darussalam, Singapore
		East Asia	Hong Kong, China; Taipei,China
		Others	Australia, New Zealand
7	Other developing Asia	Central and West Asia	Armenia*, Azerbaijan, Georgia, Kazakhstan*, Kyrgyz Republic*, Tajikistan, Turkmenistan, Uzbekistan
		South Asia	Afghanistan*, Bangladesh*, Bhutan*, India*, Maldives*, Nepal*, Pakistan*, Sri Lanka*
		Pacific	Cook Islands, Federated States of Micronesia*, Fiji*, Kiribati*, Marshall Islands*, Nauru, Papua New Guinea*, Samoa, Solomon Islands, Timor-Leste, Tonga, Tuvalu, Vanuatu
		East Asia	Mongolia*
8	United States		
9	European Union (27 countries) excluding the United Kingdom		
10	Rest of the world		

* = economies with infrastructure investment shocks (25 economies), Lao PDR = Lao People's Democratic Republic.
Source: Lee (2018).

and prices at equilibrium. An input–output accounting framework ensures that "all sources and uses of each economic good are accounted for, as are all inputs into production" (see Corong et al. [2017] for more details on the GTAP model).

For analysis, the GTAP 10 Database with the 2014 base year was aggregated into 20 industries for 10 regions. The baseline infrastructure gap data (projected infrastructure needs less investments) for 25 countries in Asia during 2016–2020 (Table 5.1 in ADB 2017a) were used as investment shocks for policy simulations. Infrastructure industries include road, rail, seaport, airport, electricity, mobile, telephone, broadband, water supply and sanitation, which were matched with the GTAP industry classification.[2]

Three shock transmission channels for infrastructure investments are defined: (i) direct impacts on infrastructure industries in Asian countries, (ii) domestic spillover impacts on other industries in the same countries using stimulated infrastructure outputs as intermediate inputs, (iii) cross-border spillover impacts on industries in other regions using the infrastructure outputs imported from the Asian countries as intermediate input. To measure the infrastructure impacts in each channel, the following technical change parameters were assumed to change: (i) output-

[2] In ADB (2017a), the infrastructure gap projections are only available for country aggregates, whereas the projected infrastructure needs are available by sector by country. As simulations in the GTAP model requires sector-specific shocks, it is assumed that sectoral distribution of infrastructure gap in a country is the same as that of infrastructure needs.

augmenting technical change in infrastructure sector *i* of region *r* [the variable name in the GTAP model: *ao(i,r)*]; (ii) infrastructure-input-*i*-augmenting technical change in industry *j* of region *r* [*af(i, j, r)*]; and (iii) import-*i*-from-region-*r*-augmenting technical change in region *s* [*ams(i, r, s)*].[3] Therefore, the difference between Channel 2 and 1 (Channel 3 and 2) provides insights on the significance of and structural understanding about the domestic (cross-border) spillover effects.

3 Given that there are few studies on the level of technical changes due to large-scale multi-country infrastructure investments and this study is mainly to examine impacts by shock transmission channels, it is assumed that *ao(i,r)* increases by the amount equivalent to 30% of infrastructure shock, *af(i, j, r)* by 15%, and *ams(i, r, s)* by 10% during 2016–2020.

8

Statistical Appendix

The statistical appendix comprises 12 tables of selected indicators on economic integration for the 48 regional members of the Asian Development Bank (ADB). The succeeding notes describe the country groupings and the calculation procedures undertaken.

Regional Groupings

- Asia consists of the 48 regional members of ADB.
- Developing Asia refers to Asia excluding Australia, Japan, and New Zealand.
- European Union (EU) consists of Austria, Belgium, Bulgaria, Croatia, Cyprus, Czech Republic, Denmark, Estonia, Finland, France, Germany, Greece, Hungary, Ireland, Italy, Latvia, Lithuania, Luxembourg, Malta, the Netherlands, Poland, Portugal, Romania, Slovak Republic, Slovenia, Spain, Sweden, and the United Kingdom.

Table Descriptions

Table A1: Asia-Pacific Regional Cooperation and Integration Index

The Asia-Pacific Regional Cooperation and Integration Index (ARCII) is a composite index that measures the degree of regional cooperation and integration in Asia and the Pacific. It comprises six dimensional indices based on 26 indicators to capture the contributions of six different aspects of regional integration: (i) trade and investment, (ii) money and finance, (iii) regional value chains, (iv) infrastructure and connectivity, (v) free movement of people, and (vi) institutional and social integration. The construction of ARCII follows two steps: first, the 26 indicators have been weight-averaged in each of the six dimensions to produce six composite dimensional indices; second, these six dimensional indices are weight-averaged to generate an overall index of regional integration. In each step, the weights are determined based on principal component analysis. For more details on the methodology and to download the data, please see Asia-Pacific Regional Cooperation and Integration Index Database. https://aric.adb.org/database/arcii.

Table A2: Regional Integration Indicators—Asia (% of total)

The table provides a summary of regional integration indicators for three areas: trade and investment, capital (equity and bond holdings), and movement of people (migration, remittances, and tourism); and for Asian subregions, including ASEAN+3 (including Hong Kong, China). Cross-border flows within and across subregions are shown as well as total flows with Asia and the rest of the world. The definition for each indicators is provided in the description below.

Table A3: Trade Share—Asia (% of total trade)

It is calculated as $(t_{ij}/T_{iw})*100$, where t_{ij} is the total trade of economy "i" with economy "j" and T_{iw} is the total trade of economy "i" with the world. A higher share indicates a higher degree of regional trade integration.

Table A4: Free Trade Agreement Status—Asia

It is the number and status of bilateral and plurilateral free trade agreements (FTA) with at least one of the Asian economies as signatory. FTAs only proposed are excluded. It covers FTAs with the following status: Framework agreement signed—the parties initially negotiate the contents of a framework agreement, which serves as a framework for future negotiations; Negotiations launched—the parties, through the relevant ministries, declare the official launch of negotiations or set the date for such, or start the first round of negotiations; Signed but not yet in effect—parties sign the agreement after negotiations have been completed, however, the agreement has yet to be implemented; and Signed and in effect—provisions of the FTA come into force, after legislative or executive ratification.

Table A5: Time to Export and Import—Asia (number of hours)

Time to export (import) data measures the number of hours required to export (import) by ocean transport, including the processing of documents required to complete the transaction. It covers time used for documentation requirements and procedures at customs and other regulatory agencies as well as the time of inland transport between the largest business city and the main port used by traders. Regional aggregates are weighted averages based on total exports or imports.

Table A6: Logistics Performance Index—Asia (% to EU)

Logistics Performance Index (LPI) scores are based on the following dimensions: (i) efficiency of border control and customs process; (ii) transport and trade-related infrastructure; (iii) competitively priced shipments; (iv) ability to track and trace consignments; and (v) timeliness of shipments. Regional aggregates are computed using total trade as weights. A score above (below) 100 means that it is easier (more difficult) to export or import from that economy compared with the European Union (EU).

Table A7: Cross-Border Portfolio Equity Holdings Share—Asia (% of total cross-border equity holdings)

It is calculated as (E_{ij}/E_{iw})*100 where E_{ij} is the holding of economy "i" of the equity securities issued by economy "j" and E_{iw} is the holding of economy "i" of the equity securities issued by all economies except those issued in the domestic market. Calculations are based solely on available data in the Coordinated Portfolio Investment Survey (CPIS) database of the International Monetary Fund (IMF). Rest of the world (ROW) includes equity securities issued by international organizations defined in the CPIS database and "not specified (including confidential) category". A higher share indicates a higher degree of regional integration.

Table A8: Cross-Border Portfolio Debt Holdings Share—Asia (% of total cross-border debt holdings)

It is calculated as (D_{ij}/D_{iw})*100 where D_{ij} is the holding of economy "i" of the debt securities issued by partner "j" and D_{iw} is the holding of economy "i" of the debt securities issued by all economies except those issued in the domestic market. Calculations are based solely on available data in the CPIS database of the IMF. ROW includes debt securities issued by international organizations defined in the CPIS database and "not specified (including confidential) category". A higher share indicates a higher degree of regional integration.

Table A9: Foreign Direct Investment Inflow Share—Asia (% of total FDI inflows)

It is calculated as (F_{ij}/F_{iw})*100 where F_{ij} is the foreign direct investment (FDI) received by economy "i" from economy "j" and F_{iw} is the FDI received by economy "i" from the world. Figures are based on net FDI inflow data. A higher share indicates a higher degree of regional integration. The bilateral FDI database was constructed using data from the in the United Nations Conference on Trade and Development (UNCTAD), ASEAN Secretariat, Eurostat, and national sources. For country pairs with missing data from 2013 to 2017, bilateral FDI estimates derived from a gravity model are used. All bilateral data available from 2001–2017 from the data sources were utilized to estimate the following gravity equation: $\ln FDI_{ijt} = \alpha + \beta_1 \ln GDP_{it} + \beta_2 \ln GDP_{jt} + \gamma \cdot X_{ijt} + \delta_i \cdot F_i + \delta_j \cdot F_j + \delta_t \cdot F_t + \nu_{ijt}$, where FDI_{ijt} is the FDI from economy "j" (home) to economy "i" (host) in year t, GDP_{it} is the gross domestic product (GDP) of economy "i" in year t, GDP_{jt} is the GDP of economy "j" at year t, X_{ijt} are the usual gravity variables (distance, contiguity, common language, colonial relationship) between economies "i" and "j", and F_j, F_i, F_t, are home, host, and year fixed effects, and ν_{ijt} is the error term. Data on distance, contiguity, common language, colonial relationship are from the Centre d'Études Prospectives et d'Informations Internationales (CEPII) and data on GDP are from the World Development Indicators of the World Bank. For more details on methodology and data sources, please see online Annex 1: http://aric.adb.org/pdf/aeir2018_onlineannex1.pdf

Table A10: Remittance Inflows Share—Asia (% of total remittance inflows)

It is calculated as (R_{ij}/R_{iw})*100 where R_{ij} is the remittance received by economy "i" from partner "j" and R_{iw} is the remittance received by economy "i" from the world. Remittances refer to the sum of the following: (i) workers' remittances which are recorded as current transfers under the current account of the IMF's Balance of Payments (BOP); (ii) compensation of employees which includes wages, salaries, and other benefits of border, seasonal, and other non-resident workers and which are recorded under the "income" subcategory of the current account; and (iii) migrants' transfers which are reported under capital transfers in the BOP's capital account. Transfers through informal channels are excluded.

Table A11: Outbound Migration Share—Asia (% of total outbound migrants)

It is calculated as (M_{ij}/M_{iw})*100 where M_{ij} is the number of migrants of economy "i" residing in economy "j" and M_{iw} is the number of all migrants of economy "i" residing overseas. This definition excludes those traveling abroad on a temporary basis. A higher share indicates a higher degree of regional integration.

Table A12: Inbound Tourism Share—Asia (% of total inbound tourists)

It is calculated as (TR_{ij}/TR_{iw})*100 where TR_{ij} is the number of nationals of origin economy "i" that have arrived as tourists in destination "j" and TR_{iw} is the total number of nationals of economy "i" that have arrived as tourists in all international destinations. A higher share indicates a higher degree of regional integration.

Table A1.a: Overall Asia-Pacific Regional Cooperation and Integration Index and Dimensional Subindexes—Asia

		Dimensional Subindexes					
	Overall Index	Trade and Investment	Money and Finance	Regional Value Chain	Infrastructure and Connectivity	Movement of People	Institutional and Social Integration
2006	0.531	0.545	0.355	0.509	0.497	0.561	0.299
2007	0.519	0.504	0.397	0.512	0.498	0.565	0.301
2008	0.536	0.524	0.455	0.490	0.504	0.565	0.308
2009	0.526	0.546	0.400	0.503	0.505	0.565	0.314
2010	0.536	0.561	0.425	0.500	0.508	0.563	0.316
2011	0.532	0.582	0.436	0.489	0.517	0.563	0.317
2012	0.529	0.567	0.391	0.494	0.518	0.568	0.318
2013	0.522	0.546	0.394	0.493	0.519	0.562	0.321
2014	0.530	0.533	0.398	0.484	0.514	0.559	0.323
2015	0.525	0.601	0.385	0.483	0.524	0.557	0.324
2016	0.530	0.565	0.396	0.488	0.529	0.555	0.325

Table A1.b: Asia-Pacific Regional Cooperation and Integration Index—Asia Subregions and Subregional Initiatives

	Central Asia	East Asia	Southeast Asia	South Asia	Oceania	ASEAN	CAREC	GMS	SASEC
2006	0.339	0.578	0.590	0.464	0.549	0.590	0.422	0.586	0.464
2007	0.334	0.547	0.586	0.470	0.527	0.586	0.428	0.583	0.470
2008	0.360	0.564	0.598	0.488	0.551	0.598	0.445	0.606	0.488
2009	0.345	0.557	0.589	0.470	0.549	0.589	0.429	0.593	0.470
2010	0.346	0.567	0.596	0.484	0.573	0.596	0.438	0.603	0.484
2011	0.368	0.565	0.601	0.494	0.559	0.601	0.433	0.608	0.494
2012	0.363	0.568	0.586	0.470	0.542	0.586	0.438	0.580	0.470
2013	0.377	0.572	0.580	0.453	0.551	0.580	0.443	0.576	0.464
2014	0.391	0.577	0.589	0.466	0.549	0.589	0.458	0.584	0.472
2015	0.383	0.563	0.589	0.468	0.529	0.589	0.447	0.586	0.480
2016	0.356	0.596	0.590	0.481	0.542	0.590	0.446	0.589	0.499

Table A1.c: Regional Integration Index—Asia versus Other Regions

	Asia	European Union	Latin America and the Caribbean	Africa
2006	0.403	0.541	0.349	0.337
2007	0.389	0.549	0.340	0.336
2008	0.401	0.547	0.342	0.343
2009	0.395	0.557	0.341	0.346
2010	0.404	0.543	0.349	0.335
2011	0.400	0.543	0.345	0.327
2012	0.402	0.544	0.352	0.336
2013	0.397	0.531	0.360	0.332
2014	0.406	0.539	0.340	0.328
2015	0.402	0.534	0.354	0.309
2016	0.408	0.533	0.360	0.305

ASEAN = Association of Southeast Asian Nations, CAREC = Central Asia Regional Economic Cooperation, GMS = Greater Mekong Subregion, SASEC = South Asia Subregional Economic Cooperation.

Notes:

(i) The ARCII for each subregion (subregional initiative) for each year is calculated by averaging the ARCII scores for all the economies in each subregion (member economies in each subregional initiative).

(ii) The economy coverage for subregions and subregional initiatives includes: Central Asia (Georgia, Kazakhstan, and the Kyrgyz Republic); East Asia (the People's Republic of China [PRC]; Hong Kong, China; Japan; the Republic of Korea; and Mongolia); Southeast Asia (Cambodia, Indonesia, the Lao People's Democratic Republic [Lao PDR], Malaysia, the Philippines, Singapore, Thailand, and Viet Nam); South Asia (Bangladesh India, Nepal, Pakistan, and Sri Lanka); Oceania (Australia and New Zealand);
ASEAN (Cambodia, Indonesia, the Lao PDR, Malaysia, the Philippines, Singapore, Thailand, and Viet Nam); CAREC (the PRC, Georgia, Kazakhstan, the Kyrgyz Republic, Mongolia, and Pakistan); GMS (Cambodia, the PRC, the Lao PDR, Thailand, and Viet Nam); SASEC (Bangladesh, India, Nepal, and Sri Lanka).

(iii) The regional integration index for each region is calculated in the same method as ARCII but is based on worldwide normalization, i.e. normalizing raw indicator values using global minimum and maximum values.

Sources: Asia-Pacific Regional Cooperation and Integration Index Database. https://aric.adb.org/database/arcii (accessed September 2018); and methodology from C.Y. Park and R. Claveria. 2018. Constructing the Asia-Pacific Regional Integration Index: A Panel Approach. ADB Economics Working Paper Series. No. 544. Manila: Asian Development Bank (ADB); H. Huh and C.Y. Park. 2018. Asia-Pacific Regional Integration Index: Construction, Interpretation, and Comparison. Journal of Asian Economics. 54. pp. 22–38; and H. Huh and C.Y. Park. 2017. Asia-Pacific Regional Integration Index: Construction, Interpretation, and Comparison. ADB Economics Working Papers. No. 511. Manila: ADB.

Table A2: Regional Integration Indicators—Asia (% of total)

	Movement in Trade and Investment		Movement in Capital		People Movement		
	Trade (%) 2017	FDI (%) 2017	Equity Holdings (%) 2017	Bond Holdings (%) 2017	Migration (%) 2017	Tourism (%) 2016	Remittances (%) 2017
Within Subregions							
ASEAN+3 (including HKG)[a]	46.8 ▼	50.7 ▼	15.0 ▼	10.7 ▲	38.3 ▼	69.9 ▼	32.6 ▼
Central Asia	7.3 ▲	5.5 ▲	0.0 ▼	0.4 ▲	9.2 ▼	52.5 ▼	6.7 ▲
East Asia	36.3 ▼	48.2 ▼	10.6 ▼	7.5 ▲	33.1 ▼	69.4 ▼	35.5 ▼
South Asia	5.6 ▼	0.2 ▲	0.2 ▼	1.7 ▼	23.4 ▼	23.2 ▲	9.4 ▼
Southeast Asia	22.3 ▼	19.6 ▼	6.4 ▼	7.4 ▼	32.4 ▼	41.7 ▼	12.4 ▼
The Pacific and Oceania	6.2 ▼	7.0 ▲	3.2 ▼	2.1 ▲	56.5 ▲	29.6 ▼	28.9 ▲
Across Subregions							
ASEAN+3 (including HKG)[a]	11.4 ▲	2.4 ▼	3.6 ▼	5.9 ▲	8.6 ▼	10.7 ▲	3.0 ▼
Central Asia	24.1 ▼	12.8 ▼	11.9 ▲	16.3 ▲	0.4 ▼	2.1 ▼	0.7 ▼
East Asia	20.0 ▲	5.2 ▲	3.1 ▼	7.6 ▲	13.9 ▼	10.9 ▲	15.4 ▲
South Asia	34.5 ▲	36.4 ▲	34.9 ▲	7.8 ▼	5.7 ▼	23.9 ▼	5.8 ▲
Southeast Asia	45.8 ▲	32.8 ▼	33.5 ▼	16.2 ▲	14.5 ▼	40.4 ▲	13.8 ▲
The Pacific and Oceania	64.0 ▲	40.7 ▲	11.2 ▲	11.9 ▲	5.6 ▼	39.5 ▲	13.8 ▼
TOTAL (within and across subregions)							
Asia	**57.8** ▲	**50.2** ▲	**18.1** ▼	**16.4** ▲	**34.7** ▼	**78.0** ▼	**27.7** ▼
ASEAN+3 (including HKG)[a]	58.2 ▲	53.2 ▼	18.6 ▼	16.6 ▲	47.0 ▼	80.6 ▼	35.6 ▼
Central Asia	31.4 ▼	18.3 ▲	12.0 ▲	16.8 ▲	9.6 ▼	54.6 ▼	7.3 ▲
East Asia	56.3 ▲	53.4 ▲	13.7 ▼	15.0 ▲	47.0 ▼	80.3 ▼	50.9 ▼
South Asia	40.1 ▲	36.6 ▲	35.1 ▲	9.5 ▼	29.1 ▼	47.2 ▲	15.2 ▼
Southeast Asia	68.2 ▲	52.4 ▼	39.9 ▼	23.5 ▲	46.9 ▼	82.1 ▼	26.2 ▼
The Pacific and Oceania	70.2 ▲	47.7 ▲	14.3 ▼	13.9 ▲	62.1 ▲	69.0 ▲	42.8 ▼
With the rest of the world							
Asia	**42.2** ▼	**49.8** ▼	**81.9** ▲	**83.6** ▼	**65.3** ▲	**22.0** ▲	**72.3** ▲
ASEAN+3 (including HKG)[a]	41.8 ▼	46.8 ▲	81.4 ▲	83.4 ▼	53.0 ▲	19.4 ▲	64.4 ▲
Central Asia	68.6 ▲	81.7 ▼	88.0 ▼	83.2 ▼	90.4 ▲	45.4 ▲	92.7 ▼
East Asia	43.7 ▼	46.6 ▼	86.3 ▲	85.0 ▼	53.0 ▲	19.7 ▲	49.1 ▲
South Asia	59.9 ▼	63.4 ▼	64.9 ▼	90.5 ▲	70.9 ▲	52.8 ▼	84.8 ▲
Southeast Asia	31.8 ▼	47.6 ▲	60.1 ▲	76.5 ▼	53.1 ▲	17.9 ▲	73.8 ▲
The Pacific and Oceania	29.8 ▼	52.3 ▼	85.7 ▲	86.1 ▼	37.9 ▼	31.0 ▼	57.2 ▲

▲ = increase from previous period, ▼ = decrease from previous period.
HKG = Hong Kong, China.
[a] Includes ASEAN (Brunei Darussalam, Cambodia, Indonesia, the Lao People's Democratic Republic, Malaysia, Myanmar, the Philippines, Singapore, Thailand, and Viet Nam) plus Hong Kong, China; Japan; the People's Republic of China; and the Republic of Korea.
Trade—national data unavailable for Bhutan, Kiribati, Nauru, Palau, Timor-Leste, and Tuvalu; no data available on the Cook Islands, the Federated States of Micronesia, and the Marshall Islands,.
Equity and Bond holdings—based on investments from Australia; Bangladesh (start from 2013); Hong Kong, China; India; Indonesia; Japan; Kazakhstan; Malaysia; New Zealand; Pakistan; Palau (start from 2015); the Philippines; the Republic of Korea; Singapore; and Thailand. Africa: Reporters are Liberia (start from 2012), Mauritius, and South Africa. Latin America and the Caribbean: Reporters are Argentina, the Bahamas, Barbados (start from 2003), Bolivia (start from 2011), Brazil, Chile, Colombia, Costa Rica, Honduras (start from 2014), Mexico (start from 2003), Panama, Uruguay, and Venezuela. North America: Reporters are the United States and Canada. Euro Area/European Union: Reporters are Austria, Belgium, Bulgaria, Cyprus, Czech Republic, Denmark, Estonia, Finland, France, Germany, Greece, Hungary, Ireland, Italy, Latvia, Lithuania (start from 2009), Luxembourg, Malta, the Netherlands, Poland, Portugal, Romania, Slovak Republic, Slovenia (start from 2009), Spain, Sweden, and the United Kingdom. Middle East: Reporters are Bahrain, Egypt, Kuwait (start from 2003), Lebanon, and Saudi Arabia (start from 2013). Otherwise, data start from 2001. Intraregional share not comparable to previously released issue due to data availability.
Migration—share of migrant stock to total migrants in 2017 (compared with 2015).
Tourism—share of inbound tourists to total tourists in 2016 (compared with 2015).
Remittances—share of inward remittances to total remittances in 2017 (compared with 2016).
Sources: ADB calculations using data from Association of Southeast Asian Nations Secretariat. ASEANstats Database. https://www.aseanstats.org/ (accessed July 2018); ADB. Asian Regional Integration Center. https://aric.adb.org/; CEIC (accessed July 2018); Eurostat. Balance of Payments. http://ec.europa.eu/eurostat/web/balance-of-payments/data/database (accessed June 2018); International Monetary Fund (IMF). Direction of Trade Statistics. http://imf.org/en/data (accessed August 2018); IMF. Coordinated Portfolio Investment Survey. http://data.imf.org/CPIS (accessed March 2018); Department of Economic and Social Affairs, United Nations. Trends in International Migrant Stock. http://www.un.org/en/development/desa/population/migration/data/estimates2/estimates15.shtml (accessed July 2018); United Nations Conference on Trade and Development. Bilateral FDI Statistics. http://unctad.org/en/Pages/DIAE/FDI%20Statistics/FDI-Statistics-Bilateral.aspx (accessed June 2018) and World Investment Report 2018 Statistical Annex Tables. http://unctad.org/en/Pages/DIAE/World%20Investment%20Report/Annex-Tables.aspx (accessed June 2018); United Nations World Tourism Organization; and IMF. World Economic Outlook Database April 2018. https://www.imf.org/external/pubs/ft/weo/2018/01/weodata/download.aspx (accessed June 2018).

Table A3: Trade Shares—Asia (% of total trade)

	Partner					
		of which				
Reporter	**Asia**	**PRC**	**Japan**	**EU**	**US**	**ROW**
Central Asia	**31.4**	**16.6**	**1.2**	**29.1**	**2.4**	**37.1**
Armenia	19.0	9.4	1.3	24.3	3.2	53.5
Azerbaijan	19.9	6.5	0.9	36.2	3.9	39.9
Georgia	29.0	8.8	1.4	26.6	3.6	40.7
Kazakhstan	25.8	13.5	1.7	38.7	2.2	33.2
Kyrgyz Republic	47.5	25.3	0.6	8.6	2.5	41.4
Tajikistan	34.6	11.3	0.3	7.5	0.7	57.2
Turkmenistan	62.5	54.8	0.7	11.1	2.6	23.9
Uzbekistan	44.3	20.2	0.6	10.6	0.7	44.4
East Asia	**56.3**	**15.6**	**6.0**	**12.4**	**12.7**	**18.6**
China, People's Republic of	46.7	0.0	7.4	15.1	14.3	23.9
Hong Kong, China	78.5	49.2	4.6	7.5	6.4	7.5
Japan	56.8	21.7	0.0	11.3	15.3	16.6
Korea, Republic of	58.9	23.0	7.8	10.6	11.5	19.1
Mongolia	72.5	63.4	3.6	11.4	2.1	14.0
Taipei,China	72.6	30.3	10.0	8.6	10.4	8.5
South Asia	**40.1**	**12.6**	**2.2**	**14.1**	**9.0**	**36.9**
Afghanistan	69.9	18.1	2.9	1.5	1.0	27.6
Bangladesh	44.2	14.1	3.0	23.2	6.7	26.0
Bhutan	96.6	0.5	0.5	2.1	0.1	1.2
India	37.5	11.4	2.0	13.1	9.5	40.0
Maldives	64.4	10.0	1.1	10.5	2.3	22.8
Nepal	83.8	11.9	0.6	4.0	1.5	10.7
Pakistan	43.3	21.3	3.1	16.7	8.0	32.1
Sri Lanka	55.1	13.1	3.9	15.8	10.7	18.5
Southeast Asia	**68.2**	**16.8**	**8.4**	**10.2**	**9.1**	**12.6**
Brunei Darussalam	89.1	10.5	20.2	4.8	3.7	2.4
Cambodia	63.4	23.2	5.2	19.2	9.3	8.1
Indonesia	69.9	17.5	9.7	8.6	7.9	13.6
Lao PDR	93.7	24.4	2.2	4.5	1.0	0.7
Malaysia	68.9	15.9	7.5	9.6	8.6	12.9
Myanmar	85.4	34.4	5.9	7.0	2.9	4.6
Philippines	72.8	15.3	13.3	10.0	10.7	6.5
Singapore	69.2	14.4	5.5	10.4	8.5	11.8
Thailand	65.8	16.1	11.8	9.7	9.0	15.5
Viet Nam	63.1	20.3	7.9	12.0	11.5	13.3
The Pacific	**84.0**	**18.0**	**8.2**	**8.6**	**3.1**	**4.2**
Fiji	81.9	13.0	3.8	5.4	7.7	5.0
Kiribati	89.0	4.7	4.4	1.4	6.5	3.1
Marshall Islands	84.7	21.8	8.9	10.9	2.3	2.1
Micronesia, Federated States of	58.2	4.9	5.1	0.1	12.3	29.4
Nauru	80.6	0.8	7.3	0.3	1.9	17.3
Palau	37.2	11.5	14.1	1.6	28.8	32.4
Papua New Guinea	87.1	14.8	9.8	8.3	1.7	2.9
Samoa	82.1	8.1	4.1	2.6	10.4	4.9
Solomon Islands	89.9	41.0	1.9	6.3	1.3	2.5
Timor-Leste	76.0	27.5	3.8	10.5	1.4	12.1
Tonga	85.2	7.7	7.2	1.5	11.2	2.1
Tuvalu	77.6	1.3	4.9	2.0	4.3	16.1
Vanuatu	56.6	5.6	2.5	3.4	2.7	37.4
Oceania	**69.3**	**27.1**	**10.5**	**11.8**	**7.8**	**11.1**
Australia	70.2	28.2	11.1	11.5	7.3	11.0
New Zealand	64.0	20.5	6.8	13.8	10.3	11.9
Asia	**57.8**	**16.1**	**6.4**	**12.2**	**11.3**	**18.7**
Developing Asia	**57.4**	**14.9**	**7.0**	**12.3**	**11.0**	**19.3**

EU = European Union, Lao PDR = Lao People's Democratic Republic, PRC = People's Republic of China, ROW = rest of the world, US = United States.
Notes: Calculations use bilateral trade data. The mirror trade approach was used to fill-in missing data.
Source: ADB calculations using data from International Monetary Fund. Direction of Trade Database. https://www.imf.org/en/Data (accessed August 2018).

Table A4: Free Trade Agreement Status—Asia

Economy	Under Negotiation: Framework Agreement Signed	Under Negotiation: Negotiations Launched	Signed But Not Yet In Effect	Signed and In Effect	Total
Central Asia					
Armenia	0	5	2	11	18
Azerbaijan	0	0	0	10	10
Georgia	0	0	1	13	14
Kazakhstan	0	7	2	11	20
Kyrgyz Republic	0	5	2	11	18
Tajikistan	0	0	0	8	8
Turkmenistan	0	0	0	6	6
Uzbekistan	0	0	0	10	10
East Asia					
China, People's Republic of	0	9	2	17	28
Hong Kong, China	0	2	2	5	9
Japan	0	7	2	15	24
Korea, Republic of	0	10	1	16	27
Mongolia	0	0	0	1	1
Taipei,China	0	1	0	8	9
South Asia					
Afghanistan	0	0	0	2	2
Bangladesh	0	2	1	3	6
Bhutan	0	1	0	2	3
India	1	15	0	13	29
Maldives	0	1	2	1	4
Nepal	0	1	0	2	3
Pakistan	0	7	1	10	18
Sri Lanka	0	2	0	6	8
Southeast Asia					
Brunei Darussalam	0	1	2	8	11
Cambodia	0	1	1	6	8
Indonesia	0	8	3	9	20
Lao People's Democratic Republic	0	1	1	8	10
Malaysia	1	4	3	14	22
Myanmar	1	2	1	6	10
Philippines	0	2	1	8	11
Singapore	0	9	2	22	33
Thailand	1	8	1	13	23
Viet Nam	0	4	2	10	16
The Pacific					
Cook Islands	0	0	1	3	4
Fiji	0	0	1	4	5
Kiribati	0	0	1	3	4
Marshall Islands	0	0	1	4	5
Micronesia, Federated States of	0	0	1	4	5
Nauru	0	0	1	3	4
Palau	0	0	1	3	4
Papua New Guinea	0	0	1	5	6
Samoa	0	0	1	3	4
Solomon Islands	0	0	1	4	5
Tonga	0	0	1	3	4
Tuvalu	0	0	1	3	4
Vanuatu	0	0	1	4	5
Timor-Leste	0	0	0	0	0
Oceania					
Australia	0	7	3	12	22
New Zealand	0	6	2	11	19

Notes:

(i) Framework Agreement signed: The parties initially negotiate the contents of a framework agreement (FA), which serves as a framework for future negotiations.

(ii) Negotiations launched: The parties, through the relevant ministries, declare the official launch of negotiations or set the date for such, or start the first round of negotiations.

(iii) Signed but not yet in effect: Parties sign the agreement after negotiations have been completed. However, the agreement has yet to be implemented.

(iv) Signed and in effect: Provisions of FTA come into force, after legislative or executive ratification.

Source: ADB. Asia Regional Integration Center. https://aric.adb.org/ (accessed August 2018).

Table A5: Time to Export and Import—Asia (number of hours)

	Time to Export		Time to Import	
	2016	2017	2016	2017
Central Asia	**189**	**195**	**76**	**79**
Armenia	41	41	43	43
Azerbaijan	62	62	68	68
Georgia	50	50	17	17
Kazakhstan	261	261	8	8
Kyrgyz Republic	41	41	108	108
Tajikistan	141	141	234	233
Turkmenistan	–	–	–	–
Uzbekistan	286	286	285	285
East Asia	**35**	**32**	**90**	**91**
China, People's Republic of	47	47	158	158
Hong Kong, China	3	3	20	20
Japan	25	25	43	43
Korea, Republic of	14	14	7	7
Mongolia	230	230	163	163
Taipei,China	48	22	51	51
South Asia	**152**	**151**	**323**	**309**
Afghanistan	276	276	420	420
Bangladesh	247	247	327	327
Bhutan	14	14	13	13
India	145	145	345	326
Maldives	90	90	161	161
Nepal	99	99	109	109
Pakistan	134	130	276	272
Sri Lanka	119	91	130	120
Southeast Asia	**68**	**68**	**105**	**102**
Brunei Darussalam	280	272	188	180
Cambodia	180	180	140	140
Indonesia	115	115	232	219
Lao PDR	228	228	230	230
Malaysia	58	55	82	79
Myanmar	288	286	280	278
Philippines	114	114	168	168
Singapore	14	12	38	36
Thailand	62	62	54	54
Viet Nam	108	105	138	132
The Pacific	**134**	**134**	**147**	**145**
Cook Islands	–	–	–	–
Fiji	112	112	76	76
Kiribati	96	96	144	144
Marshall Islands	84	84	144	144
Micronesia, Federated States of	62	62	91	91
Nauru	–	–	–	–
Palau	174	174	180	180
Papua New Guinea	138	138	192	192
Samoa	75	75	109	109
Solomon Islands	170	170	145	145
Timor-Leste	129	129	144	144
Tonga	220	220	98	98
Tuvalu	–	–	–	–
Vanuatu	110	110	174	174
Oceania	**43**	**43**	**40**	**40**
Australia	43	43	43	43
New Zealand	40	40	26	26
Asia	**50**	**49**	**112**	**112**
Developing Asia	**53**	**51**	**119**	**119**

– = unavailable, Lao PDR = Lao People's Democratic Republic.
Source: ADB calculations using data from World Bank. Doing Business Database. https://doingbusiness.org (accessed August 2018).

Table A6: Logistics Performance Index—Asia (% to EU)

	2014	2016	2018		2014	2016	2018
Central Asia	**66.5**	**55.8**	**60.0**	Indonesia	79.7	75.7	80.9
Armenia	69.2	55.9	67.0	Lao PDR	61.8	52.4	69.3
Azerbaijan	63.4	–	–	Malaysia	92.9	86.9	82.7
Georgia	64.9	59.7	62.7	Myanmar	58.2	62.4	59.0
Kazakhstan	69.8	69.8	72.2	Philippines	77.7	72.4	74.6
Kyrgyz Republic	57.2	54.7	65.4	Singapore	103.6	105.1	102.6
Tajikistan	65.4	52.3	60.1	Thailand	88.7	82.6	87.6
Turkmenistan	59.6	56.1	61.9	Viet Nam	81.6	75.5	84.1
Uzbekistan	62.0	61.0	66.2	**The Pacific**	**51.2**	**42.4**	**27.7**
East Asia	**94.8**	**95.8**	**95.5**	Cook Islands	–	–	–
China, People's Republic of	91.4	92.9	92.6	Fiji	65.9	58.7	60.4
Hong Kong, China	99.0	103.2	100.7	Kiribati	–	–	–
Japan	101.3	100.7	103.4	Marshall Islands	–	–	–
Korea, Republic of	94.9	94.3	92.8	Micronesia, Federated States of	–	–	–
Mongolia	61.0	63.6	60.9	Nauru	–	–	–
Taipei,China	96.2	93.8	92.4	Palau	–	–	–
South Asia	**77.5**	**80.1**	**77.7**	Papua New Guinea	62.9	63.7	55.8
Afghanistan	53.5	54.3	50.0	Samoa	–	–	–
Bangladesh	65.8	67.6	66.2	Solomon Islands	67.0	61.3	66.0
Bhutan	59.3	58.9	55.7	Timor-Leste	–	–	–
India	79.7	86.7	81.6	Tonga	–	–	–
Maldives	71.1	63.7	68.5	Tuvalu	–	–	–
Nepal	67.0	60.3	64.5	Vanuatu	–	–	–
Pakistan	73.1	74.1	62.1	**Oceania**	**98.0**	**94.7**	**96.8**
Sri Lanka	69.7	–	66.7	Australia	98.6	96.2	96.3
Southeast Asia	**90.3**	**86.0**	**87.6**	New Zealand	94.3	85.9	99.5
Brunei Darussalam	–	72.8	69.5	**Asia**	**92.2**	**92.0**	**91.9**
Cambodia	70.9	71.0	66.2	**Developing Asia**	**90.6**	**90.7**	**90.1**

– = unavailable, EU = European Union, Lao PDR = Lao People's Democratic Republic.
Source: ADB calculations using data from World Bank. Logistics Performance Index. https://lpi.worldbank.org (accessed August 2018).

Table A7: Cross-Border Equity Holdings—Asia, 2017 (% of total cross-border equity holdings)

Reporter	Partner					
	Asia	of which		EU	US	ROW
		PRC	Japan			
Central Asia	**12.0**	**0.0**	**8.2**	**26.4**	**52.4**	**9.2**
Armenia	–	–	–	–	–	–
Azerbaijan	–	–	–	–	–	–
Georgia	–	–	–	–	–	–
Kazakhstan	12.0	0.0	8.2	26.4	52.4	9.2
Kyrgyz Republic	–	–	–	–	–	–
Tajikistan	–	–	–	–	–	–
Turkmenistan	–	–	–	–	–	–
Uzbekistan	–	–	–	–	–	–
East Asia	**16.6**	**7.4**	**1.0**	**15.0**	**21.5**	**46.9**
China, People's Republic of	46.0	0.0	3.1	13.4	27.0	13.6
Hong Kong, China	21.8	18.7	0.8	10.7	2.8	64.7
Japan	6.9	0.9	0.0	17.0	30.5	45.6
Republic of Korea	20.0	5.2	5.8	24.0	45.2	10.8
Mongolia	68.5	0.4	0.0	13.1	13.3	5.1
Taipei,China	–	–	–	–	–	–
South Asia	**35.1**	**25.1**	**0.8**	**27.1**	**22.2**	**15.6**
Afghanistan	–	–	–	–	–	–
Bangladesh	100.0	0.0	0.0	0.0	0.0	0.0
Bhutan	–	–	–	–	–	–
India	37.5	26.9	0.8	28.5	23.5	10.5
Maldives	–	–	–	–	–	–
Nepal	–	–	–	–	–	–
Pakistan	0.6	0.0	0.0	8.5	4.0	86.9
Sri Lanka	–	–	–	–	–	–
Southeast Asia	**39.9**	**11.8**	**5.5**	**11.7**	**24.6**	**23.8**
Brunei Darussalam	–	–	–	–	–	–
Cambodia	–	–	–	–	–	–
Indonesia	56.6	13.0	0.2	0.5	38.4	4.4
Lao PDR	–	–	–	–	–	–
Malaysia	47.5	1.5	0.8	10.6	36.3	5.6
Myanmar	–	–	–	–	–	–
Philippines	9.8	0.3	3.4	37.0	51.8	1.4
Singapore	40.0	13.2	6.2	9.9	23.7	26.4
Thailand	18.8	1.4	1.8	58.3	17.2	5.7
Viet Nam	–	–	–	–	–	–
The Pacific	–	–	–	–	–	–
Cook Islands	–	–	–	–	–	–
Fiji	–	–	–	–	–	–
Kiribati	–	–	–	–	–	–
Marshall Islands	–	–	–	–	–	–
Micronesia, Federated States of	–	–	–	–	–	–
Nauru	–	–	–	–	–	–
Palau	–	–	–	–	–	–
Papua New Guinea	–	–	–	–	–	–
Samoa	–	–	–	–	–	–
Solomon Islands	–	–	–	–	–	–
Timor-Leste	–	–	–	–	–	–
Tonga	–	–	–	–	–	–
Tuvalu	–	–	–	–	–	–
Vanuatu	–	–	–	–	–	–
Oceania	14.3	1.4	5.2	11.9	45.0	28.8
Australia	11.7	1.5	5.3	12.1	46.1	30.1
New Zealand	35.0	0.6	4.5	10.9	35.7	18.4
Asia	**19.8**	**7.3**	**2.2**	**14.1**	**24.9**	**41.1**
Developing Asia	**29.8**	**13.0**	**3.0**	**12.8**	**16.6**	**40.9**

– = unavailable, EU = European Union, Lao PDR = Lao People's Democratic Republic, PRC = People's Republic of China, ROW = rest of the world, US = United States.

Source: ADB calculations using data from International Monetary Fund. Coordinated Portfolio Investment Survey. http://data.imf.org/CPIS (accessed September 2018).

Table A8: Cross-Border Debt Holdings—Asia, 2017 (% of total cross-border debt holdings)

	Partner					
		of which				
Reporter	**Asia**	**PRC**	**Japan**	**EU**	**US**	**ROW**
Central Asia	**16.8**	**0.7**	**5.2**	**25.7**	**45.5**	**12.1**
Armenia	–	–	–	–	–	–
Azerbaijan	–	–	–	–	–	–
Georgia	–	–	–	–	–	–
Kazakhstan	16.8	0.7	5.2	25.7	45.5	12.1
Kyrgyz Republic	–	–	–	–	–	–
Tajikistan	–	–	–	–	–	–
Turkmenistan	–	–	–	–	–	–
Uzbekistan	–	–	–	–	–	–
East Asia	**15.8**	**4.3**	**1.5**	**27.2**	**39.9**	**17.1**
China, People's Republic of	27.8	0.0	1.9	9.8	32.6	29.8
Hong Kong, China	48.6	24.9	8.2	15.1	20.1	16.2
Japan	7.8	0.3	0.0	31.5	44.6	16.0
Republic of Korea	15.2	2.9	2.9	21.7	41.8	21.3
Mongolia	6.9	1.5	0.0	7.7	3.5	82.0
Taipei,China	–	–	–	–	–	–
South Asia	**9.5**	**1.2**	**1.9**	**39.1**	**38.3**	**13.1**
Afghanistan	–	–	–	–	–	–
Bangladesh	12.6	1.9	2.8	58.3	16.2	12.8
Bhutan	–	–	–	–	–	–
India	0.7	0.0	0.0	7.8	88.1	3.4
Maldives	–	–	–	–	–	–
Nepal	–	–	–	–	–	–
Pakistan	20.2	0.0	1.5	1.0	18.6	60.2
Sri Lanka	–	–	–	–	–	–
Southeast Asia	**23.5**	**5.0**	**0.6**	**12.4**	**33.2**	**30.9**
Brunei Darussalam	–	–	–	–	–	–
Cambodia	–	–	–	–	–	–
Indonesia	8.6	1.8	0.2	64.2	8.7	18.5
Lao PDR	–	–	–	–	–	–
Malaysia	58.5	1.5	1.5	6.9	19.9	14.7
Myanmar	–	–	–	–	–	–
Philippines	39.5	3.9	0.9	8.7	34.2	17.6
Singapore	20.5	4.8	0.0	11.9	35.3	32.3
Thailand	60.1	15.8	12.3	7.7	6.9	25.3
Viet Nam	–	–	–	–	–	–
The Pacific	**0.0**	**0.0**	**0.0**	**0.0**	**100.0**	**0.0**
Cook Islands	–	–	–	–	–	–
Fiji	–	–	–	–	–	–
Kiribati	–	–	–	–	–	–
Marshall Islands	–	–	–	–	–	–
Micronesia, Federated States of	–	–	–	–	–	–
Nauru	–	–	–	–	–	–
Palau	0.0	0.0	0.0	0.0	100.0	0.0
Papua New Guinea	–	–	–	–	–	–
Samoa	–	–	–	–	–	–
Solomon Islands	–	–	–	–	–	–
Timor-Leste	–	–	–	–	–	–
Tonga	–	–	–	–	–	–
Tuvalu	–	–	–	–	–	–
Vanuatu	–	–	–	–	–	–
Oceania	**14.0**	**1.1**	**5.7**	**26.8**	**29.9**	**29.3**
Australia	12.4	1.2	5.8	28.6	33.3	25.6
New Zealand	27.3	0.0	4.4	10.6	0.0	62.1
Asia	**16.9**	**4.1**	**1.7**	**24.8**	**38.2**	**20.1**
Developing Asia	**30.9**	**10.4**	**3.5**	**14.4**	**30.3**	**24.4**

– = unavailable, EU = European Union, Lao PDR = Lao People's Democratic Republic, PRC = People's Republic of China, ROW = rest of the world, US = United States.

Source: ADB calculations using data from International Monetary Fund. Coordinated Portfolio Investment Survey. http://data.imf.org/CPIS (accessed September 2018).

Table A9: Foreign Direct Investment Inflow Share-Asia (% of total FDI inflows)

	Partner					
		of which				
Reporter	**Asia[2]**	**PRC**	**Japan**	**EU**	**US**	**ROW**
Central Asia	**18.3**	**5.9**	**1.8**	**20.7**	**4.1**	**37.2**
Armenia	5.0	3.6	–	21.2	1.0	72.9
Azerbaijan	1.1	0.6	0.5	6.5	1.6	90.7
Georgia	32.0	2.8	1.2	40.0	4.0	24.0
Kazakhstan	25.6	7.0	3.4	31.1	7.5	35.8
Kyrgyz Republic	398.3	323.0	17.0	106.9	7.9	-413.1
Tajikistan	28.1	14.6	7.6	10.3	19.2	42.4
Turkmenistan	–	–	–	–	–	–
Uzbekistan	–	–	–	–	–	–
East Asia	**53.4**	**6.4**	**3.5**	**10.1**	**5.7**	**30.8**
China, People's Republic of	79.6	–	2.4	4.8	1.9	13.7
Hong Kong, China	25.1	14.4	3.7	10.4	7.1	57.4
Japan	31.2	5.8	0.0	11.7	4.9	52.2
Korea, Republic of	33.2	7.5	10.8	31.4	27.6	7.8
Mongolia	40.8	25.7	3.8	13.5	4.7	41.0
Taipei,China	47.1	8.2	19.7	99.3	6.6	-53.0
South Asia	**36.6**	**4.9**	**4.0**	**18.9**	**5.4**	**39.1**
Afghanistan	39.1	39.1	–	27.5	–	33.4
Bangladesh	21.6	3.9	2.6	15.7	4.2	58.5
Bhutan	166.0	–	–	73.8	121.4	-261.2
India	35.9	0.4	4.3	19.7	5.5	39.0
Maldives	1.8	–	1.8	3.6	4.3	90.3
Nepal	14.5	7.6	3.6	3.1	6.6	75.9
Pakistan	81.0	70.6	2.5	21.1	5.6	-7.7
Sri Lanka	5.7	2.0	1.6	4.3	3.4	86.7
Southeast Asia	**52.4**	**8.4**	**9.8**	**20.3**	**4.0**	**23.3**
Brunei Darussalam	219.2	2.2	-2.6	-127.4	-0.2	8.3
Cambodia	80.5	22.2	8.1	7.8	2.7	9.0
Indonesia	81.3	8.0	17.6	24.0	-10.7	5.5
Lao PDR	99.0	77.5	4.1	1.4	0.0	-0.4
Malaysia	72.4	16.8	12.1	25.5	-11.5	13.7
Myanmar	64.6	7.0	1.0	16.5	18.2	0.6
Philippines	10.6	0.3	0.6	17.7	4.9	66.7
Singapore	29.3	7.2	1.3	24.9	11.4	34.4
Thailand	87.0	3.3	42.3	16.1	2.6	-5.7
Viet Nam	82.3	6.0	25.4	5.7	2.4	9.6
The Pacific	**125.4**	**10.3**	**16.8**	**12.4**	**60.2**	**-97.9**
Cook Islands	162.6	–	–	1.0	–	-63.5
Fiji	17.5	2.0	2.7	0.8	13.8	67.9
Kiribati	–	–	–	–	–	–
Marshall Islands	–	–	–	–	–	–
Micronesia, Federated States of	–	–	–	–	–	–
Nauru	–	–	–	–	–	–
Palau	16.3	3.7	9.9	–	19.7	63.9
Papua New Guinea	-75.2	-6.7	-9.1	-8.2	-27.6	211.0
Samoa	–	–	–	–	–	–
Solomon Islands	66.0	–	13.7	–	48.2	-14.2
Timor-Leste	0.0	–	0.0	0.0	0.0	100.0
Tonga	15.2	–	–	8.7	–	76.1
Tuvalu	–	–	–	–	–	100.0
Vanuatu	114.6	14.2	19.4	36.0	84.6	-135.2
Oceania	**47.3**	**4.8**	**10.1**	**13.1**	**7.1**	**32.5**
Australia	44.9	5.0	10.2	13.9	7.9	33.3
New Zealand	78.4	1.3	9.7	3.2	-3.7	22.1
Asia	**50.2**	**6.6**	**5.8**	**14.1**	**5.3**	**29.9**
Developing Asia	**51.0**	**6.8**	**5.5**	**14.2**	**5.2**	**29.1**

– = unavailable, EU = European Union, FDI = foreign direct investments, Lao PDR = Lao People's Democratic Republic, PRC = People's Republic of China, ROW = rest of the world, US = United States.

Sources: Association of Southeast Asian Nations Secretariat. ASEANstats Database. https://www.aseanstats.org/ (accessed July 2018); Eurostat. Balance of Payments. http://ec.europa.eu/eurostat/web/balance-of-payments/data/database (accessed June 2018); United Nations Conference on Trade and Development. Bilateral FDI Statistics. http://unctad.org/en/Pages/DIAE/FDI%20Statistics/FDI-Statistics-Bilateral.aspx (accessed June 2018); and World Investment Report 2018 Statistical Annex Tables. http://unctad.org/en/Pages/DIAE/World%20Investment%20Report/Annex-Tables.aspx (accessed June 2018).

Table A10: Remittance Inflows Share—Asia (% of total remittance inflows)

Reporter	Partner				
	Asia	of which Japan	EU	US	ROW
Central Asia	**7.3**	**0.0**	**8.0**	**2.6**	**82.1**
Armenia	4.4	0.0	10.5	13.8	71.2
Azerbaijan	24.1	0.0	3.4	2.0	70.4
Georgia	9.2	0.0	16.8	2.4	71.6
Kazakhstan	4.2	0.0	22.2	0.8	72.9
Kyrgyz Republic	4.7	0.0	12.8	0.6	81.8
Tajikistan	12.8	0.0	4.2	0.9	82.2
Turkmenistan	–	–	–	–	100.0
Uzbekistan	–	–	–	–	100.0
East Asia	**50.9**	**7.8**	**9.0**	**27.4**	**12.7**
China, People's Republic of	52.7	6.6	9.0	25.3	13.0
Hong Kong, China	22.6	0.0	11.6	30.8	35.1
Japan	39.7	0.0	13.1	34.8	12.4
Korea, Republic of	43.4	26.6	4.5	44.8	7.3
Mongolia	45.1	0.0	20.0	0.3	34.7
Taipei,China	–	–	–	–	–
South Asia	**15.2**	**0.2**	**9.5**	**12.0**	**63.2**
Afghanistan	31.6	0.0	8.0	2.1	58.3
Bangladesh	36.2	0.2	5.5	3.3	55.0
Bhutan	97.0	0.0	1.8	0.2	1.0
India	13.0	0.2	8.7	17.0	61.4
Maldives	58.0	0.0	12.7	0.0	29.3
Nepal	21.4	0.0	3.0	4.8	70.8
Pakistan	5.4	0.2	14.0	6.7	73.9
Sri Lanka	17.0	0.6	19.1	3.1	60.8
Southeast Asia	**26.2**	**2.7**	**10.3**	**32.4**	**31.0**
Brunei Darussalam	–	–	–	–	–
Cambodia	68.8	0.3	7.4	20.8	3.0
Indonesia	40.0	0.7	4.6	2.8	52.6
Lao PDR	74.6	0.0	4.2	19.5	1.8
Malaysia	89.3	0.5	4.3	3.8	2.6
Myanmar	66.4	0.0	0.7	5.4	27.5
Philippines	18.3	3.6	7.1	33.8	40.8
Singapore	–	–	–	–	–
Thailand	37.1	4.6	25.2	27.6	10.1
Viet Nam	19.6	1.4	15.6	56.1	8.6
The Pacific	**59.3**	**0.0**	**1.9**	**26.1**	**12.6**
Cook Islands	–	–	–	–	–
Fiji	59.7	0.0	3.2	23.1	14.1
Kiribati	50.7	0.0	0.8	46.5	2.0
Marshall Islands	2.5	0.0	0.2	94.3	3.0
Micronesia, Federated States of	1.6	0.0	0.0	71.8	26.5
Nauru	–	–	–	–	–
Palau	7.1	0.0	0.4	56.0	36.5
Papua New Guinea	89.3	0.0	1.1	7.7	1.8
Samoa	64.3	0.0	0.2	12.5	23.1
Solomon Islands	88.8	0.0	2.1	4.4	4.6
Timor-Leste	93.7	0.0	5.9	0.0	0.4
Tonga	57.1	0.0	0.3	39.3	3.3
Tuvalu	77.2	0.0	1.3	5.1	16.3
Vanuatu	21.2	0.0	10.2	2.1	66.6
Oceania	**38.5**	**2.4**	**37.5**	**13.4**	**10.6**
Australia	31.5	2.7	41.8	14.9	11.8
New Zealand	84.1	0.6	9.2	3.9	2.7
Asia	**27.7**	**2.9**	**9.7**	**20.8**	**41.8**
Developing Asia	**27.4**	**3.0**	**9.4**	**20.6**	**42.6**

– = unavailable, EU = European Union, Lao PDR = Lao People's Democratic Republic, ROW = rest of the world, US = United States.
Source: ADB calculations using data from World Bank. World Bank Migration and Remittances Data. http://www.worldbank.org/en/topic/migrationremittancesdiasporaissues/brief/migration-remittances-data (accessed July 2018).

Table A11: Outbound Migration Share—Asia (% of total outbound migrants)

	Partner					
		of which				
Reporter	Asia	PRC	Japan	EU	US	ROW
Central Asia	**9.6**	**0.0**	**0.0**	**14.8**	**2.3**	**73.4**
Armenia	19.4	0.0	0.0	8.7	9.7	62.2
Azerbaijan	14.7	0.0	0.0	3.6	1.8	80.0
Georgia	11.8	0.0	0.0	20.0	3.2	65.0
Kazakhstan	1.4	0.0	0.0	26.2	0.7	71.8
Kyrgyz Republic	3.7	0.0	0.0	12.4	0.8	83.1
Tajikistan	5.9	0.0	0.0	5.7	0.8	87.6
Turkmenistan	2.5	0.0	0.0	4.2	0.9	92.3
Uzbekistan	21.7	0.0	0.0	3.7	3.0	71.6
East Asia	**47.0**	**3.3**	**9.2**	**9.4**	**29.1**	**14.5**
China, People's Republic of	51.5	0.0	7.4	10.0	24.0	14.5
Hong Kong, China	40.8	25.1	0.0	9.3	22.3	27.6
Japan	22.7	0.8	0.0	17.1	44.3	15.9
Korea, Republic of	40.1	7.6	23.7	4.0	48.0	7.9
Mongolia	39.0	0.0	0.0	25.8	0.0	35.2
Taipei,China	0.0	0.0	0.0	0.0	0.0	0.0
South Asia	**29.1**	**0.1**	**0.2**	**8.4**	**8.0**	**54.4**
Afghanistan	32.5	0.0	0.0	6.4	1.5	59.6
Bangladesh	48.9	0.1	0.1	5.1	2.9	43.1
Bhutan	89.1	0.0	0.0	4.0	0.0	7.0
India	19.7	0.1	0.2	7.5	13.5	59.4
Maldives	75.3	0.0	0.0	14.9	0.0	9.8
Nepal	50.8	0.0	0.0	5.4	6.1	37.7
Pakistan	24.3	0.1	0.2	14.0	6.2	55.5
Sri Lanka	20.8	0.3	0.6	21.4	3.1	54.7
Southeast Asia	**46.9**	**0.8**	**2.0**	**7.7**	**21.3**	**24.1**
Brunei Darussalam	77.0	0.0	0.0	12.1	0.0	11.0
Cambodia	71.0	0.0	0.3	6.6	16.2	6.1
Indonesia	42.8	1.0	0.7	4.3	2.4	50.4
Lao PDR	79.5	0.0	0.0	3.8	16.2	0.5
Malaysia	89.1	0.3	0.5	4.7	3.7	2.6
Myanmar	84.5	0.0	0.0	0.7	4.6	10.2
Philippines	15.8	1.3	4.2	8.7	36.8	38.7
Singapore	65.3	0.0	0.8	18.2	10.9	5.6
Thailand	34.5	1.7	5.2	26.7	29.2	9.5
Viet Nam	24.6	1.1	3.1	15.0	51.9	8.6
The Pacific	**64.3**	**0.0**	**0.0**	**2.8**	**19.3**	**13.6**
Cook Islands	99.9	0.0	0.0	0.0	0.0	0.0
Fiji	62.4	0.0	0.0	2.8	21.4	13.4
Kiribati	94.4	0.0	0.0	3.4	0.0	2.2
Marshall Islands	1.8	0.0	0.0	0.1	94.2	3.9
Micronesia, Federated States of	3.1	0.0	0.0	0.7	38.2	58.0
Nauru	96.3	0.0	0.0	1.2	0.0	2.5
Palau	12.2	0.0	0.0	7.4	0.0	80.4
Papua New Guinea	49.5	0.0	0.0	30.8	0.0	19.7
Samoa	69.9	0.0	0.0	0.7	15.7	13.8
Solomon Islands	91.3	0.0	0.0	8.4	0.0	0.3
Timor-Leste	89.7	0.0	0.0	10.1	0.0	0.2
Tonga	62.7	0.0	0.0	0.7	32.1	4.6
Tuvalu	78.1	0.0	0.0	1.9	0.0	20.0
Vanuatu	23.0	0.0	0.0	11.5	0.0	65.5
Oceania	**61.3**	**0.4**	**1.0**	**23.7**	**8.8**	**6.2**
Australia	26.9	1.0	1.9	45.5	16.2	11.4
New Zealand	83.6	0.0	0.4	9.6	4.0	2.7
Asia	**34.7**	**0.8**	**2.1**	**9.4**	**14.1**	**41.7**
Developing Asia	**34.4**	**0.8**	**2.1**	**9.1**	**13.9**	**42.6**

EU = European Union, Lao PDR = Lao People's Democratic Republic, PRC = People's Republic of China, ROW = rest of the world, US = United States.
Source: ADB calculations using data from United Nations. Department of Economic and Social Affairs, Population Division. International Migrant Stock 2017. http://www.un.org/en/development/desa/population/migration/data/index.shtml (accessed July 2018).

Table A12: Inbound Tourism Share—Asia, 2016 (% of total inbound tourists)

	Partner				
		of which			
Reporter	**Asia**	**PRC**	**EU**	**US**	**ROW**
Central Asia	**54.6**	**0.9**	**3.6**	**0.9**	**40.9**
Armenia	1.9	0.3	8.1	6.7	83.4
Azerbaijan	26.7	0.3	4.1	0.6	68.7
Georgia	49.9	0.2	4.2	0.5	45.4
Kazakhstan	67.8	1.8	3.0	0.4	28.9
Kyrgyz Republic	79.6	1.3	1.5	0.4	18.5
Tajikistan	–	–	–	–	–
Turkmenistan	–	–	–	–	–
Uzbekistan	–	–	–	–	–
East Asia	**80.3**	**16.1**	**2.9**	**2.4**	**14.4**
China, People's Republic of	76.3	0.0	2.2	1.6	19.9
Hong Kong, China	87.5	65.8	4.7	3.3	4.5
Japan	86.8	26.6	5.3	5.2	2.8
Korea, Republic of	86.8	47.5	3.7	5.1	4.4
Mongolia	62.5	34.2	8.8	4.1	24.5
Taipei,China	91.5	33.3	2.3	5.0	1.3
South Asia	**47.2**	**7.5**	**26.9**	**11.2**	**14.7**
Afghanistan	–	–	–	–	–
Bangladesh	–	–	–	–	–
Bhutan	56.1	16.9	22.4	13.4	8.1
India	44.8	2.9	23.1	14.7	17.3
Maldives	46.7	25.2	35.7	2.5	15.1
Nepal	66.1	14.4	20.8	7.4	5.6
Pakistan	–	–	–	–	–
Sri Lanka	50.6	13.4	39.9	2.7	6.9
Southeast Asia	**82.1**	**18.3**	**9.1**	**3.3**	**5.4**
Brunei Darussalam	88.7	18.9	8.0	1.6	1.7
Cambodia	77.3	16.7	13.1	4.8	4.8
Indonesia	77.3	13.5	12.2	2.8	7.7
Lao PDR	93.2	13.0	4.2	1.4	1.2
Malaysia	93.1	8.0	3.7	0.8	2.4
Myanmar	87.3	17.2	7.2	2.6	2.8
Philippines	68.2	11.8	9.0	15.2	7.7
Singapore	83.6	17.5	8.8	3.1	4.5
Thailand	76.5	28.2	12.7	3.0	7.8
Viet Nam	77.5	28.6	10.1	5.9	6.5
The Pacific	**84.0**	**9.1**	**5.0**	**8.1**	**2.9**
Cook Islands	86.7	0.5	6.5	4.3	2.6
Fiji	82.4	6.8	5.7	9.7	2.2
Kiribati	55.1	0.0	9.7	33.3	1.9
Marshall Islands	–	–	–	–	–
Micronesia, Federated States of	68.5	9.2	0.0	23.2	8.3
Nauru	–	–	–	–	–
Palau	90.6	47.4	2.7	5.8	1.0
Papua New Guinea	84.2	7.3	7.3	6.8	1.6
Samoa	87.8	0.0	0.0	7.3	4.8
Solomon Islands	87.0	4.4	4.3	7.9	0.9
Timor-Leste	81.9	13.3	13.1	3.9	1.1
Tonga	79.6	2.2	3.6	13.7	3.1
Tuvalu	79.5	3.0	1.7	4.9	13.9
Vanuatu	86.9	3.7	0.0	0.0	13.1
Oceania	**67.0**	**13.8**	**16.8**	**8.6**	**7.6**
Australia	65.6	14.6	17.9	8.7	7.9
New Zealand	70.5	11.9	14.2	8.5	6.8
Asia	**78.0**	**15.6**	**6.0**	**3.1**	**12.9**
Developing Asia	**77.8**	**14.4**	**5.7**	**2.8**	**13.7**

– = unavailable, EU = European Union, Lao PDR = Lao People's Democratic Republic, PRC = People's Republic of China, ROW = rest of the world, US = United States.

Source: ADB calculations using data from United Nations World Tourism Organization. Tourism Satellite Accounts. http://statistics.unwto.org/ (accessed August 2018).

www.ingramcontent.com/pod-product-compliance
Lightning Source LLC
Chambersburg PA
CBHW061220270326
41926CB00032B/4786